D0105341

Praise for
SAGEBRUSH REBEL

"*Sagebrush Rebel* is one of the most important, insightful, and inspirational books about Ronald Reagan's domestic policies since *An American Life* by President Reagan himself. It is a 'must read' for those interested in all that the President accomplished."

—**Edwin Meese III**, Ronald Reagan's attorney general

"Ronald Reagan—a life-long conservationist and environmentalist—believed people are part of the ecosystem. That was heresy to those who Reagan called 'environmental extremists,' so they lie about his record. The truth is in *Sagebrush Rebel*."

—**Mark R. Levin**, radio talk show host
and author of *Liberty and Tyranny*

"The story of Ronald Reagan's policies on natural resources and the environment has never been told, or has been distorted by his political enemies. *Sagebrush Rebel* corrects the record for the first time, with relevant insights for our policy debates over resource management today."

—**Steven F. Hayward**, Reagan biographer and author,
The Age of Reagan: The Conservative Counterrevolution: 1980–1989

"Reagan battled Carter's War on the West and confronted Big Green head on. The progressive war on western civilization is never-ending. We must take up Reagan's fight to preserve the American way of life. *Sagebrush Rebel* shows us how. Buy it now!"

—**Michelle Malkin**, syndicated columnist, best-selling author,
and Fox News contributor

"*Sagebrush Rebel* illuminates a forgotten Reagan war—not with the Soviets but environmental extremists. Students of the Reagan presidency will learn a lot from this book."

—**Paul Kengor**, professor of political science at
Grove City College and author of *The Crusader: Ronald Reagan
and the Fall of Communism* and *The Judge: William P. Clark,
Ronald Reagan's Top Hand*

"Ronald Reagan was a gifted leader who understood how to inspire the American people while substantively addressing the challenges we faced. It was my honor—and Perry Pendley's—to serve in his administration. His legacy deserves to be remembered and studied. And Perry Pendley does so again in his latest book."

—**Jim Webb**, assistant secretary of defense and secretary of the
navy in the Reagan administration; former U.S. senator from Virginia

"Reagan believed uniquely in America's future and its young people; his policies on energy and the environment ensured prosperity for decades."

—**Ron Robinson**, Young America's Foundation
and The Reagan Ranch

"The obsession of environmentalists is regulating private property, controlling growth—both human and economic—and trying to predict and alter the future. *Sagebrush Rebel* reveals President Reagan would have none of that and America is better off because of his courage."

—**Linda Chavez**, syndicated columnist and Fox News contributor

"Ronald Reagan took on the environmental doom and gloom merchants and showed the world these would-be 'Emperors had no clothes'—and with his economic miracle, he proved their dire predictions to be totally 'off base'—as to either America's economic or its ecological future."

—**Alan K. Simpson**, former U.S. senator from Wyoming

SAGEBRUSH REBEL

SAGEBRUSH REBEL

REAGAN'S BATTLE WITH ENVIRONMENTAL EXTREMISTS AND WHY IT MATTERS TODAY

WILLIAM PERRY PENDLEY

REGNERY
Publishing, Inc.
An Eagle Publishing Company • Washington, DC

Cataloging-in-Publication data on file with the Library of Congress
ISBN 978-1-62157-156-8

Published in the United States by
Regnery Publishing, Inc.
One Massachusetts Avenue NW
Washington, DC 20001
www.Regnery.com

Manufactured in the United States of America
10 9 8 7 6 5 4 3 2 1

Books are available in quantity for promotional or premium use. Write to
Director of Special Sales, Regnery Publishing, Inc., One Massachusetts Avenue NW, Washington, DC 20001, for information on discounts and terms,
or call (202) 216-0600.

Distributed to the trade by
Perseus Distribution
250 West 57th Street
New York, NY 10107

To Lis, my wife, best friend, and lawyer,
and to our sons, Perry and Luke,
who lived all this then, live it still today,
and endured the retelling of it.

CONTENTS

A NATIONAL CHRISTMAS TREE TALE

J anuary 20, 1981—Inauguration Day—was a federal holiday. As tens of thousands gathered on the National Mall for the swearing in of Ronald Wilson Reagan as president of the United States, Moody R. Tidwell III, counselor to Secretary of the Interior-designate James G. Watt, stayed behind to respond to any important calls that came into the U.S. Department of the Interior's vast but empty C Street building.

Nearby, on the north side of the Ellipse, across E Street from the south lawn of the White House, stood the National Christmas Tree. Only the Star of Hope atop the tree was illuminated. By order of President Carter, all of the other lights on the tree were to remain unlit until the hostages came home from Iran.

At 11:15 a.m., Jack Fish, the director of the National Capital Region of the National Park Service, called Tidwell to say that he had been ordered to turn on all the National Christmas Tree lights. The hostages, Fish was informed, had been released. Tidwell told him, "Let me think about it." He remained suspicious. After all, if the news were untrue, it would not be the first time Iran had lied to Carter about releasing the American hostages.

A short while later, Tidwell received a call from the last of Carter's aides to leave the White House, "Why are you ignoring President Carter's order to turn on the lights?" Replied Tidwell, "Do you know for sure that all of the hostages have been released, or is this just another rumor swirling about Washington today?"

"Yes, the hostages have been released," Tidwell was assured, "but they have not yet left Iran." Responded Tidwell just before he hung up, "Call me when all of the hostages have been released."

A short while later, the White House called again, "The hostages have been freed and they are almost to the airport. Turn on the lights."

Tidwell demurred, "Call me back when you can assure me that they are out of Iranian airspace." Bellowed the White House aide, "You are frustrating an order of the President of the United States."

Tidwell was unrepentant. "I am not about to let President Reagan be embarrassed by a screw-up of this magnitude." Ten minutes before noon, the aide called for the last time, "The hostages are almost outside Iranian airspace. Turn on the damned lights."

Tidwell decided to wait until after President Reagan made the announcement. That came during the traditional post-Inauguration luncheon with congressional leaders in the Capitol. "With thanks to Almighty God, I have been given a tag line, the get-off line everyone wants at the end of a toast or speech. Some thirty minutes ago, the planes bearing our prisoners left Iranian airspace and are free of Iran."[1] After Reagan and the other officials reached the White House, Tidwell called the reviewing stand and dictated a message that was passed on to Watt.

Watt's response: "Do the needful," which meant, "I trust you to do the right thing." Tidwell called Fish and the lights went on. A few moments later, Watt leaned forward, touched President Reagan on the shoulder and whispered, "Mr. President, to celebrate the release of the hostages, we turned on the lights on the National Christmas Tree."

"Wonderful," replied President Reagan.[2]

IN MEMORIAM

Ronald Wilson Reagan

Robert N. Broadbent

Robert F. Burford

William H. Coldiron

Russell E. Dickenson

James R. Harris

Richard R. Hite

James F. McAvoy

Daniel N. Miller Jr.

Richard Mulberry Jr.

Dallas L. Peck

Pedro A. Sanjuan

Joseph Jacob Simmons III

J. Roy Spradley Jr.

RONALD REAGAN'S
SECRETARIES OF THE INTERIOR

"I should warn you that things in this city aren't often the way they seem. Where but in Washington would they call the department that's in charge of everything outdoors the Department of the Interior?"
—RONALD REAGAN, SEPTEMBER 14, 1983[1]

James G. Watt
January 1981–November 1983

William P. Clark
November 1983–February 1985

Donald Paul Hodel
February 1985–January 1989

FEDERAL AND INDIAN LANDS

Bureau of Indian Affairs
Bureau of Land Management
Bureau of Reclamation
Department of Defense
Fish and Wildlife Service
Forest Service
National Park Service
Tennessee Valley Authority
Other agencies
Agricultural Research Service (ARS)
Department of Energy (DOE)
Department of Transportation (DOT)

Compiled by U.S. Geological Survey
1996

SCALE 1:7,500,000

nationalatlas.gov
Where We Are

The **National Atlas** of the United States of America™

PREFACE

The president's "natural resources and environmental policies," despite their importance for more than half a century, are entrusted to a federal department unknown to most Americans, the U.S. Department of the Interior. Of course, like almost any other national issue, those policies are implemented by an assortment of federal departments and agencies, including the Department of Agriculture, which houses the U.S. Forest Service and the Natural Resources Conservation Service; the Department of Defense, which is home to the U.S. Army Corps of Engineers and is also responsible for vast military reservations, especially across the American West; the Department of Energy, which is a large landowner in the Western United States; and the Environmental Protection Agency. Nonetheless, it is to the Interior Department that almost all Westerners, most knowledgeable observers, and scores of constituent and special interest groups look to learn a president's natural resources and environmental policies.

A department akin to the Department of the Interior was considered in 1789 by the first United States Congress, but the domestic responsibilities that might have resided there were combined with foreign affairs in the Department of State. Nevertheless, the idea of a "Home Department" remained a subject of discussion; in fact, presidents from James Madison (1809–1817) through James K. Polk (1845–1849) supported the idea. Finally, in response to the growth in the responsibilities of the federal government during the Mexican-American War (1846–1848), Robert J. Walker, Polk's secretary of the treasury, an outspoken champion of a domestic department, urged Congress in his report of 1848 to form a new department from various federal offices and to entrust its duties to a "Secretary of the Interior."[1] Little wonder—in three short years, the United States had annexed Texas, resolved the Oregon boundary dispute with Great Britain, and, with the end of the Mexican War, expanded its territory by more than a million square miles.[2] Walker argued that many federal offices should be in departments that were more complementary to their missions. The General Land Office, for example, did not belong in the Treasury Department, the Indian Affairs Office in the Department of War, or the Patent Office in the Department of State. Finally, Walker expressed concerned about the potential corrupting influence on the Department of the Treasury—given its desire for increased revenues—of the presence there of the General Land Office, which, in his view, was soon to be set upon by lobbyists and speculators in pursuit of great profits in the new territories.[3]

Despite sectional and party conflicts, Congress acted quickly on Walker's recommendation. The House of Representatives passed a bill on February 15, 1849,[4] and the Senate gave its approval on March 3, 1849.[5] The next day Zachary Taylor became president and days later appointed the first secretary of the interior, Thomas Ewing.[6]

Senator John C. Calhoun of South Carolina had opposed creation of the Department of the Interior, fearing, "Everything upon the face of God's earth will go into the Home Department."[7] He was prophetic. Soon the department was called the "Great Miscellany," "[a] slop bucket for executive fragments," and a "hydra-headed monster,"[8] or, more kindly, "Mother of Departments," for the tendency of agencies it adopted as orphans to become grown-up, stand-alone agencies, if not full-blown departments.[9] This potpourri served a purpose: the department became a repository for almost any and all of the functions that Congress determined were necessary to address the internal needs of the rapidly expanding country but that belonged nowhere else. Over time, offices accomplished their functions and were dismantled; others endured intact with limited responsibilities; and still others grew and split off as departments of their own.[10]

It is hardly surprising that the Department of the Interior, created in response to evolving Western issues, would have a Western focus,[11] especially after 1873, when Congress transferred territorial responsibilities from the State Department to Interior.[12] In fact, two of the department's four major bureaus were ubiquitous in the American West: the Indian Bureau, created in 1824, and the General Land Office, created in 1812. The Indian Bureau's responsibility was to implement evolving national policy regarding American Indians and their tribes, which as of 1885 included 260,000 people on 138 reservations,[13] a task made difficult for three decades by conflicts with the War Department, whose obligation it was to end "hostilities" on the frontier, from whence the Indian Affairs office had come and to where the War Department acrimoniously sought its return.[14] The General Land Office had an even more Herculean task: the massive transfer of federal lands into private hands as authorized by laws enacted in 1862 that opened up the American West: the Pacific Railroad Act,[15] the Morrill Act,[16] and the Homestead Act.[17]

Other agencies came along as a result of the department's responsibilities over the West. Interior, for example, joined with the army in resolving the international boundary with Mexico (the Mexican Boundary Commission), improved historic emigrant routes across the West (the Pacific Wagon Road Office), and supervised the organization, building, and operation of the Pacific railroads. After governors and other high officials of the Western territories were appointed by the president, they reported, beginning in 1873, to the secretary of the interior.[18] Some operations during this early period became more permanent. For example, Interior won its long running battle with the War Department, which began in the years after the Civil War, over which one was preeminent in conducting official Western exploration when the U.S. Geological Survey was created in 1879 as an Interior agency and assigned that responsibility.[19] Meanwhile, in 1872, Congress created the first national park, Yellowstone, and placed it in Interior.[20] Although other national parks followed in the 1890s, it was not until 1916 that Congress created the National Park Service to manage and operate the parks.[21]

One of the Interior Department's other two major bureaus was the Bureau of Pensions, which administered the distribution of pensions to veterans of the Union army and navy—one and a half million men by 1885.[22] By 1890, the Pension Bureau "numbered more than 6,000 agents, medical examiners, and clerks."[23] In 1930, the Pension Bureau was moved out of Interior and consolidated with the Veterans Bureau and the National Home for Disabled Volunteer Soldiers to form the Veterans Administration.[24] Interior's fourth major bureau was the Patent Office; by 1890 it was receiving more than 41,000 applications and issuing over 26,000 patents annually.[25] In 1882, the Patent Office's "agricultural division" became a part of the Department of Agriculture, a non-cabinet entity.[26] Similarly, the Bureau of Labor, which arrived at Interior in 1884, became the Department of Labor in 1888, and the Census Office, which was moved into the Interior Department in 1903, was renamed the Census Bureau under a newly created Department of Commerce and Labor in 1913. That department took over the Patent Office in 1925. The Interstate Commerce Commission began life in the Interior Department in 1887 but became an independent agency within two years.[27] Meanwhile, one of Interior's minor bureaus—a "Department of Education," which was created by Congress in 1867 as a stand-alone entity but shifted to Interior in 1869 as the Bureau of Education—was downgraded in 1929 to an "office" to remove any question as to whether it was involved in matters exclusively state and local.[28] In 1939, the Office of Education departed Interior for what would become the Department of Health, Education, and Welfare in 1953.[29]

In 1905, Congress transferred some sixty-three million acres of forest lands, which had been set aside under the Forest Reserve Act of 1891 and placed in Interior's General Land Office, to the Division of Forestry in the Department of Agriculture. The forest lands became the foundation of the National Forest System, and the division was renamed the U.S. Forest Service. Gifford Pinchot, the head of the division, became chief of the Forest Service. Meanwhile, the Reclamation Service of the U.S. Geological Survey, created to carry out the purposes of the Reclamation Act of 1902, became a separate division within Interior itself; in 1923, it became the Bureau of Reclamation.[30]

In 1910, Congress created the Bureau of Mines, following coal mine disasters, to promote minerals technology and mine safety; in 1925, the Bureau of Mines was sent to the Commerce Department but returned in 1934.[31] In 1934, Congress passed the Taylor Grazing Act, which authorized the secretary of the interior to place eighty million acres of federal land in grazing districts, which were managed by the Grazing Service. In 1946, the General Land Office and the Grazing Service together became the Bureau of Land Management (BLM), with responsibility for 342 million acres of federal surface and an additional 370 million acres of oil, gas, and mineral or subsurface rights owned by the federal government.[32] In 1977, Congress established the Office of Surface Mining Reclamation and Enforcement to regulate and oversee coal mining reclamation[33] and transferred several Interior activities to create the Department of Energy.[34]

Meanwhile, in 1940, the Bureau of Fisheries and the Bureau of Biological Survey, which originated elsewhere and were transferred to Interior in 1939, were consolidated as the Fish and Wildlife Service.[35] With them came federal wildlife refuges created by executive orders beginning in 1903, a concept that Congress sanctioned with enactment of the Migratory Bird Conservation Act of 1929.[36] In 1956, Congress reorganized the Fish and Wildlife Service into the Bureau of Sports Fisheries and Wildlife and the Bureau of Commercial Fisheries, the latter of which was transferred to the Commerce Department's National Oceanic and Atmospheric Administration in 1970. In 1974, the remaining bureau became the U.S. Fish and Wildlife Service with its responsibility for millions of acres of federal land—second only, within Interior, to the BLM—that serve as wildlife refuges.[37]

In 1950 and 1951, Interior assumed territorial responsibilities—in accordance with Congress's transfer of that authority from the Department of State in 1873—over Guam, American Samoa, and the Trust Territory of the Pacific Islands, which held the Caroline and Northern

Mariana Islands;[38] Interior had held territorial responsibility for Hawaii since its acquisition by the United States in 1898.[39] The Division of Territories and Island Possessions—created in 1934 to oversee Alaska, Hawaii, the Virgin Islands, and Puerto Rico and which, as of 1939, oversaw the Philippines—lost responsibility for the Philippines in 1946, when the islands achieved independence, Puerto Rico in 1952, when it became a commonwealth, and Alaska and Hawaii in 1959, when they became states.[40] After a number of name changes and reorganizations, in 1980 Interior's territorial duties were assigned to the assistant secretary for territorial and international affairs.[41]

This was the Department of the Interior as it existed in January 1981 when Ronald Reagan took office, over which the president gave responsibility to his secretaries of the interior, James G. Watt, William P. Clark, and Donald Paul Hodel.

INTRODUCTION

"We win and they lose," said Ronald Reagan. It was 1977, and he was explaining his Cold War strategy to Richard V. Allen, an international relations scholar who would become the first national security advisor in the Reagan administration.[1]

Allen was "flabbergasted." "I'd worked for Nixon and Goldwater and many others, and I'd heard a lot about Kissinger's policy of détente and about the need to 'manage the Cold War,' but never did I hear a leading politician put the goal so starkly."[2]

His plan was "simple," Reagan told Allen, but he recognized that others might call it "simplistic."[3] "Naïve," "primitive," and even "dangerous" were more like it.

Ronald Reagan, with his boundless faith in American ingenuity, creativity, and know-how and his confidence in the free enterprise system, believed the United States would "transcend" the Soviet Union. Before it could do so, however, President Reagan had to revive an American economy reeling from double-digit unemployment, double-digit inflation, and double-digit interest rates. He knew that the economy could not grow without reliable sources of energy. It was clear to Reagan that the economy, energy, and foreign policy were inextricably linked.

Reagan had argued for years that the nation needed to develop its rich energy and mineral resources in order to restore the economy. Furthermore, he made it clear that those resources had to come from the one-third of the country owned by the federal government as well as from the billion acres of offshore resources over which the federal government has authority. Reagan made a compelling case to the American people, and they elected him by a large margin; however, in the two decades preceding his inauguration in 1981, so-called "environmentalists" had erected some imposing obstacles to progress, and Reagan entered office with a battle on his hands.

In its heyday of the 1960s and 1970s, the environmental movement had persuaded Congress to enact a series of well-intentioned laws that proved mischievous in the hands of covetous bureaucrats, radical groups, and activist judges. These laws, together with a feckless Congress, the compliant and often duplicitous media, and a well-organized and lavishly funded environmental lobby, created a formidable impediment to the ability of President Reagan to implement his natural resources and environmental policies.

As governor of California in the late 1960s and early 1970s, Reagan had watched the environmental movement change. A fervent conservationist and an environmentalist himself, Ronald Reagan believed in being a good steward, but above all, he believed in people, who are, after all, part of the environment. That was where the split developed.

From its beginnings, the conservation movement held human beings at its center. Whether the issue was the need for humans to sustain themselves by wise use ("conservation") of nature's bounty, or the need to set aside permanently and unchanged ("preservation") a portion of God's great creation for their emotional, physical, and spiritual restoration, the focus was always on human beings. That focus changed, to Reagan's great dismay, during his lifetime.

People were no longer at the center; people were just part of the biota, no greater and often worse than any other living thing. Not only was mankind on a par with the flora and the fauna, it was the enemy of creation.

All the terrible things that had happened, were happening, and might happen could be laid at the feet of *Homo sapiens*. In fact, the worst was yet to come because human beings had drained the world of its resources. Unless they adapted to lives of scarcity and sacrifice, only pain and privation lay ahead. Even then, thought the gloomier environmentalists, it might be too late, for human beings were not only at war with their own planet, their faith in human ingenuity and their belief in technology were infantile. Their hope for a bright future was futile!

Ronald Reagan would have none of this gloom and doom. In his 1980 presidential campaign, he depicted the stark contrast between his vision of the future and that of President Carter. Reagan adhered to what one social scientist called the "human exemptionalism paradigm,"[4] according to which "human technological ingenuity can continue infinitely to improve the human situation."[5] Carter, the Earth Day organizers, and the environmental groups embraced a neo-Malthusian "ecological paradigm,"[6] which posits environmental limits on economic growth. Environmental groups saw the sharp difference and, for the first time ever, as a body, took sides in a presidential election. In September 1980, they went to the White House to praise and endorse President Carter and to denounce Governor Reagan.[7]

Environmental extremists had another reason for their rage toward Ronald Reagan; he was an unabashed Sagebrush Rebel who pledged to put an end to Carter's War on the West. He had made common cause with Westerners who were fed up with an arrogant environmental movement that was entrenched in positions of power in San Francisco, New York, and especially in Washington, where the federal bureaucracy was filled with environmental activists. Therefore, nearly a year before their White House meeting with Carter, environmental groups met in Denver to prepare for battle against Westerners and their champion, Ronald Reagan.[8]

The claim that environmental activists arose in opposition to President Reagan only after his policies became extreme is pure fiction. As a candidate, Reagan was very clear not only about what he believed—that people are part of the ecology—but also about what such a philosophical point of view means for public policy, and his intention to implement such policies. He left no room for doubt that a Reagan victory would mean the end of the business as usual—the so-called bipartisan consensus regarding natural resources and the environment—that had prevailed for two decades.

Exactly how different Ronald Reagan's point of view was from that of the past was demonstrated by the two "transition task force" reports regarding natural resources and environmental issues he received when he arrived in Washington. One—prepared by those who had served in the Nixon and Ford administrations—urged the new president to "maintain the momentum of environmental protection while allowing for some easing of regulation."[9] The president-elect quickly tossed it aside; it "was largely ignored: only three copies were ever made...."[10]

Instead, in a bold break with the past, Reagan opted for The Heritage Foundation's report, *Mandate for Leadership: Policy Management in a Conservative Administration.*[11] This famous blueprint, which "cover[ed] virtually every major policy area,"[12] called for massive changes in the Interior Department's programs, including dramatic increases in oil and gas leasing, both on the Outer Continental Shelf and on federal lands across the country, resumed leasing of federal coal lands in the West and full-scale changes throughout the vast bureaucracy.[13] Then Reagan appointed a secretary of the interior to accomplish exactly what he had promised the American people he would do, named two successors who would stay the course, and consistently backed them in their implementation of his policies.

President Reagan's aggressive energy policies, for example, have never been equaled. Of greater importance today than the specific policies that he pursued, however, is his belief in American exceptionalism and in the ability of the American people—if unfettered by burdensome regulations and given reasonable access to the nation's rich natural resources—to improve their lot. The amazing work of the energy industry in discovering, developing, and delivering previously inaccessible oil and gas resources through hydraulic fracturing technology, for example, would not have surprised President Reagan.

The story of Ronald Reagan's approach to natural resources and the environment—why it was important then and what it can teach us today—remains largely untold. One reason is the spectacular success of his foreign policy. "We win and they lose" worked. A second reason is that natural resources and environmental policies usually do not attract a lot of attention. The personalities at Reagan's Interior Department and the inflamed passions of radical environmental groups generated headlines at the time, but with the passing of that era, the media lost interest. Finally, no one has stepped back from today's perspective to examine what Reagan tried to accomplish in the area of natural resources and the environment.

In 2013, America's situation is similar to that of 1980—an economy in distress, vast natural resources locked up with no plans to put them to use, and a regulatory regime that inhibits the development of resources and the creation of jobs. What lessons can we take from President Reagan's policies and the responses to them?

In this book, I will explore what Reagan and his secretaries of the interior did in order to:

- Develop onshore oil and gas resources;
- Explore for Outer Continental Shelf energy resources;
- Ensure the use of America's uniquely vast coal resources;
- Provide for the availability of strategic and critical minerals;
- Remove burdensome regulations, shrink the bureaucracy, and control wasteful federal spending;
- Prevent a radical law from stopping projects, seizing land, and stifling jobs;
- Preserve and protect parks, refuges, and wild places for people; and
- Restore good neighbor relations with the states and the American people.

I also will highlight the response of radical environmental groups and their relentless attack on President Reagan, his policies, and the leaders to whom he gave responsibility to bring change to America. What we know today as the mainstream media also deserve scrutiny for their unwillingness or inability to get to the heart of important public policy issues raised by President Reagan. Finally, I will explore several significant issues with which most Americans are unfamiliar and, in conclusion, will explain why President Reagan's policies on natural resources and the environment were right and must be renewed if we want to restore America as "the shining city on a hill."

Reagan foresaw that the Soviet Union would collapse of its own weight, and he no doubt thought that the radical environmental movement—"environmental extremists," as he called them—would share that fate. Unfortunately, the latter has not happened—yet. That is not to say that Reagan failed in his toe-to-toe battles with environmental groups, their allies in Congress, and the media. In the 1980s, Reagan deprived these extremists of the aura of inevitability, invincibility, and infallibility with which they had been cloaked for almost two decades. Environmentalists had become a high priesthood; they were the oracles elected officials approached with reverence and awe to obtain their approval. Reagan denied them their moral high ground. When they said they spoke for the planet and the needs of all living things not human, he responded that he spoke for the dream of the American people and for unborn generations to be free and prosperous. Reagan countered the religious mysticism that drives the radical environmental movement with his own deep religious faith, which insists on the preeminence of human life. With his balanced approach to natural resources and environmental policies, he exposed the childishness of radical environmentalists, who are incapable of being satisfied, always demand their own way, and, like the tyrants they are, never bring anything to the negotiating table—not even their good will or a sense of fair play. As Reagan succinctly put it in 1983, "I do not think they will be happy until the White House looks like a bird's nest."[14]

In a curious twist of history, what allowed environmental extremists to continue to get their way was the economic recovery for which Reagan was responsible. His policies of lower taxes, reduced regulatory burdens, and a return to federalism produced years of sustained economic growth. The demands by environmental groups for restrictions, limits, or land-closures, which in tougher times would have resulted in a harsh economic burden, could be absorbed by a constantly growing economy. Entire sections of the Outer Continental Shelf could be closed, massive coal and gold deposits could be locked in the ground, and millions of acres of rich timberland could be put off limits with no perceptible adverse economic effects. Reagan's successor could be "the environmental president," another president could accede to every demand made by radical environmental groups, another could permit foreign policy concerns to distract his attention from domestic policy, and yet another could "go green" with no discernable harm to the economy or the American people.

No more. For twenty-five years, Gallup has asked people whether the economy or the environment is more important, and the environment has consistently out-polled the economy. In 2009, however, the lines crossed for the first time; those polled said the economy is more important.[15] Given the state of the economy, the outlook for the future, and the intractable demands of the environmental movement, the lines may never cross again. The discrediting of the climate-change scare,[16] the failure—after the waste of billions of dollars—of alternative energy sources to compete with hydrocarbons,[17] and the apparent indifference and even hostility of environmental groups to the economic needs of their fellow citizens have been serious blows to the environmentalists' prestige.[18]

Ronald Reagan, I am confident, will turn out to have been right about the future of radical environmentalism. That, however, is up to the generations that follow him. In the meantime, Americans have much to learn from our Sagebrush Rebel president.

CHAPTER ONE

FEDERAL LAND BELONGS TO US: TO THE PEOPLE OF AMERICA[1]

*"Why is the government so anxious to lock up this [federal] land[?]
Is it a fear that more [natural gas] strikes will be made?"*
—RONALD REAGAN, OCTOBER 10, 1978[2]

A Stainless Steel Backbone

In August 1981, in the first year of the Reagan administration, the Conservation Division of the U.S. Geological Survey (USGS) completed work on the environmental studies required by federal law for an "application for permit to drill" (APD) submitted by an energy company that had won a federal oil and gas lease on the Bridger Teton National Forest near Jackson, Wyoming. The environmental impact statement (EIS), as required by the National Environmental Policy Act (NEPA), outlined the effects of the proposed drilling, primarily on the nonhuman environment, and the methods by which the company will seek to discover energy resources, in this case most likely natural gas.[3] By winning the lease the company also had won the right, over a ten-year primary term, to explore for and, if successful, develop energy resources, "in commercial quantities," for which the company would then pay a royalty to the federal government, half of which would be delivered to the state of Wyoming.[4] First, however, in order to commence work, the company had to submit an APD, the approval of which was deemed a "major federal action significantly affecting the quality of the human environment." This triggered the NEPA review, untold man-hours of studies and mountains of paperwork, and months, usually years, of delay, even without the inevitable litigation. Ultimately, the voluminous document, a final EIS, landed on the desk of an official for final agency action, which permits any aggrieved party to go to court. The most likely "aggrieved party," if the APD were rejected, is the lessee itself. Although the federal government—in this case, the Interior Department, specifically the Bureau of Land Management and the U.S. Forest Service—might condition the manner in which the exploratory drilling was to take place, it could not deny the APD outright. The law provides that the lease is a property right, and denial of the ability to exercise that property right by drilling to discover oil and gas constitutes an "unconstitutional taking" for which "just compensation" must be paid. The federal government could say "No," but there would be a price to pay, and, depending on the value of the natural resources forgone, that is, the value of the oil and gas left in the ground, it could be a steep one.[5]

That August, the Cache Creek–Bear Thrust Environmental Impact Statement landed on my desk. I was the sole deputy assistant secretary for energy and minerals of the U.S. Department of the Interior and had responsibility for three bureaus, one of which was the USGS. Born and raised in Wyoming, I was excited to see the EIS and to learn that there was an interest in exploring a part of the Overthrust Belt—the geological feature that runs the length of the Rocky Mountains from Montana through New Mexico and is thought to contain an abundance of natural gas—close to a town of any size. I knew Jackson's electricity came from hydroelectric power generated in the Pacific Northwest and its homes were heated primarily with propane hauled in over winding and often dangerous two-lane roads. I warmed to the idea that a rich supply of natural gas might be found just south of town to provide hard-working permanent residents, as opposed to the part-timers—summer residents and winter tourists—cheap, clean, and locally produced energy.

There was yet another reason for my interest. The previous year, as the attorney to the Mines and Mining Subcommittee of the U.S. House of Representatives Interior and Insular Affairs Committee under its chairman, James D. Santini (a Democrat from Nevada), and later as a member of the team drafting the "Department of the Interior" chapter of The Heritage Foundation's *Mandate for Leadership*, I became aware of the restrictions imposed on oil and gas lessees operating south of Jackson in the Palisades area—restrictions such as "no surface occupancy" provisions that rendered any oil and gas lease a near nullity. I also had followed the battle over a proposal to conduct seismic work in the Bob Marshall Wilderness Area in northwestern Montana. Nonintrusive seismic work, conducted in the winter on snow-packed and frozen soil, would permit a better understanding of the nature of the Overthrust Belt and where the nation might find new and abundant natural gas reserves. Environmental groups objected mightily and the plan was rejected.[6] Because the federal lands near Jackson were not designated as wilderness, the limitations that stymied energy activity in the Bob Marshall did not apply—the lessee could occupy the surface, conduct seismic work, and do exploratory drilling.

A presidential appointee, Dan Miller, the assistant secretary for energy and minerals, was in my chain of command, but the man to whom I reported directly was the man who appointed me to my post, the secretary of the interior, James G. Watt. When next I saw Watt, I told him about the APD near Jackson and my recommendation that we approve it. "You'd better brief the Wyoming delegation," he replied in his typical no nonsense manner. Easily done, I thought. I knew Senator Malcolm Wallop, a Republican; we met first on the floor of the Senate when I was an attorney to Senator Clifford P. Hansen, a Wyoming Republican. Republican Congressman Dick Cheney of Wyoming was a member of the Interior Committee on which I had served as an attorney. Furthermore, I had flown to Casper to meet with him shortly after his election to offer my assistance when he became—as was all but required of the

"Gentleman from Wyoming"—a member of the committee during the next Congress. As for Senator Alan K. Simpson, another Republican, everyone in Wyoming knew him, or at least, given his phenomenal memory, it seemed he knew everyone, including me. Most importantly, Watt knew him. They met after Watt graduated from Wyoming's College of Law in 1962 and joined the U.S. Senate campaign of former Governor Milward L. Simpson, Al Simpson's father; Al was chairman of the election committee.

I arranged for a conference room in the Capitol Building and, days later, headed for the Hill. Senator Wallop was there, but Simpson and Cheney sent personal and committee staffers. The USGS, created to survey and to map the country, had provided me with its usual outstanding poster-board-backed maps of the location, which I used to deliver a short, to-the-point briefing. Wallop asked what we planned to with the APD. I told him of my recommendation to Watt.

"Perry," Wallop drawled, "I've already heard from oil men in Casper who oppose this project."

"Senator Wallop," I replied, "What did those oil men think about conducting seismic work in the Bob Marshall Wilderness Area in Montana last year?"

"They don't have summer homes in the Bob Marshall," said Wallop. Some of the staffers exchanged smiles and smirks.

"Yes sir, I understand," I said. The meeting was over. I packed up my gear and headed for the government vehicle and my ride across town, but before I got to my office, Watt had heard from the Wyoming delegation. The news was not good.

Days later, as Watt emerged from a cabinet meeting at the White House, Reagan's chief of staff, James A. Baker III, slipped alongside. Baker had just returned from a fishing trip with Cheney in Teton County, where Cheney told him about the Cache Creek APD. "What are you going to do?" asked Baker.

"I suppose I have to deny it," answered Watt.

"You need to see the president," replied Baker.

The next morning, a Friday, at nine o'clock, Baker ushered a downcast Watt into the Oval Office and then left the room. Watt knew he was letting President Reagan down, so he quickly briefed him on the issue, the controversy, and his plans to deny the APD.

"Why?" asked President Reagan.

"Three reasons," replied Watt, "Wallop, Simpson, and Cheney."

President Reagan sat back in his chair. "Jim, if you do not do it, who will? If not there, where will we drill?"[7]

Watt was encouraged and emboldened. "Mr. President," he said leaning forward, "since you are in an advice-giving mood, let me ask you about some other issues we are facing over at Interior." For the next forty-five minutes—in a meeting scheduled for ten—Watt posed the questions and President Reagan provided the answers. When Watt emerged, he held his head high, his shoulders back, and his chest forward; President Reagan had given him, in Watt's words, "a stainless steel backbone."[8]

The Master and the Servant

Watt was hardly a newcomer to the Department of the Interior. Born and raised in Wyoming, he came to Washington, D.C., as the chief legislative assistant to Senator Simpson, whose primary concerns were the policies that emerged from Interior. Later, Watt left Capitol Hill to work at the U.S. Chamber of Commerce on natural resources and environmental issues, many of which involved Interior, and then, after Nixon's election, Watt was the lawyer who guided Governor Walter Hickel of Alaska through a torturous confirmation process to become secretary of the interior. Watt became deputy assistant secretary for water and power development and later director of the Bureau of Outdoor Recreation, both at Interior.

After a short stint at the Federal Power Commission, which became the Federal Energy Regulatory Commission, Watt returned to the West as the first president of Mountain States Legal Foundation (MSLF), a nonprofit, public-interest legal foundation that represents itself and clients in litigation against various federal agencies, often the Department of the Interior.[9] In that role, Watt traveled throughout the Mountain West meeting with and speaking to individuals and groups who believed they were being besieged by federal laws and regulations. Watt, therefore, had a keen understanding of Interior, its mission, and its effect on the West.[10]

As impressive as Watt's background was, President Reagan's familiarity with the vast agency was equally impressive. California, after all, is a vast public-lands state like those in the Mountain West. Nearly half of California is owned by the federal government and managed by various departments and agencies, including the Bureau of Land Management, the Bureau of Reclamation, the U.S. Army Corps of Engineers, the U.S. Forest Service, the National Park Service, and the Department of Defense. It is also the site of American Indian tribal lands often held in trust by the federal government.[11] From 1967 to 1975, therefore, Governor Reagan dealt often with the federal government, not only, as did other governors, when it acted as a sovereign, but also when it was a California landowner and a neighbor to state and private lands.

In January of 1975, shortly after he left office, Reagan wrote and recorded thirteen radio addresses and prepared a newspaper column.[12] For almost five years—with a break only from November of 1975 through August of 1976, when he ran for the Republican nomination for president—Reagan drafted and then delivered 1,027 radio commentaries, 673 of which were written in his own hand.[13] Over two-thirds of the radio addresses concerned domestic issues, such as energy and the environment, which Reagan covered frequently.[14] He discussed, in careful but understandable detail, subjects such as oil and gas, gasoline shortages, nuclear power, endangered species, federal land use planning, coastal zone management, DDT, seal hunting, Alaska lands, federal lands, private property rights, conservation, the environmental movement, pollution, redwoods, wilderness, grazing, lumbering, mining, outdoor recreation, coal, irrigation projects, solar power, the Sagebrush Rebellion, and much more. Not only was the range of Reagan's subjects impressive, but the depth of his analysis and his understanding of them was astonishing. The ease with which he moved from department to department and bureau to bureau, often delving into arcane details that only federal bureaucrats would have reason to know, belied the image—so assiduously constructed by his opponents—of a Hollywood airhead or a huckster from the "rubber chicken circuit." Reagan's commentaries reflected the knowledge of a scholar, a keen observer, and a thoughtful analyst who knew his way from one end of Pennsylvania Avenue to the other.

When Reagan met with Watt for the first time—before Watt's nomination as secretary—the president-elect knew what Interior did. More importantly, he knew what he wanted it to do. James Watt, however, was not Reagan's first choice for secretary of the interior. In the time-honored tradition of appointing an elected politician (a senator, congressman, governor, or attorney general)—in particular, at least since World War II, one from the West—and on the advice of his friend and advisor Republican Senator Paul Laxalt of Nevada,[15] Reagan turned to the recently retired Senator Clifford P. Hansen of Wyoming. When Hansen declined,[16] Laxalt and Republican Senator James A. McClure of Idaho,[17] as well as other Western senators, recommended Watt.[18]

Reagan had never met Watt, but he knew of him and MSLF;[19] in fact, in his final radio commentary before he began his campaign for president, Reagan read from a yellow legal pad his hand-written and lightly edited discussion of a controversial MSLF lawsuit.[20] Watt had never held elected office, nor had he ever been deeply involved in his political party's activities. He had helped with Milward Simpson's successful Senate campaign and served briefly as his top aide, became a Washington lobbyist, received political appointments to three federal administrative posts, and later returned to Colorado, where he was not active politically.[21]

Reagan intended to bring about wholesale change in the federal government's domestic and foreign policies, and he planned to accomplish as much as he could administratively, that is, without the need for congressional approval. Although Republicans controlled the Senate, the House remained firmly in the grip of Speaker Tip O'Neill, a Democrat from Massachusetts, whose disdain for his fellow Irishman in the White House was clear. "You're in the big leagues now," O'Neill told Reagan in their first meeting in the Oval Office, "to set [him] straight on how things operated in Washington."[22] Reversing the policies of course in a department as big and as unwieldy as Interior required a smart, tough, knowledgeable administrator. Reagan's familiarity with the work of MSLF,[23] the recommendations of his close advisor Edwin Meese, Laxalt, and the other Western senators, and his own sense of Watt assured him that the man was perfect. When the two met in December of 1980, Reagan's instructions to Watt were straightforward, broad-reaching, and anything but simple:

- Quell the "Sagebrush Rebellion" by being a "Good Neighbor" to states, governors, county commissioners, and other local government officials;
- Open up federal lands, including the Outer Continental Shelf, to oil and gas and coal development, and for strategic and critical minerals;
- Restore National Park System and U.S. Fish and Wildlife Service lands;
- End Carter's war on Western water projects, return control of Western water to the states, and reform the old Bureau of Reclamation;
- Transfer the lands promised to Western states on admission to the Union; and
- Address the problems facing American Indians.[24]

After Watt resigned in October of 1983, while White House senior staff and others scurried to find a replacement and then leak the name to the media, Reagan quietly turned to his closest friend from California—the man he knew would continue to implement his policies—William P. Clark.[25] After Clark had been confirmed and was in place at Interior,[26] Reagan personally researched and wrote in longhand a radio address on Watt's tenure at Interior that he delivered from his California ranch on November 26, 1983. He concluded, "James G. Watt has served this nation well."[27] Earlier, after meeting with Watt to receive "a report on his stewardship," Reagan wrote, "He knew that in carrying out my policies his days would be numbered."[28]

Although Clark's demeanor differed markedly from the effusive, expansive, and exceedingly blunt Watt—Judge Clark, as he was called due to his lengthy service on the California Supreme Court and Superior Court, possessed an imposing, immovable, and inscrutable judicial temperament—his mission at Interior, on instructions from Reagan, remained the same as the one given to Watt. In fact, as he prepared to depart Interior in late 1984, Clark, in a hand-written, five-page, six-point letter to the president, wrote, "The policies begun by Jim Watt are going well and I hope to make them your quiet legacy."[29]

Like his predecessor, Clark never held elected office, but like a number of secretaries earlier in the twentieth century, he had held other appointed positions before leading Interior.[30] Clark was a confidant of the president, and his role at Interior was not limited to the bureaus and agencies there. He was most like the department's longest-tenured secretary, Harold L. Ickes, who served thirteen years under Presidents Franklin D. Roosevelt and Harry S. Truman.[31]

As Reagan's second term began with a vacancy to fill at Interior, he turned to another tried and true administrator who had never held elected office, Donald Paul Hodel. Hodel had been active in Republican politics for decades, had served twenty-one months as Watt's undersecretary, which made him, in effect, Interior's chief operating officer, and was now Reagan's secretary of energy. Clark knew that Hodel would pursue the policies that Watt had begun and that Clark had continued. In fact, it was Clark who persuaded Reagan to nominate Hodel. In his relatively brief meeting with the president to discuss the nomination, Hodel asked forthrightly, "Mr. President, I assume you want me to continue to implement the policies begun by Jim Watt?" President Reagan said, "Yes," and on January 10, 1985, he announced Hodel's nomination.[32]

That Reagan selected three seasoned administrators, one of whom was his closest and most trusted friend, who he assigned to handle only the toughest and most important of jobs,[33] demonstrates the vital role he believed the Interior Department needed to play in his administration.

Ronald Reagan on the Economy, Energy, and the Environment

In accepting the presidential nomination at the Republican National Convention in Detroit on July 17, 1980, Ronald Reagan declared:

> First, we must overcome something the present administration has cooked up: a new and altogether indigestible economic

stew, one part inflation, one part high unemployment, one part
recession, one part runaway taxes, one part deficit spending
and seasoned by an energy crisis. It's an economic stew that
has turned the national stomach.[34]

———

Those who preside over the worst energy shortage in our
history tell us to use less, so that we will run out of oil, gasoline, and natural gas a little more slowly. Conservation is
desirable, of course, for we must not waste energy. But conservation is not the sole answer to our energy needs.

America must get to work producing more energy. The
Republican program for solving economic problems is based
on growth and productivity.

Large amounts of oil and natural gas lay beneath our land
and off our shores, untouched because the present administration seems to believe the American people would rather see
more regulation, taxes and controls than more energy.

———

Make no mistake. We will not permit the safety of our people
or our environment heritage to be jeopardized, but we are
going to reaffirm that the economic prosperity of our people
is a fundamental part of our environment.[35]

Six months later, in his inaugural address, Reagan announced,

[T]his administration's objective will be a healthy, vigorous,
growing economy.... With the idealism and fair play which
are the core of our system and our strength, we can have a
strong and prosperous America, at peace with itself and the
world.

If we look to the answer as to why for so many years we achieved so much, prospered as no other people on Earth, it was because here in this land we unleashed the energy and individual genius of man to a greater extent than has ever been done before.... It is no coincidence that our present troubles parallel and are proportionate to the intervention and intrusion in our lives that result from unnecessary and excessive growth of government. It is time for us to realize that we are too great a nation to limit ourselves to small dreams. We are not, as some would have us believe, doomed to an inevitable decline.[36]

Ronald Reagan's research, analysis, and writing of his radio commentaries over the years had convinced him of several facts regarding energy—specifically oil and gas, federal lands, and the free market. First, he did not believe the federal government's estimates regarding the nation's energy present, let alone its energy future. "I don't buy the CIA's report quoted by [President Carter that] has us running out of oil in about 30 years....[37] I don't believe it will be gone in 30 or 33 years."[38] Ronald Reagan had good historical reasons for his disbelief. As he recounted in one of his radio addresses:

In 1914, the U.S. Bureau of Mines projected future production of crude oil at 5.7 billion barrels. Since then we've produced 34 billion barrels. Incidentally about that same time we were told there was no hope of ever finding oil in Texas or Kansas.

In 1920, we were told we'd be out of oil in 15 years. Nineteen years later in 1939, the Department of the Interior told us we'd run out in 13 years. Since then, we have discovered more than the total known oil reserves we had at that time.

In 1948, the proven reserves in all of the free world amounted to 62.3 billion barrels. Within 24 years, there were nine times as many. In 1949, our Department of the Interior said the end of the U.S. oil supply was in sight. We increased production in the next five years by a million barrels a day.

By 1970, known world reserves were six times as large as they were in 1950.... Significantly and contrary to much of what is being said, the amount of proven reserves is increasing faster than the rate of consumption.[39]

Second, Ronald Reagan believed that, with regard to the development of energy, the "government is not the solution to our problem; government is the problem,"[40] not only because "[t]he federal government owns one-third of the United States—that would be equal to all the land East of the Mississippi River," but also because much of that land holds vast energy resources that are off limits to the American people.[41] In late 1978, he cited Dean William Lesher of the University of Arizona College of Mines, who estimated that "50 percent of all our known energy sources are in these federal lands [y]et in 1976, they only accounted for 10 percent of our total energy production."[42] Even worse, "[i]n 1968, only about one-quarter of federal lands had been withdrawn from use. Six years later that had become three-quarters and no one knows the current rate of withdrawal."[43] Ironically, reported Ronald Reagan, in an area where "[o]ne of the richest natural gas strikes in years was made within recent months," both the Bureau of Land Management and the U.S. Forest Service "are trying to lock up an additional 90 million acres."[44]

Third, Ronald Reagan offered a simple but time-tested and true solution to the "energy crisis," one that had been abandoned by the Carter administration: "Why don't we try the free market again?"[45] He offered two solutions to "our foolishness."[46] One was to strengthen both the United States economy and the value of the American dollar.[47] Another was "decontrol of the well head price."[48] He believed that these two solutions would unleash America's entrepreneurial spirit and help unlock vast stores of known energy resources not available through lower-cost, conventional technology.[49] Reagan called for one more change: recognition that the oil and gas industry is not a monopoly, and that it is the independent operator who makes most new discoveries:

[Recently] a punitive attitude toward the oil industry has prevailed. The incentives are gone and a network of regulations makes wildcatting so high risk few are tempted. About 80% of the finding of new oil has been done—not by the giant oil companies but by independents and they have been the hardest hit by government's punitive policies.[50]

The Department of the Interior in a Conservative Administration

In the summer of 1980, while all attention was on the nominating conventions and the presidential campaigns, twenty project teams gathered in Washington, D.C., to draft a blueprint for a hoped-for Reagan administration, *Mandate for Leadership*.[51] One team, under the leadership of Robert L. Terrell, a professional staff member on the Energy and Environment Subcommittee of the House Interior and Insular Affairs Committee, drafted a chapter titled "The Department of Interior."[52]

Mandate argued that Interior's mission in the Carter administration had changed from "conservation," that is, the wise use of natural resources,[53] to "preservation" because of the perception of Carter, Secretary Cecil Andrus, and other top officials that Interior's constituency was the environmental lobby, which opposed any development of energy and mineral resources.[54] *Mandate* charged that Interior displays "an apparent timidity in discussing the energy and mineral wealth of the United States," as a result of "a new departmental constituency positioned against prudent development of domestic resources," which yields a "flaccid" "energy and minerals posture" and "a cadre of minerals professionals in the federal sector disillusioned with their scuttled policy role."[55]

After listing a series of sins of omission and commission, including several oil and gas leasing moratoria and various solicitor's opinions, *Mandate* concluded:

The federal government, America's largest and most powerful land owner, is also the nation's most powerful energy and

minerals monopolist—a monopolist whose policies and programs have created artificial scarcities, inflated prices and
national vulnerability to foreign powers.[56]

Mandate expressed concern that of the "824 million acres of public
lands subject to [oil and gas] leasing, 321 million acres, or 39 percent,
are closed to [oil and gas] leasing [and] [a]n additional 81 million acres
are highly restricted from [oil and gas] development even if they were
leased." Moreover, contrary to federal law, the Carter administration had
failed to restore withdrawn lands to eligibility for oil and gas leasing at
the same time that it expanded Wilderness Study Areas (WSAs), sharply
limiting the oil and gas activities permitted in these areas.[57]

The Reagan Administration Tackles Onshore Oil and Gas Leasing

Within days of taking office, President Reagan removed all price
controls from crude oil and refined petroleum products to encourage the
discovery, development, and delivery of known or new energy supplies.[58]
It thus fell to Interior to ensure that the search included federal lands
available for oil and gas development in accordance with federal law.[59]
Although various types of federal lands are subject to oil and gas leasing—for example, lands managed by the Bureau of Land Management
(BLM) (245 million acres),[60] the U.S. Forest Service (USFS) (190 million
acres),[61] the U.S. Fish and Wildlife Service (150 million acres),[62] and the
U.S. Department of Defense (twenty million acres)[63]—some federal holdings are statutorily off limits, including most of the National Park System
(eighty-three million acres),[64] as well as land managed by agencies such
as the BLM and USFS but designated by Congress as "wilderness."[65]

The term "wilderness," as applied to federal lands, means lands designated by Congress pursuant to the Wilderness Act of 1964 as federal
lands "where the earth and its community of life are untrammeled by
man," "where man himself is a visitor who does not remain,"and where
no motorized activity is permitted.[66] As of late 1981, there were 23.4
million acres of wilderness in the continental United States: the USFS
administered 19.7 million, the National Park Service managed three

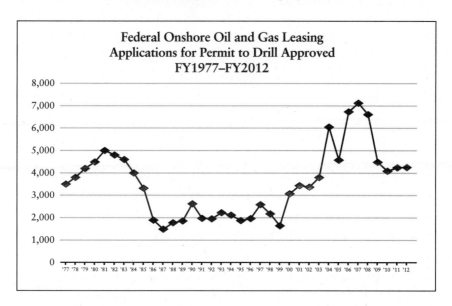

million, the U.S. Fish and Wildlife Service managed 0.7 million, and the BLM administered 12,000.[67] In passing the Wilderness Act, Congress left the designated lands open for oil and gas leasing through 1984. Because much of the national forest lands designated as wilderness were formerly "primitive" lands—high altitude, alpine areas—there was little if any interest in exploring those areas. Instead, the controversy that would erupt during Reagan's presidency involved not wilderness lands but the millions of acres tabbed by various federal agencies as "recommended wilderness," "further planning areas," and "wilderness study areas."[68]

Notwithstanding the furor whipped up by national environmental groups over oil and gas leasing activity that was never planned, proposed, or promulgated, the Reagan administration moved to develop the nation's publicly owned oil and gas resources. It could do little else. After all, as of 1981, "[l]ess than 15% of the federal onshore multiple use lands were under lease for oil and gas development; no federal onshore oil and gas leases had been issued in Alaska for 15 years; no oil shale leases had been issued since 1974; ... no tar sands leases had been issued since 1965, and geothermal energy development was stifled...."[69]

The administration moved with breathtaking speed and virtually no opposition from Congress:

- From 1981 to 1983, over ninety-three million acres of federal onshore oil and gas leases were issued—nearly twice the 51.8 million acres leased from 1977 to 1980;
- From 1981 to 1983, 14,400 oil and gas drilling permits were processed, 1,910 more than were processed in the three previous years;
- In 1982, the first federal onshore oil and gas leases in Alaska in fifteen years were issued—259 leases covering 2.8 million acres; in 1983, 915 oil and gas leases were issued covering over 1.5 million acres;
- Oil and gas regulations were streamlined—the first total revision in over twenty-five years, eliminating counter-productive and obsolete provisions and spelling out leasing procedures for 290 million acres managed by the BLM, about 300 million acres managed by other federal agencies, and some sixty-five million acres of state- or privately-owned land, where mineral rights are reserved by the federal government;
- In 1983, over 2.2 million acres were offered in a sale in the National Petroleum Reserve in Alaska (NPR-A), netting $16.7 million in high bids; in 1982, the largest federal competitive oil and gas lease sale in NPR-A history was held, offering 4.25 million acres in two sales;[70] and
- In 1987, because of the immense oil and gas potential of the coastal plain of the Arctic National Wildlife Refuge as determined by the USGS and the BLM, Congress was urged to authorize development in the region.[71]

Meanwhile, to assist Congress in its deliberations regarding various wilderness bills, Interior completed studies regarding the potential oil and gas resources on lands being considered for wilderness designation in eleven Western states, concluding that "[a]bout one-third of the wilderness lands have petroleum potential."[72] When allegations were made regarding the potential mishandling of crude oil from onshore federal and Indian leases,[73] Watt appointed a presidential commission to study the matter and make recommendations, worked with Congress to enact legislation, and in 1983, adopted "regulations [to] reverse revenue losses and ensure that the federal government, representing the general public and Indian Tribes, receives all royalties due from mineral development."[74] Furthermore, to implement a specific proposal set forth in *Mandate for Leadership*, Watt "[c]onsolidated responsibility for all mineral lease activity[, including those formerly performed by the USGS's Conservation Division,] on federal and Indian mineral leases in the [BLM], and responsibility for all mineral lease accounting functions in the Minerals Management Service."[75]

Finally, Watt took steps to ensure the integrity of the free market system of federal onshore oil and gas leasing on which Reagan's Interior Department intended to rely and to address allegations of fraud and improprieties. The department reformed its procedures for identifying tracts as competitive and noncompetitive and increased the up-front financial burden on those who wished to participate in the lottery portion of the noncompetitive oil and gas system. The department believed that this system, when properly administered, remained a highly efficient and therefore profitable means of finding oil and gas resources where few thought energy resources existed.[76] After all, as of 1981, noncompetitive onshore oil and gas leases produced 82.4 percent of the oil and 95.9 percent of the natural gas produced from federal leases.[77]

In 1983, onshore federal leases in the lower forty-eight states covered 146 million acres and accounted for 4 percent of all domestic oil and 6 percent of all domestic natural gas production. Moreover, federal onshore oil and gas activity generated a billion dollars in revenue, far more than any other onshore federal lands activity. The potential for even more energy production was great, given that, in mid-1985, federal lands were thought to contain a sixth of the nation's undiscovered oil and gas reserves.[78]

Domestic Oil and Gas Collapse—and Rebirth

Then in 1986 the unthinkable happened: the bottom fell out of the price of domestic crude oil.[79] A decade earlier, such an occurrence would

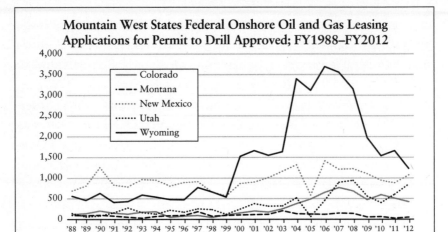

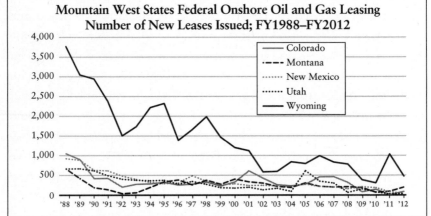

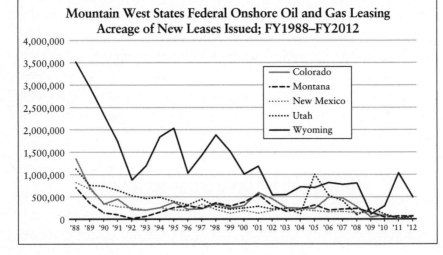

have been inconceivable. After all, in 1973, the Organization of Petroleum Exporting Countries (OPEC), led by Saudi Arabia, reduced production, embargoed deliveries to the United States, and then raised its price to nearly twelve dollars a barrel—four times the average price at the time. In 1979, Iran's revolution drove prices to twenty dollars a barrel; then Saudi Arabia raised its price to twenty-six dollars a barrel. In 1980, when war broke out between Iran and Iraq, light crude from Saudi Arabia shot to twenty-eight dollars a barrel and then up to thirty-four dollars a barrel. Experts thought that crude oil could not drop below twenty dollars a barrel and that, by the twenty-first century, crude oil would be at a hundred dollars a barrel. The petroleum industry responded by drilling wells—a lot of wells![80]

In 1982, the recession hit bottom; by the next year oil prices were below thirty dollars a barrel. The year after that, savings and loan institutions, sustained by high energy prices, began to go under. Even so, in 1985, experts thought oil would never drop below twenty-five dollars a barrel but would eventually climb toward one hundred dollars a barrel. No one expected that Saudi Arabia, with its vast oil reserves, would flood the market.[81] In December 1985, it did just that, and the "Oil Price Collapse of 1986" was underway.[82]

In Denver and across the West, major oil companies sold their leases, let their employees go, sublet their office space, and left town—for good, it would seem. But as Ronald Reagan mentioned in one of his radio commentaries, it is not the major oil companies that make the discoveries but the independents.[83] One of those independents was McMurry Oil Company (MOC) located in Casper, Wyoming, and owned by the late W. N. "Neil" McMurry, his son Neil "Mick" McMurry, and their partner John Martin. Mick McMurry said, "There were a lot of opportunities in [natural gas] and no one else believed in it," so MOC went looking for prospects "that we could believe in and afford."[84] What they found was in Wyoming, in Pinedale, 275 miles due west of Casper.

Drilling had begun in the area in 1939, but it had not yet unlocked the area's energy riches. In 1991, MOC bought three leases that had yielded unpromising results and then acquired additional BLM leases. MOC consulted with the nation's top fracturing experts to discover how to "unlock" the tight shale formations.[85] This, of course, was the very type of "[un]conventional technology" that Ronald Reagan knew would be required to develop America's energy resources.[86] MOC had hoped to produce a million cubic feet of natural gas a day from its three wells, but in September of 1993 MOC was reporting two million cubic feet a day. More BLM leases and more drilling and discoveries followed. In November of 2001, as a result of its use of innovative new technologies, MOC's success attracted other operators into Wyoming; the "majors" were back in the Rockies.[87]

Mick McMurry recently reminisced about the early days working with the BLM. "We did up an EA (environmental assessment) in a month and I was moving dirt with my bulldozer all the while. When the EA was final, we were spudding within the day." But no more, says Mick McMurry. Today, a full-blown EIS is required that can fill a small room with documents. "And then there's the sage grouse," adds Mick McMurry. Little wonder that the fracturing breakthrough achieved in west-central Wyoming on federal lands is now underway across the country—almost everywhere but on federal lands. The Barnett, the Haynesville, the Fayetteville, the Marcellus, the Utica, where the oil and gas industry is using hydraulic fracturing to discover, develop, and deliver vast amounts of oil and natural gas, are on state or private lands; leasing of and development on federal lands is not part of this amazing success story.[88]

Worse yet, President Obama's Environmental Protection Agency has waged a relentless war against fracturing, while Obama's Interior Department plans regulations to remove the fracturing permitting process regarding oil and gas activity on federal lands from the hands of individual states and is dragging its feet on the leasing and developing of federal onshore oil and gas properties. At the same time, the administration is spending billions of dollars on "green energy" sources, given the historic prejudice of environmental groups against all hydrocarbon energy sources such as coal, oil, and even clean natural gas.[89] In doing so, they reject Reagan's insight that the marketplace will provide real solutions to the nation's energy problems if they will simply let it work.[90] Instead, Obama and the "experts" who surround him think they know better.[91]

In 2012, Harold Hamm, the Oklahoman who owns Continental Resources, was part of a small meeting with President Obama. Hamm knew that he had only a couple of minutes to make his case; he wanted those minutes to count. "I told him of the revolution in the oil and gas industry and how we have the capacity to produce enough oil to enable America to replace OPEC."

Obama brushed the remarks aside. "Oil and gas will be important for the next few years," said Obama. "But we need to go on to green and alternative energy. [Energy] Secretary [Steven] Chu has assured me that within five years, we can have a battery developed that will make a car with the equivalent of 130 miles per gallon."

"Even if you believed that," says Hamm, "why would you want to stop oil and gas development?"[92]

Three decades after Ronald Reagan came into office determined to provide for America's energy future, oil and gas leasing and permitting on federal lands onshore are declining by the year. With a third of the country's onshore lands in the hands of the federal government, is it too much to ask that the federal government become part of America's energy future to the overwhelming economic benefit of the American people?[93]

———

The greatest future source of oil and natural gas, however, is off America's shores, beneath the Outer Continental Shelf.

CHAPTER TWO

LARGE AMOUNTS OF OIL AND GAS—OFF OUR SHORES[1]

"What are the facts? [I]n Louisiana[,] where there was great offshore [oil and gas] drilling and production[,] the fish catch increased 400 percent."
—RONALD REAGAN, JUNE 5, 1978[2]

Cover-up in Washington's Energy Game

I n a radio commentary in October of 1977, Ronald Reagan referred to the surprising news that the director of the U.S. Geological Survey, Dr. Vincent McKelvey, had been fired.[3] "In 98 years," he said, "the agency has only had nine directors. They are nominated by the National Academy of Sciences and Presidents have always accepted them and not fired them."[4] Unfortunately for Dr. McKelvey, Reagan observed, he had blown a "hole in the [White House] script" that "we'd be running out of fuel before the turn of the century...."[5] McKelvey, "an expert on geology but a rank amateur on politics," had "mentioned a 4000 year supply of geo-pressured gas in the Gulf of Mexico, also a large amount of oil still to be found in the United States." It got worse:

The White House quickly covered with a CIA report (you
remember the CIA) that the Russians would run out of oil by
1985 and start buying it from the Arabs. Dr. McKelvey, sincerely interested in helping out, said, "No, the Russians are
floating on a sea of oil."[6]

Accepting the presidential nomination of the Republican Party three years
later, Reagan declared, "America must get to work producing more
energy [from oil and gas deposits] off our shores...."[7] Not surprisingly,
given offshore energy's importance, the people at work that summer of
1980 on *Mandate for Leadership* addressed the same topic:

> During the past four years, [Outer Continental Shelf] OCS oil
> and gas leasing has not been recognized as an important com-
> ponent of short-term domestic energy supply, and thus, as one
> of the most vital tools the U.S. has to reduce or minimize
> OPEC supply interruptions and price pressures in both the
> short and medium range.[8]

As a result, concluded *Mandate*, the Carter administration's OCS oil
and gas program suffered from a number of "[d]eficiencies," including
"a timid OCS schedule," the exclusion from leasing plans or the infre-
quent leasing of "high potential areas," and "[l]imitations on the scope
of sales," as well as other procedural and bureaucratic road blocks amidst
wasteful and time-consuming federal spending.[9]

Mandate proposed a series of short-term and long-term action items:

- A new five-year leasing schedule featuring:
  - More sales and larger acreages;
  - Faster sales in high-prospect areas;
  - More repeat sales in high-prospect areas;
  - Simplified administration;
  - A streamlined EIS process for repeat sales;
  - An increase in the size or composition of California sales;
  - An increase in the size of sales in the Gulf of Mexico;

- Termination of duplicative and expensive studies;
- Return of all OCS leasing to the Interior Department.[10]

Mandate called for "reorganization of OCS authority in the Interior Department" because the "[p]resent organization only encourages turf battles, a lack of accountability, and bureaucratic cartwheels for day-to-day functioning." Putting "OCS authority" under a single leader "would contribute substantially to the formulation and timely execution of an aggressive OCS schedule."[11]

The Federal OCS Oil and Gas Program

In 1946, President Truman ordered development of the energy resources in the OCS.[12] In 1952, General Eisenhower made an election year promise to resolve the dispute between the federal government and coastal states over ownership of the OCS to permit exploration for and development of oil and gas resources owned by the federal government.[13] In 1953, Congress statutorily resolved the long-running dispute,[14] enacting legislation that defined the OCS to include "all submerged lands lying seaward and outside of the area of lands beneath navigable waters as defined [elsewhere in federal law], and of which the subsoil and seabed appertain to the United States and are subject to its jurisdiction and control,"[15] and authorized the secretary of the interior to put federal OCS tracts up for bid and subsequent lease.[16]

In 1954, Interior held its first OCS lease sale, this one in the Gulf of Mexico off the coast of Louisiana—the site of state oil and gas production since 1938—which brought $116,378,476 worth of bonus bids into the U.S. Treasury.[17] Federal law regarding OCS oil and gas leasing would not change for another decade and a half.[18]

One year after production began in 1968 on the first federal lease in the Santa Barbara Channel off the California coast, a blowout and spill occurred in federal waters, ushering in the nascent environmental movement.[19] In 1970, the National Environmental Policy Act (NEPA) and the Clean Air Act were passed,[20] followed in 1972 by enactment of the Coastal Zone Management Act (CZMA) and the Marine Mammal

Protection Act,[21] and in 1973 by passage of the Endangered Species Act.[22] In 1977, the Clean Water Act passed,[23] and in 1978, Congress made major revisions to the Outer Continental Shelf Lands Act,[24] mandating a five-year leasing program, formalizing environmental studies, and requiring coordination and information-sharing with various affected parties, especially the states.[25] Finally, in 1980, Congress amended the CZMA.[26]

When Reagan took office, the OCS oil and gas program was all but moribund. Since 1953, out of nearly a billion acres, only 17.9 million acres of the OCS had ever been leased for oil and gas development, and at the end of 1979, a scant 10.3 million acres remained under lease.[27] Nonetheless, the OCS leases issued prior to 1977 still accounted for 17 percent of all domestically produced oil and gas.[28] The need to do more was obvious, especially following the 1977 Arab oil embargo and given Interior's view that "85% of the crude oil still to be discovered in America is likely to come from public lands, 67% of that from offshore drilling."[29]

President Reagan's charge to Secretary Watt regarding OCS oil and gas leasing was clear: government will not be the problem; it will be part of the solution. Reagan's twin goals of national energy self-sufficiency and economic recovery required that Watt abandon the Carter administration's recently adopted (June of 1980) but extremely limited five-year OCS leasing plan.[30] In July of 1982, Watt announced that, rather than trying to identify the most promising OCS tracts for development of oil and gas resources, the Interior Department's plan, over its five-year life, would make the entire OCS, an area estimated to contain one billion acres, available for leasing.[31] Only a very small portion of the OCS would be leased annually, of course.[32] The decision on where to search for energy, however, would not be made by government bureaucrats with little or no expertise and experience and absolutely no stake in the results. Instead, it would be made by companies that paid the millions of dollars in bonus bids to acquire the leases and the tens or hundreds of millions of dollars to explore for and produce oil and gas. Watt's proposal for forty-one OCS lease sales over five years made available twenty times more acreage than Andrus's 1980 proposal of fifty-five million acres in thirty-six sales, and twenty-five times more acreage than had been offered for lease from 1954—when federal OCS oil and gas leasing began—to 1980.[33] In fact, over the course of all federal OCS leasing, just forty-one million acres had been offered for lease and only nineteen million acres had been leased.[34]

Watt argued that the Reagan administration's OCS oil and gas leasing program would "enhance ... national security, provide jobs, and protect the environment while making America less dependent on foreign oil sources."[35] In fact, according to *Business Week*, with Congress unwilling to seriously consider abolishing the U.S. Department of Energy or to expeditiously decontrol natural gas prices, Watt's OCS program was "the only active energy policy proposal during the first term of the Reagan administration."[36] Watt's objective was simple, "to inventory and ultimately [to] develop the hydrocarbon resources of the Outer Continental Shelf."[37] To critics who argued that, even with the Reagan administration's aggressive OCS program, it would take 137 years to evaluate the energy potential of the federal OCS, Watt answered with the charge given him by Reagan in the Oval Office in September 1981—"If not us, who? If not now, when?"[38] The Reagan administration's OCS program:

- Increased substantially the rate of OCS leasing—average sale areas went from 900,000 acres under Andrus's plan from 1977 through 1982 to about twenty-four million acres in 1983 and 1984 under Watt;[39]
- Entered "frontier," or largely unexplored, areas with great oil and gas potential earlier:
  - Through 1980, only 0.6 percent of Alaska's OCS areas had been made available for leasing and only 0.2% had been leased; worse yet,
  - Through 1982, under the Andrus plan, only 10 percent of the acreage leased was in frontier regions outside producing areas in the Gulf of Mexico and the Santa Barbara Channel;[40] and
- Streamlined the paperwork process required to conduct OCS oil and gas lease sales from the forty-two months once necessary to just twenty-one months.[41]

Meanwhile, Watt's decision—in early 1982, prior to announcing his new five-year OCS plan—to create the Minerals Management Service dramatically increased the efficiency of the OCS oil and gas program.[42] By stripping the program's pre-leasing activity from the Bureau of Land Management and its post-leasing efforts from the Conservation Division of the U.S. Geological Survey, Watt ended a long-running, often acrimonious, and inefficient turf battle between the two old-line Interior bureaus. Creation of a unified minerals agency, akin to those throughout the Western world, would dramatically increase the agency's efficiency for nearly three decades.[43]

Environmental groups, some coastal state officials, and Democratic legislators objected, but to no avail.[44] President Reagan supported the plan, and it appeared that the public was with him.[45] Meanwhile, Watt negotiated successfully with coastal states, which ensured that nine of ten scheduled OCS lease offerings were held on time or with only minor delays.[46] Watt signed a memorandum of understanding (MOU) with both North Carolina and Florida prior to the South Atlantic lease offering held in 1983.[47] Watt signed two MOUs with Alaska to ensure the success of the Norton Basin and St. George Basin sales, which yielded $2.9 billion in bonus bids.[48] In addition, Watt signed an MOU with California's secretary of environmental affairs, which provided for "tract deferrals; stipulations and lessee advisories; consultation in protecting marine life; elaboration of air quality standards; protect[ion of] fishing interests; and, [allowance for the] initial processing of oil at onshore facilities."[49] Finally, Watt's decision to conduct Sale No. 53 off the California coast over the objections of environmental groups was vindicated when drilling in the Santa Maria Basin revealed the largest oil discovery since Prudhoe Bay.[50]

The five-year program was the target of litigation, of course, when it went final in July of 1982.[51] In July of 1983, however, the U.S. Court of Appeals for the District of Columbia upheld the administration's five-year OCS program.[52] In a stunning setback for the coastal states and environmental groups that filed suit, the three-judge panel, upon consideration of the mandate by Congress that the five-year plan "promote the swift, orderly, and efficient exploration of our almost untapped domestic oil and gas resources in the Outer Continental Shelf," held that "the [Reagan] program went beyond what was required by the statute."[53]

To the assertion by the program's opponents that area-wide leasing resulted in a "fire sale" of OCS tracts,[54] the panel answered that federal law "does not mandate the maximization of revenues, it only requires receipt of a fair return," which the program assures.[55] To the argument by the program's opponents that making the entire OCS available was "too much, too soon,"[56] the panel ruled that the five-year program is "'pyramidic in structure, proceeding from broad-based planning to an increasingly narrower focus as actual development grows more imminent' ... an area included in the program may be excluded at a latter stage."[57] To the allegation by the program's opponents that Watt had not properly considered the "environmental impact,"[58] the panel responded, "[a]fter reviewing the Secretary's analysis and methodology, we conclude that he has met the obligation imposed upon him by [federal law.]"[59]

Six months later, the Supreme Court of the United States handed the Reagan administration yet another victory over California, which had asserted that Interior's plan to conduct Lease Sale No. 53 in federal waters off California's shores was an activity "directly affecting" the California coastal zone. Secretary Andrus had removed 128 tracts but left 115 tracts in the proposed sale; California demanded the removal of more tracts and complained that the failure to do so would cause Lease Sale No. 53 to "directly affect" the California coastal zone. On behalf of the 5-4 Court, Justice O'Connor wrote that Congress did not intend for OCS leasing to fall within the "consistency" provision of the Coastal Zone Management Act (CZMA).[60] In short, states like California would not be able to scuttle federal OCS oil and gas leasing by alleging violations of the CZMA.

Rebuffed by the administration and the courts, opponents of Reagan's OCS program turned to Congress. Beginning in fiscal year 1982, Congress included language in its annual appropriations bills barring Interior from implementing the OCS program with regard to specific OCS areas totaling tens of millions of acres.[61] The ban, renewed annually with ever increasing acreage, continued for years.[62] The moratoria created uncertainty for companies seeking to spend tens of millions of dollars to explore for and develop OCS oil and gas resources, effectively blinding the country to its valuable energy resources.[63] In response to the moratoria, Secretary Clark testified, "If a foreign power had managed to do to us what we have done to ourselves, to shape our energy policy so disastrously, we would call it an act of war."[64] When the time came in 1987, Secretary Hodel adopted the Reagan administration's second five-year OCS oil and gas-leasing plan, which continued to offer the entire OCS.[65]

Into the Deep Water

The nation's offshore oil and gas industry, its ancillary companies, and the local communities across the country who make their living in the energy sector supported the Reagan plan enthusiastically.[66] For one thing, the availability of an entire planning area as opposed to the federal government's rationing of tracts through a tedious nomination and selection process ensured that a company would get the tracts it thought were most promising and could test out its theories about an area's geology.[67]

Moreover, under the Reagan plan, the private sector paid for the costly research into what the public's offshore lands held, and those whose investment and insight proved successful benefitted right along with the American people, who gained not only new supplies of energy but also the jobs and revenues that new economic activity generated. Even though the 1981–1982 recession had depressed oil demand,[68] *Newsweek* reported in May of 1983 that "[w]hile rigs stood idle in the inshore shallows of the Gulf of Mexico, more than 1,200 oilmen gathered … in New Orleans' Superdome to testify to their faith in the health of their industry."[69] The Central Gulf of Mexico lease sale—the first OCS sale using the Reagan administration's new area-wide approach—offered 37.9 million acres for lease and harvested a record $3.47 billion in high bonus bids.[70] Many of the tracts leased were deepwater tracts, that is, beyond depths of 1,000 feet, an area where government geologists saw little potential.[71]

Shell Oil, which had won the majority of the deepwater tracts at the May of 1983 sale, began drilling immediately.[72] In October of 1983, Shell made a "major discovery" at "Bullwinkle," which came to be known as the deepwater "Mini-Basin Play."[73] In the next Central Gulf of Mexico sale, in April of 1984, other companies, aware of Shell's discovery, moved quickly to bid on deepwater tracts. Nonetheless, at the May of 1985 Central Gulf of Mexico sale, Shell again dominated, winning eighty-six of 108 deepwater tracts, including out to depths of six thousand feet.[74] During this period, 1985–1986, oil prices collapsed to ten dollars a barrel, leading to the "inevitable disassembly of the offshore system and its onshore support network for the Gulf of Mexico."[75]

Meanwhile, the industry, which had been optimistic about exploring offshore Alaska, "lost its craving for the Arctic" after a number of dry holes and slumping oil prices.[76] Low oil prices would have ruined the industry's appetite for the Gulf of Mexico too but for the Reagan OCS plan, which enabled a company to access what it believed to be promising deepwater tracts in which no other company had an interest.[77] Lowering the minimum bid from $900,000 to $150,000, which allowed companies to acquire entire basins for ten years for only a few million dollars, encouraged energy companies to take a longer view.[78]

The deregulation of natural gas in 1989 caused prices to plummet, which benefitted consumers as Reagan intended, but hurt producers in the Gulf of Mexico's gas-prone continental shelf, which drove energy companies into the oil-rich deepwater. Then, in December of 1989, Shell announced a major discovery at "Auger," which was estimated later to contain 220 million barrels of oil equivalent, in the Garden Banks area nearly 140 miles off the Louisiana coast.[79] The same year, Shell drilled into "Mars" in a field directly south of the mouth of the Mississippi River in three thousand feet of water on leases purchased in 1985 and in 1988 for $5.3 million.[80] Mars, twice the size of Auger, was "the largest field discovered in the Gulf of Mexico in 25 years."[81]

Over the next five years, notwithstanding depressed oil and gas prices, companies bought up 1,500 deepwater OCS tracts.[82] Then, once news of the remarkable productivity of Auger and Mars broke, "the Gulf

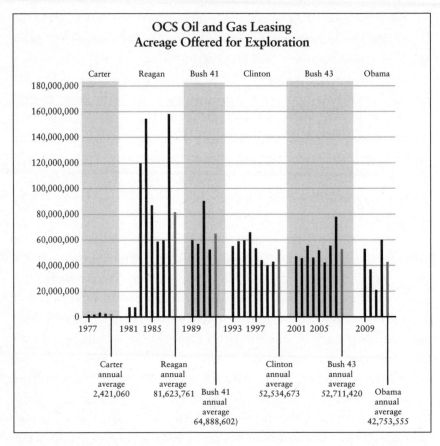

of Mexico became the hottest oil play in the world."[83] Over the next several years, major oil companies and contractors in the offshore-service industry came up with new technologies—including digital, three-dimensional seismic imaging—to find new reserves and to enhance old ones. Meanwhile, drilling and subsea engineering advanced by leaps and bounds.[84]

Reagan had been proved right. His vision of the potential of offshore energy resources and his aggressive push for the development of those resources, despite opposition from Congress and subsequent administrations, opened up vast offshore areas and provided opportunities for energy companies to explore deeper waters. The result was an increase in oil and gas reserves and government revenues, as well as thousands of high-paying jobs. Reagan's foresight and free market policies encouraged the marvelous technological advances that yielded remarkable energy, economic, and environmental benefits. Had his policies been allowed to continue, significantly more offshore oil and gas exploration and production and the resultant economic activity would be going on today.

Back to Square One: The Gulf in Economic Shambles

In July of 2008, President George W. Bush lifted the OCS moratorium adopted by his father, President George H. W. Bush, and continued by President Clinton. This allowed Interior to prepare for a new five-year plan, which would include the newly opened areas, to run from 2010 through 2015.[85] In September of 2008, Congress permitted the OCS moratorium to expire and enacted an appropriations bill that did not contain the Interior funding bans, except for a moratorium on the eastern Gulf of Mexico, first adopted in 2007.[86] In January of 2009, President Bush released his new five-year plan, which provided for leasing in four areas off Alaska, two areas off the Pacific Coast, three areas in the Atlantic Ocean, and two areas in the Gulf of Mexico.[87]

Shortly after taking office, President Obama froze the Bush five-year plan to initiate a study of the program, which ran for nearly three years, with a series of lease sale cancellations in the process.[88] Then, in late 2011, Obama announced a new five-year plan that cancelled five of the Alaska sales and killed all OCS leasing off the Pacific and Atlantic coasts, including a proposed lease off Virginia.[89] Finally, contrary to the advice of a panel of experts it had selected to study OCS oil and gas leasing following the BP blowout,[90] the Obama administration handcuffed the federal OCS program with the imposition of drilling moratoria on existing leases in the Gulf of Mexico and Alaska.[91]

Gulf Drilling Revival

In June of 2011, ExxonMobil announced two major oil discoveries and a gas discovery in the Gulf of Mexico. Drilling in several blocks of federal leases at a point 280 nautical miles southeast of Houston and 250 nautical miles southwest of New Orleans in over seven thousand feet of water, ExxonMobil made the largest discovery in the Gulf of Mexico in a decade. "We estimate a recoverable resource of more than

Areas Open for Energy Exploration under President Reagan's 1982 OCS Oil and Gas Leasing Program

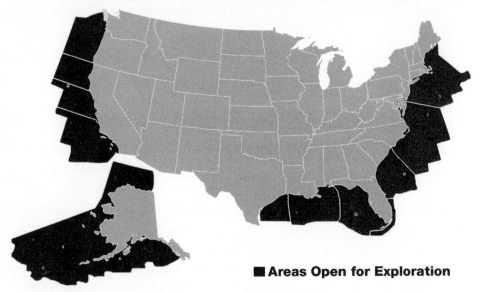

■ Areas Open for Exploration

Areas Closed to Energy Exploration under President Obama's 2012 OCS Oil and Gas Leasing Program

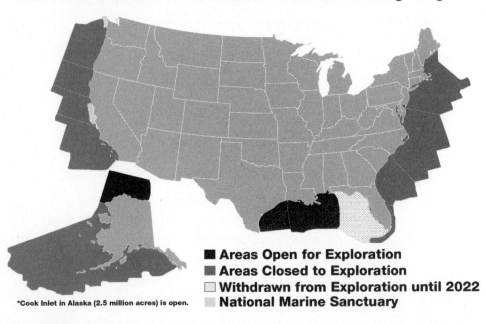

*Cook Inlet in Alaska (2.5 million acres) is open.

■ Areas Open for Exploration
■ Areas Closed to Exploration
▨ Withdrawn from Exploration until 2022
■ National Marine Sanctuary

700 million barrels of oil equivalent combined in our Keathley Canyon blocks," said Steve Greenlee, president of ExxonMobil Exploration Company. "More than 85 percent of the resource is oil with additional upside potential."[92]

The *Wall Street Journal* labeled the announcement "A Gulf Drilling Revival" and editorialized that the discovery and the innovative work that led to it demonstrated the triumph of "reality" over "politics."[93] ExxonMobil's discovery shows, declared the *Journal*, "how technology and innovation have opened up oil and gas resources that were impossible to detect, much less reach and develop, only a few years ago." The "great energy irony of recent years is that governments have thrown hundreds of billions of dollars at wind, solar, ethanol and other alternative fuels, yet the major breakthroughs have taken place in the traditional oil and natural gas business." This latest breakthrough, concluded the *Journal*, "is a display of the animal spirits that still live in the U.S. energy industry, notwithstanding the political efforts to stifle them."[94]

The *Journal* had reason to celebrate. After the Deepwater Horizon oil spill in April of 2010, the misguided federal response, and the prolonged federal moratorium on offshore oil and gas activity,[95] as well as counterproductive and burdensome new rules and regulations and the usual federal agency reorganization that accompanies public relations disasters, some wondered if the nation's offshore oil and gas program would ever resume. After all, as days turned into weeks and then months, ships set sail for Africa and South America with expensive drilling rigs in tow.[96] Costing their owners more than a million dollars a day, these rigs could not be allowed to sit idle while Washington politicians decided if they wanted to develop America's offshore energy resources.

———

President Reagan came to Washington to energize the American economy and end communism by developing the nation's rich energy resources. He did that by sending entrepreneurs far offshore in American waters. Meanwhile, out West, he had a growing rebellion to quell.

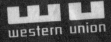
SLB044(1259)(4-022173S325)PD 11/20/80 1259

ICS IPMMTZZ CSP

2026341662 TDMT WASHINGTON DC 72 11-20 1259P EST

PMS DEAN RHODES CARE JOHN HARMER, DLR

LITTLE AMERICA HOTEL ROOM 1609

SALT LAKE CITY UT

DEAR DEAN PLEASE CONVEY BEST WISHES TO ALL MY FELLOW "SAGEBRUSH
REBELS" FROM MY PERSONAL CONTACT WITH YOU AS WELL AS OTHERS ATTENDING
THE LASER CONFERENCE, I'M CONFIDENT THE CONFERENCE WILL BE
PRODUCTIVE. I RENEW MY PLEDGE TO WORK TOWARD A "SAGEBRUSH SOLUTION".
MY ADMINISTRATION WILL WORK TO INSURE THAT THE STATES HAVE AN
EQUITABLE SHARE OF PUBLIC LANDS AND THEIR NATURAL RESOURCES. TO ALL
GOOD LUCK AND THANKS FOR YOUR SUPPORT

RONALD REAGAN

NNNN

SF-1201 (R5-69)

CHAPTER THREE

FROM SAGEBRUSH REBELS TO GOOD NEIGHBORS

*"From the Rockies, across the deserts and all the way
to the Pacific the western states are voicing their angry resentment
of a powerful absentee landlord—the Federal government,
which has overlaid the West with controls and regulations
as irksome as barb wire was in an earlier day."*
—RONALD REAGAN, OCTOBER 2, 1979[1]

There's a New Sheriff in Town

On November 20, 1980, as President-elect Reagan worked out of an office near the White House preparing for the big job that lay ahead of him, he took time from his busy schedule, which included a meeting in the Oval Office, to send a telegram to old friends in Salt Lake City.[2] There a group of Westerners—"sagebrush rebels" the media called them derisively, a nickname they enthusiastically embraced[3]—was meeting to discuss how to deal with a neighbor that was rich, powerful, and a bully. That bad neighbor was the federal government. Although its hired hands were from separate outfits and wore different uniforms, they

37

all spoke with one voice and expected to be obeyed. The rebels did not like it, and they were figuring out what to do about it.[4]

Their friend Ronald Reagan—a Californian who loved the West, the outdoors, and above all, freedom, and who, as a former governor, had dealt with that ornery neighbor—had gone off to take over its entire operation. As busy as he was now, he paused to wish them well in their deliberations, to tell them he was one of them, and to report, after a fashion, that there was a new sheriff in town.

The president-elect's telegram read:

> PLEASE CONVEY BEST WISHES TO ALL MY FELLOW SAGEBRUSH REBELS ... I RENEW MY PLEDGE TO WORK TOWARD A SAGEBRUSH SOLUTION. MY ADMINISTRATION WILL WORK TO INSURE THAT THE STATES HAVE AN EQUITABLE SHARE OF PUBLIC LANDS AND THEIR NATURAL RESOURCES. TO ALL GOOD LUCK....[5]

With all that had been going on in the American West for the last four years, Reagan's telegram was welcome news. Moreover, it showed that, unlike most politicians who, once elected, quickly forget the concerns of those who elected them, Reagan remembered and remained committed to fulfilling his promises.

War on the West

Colorado Governor Richard Lamm, a Democrat, said the Carter administration was a "western nightmare.... At no time did he have a western strategy. Out of uninterest or contempt, or both, Carter went to the Rocky Mountain West only four times in his term."[6] The importance of the president's attitude becomes apparent when one considers the amount of federal land in the Western states.[7] Although the federal government owns one-third of the country's landmass, most states have little, if any, federal land. It is a different story out West, however. The federal government owns nearly a third of Colorado, Montana, New Mexico, and Washington; roughly half of Arizona, California, Oregon, and Wyoming; and almost two-thirds or even more of Alaska, Idaho, Nevada, and Utah.[8] By comparison, the three non-Western states with the most federal land are New Hampshire (14 percent), Florida (13 percent), and Michigan (10 percent).[9] Even worse, in many Western states, federal ownership exceeds 90 percent of the land in scores of vast rural counties.[10] These percentages do not include tribal lands, as to which the secretary of the interior retains trust responsibilities.[11]

A president's views on the West, as well as those of his secretary of the interior, will be scrutinized carefully by Westerners and their leaders. Federal policies are enormously important not only to a Western governor but also to the entity that manages the state's lands, as well as to the county commissioners, especially in rural counties with massive federal land holdings. An administration's policies regarding a host of Interior Department agencies and bureaus affect Western states in ways that other Americans never think about.

Two agencies of particular importance in the lives of Westerners are the Interior Department's Bureau of Land Management (BLM), which controls nearly 250 million acres, and the Department of Agriculture's U.S. Forest Service (USFS), which manages more than 190 million acres.[12] Despite the USFS's location in Agriculture, it is the Interior secretary, as the official who manages energy and nonfuel minerals beneath national forests, whose role is of greater importance to the West. The acreage controlled by the BLM and the USFS exceeds that of Alaska; it also exceeds the acreage of the next three largest states (Texas, California, and Montana) and Colorado combined. These lands are managed in accordance with "multiple-use" principles. That is to say, these lands are to host a variety of activities, including energy and mineral development, logging, grazing, and recreation, to name a few.[13]

Multiple-use was introduced in 1960 in the management of national forests and then extended to BLM lands in 1976. Something big happened during the intervening years—the arrival of the environmental movement. Beginning with the National Environmental Policy Act (1969) and continuing through a plethora of other federal laws, Congress dramatically enhanced the power of the "public" to intervene in land-use decision making. For decades the only people interested in such parochial issues as grazing on barren expanses of Western land were the Westerners who were affected by the decisions of federal agencies. Now scores of environmental groups that were not affected by federal decision making but were interested stepped forward as the hyper-engaged public.[14] These groups had their own interpretation of multiple-use, which leaned heavily toward limited use, occasionally permitting recreation but usually favoring preservation or non-use. Not only did environmental groups intervene in land-management decision making, but they also lobbied assiduously for congressional oversight and more restrictive federal laws and litigated aggressively in federal court.

Nonetheless, it was not the federal legislation that provoked the "Sagebrush Rebellion."[15] It was the policies of the Carter administration—especially the views of Secretary of the Interior Cecil Andrus—that infuriated Westerners. Carter and Andrus viewed themselves as environmentalists and staffed their offices with people from the movement.[16] Almost immediately, Carter went after Western water projects, identifying those he refused to fund.[17] A reporter for the *Los Angeles Times* called it a "hit list [that] was anathema to the West."[18]

Andrus, supposedly not consulted before the White House launched the assault, made his prejudices clear by tarring users of public lands—ranchers, miners, oil men, and probably loggers, although he was once a logger himself—as "the rape, ruin and run boys."[19] The Carter administration may have seen those who engaged in these economic activities as the enemy, but most Westerners, including governors, senators, congressmen, and county commissioners, knew them as friends, neighbors, important contributors to state and local economies, and even, in the case of ranchers, descendants of original homesteaders.[20]

In June of 1977, the Carter administration demonstrated that the assault on Western water was only a preview of coming attractions when it issued, "the [Interior] Department's broadest assault upon western water law."[21] In a seventy-two-page opinion by its top lawyer, the solicitor, Interior "sought to reverse not only the thrust of the legal commentators['] conclusions on federal-state relations in water law, but [also] the efforts of Congress and the recent rulings of the U.S. Supreme Court."[22]

Worse, the solicitor "fashioned out of little more than whole cloth, a heretofore unknown doctrine giving the Department the right to take western water without observing either State substantive or procedural law."[23] Westerners had controlled their most precious resource, water, through state law ever since the gold-panning days, and the opinion sparked outrage. Andrus's belated assertion that the opinion was a last resort, to be used only if Interior did not get its way through "bilateral agreements"—was unpersuasive.[24]

All these things happened in Carter's first six months, and soon the Sagebrush Rebellion was raging across the West.[25] Three years later, the 1980 election sent to the White House a president who saw himself as an environmentalist *and* a Sagebrush Rebel.[26] Little wonder that, as soon as he took office, Reagan moved as aggressively as Carter had done, but in the opposite direction.[27]

The Federal Government Should Be a Good Neighbor

When President-elect Reagan met with James Watt in December of 1980 and brought up the Sagebrush Rebellion, Watt responded with a phrase he had heard from Walter Hickel, President Nixon's first secretary of the interior, who as governor of Alaska had had his fill of domineering federal bureaucrats from Washington. "The federal government should be a good neighbor to the West," declared Watt. Reagan quickly nodded his assent, and Watt had his marching orders.[28]

In January of 1981, on his first Monday as interior secretary, Watt wrote to all fifty governors pledging that his department would be "exercising its responsibilities in full and complete recognition of the vital role of the States in the federal system."[29] For Watt, simply enunciating President Reagan's "good neighbor" policy was not enough; he also took personal responsibility for the actions of the vast bureaucracy and asked each governor to communicate his ideas and concerns directly to Watt.[30] Then Watt set about to revise the Carter policies, rules, and regulations that had so antagonized the West—grazing, water law, and land lock-up, for example—and that had outraged many other states, including Eastern coal-mining states. Watt promised that he and his top officials would not leave their Washington offices except for the "most essential" travel for the first six months of the new administration.[31] Watt wanted to ensure that when he and other top officials went "on the road," they would be proclaiming to audiences what they had actually done, not promising what they hoped to accomplish in the future.[32]

Watt's first travels as secretary included a trip home to Wyoming to address Western governors in Jackson Hole.[33] With the Grand Tetons in the background and the meandering Snake River Valley in the foreground, Watt stood in a "barn-like building," at the head of a horseshoe-shaped conference table at which sat all the Western governors with staff, reporters, and observers arrayed behind them.[34] As one Western reporter put it, Watt—"[l]anky, loose, [in] Western boots[,] [with a] country-boy smile as wide as this endless valley[,] [and wearing a]n open-neck cow-puncher's shirt in vivid colors of the range"—addressed President Reagan's vision for America and the West and answered questions and acceded to requests and demands.[35] The *Washington Post* reported, "In a 3½-hour session ... Watt had the once-hostile governors eating out of his hand. And he had some choice morsels for them."[36] When he announced the end of the Carter administration's preemption of Western water rights, Governor Bob List of Nevada exclaimed, "If I'd been on my horse, I'd have fallen off. In the past, we had to bleed on the floor to get any help from Interior."[37] Watt later recalled, "I made a big point out of our intention to give the States what had been promised to them at Statehood—land.... I kept asking the Governors what they wanted and if it were at all possible, I promised to do it."[38] When it was all over, *Newsweek* reported, "Even the most skeptical Westerners had to admit that Watt deserved much of the credit for dissipating their cause—by easing tensions between them and the federal government."[39]

Watt flew to Denver, where he met with Governor Lamm and his entire natural resources team. Lamm had criticized the Carter administration's attacks on Western states as "the Second Civil War," and Watt intended to end the hostilities.[40] He reported, "I listened to his complaints and agreed with every one of them and I promised to correct Interior's position." When Watt and Lamm emerged to meet the media that had followed the secretary from Washington to Jackson Hole to Denver,

Lamm declared that he and Watt had reached agreement on all of Colorado's issues, but that he opposed what Watt was doing elsewhere.[41] Watt then traveled to Phoenix for a lengthy meeting with Governor Bruce Babbitt, a Democrat, and his natural resources officials. Babbitt echoed Lamm's two-part answer. The last stop on Watt's Western tour was Salt Lake City, where he met with another Democratic governor, Scott M. Matheson, the chairman of the Western governors' group. Matheson broke ranks with his fellow Democrats, announcing, "I support everything Secretary Watt is doing."[42]

After four years of Carter's "War on the West," Reagan's "good neighbor" policy was a welcome relief to Western governors, Democrats and Republicans alike. The Interior Department did exactly what Watt promised in his meetings with Western governors:

- It revoked the Solicitor's Opinion of 1977 that reversed decades of water law and empowered the federal government to seize Western water;[43]
- It conveyed 328,286 acres of federal land to Western states from 1981 through 1983 to support their public school systems. Only 3,859 acres had been transferred for that purpose from 1977 through 1980;[44]
- After inviting Western governors to identify "small parcels of federally-owned land that could be put to better use locally for beneficial public purposes," it transferred 185,000 acres through low-cost leases to state and local governments for park and public purposes;[45]
- It implemented innovative cooperative management agreements to increase the involvement of state and local agencies, recreationists, wildlife groups, ranchers, and other public land users by sharing responsibility for such activities as maintenance, protection, development, and enhancement of natural resources;[46]
- It rewrote 91 percent of the permanent Office of Surface Mining regulations, which permitted states to assume responsibility for surface mining reclamation in accordance

with each state's geology, topography, and climate. As a result, all twenty-four major coal-producing states had regulatory primacy, and 99 percent of the nation's operating coal mines were under state regulatory control, as envisioned by Congress;[47]

- It developed a Cooperative Audit Program in which the Minerals Management Service worked with Western states to identify past-due federal oil and gas royalties and distributed $10.25 million to the states;[48]

- It approved a ten-year timber management plan for the two million acres of the "Oregon and California Railroad Grant" lands in Western Oregon, which provided for harvesting 1.1 billion board feet annually, thereby sustaining over fifteen thousand jobs;[49]

- It adopted a Rangeland Improvement Policy regarding grazing to reduce the Bureau of Land Management's overhead expenses and increase the funding for range improvements, to eliminate unwarranted subsidies, and to enhance the legal standing of ranchers;[50]

- It approved OCS oil and gas leasing programs that substantially increased consultation with state and local governments and provided states with "greater opportunities … throughout the planning and leasing process";[51]

- It joined with the Drug Enforcement Administration to rid public lands of illegal cultivators of marijuana to protect the safety of public land users;[52]

- It encouaged increased investment from public land users to develop water projects, fencing, and other range improvements—the private sector spent $529,000 in fiscal year 1982 and $1.7 million the next fiscal year;[53]

- It established the Royalty Management Advisory Committee, made up of members from "States, Indian groups, industry, public utilities, and the general public," to identify improvements regarding federal royalty collection and auditing;[54]

- It refined the responsibilities of states and the federal government in the stewardship of fish and wildlife and reaffirmed that states have the lead role in managing resident fish and wildlife.[55]

A Special Case: Alaska

In 1981, Alaskans were still livid over their state's treatment by the Carter administration. When Alaska was admitted to the Union in 1959, nearly its entire landmass was federally owned; therefore, Alaska was granted the right to select 104 million acres, out of 375 million acres, to manage for the benefit of its residents.[56] In less than eight years, Alaska selected twenty-six million acres. Then Interior Secretary Stewart Udall—who served during the Kennedy and Johnson administrations—put a freeze on further land selections to protect any claims that might be asserted by Native Alaskans.[57] The discovery of oil at Prudhoe Bay in 1968 made resolution of the issue by Congress a matter of urgency. As a result, in 1971, Congress passed the Alaska Native Claims Settlement Act, which allowed the Native community to select forty-four million acres.[58]

Environmentalists, upset that too much of the land they coveted would be selected by the state and Native Alaskans for development, demanded the inclusion in the act of a provision—Section 17(d)(2)—that ordered the interior secretary to withdraw eighty million acres for future designation by Congress as parks, refuges, wild and scenic rivers, and national forests.[59] The deadline for this congressional action was 1978, and as it neared, the Carter administration, impatient and worried, decided to force Congress's hand. The administration unilaterally withdrew one hundred million acres from any use by the state or Native Alaskans.[60] Alaska promptly sued, charging that the administration had failed to comply with the National Environmental Policy Act.[61] In a lame duck session at the end of 1980, Congress passed (over the objections of the Alaskan delegation) the Alaska National Interest Lands Conservation Act (ANILCA), which revoked all of the withdrawals of the Carter administration and substituted congressional designations that put one

hundred million acres permanently in federal enclaves, doubled the acreage of national parks and refuges, and tripled the amount of land declared
to be wilderness.[62] Through all of this, Alaska pressed for Interior to
convey the lands to which it was entitled by federal law, but the department grudgingly transferred only portions of that land.

The new Reagan administration sought in March of 1981 to heal the
wounds from the long battle over Alaska's lands, sovereign rights, and
the failure of the federal government to deliver on promises made when
Alaska became a state. In a public meeting billed as "Alaska Day" at the
Interior Department, Watt—with Alaska's governor, Jay Hammond,
Senators Ted Stevens and Frank Murkowski, and Representative Don
Young (all Republicans) at his side—signed seven policy directives to
resolve scores of disputes, to deliver on earlier promises, and to assure
Alaska that ANILCA would not create a "permit lifestyle" in the state
where every activity required federal permission.

A short time later, the Reagan administration settled Alaska's lawsuit,
agreeing to accelerate land conveyances to Alaska and not to use presidential authority to make more federal land withdrawals. The Interior
Department included the latter provision over the objections of federal
lawyers.[63] Finally, the National Park Service, the U.S. Fish and Wildlife
Service, and the Bureau of Land Management each signed a Memorandum of Understanding with the Alaska Department of Fish and Game
ceding to the state the lead on fish and wildlife management matters.
These agreements, now over thirty years old, are still in place and working well.[64]

By the time President Reagan took office, Alaska had received less
than half the lands to which it was entitled after its admission into the
Union, and Native Alaskans had received only one-third of the land due
to them.[65] The Reagan administration moved quickly. From January of
1981 through 1983, Alaska received thirty million acres, more than had
been conveyed by any previous administration, and received a commitment of land transfers at the rate of thirteen million acres annually. In the
same period, Native Alaskans received eleven million acres, which constituted nearly 60 percent of their entitlement, and an additional fifteen
million acres were transferred by the end of 1988.[66]

A host of issues still confronted the state of Alaska and Alaskan Natives, but Reagan's Interior Department established early on that it wanted a cordial relationship. There would be times when the state and federal leaders would disagree, but the views of Alaskans would now be heard and respected.[67]

Land Sales and Land Exchanges

The very nature of federal land ownership in the American West results in frequent intermingling of federal, state, and private lands, including isolated tracts of lands owned by one entity in the midst of a vast tract owned by another. That type of ownership makes management difficult and costly for the landowner, whether a federal agency, state, or private party. As part of the Reagan administration's good neighbor policy, the Interior Department was committed to resolving these conflicts to the benefit of its state and private neighbors as well as the federal agencies involved.

Congress had long recognized the need for such actions. In fact, days after Reagan's election, Congress passed a complex bill to resolve land conflicts in Nevada, the Western state with the most federal land, legislation that required implementation by Reagan's Interior Department and the U.S. Forest Service.[68] Interior, however, committed to resolve land conflict issues without the delay involved in congressional action.[69] For example, the Bureau of Land Management, after careful consultation with state and local governments, identified scores of small tracts to ensure more efficient management of federal, state, and private lands.[70] As validation of the administration's efforts, Congress enacted another major land exchange bill involving the BLM, but this time, the other agency involved was the U.S. Fish and Wildlife Service. Again it fell to Interior to implement the legislation.[71]

These sales and exchanges, undertaken pursuant to federal law, must be distinguished from an initiative set forth in February of 1982 in Reagan's fiscal year 1983 budget. That plan, developed by the Council of Economic Advisors and known as the "Asset Management Program," envisioned selling a scant thirty-five million acres of federal land—5 percent of all federal land—over a five-year period, with expected revenues of $1 billion in fiscal year 1983 and $4 billion annually from fiscal 1984 through fiscal 1987, for a total of $17 billion.[72] Indian trust lands, national parks and monuments, wildlife refuges, and historical and environmentally critical sites were excluded. Subsurface mineral rights would be sold only if the federal lands had no mineral value.[73] In addition to generating revenue, selling land to the private sector would reduce future federal expenditures for the payment-in-lieu-of-taxes program.[74] In addition, no additional appropriations were required to manage the program.[75]

The Asset Management Program was managed by the Property Review Board, a cabinet-level board that was established by presidential order, with the responsibility of developing policies on the "acquisition, utilization and disposition of federal real property," determining which lands to sell, and establishing annual targets for land sales.[76] In 1982 the board ordered a survey of all lands administered by the Departments of Interior and Agriculture and the Corps of Engineers; the two departments, however, limited their review to lands managed by the Bureau of Land Management and the U.S. Forest Service.[77] The BLM's survey built upon one conducted in 1964 and identified 11.5 million acres of land that were expensive to administer. Yet another survey selected three million acres for disposal and twenty-two million acres as unclassified.[78] Meanwhile, Watt announced that Interior would not dispose of federal lands with known mineral deposits.[79] In March of 1983, the BLM announced the initial results of its survey of the 175 million acres of BLM managed land in the continental United States: thirty million acres were to be retained; 140 million acres needed further study; and a trivial 2.6 million acres, or 1.5 percent of all BLM lands in the lower forty-eight states, were identified for sale or transfer. Of those 2.6 million acres, BLM intended to offer 250,000 acres for sale in fiscal year 1984, resulting in anticipated revenues of $300 million.[80] In other words, the BLM planned to offer for sale an infinitesimal 0.14 percent of its land holdings in the lower forty-eight states.

Environmental extremists, nevertheless, purposefully distorted the program with the help of the media, which failed to inform the public of how narrow a range of federal lands would be considered for sale or of how little land would actually be put on the block for disposal.[81] The media were more interested in inflammatory headlines.[82] Thus uninformed and even ill-informed, public and political opposition grew.[83] In July of 1983, Watt announced that the BLM would no longer participate in the Asset Management Program; instead, under its existing authority, the BLM would dispose only of costly, burdensome, surplus lands more effectively utilized by state or private holders.[84] Watt's decision was neither an act of defiance of President Reagan nor an admission of defeat at the hands of the administration's opponents. Instead, the Reagan administration proclaimed that, at least as to the Interior Department, it could be a good neighbor and thoughtfully review land management policies using federal laws enacted by Congress.[85]

Water for the West

Early in 1981, Watt learned that the New Melones Dam and Reservoir along the Stanislaus River in California's Calaveras and Tuolumne Counties, thirty miles or so east of Stockton, was ready to be filled. Having authorized the project in 1944 to prevent flood damage caused by rain and melted snow on some 35,000 acres of agricultural land, Congress modified its purposes in 1962 to include irrigation, power generation, wildlife and fisheries enhancement, recreation, and water quality improvements.[86] Although the U.S. Army Corps of Engineers began construction in 1966, the opposition of those angered by the loss of white-water rafting opportunities and the purported loss of wildlife habitat kept the dam from being completed until 1978. The spillway and powerhouse were not finished until 1979, when the facility was turned over to the Bureau of Reclamation and the Interior Department.[87] Watt was told that in the past, protesting rafters had chained themselves to rocks at the river's edge, and it was feared that some of them might have returned. "Fill it up," Watt said. "They'll leave."[88] One more stalled Western water project was on its way to completion.[89]

Carter's War on the West was over, especially his efforts—beginning with the famous "hit list"—to keep Westerners from controlling their water. Under Reagan, the Interior Department set about to put states back in control of their water resources, to improve the quantity of delivered water, to ensure faster, more efficient water project planning and construction, and to create financial partnerships with the private sector to develop new water resources.[90] In the American West, as President Reagan himself was well aware, water projects ensure reliable and safe supplies of drinking water, provide for irrigation of the agricultural miracle that is the West, produce hydroelectric power, enhance wildlife habitat, and generate new recreation areas.[91] In 1983 alone, to achieve those vital goals, the Interior Department:

- Awarded 113 construction contracts, valued at $274 million, for ongoing construction at multi-purpose water projects in seventeen states, which yielded 15,070 work-years of direct and indirect non-federal employment;[92]
- Ended over a decade of delay and allocated Central Arizona Project water to "12 Indian communities, 85 entities needing municipal and industrial water and 23 irrigation districts," and opened the first public recreation area at the Central Arizona Project—the new Scottsdale Horsemen's Park adjacent to the Granite Reef Aqueduct;[93]
- Reached agreement with California's Friant Power Authority to build three hydroelectric power plants on Bureau of Reclamation facilities at Friant Dam—with an installed capacity of 30,500 kilowatts—and concluded yet another agreement with the Madera-Chowchilla Power Authority to begin construction on a power plant with an installed capacity of 1,800 kilowatts on the Madera Canal, California;[94]
- Dedicated the third power plant and a visitor center at Grand Coulee Dam on the fiftieth anniversary of the start of construction of "the largest hydroelectric generating complex in the world;"[95]
- Published the first National Water Summary to report on "the quantity and quality of the Nation's water supply and

the destructive impacts of natural events like flooding and drought," to aid decision makers at the federal, state, and local level and in the private sector;[96]

- Enhanced recreational opportunities and wildlife habitat at several Bureau of Reclamation facilities,[97] including:
  - Setting aside 10,000 acres for wildlife habitat—managed by the Oklahoma Wildlife Conservation Department—and 8,900 acres for a natural scenic recreation area—managed by the Oklahoma Tourism and Recreation Department—at the McGee Creek Project;
  - Setting aside 16,000 acres of federal land as waterfowl habitat, with plans to acquire another 26,000 acres for fish and wildlife habitat, at the Garrison Diversion Unit irrigation project in North Dakota in cooperation with the state, the Garrison Conservancy District, and the U.S. Fish and Wildlife Service; and,
  - Establishing interpretive facilities at Grimes Point Archeological District near the Truckee-Carson Irrigation District in Nevada as a joint project with the Bureau of Land Management to inform visitors about the natural and cultural history of the area;[98]
- Completed reviewing all statutes, rules and regulations, manuals, and internal directives to ensure that they conformed to Reagan's view that states have primacy over water rights, management, and allocation after vacating the Solicitor's Opinion issued by Carter's Interior Department that took jurisdiction over Western water from states.[99]

With President Reagan's Federalism Executive Order,[100] the successful updating of the Reclamation Act of 1902,[101] and the adoption of the administration's new cost-sharing policies regarding future reclamation projects,[102] the Interior Department addressed the challenging economic and environmental realities of the 1980s that affected Western water projects by:

- Negotiating joint federal-state funding to raise the Buffalo Bill Dam in Wyoming and to add hydroelectric generating capacity;[103]
- Negotiating, and renegotiating after congressional action, a cost-sharing plan with non-federal interests for the Central Arizona Project;[104]
- Negotiating an agreement with California for joint operation of the Central Valley and state water projects to meet state water-quality standards in the delta area;[105]
- Adopting a policy to facilitate "willing buyer–willing seller" transfers of water from Bureau of Reclamation and Bureau of Indian Affairs projects to increase the efficiency of existing federal water projects;[106] and
- Resolving litigation regarding contract disputes over price and availability of water, which permitted environmental clean-up and resolved water-rights claims by American Indians that prevented endless litigation.[107]

President Reagan's steadfast defense of Westerners and Western states was nowhere more evident than in the policies undertaken regarding water policy. That aspect of the War on the West was over and the rebellion to which it gave rise quelled.

An Executive Commitment to Federalism

In President Reagan's first inaugural address, he declared:

> It is my intention to curb the size and influence of the Federal establishment and to demand recognition of the distinction between the powers granted to the Federal Government and those reserved to the States or to the people. All of us need to be reminded that the Federal Government did not create the States; the States created the Federal Government.[108]

In a key legislative victory for federalism, the Interior Department supported efforts to amend the Quiet Title Act to exempt states from the law's requirement that any challenge to an adverse federal claim to land owned by the state must be filed within twelve years of learning of the adverse claim.[109] Reagan called the revision, "a significant victory for principles of federalism."[110]

Reagan issued Executive Order 12612—titled simply "Federalism"— "to restore the division of governmental responsibilities between the national government and the States that was intended by the Framers of the Constitution" and to require that "the principles of federalism established by the Framers guide the Executive departments and agencies in the formulation and implementation of policies...."[111] Executive Order 12612, recognized "fundamental federalism principles," including that federalism is "rooted in the knowledge that our political liberties are best assured by limiting the size and scope of the national government," that "[t]he people of the States created the national government when they delegated to it those enumerated governmental powers," that "[t]he constitutional relationship among sovereign governments, State and national, is formalized in and protected by the Tenth Amendment to the Constitution," and that, "[i]n most areas of governmental concern, the States uniquely possess the constitutional authority, the resources, and the competence to discern the sentiments of the people and to govern accordingly."[112] Finally, Executive Order 12612 set forth several "federal policymaking criteria," among which was the requirement that "Executive departments and agencies" "closely examine the constitutional and statutory authority" for proposed federal action "that would limit the policymaking discretion of the States" and thereafter "assess the necessity for such action."[113]

President Reagan's strong views regarding federalism and the role of states vis-à-vis the federal government, expressed from his first minutes in office, ensured that his secretaries of the interior would fulfill their responsibilities in accordance with the commands of the Constitution regarding dual sovereignty and the Tenth Amendment, by whatever name that policy was known. It was clear that Reagan liked the idea of being a good neighbor, whether implemented by Watt, or Clark, or Hodel. As he once promised a Western audience, under his leadership, he turned "the Sagebrush Rebellion into the Sagebrush Solution."[114]

The War on the West Resumes

In 1998, President Bill Clinton revoked Reagan's executive order on federalism and substituted his own views of the proper balance between the federal government and states, especially Western states.[115] By then however, Westerners were already well aware of what Clinton thought of the West. In 1996, as he campaigned for reelection, Clinton had issued a unilateral decree to create a national monument in Utah and thereby to kill a vast coal mine that would have provided hundreds of jobs, generated electricity, and brought needed revenue to a rural part of that state.[116] Clinton did not care; environmental extremists demanded it and Clinton gave it to them.[117] It was a pattern that Clinton repeated, over the years and all across the West.[118]

President Obama revived the War on the West with a vengeance in his first term, and Westerners look forward to his second term with well-grounded dread. Obama, his officials, and agencies have waged a war on coal, an economic mainstay of several Western states.[119] Obama, his officials, and agencies have waged a war on the exploration for and development of oil and gas resources, including relentless efforts to besmirch, bloody, and ban hydraulic fracturing, the technology that has unlocked America's remarkable storehouse of oil and natural gas and restored state and local economies across the country.[120] In fact, days after Obama's reelection, Interior Secretary Salazar eviscerated Colorado's oil shale program.[121] Obama, his officials, and agencies, often in collusion with radical environmental groups, have used the Endangered Species Act to cripple or kill Western economic activity.[122] Obama and his officials have removed federal land from economic and recreational activities. In fact, on Obama's desk sits a memorandum from Salazar on millions of acres all across the West that Obama can close, with a stroke of the pen, under the Antiquities Act, just as his predecessor Clinton did.[123]

How angry is the West? Governor Matt Mead of Wyoming, a Republican and a mild-mannered, soft-spoken rancher and lawyer, is livid over what Obama's regulations will do to oil and gas development, not to mention what banning coal-powered plants will do to Wyoming's top industry.[124] Utah passed a law ordering the state to fight for possession of federal lands.[125] The Arizona legislature passed a similar bill, but Governor Jan Brewer vetoed it; nonetheless, she "share[s] Arizona's frustration" in dealing with the federal government.[126] Other Western states express similar aggravation, annoyance, and anger; Westerners' fury continues.[127]

A new Sagebrush Rebellion is underway. Whether the mainstream media will make of it what they did of the one that took Ronald Reagan to Washington remains to be seen. Whether that matters is yet another story.

"ONWARD, CHRISTIAN SOLDIER!"

CHAPTER FOUR

"WE PRINT WHAT WE KNOW—SO WE PRINT LIES"[1]

"[T]he Eastern media[:] I'll confess, to me they were the hostile press. But we were even because to most of them I was that [N]eanderthal reactionary from out west."
—RONALD REAGAN, SEPTEMBER 21, 1976[2]

A Successful Congressional Appearance

I n February of 1981, James Watt agreed to testify before the House Interior and Insular Affairs Committee in what some on the panel and its staff called his "House confirmation hearing." Of course, the only body with constitutional authority to provide "advice and consent" to the "appointment" of "officers of the United States" is the Senate;[3] hence "confirmation hearings" are conducted only by Senate committees. The House of Representatives, however, chafes under what it views as the public's misconception that the House is less important than the Senate and its better known personalities. In fact, the term "lower house," although often said internationally in reference to the more powerful house, is never spoken aloud by members of the House of Representatives or staff.[4] Instead, the House seeks every opportunity to bring attention to itself. Watt's "House confirmation hearing" was such an opportunity.

Of course, the hearing made sense from a purely practical standpoint. As its name indicates, the jurisdiction of the committee chaired by Representative Morris K. Udall, a Democrat from Arizona and the brother of former Secretary of the Interior Stewart Udall, was at the time an exact fit to the statutory obligations of the Interior Department, and all Interior-related legislation, save for appropriations bills, passed through the committee.[5] Furthermore, Watt relished the opportunity to appear before the committee and its mostly Western members. He was proud to represent President Reagan, eager to speak for himself, rather than through the media, regarding the changes the president sought at Interior, even at this early date, and optimistic about his ability to persuade those who had not yet met him of his sincerity, candor, and accessibility. I had been an attorney to the committee before my appointment at Interior, so Watt asked me to join him at the witness table. I was pleased to sit beside him, although I knew my role would be limited. Watt had an encyclopedic mastery of Interior and its activities and a principled philosophy of governance, tempered by a modest willingness to admit he did not know an answer but was willing to find out.

The hearing opened and proceeded cordially with courteous, friendly comments by congressmen, Republicans and Democrats alike, and straightforward questions, many of which were directed to subjects of most interest to the members themselves or to their constituents. Watt answered every question forthrightly and was his usual sociable self; in turn, the members seemed genuinely pleased with his answers and with their ability to speak to a secretary directly. Because an administration witness was usually an assistant secretary, deputy assistant secretary, like me, or a bureau chief, there were smiles all around.

Perhaps to add to the House's "inferiority complex," media attendance was light. When the hearing began, there were no television cameras, only one or two reporters, and none of the photographers who usually crouch in the "well" between the witness table and the elevated committee dais. Then, midway through the proceedings, a lone photographer, a camera hanging from his neck, crawled past me, centered himself in front of Watt and me, and lifted the camera to his face. I knew he wanted a photograph of Watt but I did not know if I would be in the frame. Just in case I was, I stared intently at the member to whom the secretary was speaking. Moments passed. Another member asked a question that Watt answered. Then another member asked a question; Watt answered and on it went. Still I had not heard the click of the shutter. I stole a quick look at the photographer. He was sitting cross-legged, his elbows on his knees, the camera at his face, a finger poised above the shutter release button. It reminded me of my days on the Marine Corps rifle range holding an M14 in the sitting position: the sling wrapped around my arm, the butt tight into my shoulder, the stock pressed against my cheek, my finger upon the trigger, taking out the slack. Breathe in, I thought, and hold it, and squeeze. Still the photographer did not take the shot. What was he waiting for?

Then Watt did it. He pulled his thick glasses partially away from his face, lifted the temples, and looked through the bottom part of the lenses. It was an odd motion; I did not recall seeing him do it before. Just then, the photographer's shutter clicked. I looked and saw the camera hanging from his neck as he crawled away, his job finished. Then, I realized: he wanted the distorted shot of Watt's eyes peering through his thick lenses. In the months ahead, I would see that shot often. It became the go-to shot for the media when it wanted to portray Watt negatively for an unfavorable news story.

The hearing proceeded uneventfully and typically as members passed in and out to ask their questions and depart for other business. Soon almost no one remained but the chairman. The committee gaveled to a close. Watt shook hands with political appointees and career civil servants who had followed us up to Capitol Hill and other well-wishers, turned to me with a "well-done" nod and smile, and walked quickly through the door. I lingered with former colleagues before returning to Interior. I was pleased. Everything had gone well: friends were encouraged, opponents were mollified, at least for the moment, and no blood was drawn. Except for the photographer, the hearing was a nonevent.

Then, a few months later, early one bright June morning at my home in Arlington, I opened the *Washington Post* and turned to the editorial page.

A Lie Goes around the World

Herb Block, known as "Herblock," was the *Washington Post*'s only political cartoonist and the nation's best known. He loathed President Reagan. According to the Library of Congress, "Reagan appalled Herblock in a way that only Joseph McCarthy and Richard Nixon had done before."[6] The cartoonist himself wrote:

> Ronald Reagan had not only run against the federal government when he first campaigned for the presidency; he continued to run against it while heading it. So there might be considered a certain logic to his efforts to get around government rules and restrictions when they interfered with what he and his band of performers wanted to do.[7]

Herblock would spend the next eight years savaging President Reagan in the crude, crass, and even cruel way of which he was the master. If the opportunity for an attack presented itself, he would not be deterred by the absence of supporting facts. Watt, whose tall, lean figure, bald head, and Coke-bottle glasses not only made him easily recognizable but also a snap to draw, was a frequent target.[8]

In a cartoon titled "Onward, Christian Soldier!" Herblock portrayed Watt leading a bulldozer labeled "Timber and Mining Interests" that was driven by a grinning, cigar-smoking businessman toward a forested area, protected by a sign that read, "U.S. Lands and Resources," with snow-capped peaks in the distance, while a shocked Uncle Sam looks on. Watt, oddly and inaccurately drawn with prominent buckteeth, carries a sign reading, "Why Save It? THE END IS NEAR."[9]

Herblock's vicious attack on Watt was unique; as the lawyers say, it was *sui generis*—one of a kind. Of course, it was vicious, mean-spirited, and deeply personal.[10] Its major defect, however, was that it was a lie. I was not present for most of Watt's interviews, personal appearances, and congressional testimony—I had an office to run and three bureaus to oversee—but I *was* present when he said the very words that gave rise to this scurrilous cartoon. It was the February "House confirmation hearing" that had gone so smoothly. Watt had said, I knew, precisely the opposite of what Herblock said he said. I scrambled to find the transcript.

> *Mr. Weaver* [Democrat from Oregon]: I believe very strongly that we should not, for example, use up all the oil that took nature a billion years to make in one century. We ought to leave a few drops of it for our children, their children. They are going to need it.... I wonder if you agree, also, in the general statement that we should leave some of our resources—I am now talking about scenic areas or preservation, but scenic resources for our children? Not just gobble them up all at once?
>
> *Secretary Watt*: Absolutely. That is the delicate balance the Secretary of the Interior must have, to be steward for the natural resources for this generation as well as future generations. I do not know how many future generations we can count on before the Lord returns, whatever it is we have to manage with a skill to leave the resources needed for future generations.
>
> *Mr. Weaver*: Mr. Chairman, I want to conclude, if I might, seeing the Secretary brought up the Lord, with a story.[11]
>
> *The Chairman*: The conversation will be in order.
>
> *Mr. Weaver*: In my district, Mr. Chairman, there are some who do not like wilderness. They do not like it at all. I would

try to plead with them. I go around my district and say do you not believe—I would plead with their religious sensibilities—that we should leave some of our land the way we received it from the Creator? I have said this frequently throughout my district. I got a letter from a constituent.... He said, "Mr. Weaver, if the Lord wanted to leave his forest lands, some of them in the way that we got them from Him," he said, "why did He send His only Son down to earth as a carpenter?" [Laughter.]

That stumped us. That stumped us until one of my aides, an absolute genius, said that the Lord Jesus before He determined His true mission spent 40 days and 40 nights in the wilderness. [Laughter.][12]

Herblock never recanted and few members of the media ever had the curiosity to investigate whether there was any factual basis for the cartoonist's assertion that Watt said anything of the kind;[13] instead, the media mindlessly repeated the tall tale generated by Herblock's cartoon and the fictional claims about Watt lived on over the decades.[14]

Herblock's smear of James Watt went underground in the administration—that is, it was not part of public discussion; however, it carried a lasting taint.[15] Those who supported Reagan's policies, but did not know Watt, had no reason—other than a healthy skepticism of anything in the *Post*—to know that Herblock's cartoon had no basis in fact.[16] Therefore, they assumed that there must be some truth to it, questioned Watt's wisdom, common sense, or even sanity, and doubted whether anyone who harbored such views could or should long survive as a cabinet officer.[17]

Politicians and members of the media who opposed Reagan—the Neanderthal—took the cartoon as proof that Watt was a Bible-thumping, fundamentalist nitwit. On Capitol Hill, K Street, and elsewhere in and around Washington, the cartoon was part of a *sotto voce* campaign against Watt and, by association, Reagan.[18] To radical environmental groups that had sided with Carter in the 1980 election, Watt's alleged statement was a double blasphemy.[19] It confirmed their suspicion that Christians believe, because they were placed in dominion over all of the earth, that they are relieved of any stewardship responsibilities.[20] Furthermore, it placed environmental group leaders' worldview, which many of them embraced with an almost religious fervor, in direct conflict, not just with a differing political or public policy agenda—for example, a desire to promote the economy by using natural resources to create wealth—but also with an opposing theology,[21] an ideology that threatened to rob them of their moral superiority and ethical high ground.[22] So, armed with Herblock's imaginary quotation and the inflammatory columns of left-leaning journalists, environmental extremists, their well-funded groups, as well as congressional and other allies, embarked upon a long-term attack on Watt—and by association President Reagan.[23] The media went happily along for the ride.[24]

Reagan knew that Herblock's target was not Watt—he was merely collateral damage—but Reagan himself and his policies.[25] On mornings like the one on which the Herblock cartoon appeared, Watt would get a call from the White House. It was either Edwin Meese or Judge Clark, who declared simply, "I have just been meeting with the president, and he has read the story in this morning's paper and wants you to stand tall and never back up."

Reagan's steadfastness in the face of media attacks inspired those who worked for him and demonstrated his belief that it was up to him, his appointees and their staffs, and the federal career employees who worked for them to determine their agenda and to stick to it.[26] It is all too easy for a news story, political cartoon, or rumor to send the top people from an entire department or even several departments, as well as the White House staff, scurrying to "put out a fire," by responding to inquiries from an ever growing list of reporters and by calming matters on Capitol Hill to prevent uninformed condemnations accompanied by threats of hearings, inquiries, or investigations. That is the case in any administration, but it was especially true for the Reagan administration, which challenged the orthodoxy of the day, especially on natural resources and environmental policies.

Reagan never flinched from defending his outspoken secretary, from the earliest days, even before his formal nomination, and through his early departure and even afterward. The reason was simple: Watt was doing, as Clark and Hodel would do later, exactly what Reagan wanted done. In December of 1980, Reagan told reporters, "Jim Watt has only opposed environmental extremists. I think he's an environmentalist himself, as I am."[27] In August of 1981, Reagan stated unequivocally:

> Jim Watt has my full support because I think that we have been victimized by some individuals that I refer to as environmental extremists. Now, I think I'm an environmentalist. But I do think there has been a lot of irrationality about Jim. And what Jim's trying to do is maybe a little like getting a mule's attention—you hit it in the forehead with a two-by-four first.[28]

In an interview with the *Los Angeles Times* in January of 1982, the president was asked if Watt were a "political liability." He replied, "No ... environmental extremism [is] going beyond all bounds of reason.... And I think that Jim Watt ... is going to restore some common sense."[29]

Notwithstanding Reagan's steadfast defense of his natural resources and environmental policies in general and Watt in particular, the media kept at it. At every opportunity it seemed, the media asked once again whether Reagan's support had waned. The media did so relentlessly for several reasons.

First, these issues—tangled as they are in scores of federal laws, agencies, and regulations—are not easily understood, especially by reporters with limited time to scan a press release or fact sheet, ask questions, and file or film a report. The easier approach, therefore, is to repeat the wild assertions of environmental groups. Of course, that approach serves the reporter's self-interest: it increases the likelihood that the story will be used.

Second, reporters' willingness to give heed to the sky-is-falling rhetoric of environmental groups made them susceptible to the ploy of discussing not what Reagan's Interior Department *was* doing but what it *intended* to do, or more likely, what it *might* do in the future.[30] What the department was doing—for example with regard to oil and gas development in the Outer Continental Shelf—was bold enough without considering and giving credibility to the outlandish and even absurd claims by environmental groups.[31]

Third, the media believed that anyone as outspoken as Watt—who said what he meant and meant what he said and who considered it a virtue that the private Watt be exactly the same, word-for-word, as the public Watt—was not long for the political world, and the press wanted to be there when lightning struck and Watt was incinerated.[32] Because they wanted to be there when it happened, they began a "death watch," attending Watt events in hopes that this would be the occasion for his departure and they would have the film.[33]

Finally, members of the White House staff too often offered their unsolicited views on the wisdom of goings-on at the Interior Department, the effect of those policies on Reagan's political future, and the likely longevity of officials implementing those policies. They had their own reasons for doing so, which may have included disagreements on policy, a desire to maintain media contact by being a ready source for a good quotation or inside information, or a sincere belief that President Reagan was ill-served and was endangered by the actions or advocacy of others in the administration. Unfortunately, as facts would bear out, enough problems occur naturally during any presidential administration without fomenting them.

Contempt of Congress—Disputed Principles

In the fall of 1981, a House subcommittee sought documents from the White House regarding an issue that had been discussed at the Cabinet Council on Natural Resources and Environment, specifically, Canada's discriminatory actions against United States energy companies and whether the retaliatory provisions of the federal Mineral Leasing Act should be invoked against Canada.[34] White House lawyers, in consultation with the Department of Justice, decided to withhold the documents and assert executive privilege. Watt, as chairman of the Cabinet Council group, as secretary of the department responsible for enforcement of the

Mineral Leasing Act, and as author or transmitter of some of the documents that reached the White House, was asked to assert the privilege on the president's behalf.

Watt was not only willing, he was eager to do so. That the privilege existed in some specific circumstances he had no doubt. Watt was a lawyer. He studied and practiced constitutional law and, as a political appointee in Washington in the 1970s, he closely followed the federal court proceedings in connection with President Nixon's unrestrained and unsuccessful attempts to exercise executive privilege. Watt, however, was not his own lawyer nor was he President Reagan's lawyer. He was only the vehicle through which the president would exercise a right he and every president must have to perform his constitutional duties. If President Reagan's White House lawyers, in consultation with the attorney general, believed a privilege existed, Watt was delighted to assert it on behalf of the president. Watt had private doubts based on his review of some of the documents, but to his mind, his personal views on the subject were irrelevant.[35]

The Constitution is silent regarding "executive privilege," the authority accorded the executive branch to bar encroachments by Congress and the judiciary; nevertheless, presidents from Washington on have asserted that right, relying on the constitutional principle of separation of powers. It was not until 1974, however, that the Supreme Court of the United States declared, for the first time, that the doctrine of executive privilege does have a constitutional basis, to wit, "the supremacy of each branch within its own assigned area of constitutional duties" and in the separation of powers.[36]

Later, the Court held the privilege is not absolute, but qualified; that is, limited to communications "in performance of [a president's] responsibilities ... of his office ... and made in the process of shaping policies and making decisions." The privilege is also subject to the "substantial public interest" in Congress's right to exercise its "broad investigative powers" to examine documents.[37] Finally, in addressing Congress's right to executive branch information, the Court makes no distinction between whether Congress is engaged in a legislative function—enacting, amending, or repealing laws—or is exercising an oversight responsibility—"probes into departments of the Federal Government to expose corruption, inefficiency or waste."[38]

Based on this last distinction, in October of 1981, Watt, on behalf of President Reagan, presented the House subcommittee with a memorandum he received from the president asserting the president's first claim of executive privilege and ordering Watt not to produce the requested documents.[39] It was Watt, of course, who was threatened with a contempt of Congress resolution; in fact, the Justice Department attorney who accompanied Watt was advised that he "might face a conflict of interest in advising Watt [because] Justice ... would be called upon to prosecute if Watt were charged with contempt."[40] Needless to say, it was not the president or the attorney general or the Department of Justice that was skewered in the media. Instead, it was Watt, as the *Post* headlined when the set battle opened, "Executive Privilege Invoked to Back Watt."

Although some documents were provided to the subcommittee, in less than six weeks, the subcommittee moved ahead with plans to hold Watt in contempt of Congress.[41] In early February of 1982, the subcommittee voted eleven to six to declare Watt in contempt, even though all but seven of the thirty-one requested documents had been provided to the subcommittee.[42] Watt was sanguine, opining that he expected Congress to rule that he was in contempt;[43] in fact, he said he would rather go to jail than to retreat from President Reagan's claim of executive privilege.[44] As if to hurry him on his way, less than two weeks later, the full committee voted twenty-three to nineteen, generally along party lines, to pronounce Watt in contempt.[45] The media were having a field day with the story; it was front-page news across the country, with Watt's name in the headlines, in editorials, and in political cartoons.[46]

One day, as the contempt citation was making its way to the House floor,[47] Watt encountered White House counsel Fred Fielding on the stairs at the White House. He learned that Fielding had been on Capitol Hill attempting to resolve quickly and without rancor another potential executive privilege matter; however, this one involved Department of Justice documents and its officials themselves.

"Why?" asked Watt.

"The General is concerned about negative press directed at him personally," Fielding replied.

"General who?" countered Watt.

"Attorney General [William French] Smith," said Fielding.

Watt was livid, "I'm being held in contempt of Congress for defending the President's right to exercise executive privilege but Bill is worried about himself." Fielding stood mute. "You get back up to the Hill and put an end to this right now," Watt declared to the startled Fielding.

The matter of the contempt citation against Watt ended without media notice. Nonetheless, long after it was over, Watt headlined muckraking exposés.[48]

Long Knives–Displaced Loyalties

White House chief of staff Edwin Meese famously and frequently declared, "Those who know aren't talking and those who are talking don't know."[49] Nonetheless, people inside the White House were talking, and whether they "knew" or not, members of the media were listening and reporting what was said.[50] The problem of White House leaks was particularly vexatious to Reagan, who made frequent mention of the problem in his diaries.[51] At one point, in fact, he took the extraordinary step of excluding everyone but cabinet officers from meetings—no more "back benchers," he wrote.[52] Reagan knew some leaks were due to "in house rivalry in the staff," "by subordinates in behalf of their bosses," which "come from the 2nd echelon in [a principal's] department."[53] "I'm afraid it has reached a point where the axe must fall," he declared.[54]

Unfortunately, the axe did not fall in time to prevent an apparent rivalry or ill will from erupting into a media circus regarding Watt, the National Park Service (NPS), and the annual Independence Day celebration on the National Mall.

In 1980 and 1981, the Beach Boys performed on the Fourth of July on the National Mall—a unit of the National Park System, which is part of the Department of the Interior. In 1982, however, a group called the Grass Roots performed. Afterward, the NPS received complaints regarding the arrests by the U.S. Park Police of some fifty-two adults for assault and disorderly conduct, a "smoke-in" by five hundred persons flaunting marijuana laws, and the treatment of over six hundred people at medical facilities, many for drug-related problems.[55] One of the complaints was from the Washington, D.C., chapter of Parents for Drug-Free Youth, which contacted Watt directly.[56] In November of 1982, after discussions with NPS officials—Watt declined White House recommendations to name a political appointee as NPS Director; instead, he selected a long-time career NPS civil servant—Watt signed a memorandum to the NPS stating the "imperative" to "get entertainment ... that will attract the family." The NPS believed, and Watt agreed, that selecting different entertainment might change the crowd from primarily college-age persons to a diverse gathering that would include more families. The result, the NPS hoped, would be less drug use and unruly behavior.

In April of 1983, Watt met in his office with a reporter from the *Washington Post* regarding his efforts in support of the United States Holocaust Memorial Museum. The interview was nearly at its end when the reporter asked, "Is there anything else, Mr. Secretary?" Watt volunteered the efforts of the NPS to prevent a reoccurrence of the unpleasantness on the mall during the Fourth of July celebration of the year before and had Doug Baldwin, his press secretary, provide the reporter a copy of the memorandum to the NPS. Watt and his wife, who was present for the interview, said a few words about their hopes for the upcoming Independence Day celebration. The following week, the *Post* featured a story about Watt on its front page, not in support of the museum, but in opposition to a particular brand of music thought to attract, in Watt's words, "the wrong element."[57] The page-one article, "Watt Outlaws Rock Music on Mall for July 4," was a straight-forward, factual discussion of Watt's decision, with comments from NPS officials about the 1982 concert, a lengthy biographical sketch of the planned "head-liner" for the 1983 event, Wayne Newton, which noted his support for President Reagan and that he is "of American Indian descent," along with the reporter's gentle chiding of Watt for his mischaracterization of prior head-liners as hard rock performers:

In the lexicon of rock, the secretary is not technically correct: Hard rock means loud guitars, heavy drums, a hard beat and frequently high-pitched vocals. The Grass Roots, last year's top group in an afternoon of music on the Washington Monument grounds before the fireworks, plays light, melodic pop-rock, as do the Beach Boys.[58]

The next day, the *Post* again put the Watt story on the front page, "Watt Sets Off Uproar With Music Ban." Not surprisingly, statements were issued by both the Beach Boys ("unbelievable") and the Grass Roots ("un-American")—after all, for aging rock stars no publicity is bad publicity; a local radio station that had sponsored the last three Fourth of July pop concerts solicited listener reaction; and, one radio talk show host led off, before taking calls from listeners, by labeling Watt a nerd.[59] A pro-marijuana lobby threatened to sue, and even the local branch of the ACLU was asked its opinion of the defensibility of Watt's actions.[60]

What was surprising, however, was the response of "official Washington." The *Post* reported, "[t]he vice president of the United States issued a statement—'[The Beach Boys are] my friends and I like their music.'—and the president's deputy chief of staff felt compelled to comment."[61] In a television interview, Michael Deaver, the deputy chief of staff, called Watt's act "unfortunate," and added derisively, "Anyone who thinks [the Beach Boys] are hard rock would think Mantovani plays jazz."[62] Most significantly, the first lady became involved. She spoke by telephone to Watt to express her dismay that he had cancelled a twenty-year contract for the Beach Boys to perform on the mall (there was no *contract*—the *Post* had reported that the Beach Boys had a twenty-year *career*). Her children, she told him, grew up with the music of the Beach Boys and "[the band members] are fine, outstanding people."[63] Later, Mrs. Reagan telephoned the Beach Boys, presumably to express her support.[64]

At the White House, after taking the telephone call from the first lady, Watt was ushered aside by senior staff.[65] Craig Fuller, the cabinet secretary;

David Gergen, the director of communications; and Deaver told Watt, "We need to get this behind us." They asked him to pose with President Reagan while receiving a bronzed fiberglass foot with a hole in it—what they described as a traveling "shoot-yourself-in-the-foot award"— and then take questions from the press. Watt did as he was asked, but after it was over, he bristled at Gergen's suggestion that he was a "good sport."

"I am not a good sport. I am a good soldier. I will do anything necessary to help Ronald Reagan," Watt replied.[66]

For Reagan, who presented the award with a twinkle in his eye and quipped later that he had "called in Ambassador Phil Habib to settle the Jim Watt/Beach Boys controversy," the episode was a nonevent. Although the Watt presentation interrupted his lunch with Vice President Bush, his diaries contain no entry regarding the matter.[67] On the other hand, the experience was humiliating for Watt, who realized that the White House staff could easily have arranged his resignation.[68] Moreover, the staff's judgment that Watt had endangered the president, a questionable conclusion, exposed him and ultimately Reagan to public ridicule. In the long run, the episode robbed Watt of the political capital he would need for the future.

No doubt the senior White House staff was proud of itself for getting "through the crisis of the Beach Boys on the Mall," but what kind of crisis was it anyway?[69] It smacked of jealousies and turf battles. Watt never mentioned the Beach Boys, did not ban them from the mall, and sought only to preserve a modicum of safety and decorum at an event for which his department was responsible. That he was a nerdy, tone-deaf, musical agnostic and hence uninformed regarding hard rock may have made him a joke to the sophisticates around the Oval Office, but it did not make him a threat to President Reagan or to the fulfillment of the president's agenda at Interior. Nonetheless, the White House staff not only turned a frivolous one-day story into three days of front-page coverage and a story with film on the evening news of every television network, it also created a myth that lives on today.[70]

The Good News and the Bad News

The Department of the Interior may be huge, with vast responsibilities that stretch from border to border and coast to coast—and even deep into the ocean—and statutory obligations that involve some of the nation's best-known and most recognizable landmarks, but few Americans ever give it a thought. Of course, Westerners are familiar with the Interior Department—it is their neighbor, and it affects their backyards, local economies, and recreational pursuits.[71] The rest of the country ought to care whether federal lands produce energy to their full potential, whether America's parks, wildlife refuges, and wilderness areas are well managed, and whether laws like the Endangered Species Act are achieving their purposes or merely stifling economic activity and undermining property rights.[72] People, however, are busy and most of the time, the activities of the nation's biggest landlord go unnoticed.[73]

There are exceptions, of course, such as when energy prices skyrocket and the public learns that millions of acres of the Outer Continental Shelf, managed by the Department of Interior and thought to contain abundant supplies of oil and natural gas, are off-limits to exploration and development as a result of congressional moratoria.[74] Then political leaders decry the senseless "lock-up" of desperately needed energy and demand, for example, "Drill Here; Drill Now." Finally, the public notices and sometimes, to some greater or lesser degree, Congress responds.

At other times, a natural or man-made disaster, like the Santa Barbara oil spill of 1969, the Yellowstone National Park fires of 1988, or the BP blowout of 2010 makes the news, and the media remind the public of what it may have forgotten or never knew. Among the forgotten facts: the federal government owns a third of the nation's landmass and over a billion acres off its coast, drilling for oil and gas is exceptionally costly and mostly safe but can be dangerous if care is not taken, and timberland not managed in accordance with good forestry practices can become an inferno. The media will continue to remind the public of these things as long as they are newsworthy and then they will move on to other matters and the public will forget.

Environmental groups, of course, are especially interested in the public's lands, which they believe should be managed in a particular manner. Keeping those lands and their resources before the public eye is necessary for fund-raising and lobbying, so they portray every proposal or plan regarding them as looming disasters that only they and an enlightened and enraged public, with the assistance of the media, can prevent. At times, the media are complicit in these efforts, but the Chicken Little rhetoric eventually loses its force.

During the Reagan administration, consistent with their decisions in 1979 and 1980 to abandon nonpartisanship, endorse Carter, and attack Reagan, environmental groups were more aggressive than ever in their attempts to persuade the media and the American public of what would later be called an impending "ecological holocaust."[75] To a degree, the administration's policy initiatives lent themselves to such a crude caricature, as environmental groups decried leasing of THE ENTIRE OUTER CONTINENTAL SHELF—A BILLION ACRES, FIRESALES OF PUBLIC RESOURCES, and OIL AND GAS DRILL-ING IN THE NATIONAL PARKS. For a while, the histrionics worked, but the apocalyptic headlines eventually became shop-worn, and the facts caught up with them. The administration was not leasing a billion acres; it was only allowing the oil and gas industry to determine the best place to look for new energy supplies. Bonus bids, which dropped due to the number of tracts offered for leasing, would be more than compensated for by royalty payments, not to mention taxes and the creation of new jobs, when oil or gas was discovered and produced in commercial quantities. The Interior Department, moreover, was not leasing, drilling, or mining in the national parks. That was barred by federal statute; in fact, it had never even been considered as a policy option.

The Interior Department remained in the news, however, because of Watt's willingness to challenge assertions by environmental groups and political opponents. As *Newsweek* reported in June of 1981:

> What environmentalists find so infuriating about Watt is not just that he disagrees with them, but that he challenges their most deeply held convictions.... He opposes them on their own terms, matching his idealism with theirs. He undercuts

their basic claim to legitimacy, which is that they alone are
disinterested champions of the commonweal.[76]

As this *Newsweek* story demonstrates, not all Washington-based press
coverage of Interior and Watt was negative, though most of it was. Outside of Washington, however, the coverage tended to be positive.[77]

Watt's willingness not only to respond to attacks on the administration's policies but also to challenge the presumption that environmentalists alone spoke for the environment was always newsworthy. Conflict
makes news, and the conflict between Watt and environmental groups
could not have been starker. Moreover, the secretary relished the battle,
often telling reporters that, having been briefed by environmental group
leaders, they would know what questions to ask and Watt could set them
straight.[78] Brilliant, articulate, with almost total recall of the minutiae
of the department, and armed with charts and graphs, he was an intim-
idating adversary and an inspiring advocate for President Reagan's
policies.

Watt was something else, which is another reason his Interior Department remained in the news; he was outstanding copy.[79] Although he could
be charming, he was combative and contentious. He did not suffer fools
gladly, and while intensely loyal to his friends, he regarded opponents
warily. His brilliance and eloquence had a downside; he sought the clever
and catchy phrase, which resonated with audiences but rang hollow,
harsh, or even hateful in print. Little wonder that those who met him or
heard him speak loved him, but those who knew of him only from media
reports thought otherwise.[80] He was, as the media reported, a lightening
rod, and he knew it. He also knew that one day a bolt from the blue
would take him out.

A Fatal, Self-Inflicted Wound

On September 21, 1983, I sat along the wall in a long conference
room on the Interior Department's fifth floor. A group of industry leaders
sat at the table listening to presentations by various assistant secretaries
on Interior's activities and getting answers to their questions. We were

killing time, waiting for Watt to return from a talk to the U.S. Chamber of Commerce, his former employer and one of the Reagan administration's most loyal supporters. Suddenly the double doors to my left flew open, and Watt entered and strode to the head of the table. The assistant secretary speaking stopped, welcomed his boss to the meeting, and sat down. Watt looked over the audience of businessmen and his fellow Interior employees and smiled.

Something was wrong. I turned to his aide Emily DeRocco, who accompanied Watt at local appearances, had entered with him and now sat beside me. "What's wrong with Jim?" I asked.

"We have a problem." She paused, "Jim misspoke."

"Deny it," I laughed, remembering my days on Capitol Hill when senators who uttered some thoughtless comment or other, on being assured that no one recorded the offense, denied or modified it into acceptable language.

"The Chamber filmed it."

"Get the film; it's the Chamber," I advised.

"They already gave it to CBS."

Sure enough, later that night on CBS News, I heard Watt, describing a blue-ribbon panel he had assembled to review Interior's coal leasing program, declare, "We have every kind of mix you can have. I have a black, I have a woman, two Jews and a cripple. And we have talent." Then I watched the credits roll—with thanks to the U.S. Chamber of Commerce.[81]

President Reagan stood by Watt. "The president considers the matter closed. It's behind us," a White House spokesman announced a week after the episode.[82] Chief of Staff Edwin Meese declined Watt's repeated offers to resign.[83] Nonetheless, a number of congressional Republicans threatened to join Democrats in passing a resolution calling for Watt's ouster.[84] Moreover, his Western supporters on Capitol Hill remained silent.[85] Thus, on October 9, 1983, Watt read from his letter of resignation to President Reagan, "my usefulness to you … has come to an end. A different type of leadership at the Department of the Interior will best serve you and the nation."[86] A statement issued by President Reagan from Camp David declared, in part:

Jim has done an outstanding job as a member of my Cabinet and in his stewardship of the natural resources of the nation. He has initiated a careful balance between the needs of people and the importance of protecting the environment. His dedication to public service and his accomplishments as secretary of interior will long be remembered.[87]

In his diary that night, Reagan wrote:

Sun. evening Jim Watt called from Calif. & tendered his resignation as Sec. of Interior. I accepted with real regret. He's done a fine job. True he has an unfortunate way of putting his foot in his mouth but he's really the victim of a 2½ year lynching. He knows he no longer can be effective with Congress so he's being a bigger man than his detractors.[88]

Ten days later, Reagan added:

Jim Watt came by. He's in good spirits. He knew that in carrying out my policies his days would be numbered. Actually he thought he would have had to leave sooner than he did. He gave me a report on his stewardship & it reveals the hypocrisy of the Environmental lynch mob. I don't think the Dept. of Interior or our Nat. Parks & wild lands have ever been in better shape.[89]

On November 26, 1983, from Rancho del Cielo, his ranch near Santa Barbara, California, Reagan delivered his weekly radio address on what he called the "change of management over at the Department of the Interior." He had studied Watt's thick report, distilled its essence, and written out by hand his comments on Watt's stewardship: "James G. Watt has served this nation well. And I'm sure William Clark will do the same."[90] After all, the policies at Interior were not Watt's or Clark's policies; they were Reagan's. Furthermore, it was not those policies that ended Watt's tenure; he had been targeted, tainted, and toppled by the media, though he helped them with his outspokenness. Watt's departure was not a referendum on Reagan's policies. It merely reflected the degree to which Watt, the man and his image, not his implementation of Reagan's policy, had become radioactive. Indeed, it could be argued that from the day of the Herblock cartoon he was a dead man walking.[91]

Calming the Waters

William Clark arrived at Interior as President Reagan's top hand with two main directives: continue the initiatives begun by Watt and "calm the waves,"[92] "especially as Reagan's reelection campaign was commencing."[93] The president knew that Clark, one of his closest associates, was uniquely equipped to achieve the latter objective. Watt and Clark shared a profound commitment to Ronald Reagan,[94] but they could not have been more different. Clark was "lower-keyed," "careful in his approach and his words," non-confrontational, "amiable and conciliatory."[95] Moreover, in a town filled with people in love with the sound of their own voices, Clark found no need to utter a word or even to nod his head. His years on the bench had taught him to maintain a judicial temperament, listening politely until, in the quiet of his chambers, he issued the only statement he would deliver—his ruling.

That temperament, however, did not exempt Clark from attacks by liberal Democrats, assertions by the press—including cartoonists—that he was unqualified or worse, and assaults by environmental groups; he was, after all, Ronald Reagan's man.[96] The Senate confirmed him, nevertheless, by a vote of seventy-one to eighteen, and after putting his people in some of the top Interior positions, Clark took over as secretary.[97]

Clark met early and often with the heads of the various environmental groups and made Interior more accessible to them.[98] He schmoozed with Chairman Udall as well as other Capitol Hill leaders, even seeking their advice.[99] He called for "convergence" on the nation's national security, economic, and environmental needs, cautioning "it takes two or more to converge."[100] As if to prove his point, the Wilderness Society continued to decry President Reagan's "devastating" policies.[101]

Clark bypassed the Office of Management and Budget—as only the president's top hand could do—nullifying its opposition to irrigation and flood-control projects and its unwillingness to pay the full cost of repairing unsafe dams.[102] Clark also plucked some low-hanging public relations fruit: removing the Grand Canyon as a potential dam site, returning 132,000 unneeded acres to the Hualapai Indians who live at the bottom of the canyon, and adopting a ground water protection program.[103] He also prosecuted "polluters with renewed vigor," slightly slowed the "rush to develop energy and mineral resources on public lands," and revived "federal acquisitions of parklands."[104] Clark's goal was to remove the environment as an issue against President Reagan in his 1984 reelection campaign, and he achieved it. Clark disarmed his critics, wrote *U.S. News & World Report*, and left them "floundering."[105]

Meanwhile, Clark received unsolicited assistance from an unexpected source. Former President Jimmy Carter, thankful for Clark's kindness in his briefings on security issues, not only called his "green friends" to urge that they not oppose Clark's nomination, but also invited Clark for a weekend of quail hunting. They became friends. As a result of that friendship, Carter advised former Vice President Walter Mondale to abandon his plans to run "hard against Reagan and the Department of the Interior on the environmental legacy left by James Watt." Carter admonished Mondale, "Don't you touch Bill Clark. He's the only person in the Reagan administration that has been decent to me and Rosalynn. Besides, he's doing a good job at Interior." After losing forty-nine states to Reagan in 1984, Mondale blamed Clark for his defeat.[106]

In spite of these successes, Clark remained disappointed that Congress barred the administration from opening up the energy resources on the Outer Continental Shelf.[107] But when he stepped down as interior secretary in early 1985, the *Washington Post* and the *New York Times* ran glowing, almost poetic, tributes, depicting him riding his horse through Rock Creek Park and into the California sunset.[108]

Not with a Bang . . .

Donald Hodel, who had moved from second in command at Interior to head the Department of Energy, agreed to replace Clark. Eager to leave Washington and return to the West, Hodel accepted the transfer reluctantly. Clark was insistent, and eventually the first lady intervened. Hodel was confirmed quickly with only one "no" vote (from William Proxmire, a Democrat from Wisconsin).[109] In his meeting with the president prior to his appointment, Hodel had asked simply, "Mr. President, I assume you want me to continue to implement the policies begun by Jim Watt?" President Reagan said, "Yes," and after some casual small talk, Hodel was out the door.

A lawyer but not a judge, Donald Hodel was no William Clark. He was thoughtful but not taciturn, and despite his personal friendship and collegial working relationship with Watt, he was no Watt either. He saw no need to toss the media any red meat, and his statements were plain vanilla. At his first press conference, he eschewed engagement; instead, he disarmed and deflected. Asked if he were a Watt clone, he neither abandoned his friend nor attempted to parse. "You mean do we both comb our hair the same way?" he smiled as he stroked his nearly bald pate. The laughter led to the next question. "Do you intend to turn the buffalo to face to the right like Watt did?" Watt had famously turned the mascot on the Interior Department's seal to face in his politically preferred direction.[110] Hodel leaned over the podium to view the Interior seal and its buffalo. "He looks like he's facing to the right to me." More laughter followed. Reporters learned that Hodel would not take the bait and if he did respond, his answers would be long-winded, boring, and totally unquotable.

Nonetheless, Washington being Washington, Hodel somehow engendered media controversy. There was a dust-up in early 1986 when he removed Lee Iacocca from one of two panels on which he served to raise and spend funds for the restoration of the Statue of Liberty and Ellis Island.[111] Iacocca called his termination "un-American," and various politicians rebuked Hodel; however, the ethical issues raised by Iacocca's ability as chairman to direct how the funds he raised would be spent and the apparent support from the National Park Service for Hodel's decision muted the issue.[112] The next day, as "leading Democrats" made "political hay over Iacocca's abrupt ouster," Hodel admitted that he "deliberately skirted the White House" in making his decision; but, by then the story was no longer page-one news.[113]

A little over a year later, there was another small flap when White House or Environmental Protection Agency staff, frustrated by Hodel's opposition to the Montreal Protocol, leaked a report that he opposed the EPA's costly plan to deal with the hole in the ozone, falsely claiming that Hodel argued that Americans should be told to make "wider use of hats, sunglasses and sun-screening lotions."[114] Environmental groups assailed Hodel, and some demanded that he resign.[115] The secretary insisted that he had never made such a recommendation but was challenging the science to provide more options for President Reagan. The hit job worked, however. Hodel was *persona non grata* at Montreal Protocol discussions.[116] Soon, that story disappeared as well.

The most important media event of Hodel's tenure at Interior was a nonevent. In July of 1985, the Beach Boys, having been invited to return during Clark's tenure, were back for the Fourth of July on the National Mall. This time, however, the complaints came from the *Washington Post*.[117] The Beach Boys were not only old, they were slow, opening two hours late. "[T]he crowd was getting restless," the paper reported, and at one point, the band's Mike Love announced, "The Park Service has asked us to end the show as quickly and quietly as possible."[118] Days later, Hodel was at the White House standing at a window looking out at the Washington Monument, awaiting lunch. Nancy Reagan approached, "Don, don't you think it's about time to end the Beach Boys for July 4th?" she asked. "Absolutely," the secretary replied. Hodel gave the order, the National Park Service complied, and the next month while he was touring national parks out West the story broke. Hodel braced for a media tempest that never came. A report that the Beach Boys were banned from the National Mall for the Fourth of July was apparently no longer newsworthy.

The media appeared to have lost their taste for the "war against the environment" at Reagan's Interior Department. For the first time in years, the department did not regularly make the front page. In part this was the result of the fact that Reagan's policies as implemented by Watt and continued by Clark and Hodel were old news, no longer timely, or at least not of sufficient magnitude to warrant major news coverage. Moreover, the Interior Department could not compete with the Iran-Contra scandal, which consumed the latter half of Reagan's second term.[119] Hodel happily disappeared from the public view.[120]

Entering 1988, the administration went into election year mode. In the eighteen months prior to January of 1989, Hodel had advised his appointees and staff to implement any standing policies and to prepare anything new to be published in the *Federal Register* after the election in recognition of the fact that, in an election year, even good ideas are potential targets for partisan attacks. As soon as the election was over and during a three-day period, Hodel met with officials and staff to discuss and decide the remaining issues. As Hodel awaited the release of the Reagan administration's last batch of *Federal Register* notices, he realized he was superfluous to the operation of the department. All the decisions he would make had been made and the implementation of those decisions was in the hands of others. He could finish his tenure as secretary from the Federal Center in Denver.

The *Washington Post* ran a gossip column squib on Hodel's strange disappearance and his apparent lack of interest in the job, but it ran in the "Style" section, a far cry from the early 1980s when Interior was front-page news. At the end of the president's term, the Interior Department and its agencies published seventy-three notices of proposed rulemaking. By this time, however, the *Post* was stymied. Watt, Clark, and now Hodel were all gone. It was just the bureaucrats in the final stages of implementing President Reagan's policies. For the media and its coverage of those policies, it all ended with a whimper.

Not Your Father's Media

The news media have changed dramatically since Ronald Reagan came to Washington in 1981. Of course, the *New York Times* and the *Washington Post* still dominate the print media, and the national news networks report nightly on a day's or week's events. The thinly veiled, left-leaning bias that some detected in the coverage of Reagan's Interior Department, however, has been transformed into what lawyers would call "open and notorious" advocacy for the left.[121] Bernard Goldberg, the CBS veteran and *New York Times* bestselling author, puts it this way: The mainstream media, "abandoning even the pretense of objectivity, moved from media bias to media activism" in the 2008 election, when, "moving from their usual unthinking liberal bias to crass partisanship of the crudest kind," they "practically act[ed] as spin doctors for the presidential campaign of Barack Obama."[122] On a host of other environmental issues—climate change stands out—the media gave up all objectivity and took on the role of advocates.

A countervailing change, however, took place over the decades since Ronald Reagan left the Oval Office—the growth of talk radio, cable news, and the World Wide Web and the blogosphere. It is impossible to overestimate the contribution these alternatives to the mainstream media have made to political discourse.[123]

Reporting in the blogosphere, this time by *Powerline*, exposed the outrageous lie that the media had told for a quarter-century—namely, that James Watt's religious beliefs made him incapable of being a good steward or performing his duties as secretary of the interior. *Powerline* forced an apology from Bill Moyers, a correction in the *Washington Post*, which led to an op-ed opportunity for Watt, and a concession of sorts from the *Minneapolis Star Tribune*.[124] If a conservative were to be slandered today in the manner in which Watt was for decades, no doubt Rush Limbaugh, Fox News, and scores of bloggers would quickly reveal the lie.

———

Although the main-stream media must now share the public stage with others with divergent views, the environmental extremists who battled Ronald Reagan throughout the 1980s are stronger than ever. It is the responsibility of the American people to understand them fully and learn where they want to take this country and all of Western civilization.

CHAPTER FIVE

MODERN DAY LUDDITES[1]

"People are ecology too and most of us are looking for answers that will preserve nature to the greatest extent possible consistent with the need to have places where we can work & live."
—RONALD REAGAN, FEBRUARY 27, 1975[2]

The Politics of Personal Destruction

O n a sunny but brisk late December day in 1980, James Watt and I walked down a Denver street from his Mountain States Legal Foundation (MSLF) office, past a clot of reporters, and into a small conference room in the Brown Palace Hotel.[3] I had flown into town the night before after spending a week at the Library of Congress in Washington searching for public statements by Watt in his previous stints in the nation's capital. Weeks earlier, Watt had telephoned me using the White House switchboard. "They can find anyone, anywhere," he laughed when I asked how he tracked me to a friend's house in White Bear Lake, Minnesota. Then he asked me to perform the service for him that he had performed twelve years earlier for Governor Walter Hickel of Alaska, which was to serve as his aide in the confirmation process.

Watt was the young lawyer who briefed and grilled Hickel prior to his Senate confirmation hearing and later helped him answer the scores of questions submitted to him by various senators. Some of those questions had originated within Interior itself among the bureaucrats who would eventually work for Hickel if he were confirmed.[4] Hickel's confirmation had been brutal. Muckrakers savaged him, leading newspapers opposed him, and senators and leaders of environmental groups testified against him.[5] A popular governor who had been a developer in Alaska's territorial boom days, Hickel was unprepared for the environmentalist ambush. After his confirmation, hoping to persuade his detractors that he was a moderate and an environmentalist, he moved politically to the left. In time, his leftward movement, not on environmental issues but with regard to the Vietnam War, got him fired.[6] Watt concluded, "[Y]ou can't outrun an environmentalist to the left."[7]

Watt was still at Interior—awaiting both his nomination by President Ford to the Federal Power Commission and his confirmation by the Senate—when Ford named the interior secretary, Rogers C. B. Morton, as the new secretary of commerce and replaced him at Interior with the former governor of Wyoming, Stanley K. Hathaway.[8] Orphaned as a young boy and raised by relatives on Wyoming's eastern plains, Hathaway was a highly decorated gunner in the army air corps in World War II. In his two terms as governor, he created the Wyoming Department of Environmental Quality and then established a permanent trust fund with the proceeds from mineral development.[9]

Notwithstanding his impressive record, Hathaway was savaged when he arrived in Washington. After a contentious confirmation process, he lasted less than four months in office.[10] A good, gentle, and quiet man, Hathaway did not understand the personal attacks from environmental groups and their allies in the Senate, refused to respond in kind to their relentless assault, and internalized the vigorous, varied, and vicious beatings he absorbed daily.[11] Watt, who was in frequent contact with family, friends, and colleagues, watched in horror as a Wyoming neighbor was vilified.[12] He concluded that, by remaining silent, Hathaway had not effectively stilled his opponents but had emboldened them to press their attack. He resolved that, were he ever in Hathaway's shoes, for his own sanity, and given his personality, he would not remain silent but would return fire with fire. He might be driven from office, but he would not be driven mad—and he would go down swinging.[13]

On our walk that morning, Watt reflected on what he learned from working with Hickel and watching Hathaway and reviewed his strategy for the confirmation hearing in January as well as what he expected from me. Working for Watt, I had an easier job than Watt had working for Hickel. The Senate was now overwhelmingly Republican. Reagan's landslide victory had given him a mandate, and he deserved the confirmation of his appointees, barring a major scandal. Watt was an experienced Interior hand, unlike Hickel and Hathaway. He knew what he wanted to say, how to answer questions—to maintain total flexibility in his job to accomplish what Reagan wanted—and where in Interior the most nettlesome issues lay unresolved. My job was to find landmines that he had forgotten. I found none but reminded Watt of the testimonies he had delivered.

That morning presented a different challenge. Watt had asked sixteen leaders of Colorado environmental groups to sit down with him before his confirmation hearings.[14] The Colorado environmentalists knew Watt only from his work as MSLF's president. Although Watt had been outspoken in many fundraising appearances before oil and gas, mining, ranching, and forestry groups regarding the threat to economic activity posed by environmental groups, much of MSLF's litigation—such as challenges to the Windfall Profits Tax, the presence of wild horses on federal land and private grazing allotments, and extension by Congress of the time to ratify the Equal Rights Amendment—had not involved the other groups directly.[15] Watt hoped, therefore, that the Coloradoans would see him as a straight-shooting, decent, and honest Westerner they knew and one with whom they would usually disagree but against whom they did need not to launch a preemptive strike.

The meeting went well enough—the leaders were still nursing their wounds from the November election results, although Senator Gary Hart, a Democrat, had won a close reelection battle—and Watt pledged to hear their grievances once in office.[16] Then he cautioned with a broad smile, "Just so you know, however, shrillness will affect my hearing." I immediately thought it ham-handed but tried to keep a poker face. Let them discover the consequences of unprovoked, irresponsible, and baseless attacks, I thought, but I held my peace. As I feared, several in the group did not take it well.

"Are you trying to muzzle us, Jim?" one suggested; others nodded.

"I think we all know what I am talking about," Watt concluded. The meeting broke up and we all shook hands. As Watt and I emerged into the bright sunshine and slipped, without comment, past the reporters and cameramen, I wondered if his veiled threats had soured the mood.[17] I need not have worried. To a man, those local environmental leaders respected Watt's willingness to attempt to build a bridge and made only general comments, including "I want to hear more."[18] By the time Watt got to his confirmation hearings, however, the environmental groups—from headquarters in San Francisco, New York, and Washington—had been blasting away for days in a personal, personnel, and policy assault on the Reagan administration that would never end; in fact, it continues to this day.[19]

Environmental Groups Choose Sides

Today, environmental groups pretend that they were not all that enamored with President Carter,[20] that Governor Reagan's record in Sacramento was not one of outright opposition to environmental initiatives, that environmental issues were largely absent from the presidential campaign of 1980, and that as Reagan's inauguration approached, his agenda on environmental issues was still unknown.[21] In truth, the environmental groups were tied closely to Carter, and many of their colleagues had gone to work for him, especially in the Interior Department. For example, they teamed up with Carter, the United Mine Workers, and others to add a "local coal amendment" to the Clean Air Act Amendments of 1977, barring importation of Western coal into the Midwest to meet the emission requirements of federal law. Certainly no friends of underground coal mining, these groups sought instead to prevent the open-pit mining of low-sulfur coal in eastern Montana and Wyoming.[22]

Environmentalists saw Reagan as such a serious threat that they took the unprecedented step of endorsing, supporting, and campaigning for Carter.[23] Reagan's views on economic, natural resources, and environmental issues were well known, and the environmental lobby opposed them. Marion Edy of the League of Conservation Voters said, "[Reagan's] ignorance of environmental issues is real, not a figment of the media's imagination."[24] Russell Peterson, a former Republican governor of Delaware who represented the National Audubon Society, pronounced Reagan and his party guilty of a "basic misunderstanding of the important issues such as energy.... [T]hey don't understand that a healthy economy depends on a healthy environment...."[25] Brock Evans of the Sierra Club said it was time that environmentalists "started acting like the other guys around town and started getting active on the political front."[26] The endorsement of Carter by these twenty-two groups, on behalf of their ten million members, concluded the *New York Times*, "marks another step in the politicization of the environmental movement in recent years."[27] Despite their later insistence that it was Reagan who politicized environmental issues, in truth it was the environmentalists who did so.

Nearly a year before the leading environmentalists endorsed Carter in September of 1980 and went to war against Reagan, they met in Denver to prepare a response to the growing Sagebrush Rebellion.[28] Reagan's close friend Senator Paul Laxalt of Nevada, one of the first politicians to identify himself as a Sagebrush Rebel, introduced legislation on the subject.[29] There was little question that Reagan would embrace the Sagebrush Rebellion, which he did early and enthusiastically.[30]

The Sagebrush Rebellion was more than the angry response of Westerners who depend on federal land for economic and recreational activities to the War on the West waged by Carter.[31] It was also the reinstitution of the political debate that had characterized the conservation movement from its earliest days at the dawn of the twentieth century, that is, the battle between preservation and conservation.[32]

It was much more, however. It was additionally a battle between two competing systems of government: between big and powerful New Deal-style government run by progressives and technocrats, like Carter himself, and a limited government that emphasized individual and economic freedom. At the same time, Westerners who viewed themselves as the true environmentalists challenged the moral high ground claimed by environmental groups in their advocacy of "an ecological conscience" and "a land ethic." Although the entire country was hurting economically, the West believed itself to be the most beleaguered because it was besieged by the federal government.

Sagebrush Rebels decried the "environmental consensus" as the source of their problems. More than any other region, the American West was a victim of the scores of environmental laws adopted during the previous two decades. As a result, Sagebrush Rebels asserted that economic well-being was more important than ecological well-being, a term that, as a high priesthood of environmental wisdom, only environmental groups and their leaders could define and determine if and when national policy is consistent with it.

It was natural for a Sagebrush Rebel like Reagan to articulate these concerns in the 1980 campaign. His support of the Sagebrush Rebellion, however, was not the first sign that Reagan's views on natural resources and the environment diverged from those that had prevailed for years in Washington. After he left the governor's mansion in Sacramento and began his radio show, he spoke out consistently on those issues. He made no secret of his opinion of "environmental extremists" and the crazy laws and policies they championed.[33]

By 1980, the "apocalyptic predictions about the failures of big government" that Reagan had been making for years "were coming true,"[34] as one biographer put it. Reagan had an explanation, of course, not only for the country's economic ills but also for its enduring and confounding foreign policy problems. In short, energy! Inflation, unemployment, and foreign affairs, Reagan reasoned, were all influenced by oil shortages. He asserted that, for the first time in American history, the country faced "three grave crises at the same time. [1] Our economy is deteriorating. [2] Our energy needs are not being met. [3] And our military preparedness has been weakened to the point of immediate danger."[35] Nonetheless, America, he asserted, "doesn't have to be in the shape that it is in.... We do not have to go on sharing in scarcity with the country getting worse off [and] unemployment growing.... All of this can be cured and all of it can be solved."[36]

In his acceptance speech at the Republican National Convention, Reagan said Carter failed to search for and develop the energy that America possesses in abundance because he "seems to believe the American people would rather see more regulation, taxes and control than more energy."[37] America's "environment[al] heritage" will not be jeopardized, Reagan said, but "we are going to reaffirm that the economic prosperity of our people is a fundamental part of our environment."[38]

That fall, in a debate seen by a hundred million viewers, Reagan faulted Carter for not exploring the Outer Continental Shelf, where "there are vast [energy] supplies to be found." He also blamed "environmental extremists [and] a tiny minority opposed to economic growth" for locking up federal lands that hold "probably 70 percent of the potential oil in the United States."[39] So stark was the choice presented between Reagan and Carter—they discussed public land issues in "such extreme, polarized terms"—that one observer concluded, "[d]uring the 1980 presidential campaign, the future of the public lands became a primary issue among Republicans and Democrats." In fact, "[h]ad no other issues been at stake," the election might be viewed as a "national referendum on whether [public lands] ought to be preserved or developed...."[40]

Environmental groups, those whom Reagan called "environmental extremists," were right to see him as a threat. He challenged their views that the needs of nature took priority over the needs of mankind, their claim of moral rectitude, and their assertions that they alone spoke for nature, for most Americans, and for the future of the planet. Reagan insisted that he could, in the words of one former environmentalist, "oppose environmentalists without opposing the environment."[41] Reagan was about to present the first presidential challenge to the moral authority of the environmentalist establishment that had reigned unchallenged in Washington.

Not Your Grandfather's Environmental Movement

Reagan's biographer Lou Cannon wrote that the president "considers himself a conservationist, an outdoorsman and a lover of nature" and, "[a]s a rancher of varying sorts for more than four decades[,] is a careful steward of his own land [who] believes in the value of open space, for himself and his countrymen."[42] As governor, Reagan built an impressive record on environmental issues:

> In California the Reagan administration added 145,500 acres of land and two underwater Pacific Ocean preserves to the state park system. He signed legislation requiring auto emission controls that were more stringent than the controls required by federal law. Given a choice between alternative measures to protect California's few remaining wild rivers, Reagan signed the more environmentally protective of the two bills. In 1968 he defied the state's influential dam-building establishment and the Army Corps of Engineers by saving scenic Round Valley from a high dam which would have flooded it. Reagan said that the building of the dam would violate a treaty made long ago with a tiny Indian tribe. "We've broken too damn many treaties," he said.[43]

Cannon writes that Reagan "evolved into a balancer of environmental and development claims and tried to work with moderates in both camps."[44] As he declared in a 1973 speech:

> We do not have to choose between the environment and jobs. We can set a common-sense course between those who would cover the whole country with concrete in the name of progress, and those who think you should not build a house unless it looks like a bird's nest or rabbit hole.[45]

An example of this common-sense course was Reagan's compromise in the creation of the 53,000-acre Redwood National Park, which Congress established from federal land, two state parks, and additional property bought from lumber companies.[46] Nonetheless, according to Cannon, Reagan's "prodevelopment positions made him a target for environmental groups in the 1966 gubernatorial campaign."[47] For Ronald Reagan, the worst was yet to come from environmental groups.

There were fissures in the conservation or environmental movement from the beginning.[48] At first the division was between those who wanted unrestrained use of federally owned land for economic activity and those who sought to conserve the land to ensure its "wise use" over time, including for the economic needs of future generations.[49] The conservation ethic prevailed, and national forests were created to ensure the use, then and into the future, of their timber and water, while preserving them for recreation.[50] The national parks and national monuments were likewise created, not for the use of their economic resources, but as "pleasuring grounds" for the American people both now and for generations to come.[51]

In the 1960s, however, a new cadre of doomsayers viewed the conservation ethic as inadequate to the task of protecting the planet from emerging dangers. Rachel Carson published *Silent Spring* in 1962, the first installment of what became "the favored genre of environmentalist writers: alarmism."[52] In 1964, Stewart L. Udall published the federal lands or "open space" companion piece to Carson's attack on pesticides.[53] In 1968, Paul R. Ehrlich published *The Population Bomb*, yet another alarmist screed, this one filled with neo-Malthusian predictions of unavoidable catastrophe.[54] In April of 1970, environmentalists celebrated the first Earth Day, and in 1972, the Club of Rome published its doomsday warning, *The Limits to Growth*.[55] In 1964, environmentalists celebrated the passage of the Wilderness Act, the culmination of fifteen years of lobbying, which set aside federal land not for "wise use" or even as "pleasuring grounds" but as land "where man himself is a visitor who does not remain."[56] By the 1970s, the evolving environmental movement was showing abundant signs of becoming anti-technology, anti-civilization, anti-humanity, anti-intelligence, and even anti-Western civilization.[57]

Before that first Earth Day, the predominant view of man's relation
to the rest of nature was what one environmental historian has called the
"human exemptionalism paradigm," which saw "life's possibilities and
nature's bounty as infinite and humans as essentially omnipotent":

> They assume that human technological ingenuity can continue
> infinitely to improve the human situation as long as it is unfet-
> tered by unnecessary restrictions and self-imposed limitations.
> In this view, it is imperative to use natural resources to pro-
> mote human welfare through economic growth.[58]

Earth Day organizers, on the other hand, promoted the opposing "ecological paradigm," which held that "environmental limits are real."[59]

As environmental groups abandoned their conservation roots and
asserted that mankind was not part of the solution but was part of the
problem and that nature itself was to be valued more than man, rising to
the level of "nature mysticism," something else happened.[60] The movement took on the "trappings of a religion," which included:

> Inspired leaders and true believers, revered dogmas and irre-
> proachable belief, a sense of awe and cosmic unity, community
> bonds, a sense of distinctiveness and moral superiority to
> non-believers, promises of salvation and healing, the urge to
> convert and redeem others as expressed in a missionary service
> to unbelievers, apocalyptic visions of the end of the world—
> and even a number of denominations preaching variations on
> the central dogma....[61]

A conflict decades in the making erupted between two old-line environmental groups—the Sierra Club, founded in 1892, and the Save the
Redwoods League, founded in 1918—headquartered across the street
from each other in San Francisco:

> At the turn of the century, [they] had accepted a world view
> in which man's technological progress was compatible with

the progressive, directional action of evolution. [Over the
years,] [t]he League retained this older idealism, stoically
adhering to its conservative politics.... The Sierra Club abandoned the philosophy of [its founders] for that of [others],
who found no will, no knowledge beyond the natural order.
Evolution was random. A nondirectional universe comple-
mented a technology that appeared as destructive as it was
beneficent. Technology was not divinely programmed progress. Indeed, it may be no more than the random movement
of the human parasite through an indifferent cosmos.[62]

The two organizations clashed over the creation of a Redwood National
Park in the 1960s. The Sierra Club engaged in an alarmist nationwide
campaign, demanded congressional action, and urged land acquisition
by eminent domain. The League, on the other hand, pressed for a cooperative approach between park proponents and landowners, a smaller
and more manageable park, and acquisition of private property by
purchase. "With the shrillness of one betrayed, the Sierra Club turned
the division between the once-friendly San Francisco groups into a
nationally publicized schism [and in doing so] rejected an image that
looked like an old photograph of itself."[63]

Governor Reagan, whose views were closer to the League's and who
had agreed reluctantly to the creation of the national park, rebelled when
the Sierra Club and liberal California Democrats later pushed to expand
the park, explaining his objections in a number of his radio addresses.[64]
Reagan often said that he did not leave the Democratic Party; it left him.[65]
So it was with the old-line conservation movement, which had become
the new, post-Earth Day environmental movement; it left Ronald Reagan.

President Jimmy Carter, on the other hand, embraced the new environmental ethic and populated his administration with members of the
movement, whom one Washington insider described as

... a new kind of individual not formerly part of the Washington scene. They are the environmentalists, the consumer-advo-
cates and others from what is loosely called the counterculture.

The strength of the new men and women who dot the Carter
Administration and who came out of a gaggle of activist organizations is that they feel in possession of moral legitimacy.[66]

Irving Kristol saw this "New Class" of highly educated and affluent
public sector leaders much more darkly:

> Though they continue to speak the language of "progressive
> reform," in actuality they are acting upon a hidden agenda:
> to propel the nation from that modified version of capitalism
> we call "the welfare state" toward an economic system so
> stringently regulated in detail as to fulfill many of the tradi-
> tional anti-capitalist aspirations of the Left.[67]

When the energy crisis hit, Carter responded by embracing wholeheartedly the "ecology paradigm": natural resources were limited, and mankind would just have to get used to permanent scarcity. Reagan, of course,
embraced the "human exemptionalism paradigm," so he drew the unrelenting enmity of environmental groups, which by this time had become
an arm of the Democratic Party.[68]

The Unrelenting Attack

The opposition by environmental groups to James Watt's nomination
as secretary of the interior was unanimous and so shrill as to descend into
self-parody: "Were [Watt] to become Secretary of the Interior … the war
against the earth would step up in pace and this country and the globe
are not likely to reach the year 2,000 intact."[69]

In the late spring of 1981, as news of the media's distorted report of
Watt's testimony in answer to Congressman Weaver's question became
more widely known, environmental groups opened up with both barrels
on Watt's religious views.[70] In the July–August 1981 issue of *Sierra*, the
Sierra Club declared, "Watt seems to think he has divine sanction for his
efforts to turn our natural resources over to concessioners and developers."[71]

In fact, "virtually every major environmental journal had something to say about Watt's religion, all of it scurrilous and abusive."[72]

Notwithstanding the unrelenting attacks, Watt agreed to meet with ten environmental leaders in May of 1981 to review a ten-point list of demands to which they sought the secretary's agreement.[73] To their surprise, Watt signed off on seven of the ten items, a "gentleman's C" in any college and more than enough in politics, the "art of the possible."[74] It was not enough for the environmentalists, however. They had their narrative, and it did not include saying that Watt did anything right.[75] Nonetheless, behind closed doors, they worked with Interior officials to reach agreements on various issues.[76]

The environmental groups, which had endorsed Carter, opposed Reagan, and assailed Watt, had worked out plans with their allies on Capitol Hill.[77] The National Wildlife Federation announced that an opinion poll of four thousand of its 4.5 million members urged the organization to call for Watt's resignation.[78] Watt completed the survey himself, with its skewed questions, and then announced, "I also fired James Watt."[79] Meanwhile, the Sierra Club was gathering 1.1 million signatures on its "Dump Watt" petition.[80] Not to be outdone, the Wilderness Society issued a four-pound volume, *The Watt Book*, that James K. Kilpatrick called "a labor of loathing."[81]

The attack on Watt continued and received great coverage in the national media—although not out West—which was the purpose of the exercise,[82] not because of Watt's policies, pronouncements, or personality, but because he was implementing the policies of Reagan so effectively.[83]

President Reagan and the Environmentalists

Ronald Reagan staked out his territory in support of James Watt early on. Shortly after rumors of Watt's nomination broke and as environmental groups opened fire, President-elect Reagan provided personal cover for his likely nominee by putting the controversy in context: "Jim Watt has only opposed environmental extremists. I think he's an environmentalist himself, as I am."[84]

The meeting with James Watt from which the secretary famously emerged with a "stainless steel backbone" took place in September of 1981. Reagan wrote in his diary later that evening, "Met with Jim Watt. He's taking a lot of abuse from environmental extremists but he's absolutely right. People are ecology too and they can't forage for food and live in caves."[85]

Watt was not the only one taking a lot of abuse. Environmentalists sought to discredit not only Watt but also Reagan and everyone else in his administration who was implementing his policies.[86] Environmental extremists, as President Reagan termed them, were relentless in their attacks, but one man in particular carried the attacks to an obsessive degree. The legendary photographer Ansel Adams began writing "a letter a day to newspapers and congressmen decrying President Reagan's 'disastrous' environmental policies and his interior secretary, James G. Watt."[87] He warned of "a catastrophe," "a tragedy," and "the Pearl Harbor of our American Earth."[88] Then, in May of 1983, Adams declared flatly, "I hate Reagan."[89] That got the president's attention. He told a top aide, "I want to talk to this man, Adams, to find out why he dislikes me so much."[90]

Meanwhile, Reagan decided it was "time to clear the air and straighten out the record on where my administration stands on environmental and natural resources management matters," which was how he began his weekly radio address in mid-June, 1983.[91] After some opening remarks on the new leadership at the Environmental Protection Agency, Reagan transitioned,[92] "But, that's enough about me."

> The Secretary of Interior, Jim Watt, is the prime target for those who claim that this Administration is out to level the forests and cover the country with blacktops. Someone in the press the other day said if Jim discovered a cure for cancer, there are those who would attack him for being pro-life.
>
> Let's go back a little first and set the stage. Jim rides herd on all the national parks and most of the 80 million acres of national wilderness. There are other things, like wildlife refuges, which up the total considerably. In fact, the Federal

Government owns one-third of all the land of the United States.

When he came to Washington [two and a half] years ago, Jim found that visitor facilities in our national parks had been allowed to deteriorate to the point that many failed to meet standards for health and safety. It's being corrected. The National Park Service has made a major effort to improve maintenance at the parks that so many Americans love and love to visit. And today, they provide a wider, more beautiful variety of outdoor splendor than you can find anywhere else in the world.

Not too long ago, however, a new firestorm was raised about our wilderness lands. The perception was created that Secretary Watt was turning some of these lands loose from wilderness classification and government ownership. I should point out that wilderness lands are areas of such wild beauty that they're totally preserved in their natural state. No roads violate them, and no structures of any kind are allowed, and there are now almost 80 million acres of such land.

So, what was the fire-storm all about? Well, hang on, and follow me closely. As a result of legislation passed several years ago, a study was made of some 174 million acres of land to see if any or all of it should be declared wilderness and added to the present 80 million acres. Conditions were imposed in the review procedures to ensure that wilderness standards would be met.

If, for example, there were roads on the land, it was inel-igible. It was ineligible if there was any dual ownership by other levels of government or if title to mineral rights was held by individuals or governments. Also, with limited exceptions, any package had to contain no less than 5,000 acres to be eligible. The study had been going on under the previous Administration, and some 150 million of the designated 174 million acres had already been turned down by previous

Administrations as being ineligible for wilderness classification.

Now, think hard now. Do you recall hearing one word about this or any attack being made on anyone at the time? I don't. When we arrived, there were still about 25 million acres to be studied. A few months ago, another 800,000 acres—that's a fraction of what the previous Administration rejected—were disqualified as not meeting wilderness qualifications. Yet, the reaction this time was instantaneous, volcanic in size, and nationwide in effect: "Jim Watt was giving away wilderness land. Our children and grandchildren would be deprived of ever seeing America as it once was."

Well, nobody bothered to mention that our Administration has proposed to the Congress addition of another 57 wilderness areas encompassing 2.7 million acres. That's more than three times as much land as was disqualified. Nor did anyone mention that I've already signed legislation designating sites in Indiana, Missouri, Alabama, and West Virginia as new wilderness areas.

The truth is that our National Park System alone has grown to 74 million acres, and almost 7,000 miles of river are included in our National Wild and Scenic River System. We have 413 wildlife refuges totaling some 86.7 million acres. This record is unmatched by any other country in the world.

Our environmental programs also are the strongest in the world. Last year, expenditures by business and government to comply with environmental laws and regulations were estimated at over $55 billion, or $245 per man, woman, and child in the United States.

We have made a commitment to protect the health of our citizens and to conserve our nation's natural beauty and resources. We have even provided financial and technical support to other nations and international organizations to protect global resources. Thanks to these efforts, our country remains "America the Beautiful." Indeed, it's growing more healthy and more beautiful each year. I hope this helps set the record straight, because it's one we can all be proud of.

Till next week, thanks for listening, and God bless you.[93]

It was classic Ronald Reagan, putting a set of complex issues in simple, straightforward language. Of course, Reagan had facility with the subject matter—he had been involved in these issues since he was governor of California, and he had researched, written, and spoken about them for years. Now he was ready to meet Adams, which he did a couple of weeks later in Beverly Hills, calling him "the great nature photographer." Reagan wrote about the meeting in his diary:

> He has expressed hatred for me because of my supposed stand on the environment. I asked for the meeting. I gave him chapter & verse about where I really stand on the environment & what our record is. All in all the meeting seemed pleasant enough & I thought maybe I'd taken some of the acid out of his ink. Then I read the story of the meeting as he'd given it to the press. I'm afraid I was talking to ears that refused to hear.[94]

Sure enough, Adams emerged from the meeting unassuaged. He assailed Reagan personally—faulting his intelligence, imagination, and "aura"—and attacked his policies and the people appointed to implement them. At the end of its story about the incident, however, the *Washington Post* reported that "[f]or all his intense anger at [Reagan and Watt], Adams said he is hard-pressed to document widespread environmental damage from their policies."[95]

In October of 1983, when Watt "tendered his resignation," Reagan "accepted with real regret," noting, "He's done a fine job."[96] The president's formal statement regarding Watt's performance was laudatory, as one might expect of such a statement, but he wrote in his diary, "[Watt is] really the victim of a 2½ year lynching. He knows he no longer can be effective with Congress so he's being a bigger man than his detractors."[97] A week later, after meeting with Watt, Reagan went into further detail, "He gave me a report on his stewardship & it reveals the hypocrisy of the Environmental lynch mob. I don't think the Dept. of Interior or our Nat. Parks & wild lands have ever been in better shape."[98] So pleased was Reagan with the detailed report that he made it the basis for one of his weekly radio addresses. For the first time, Reagan had in his hands a detailed and thorough presentation of Watt's accomplishments on all aspects of Interior's diverse mission—not just on Outer Continental Shelf oil and gas leasing. He obviously liked what he read. Moreover, given his remarkable memory, he was armed for future confrontations with environmental extremists.[99]

After Watt's departure, William Clark did exactly as Watt had done: he met with the leaders of the environmental groups, heard their concerns, and tried to persuade them that the Interior Department was implementing the law, not only with regard to energy and mineral issues but also regarding parks, refuges, and wildlife.[100] There was one crucial difference between Watt and Clark—Clark could get the environmental group leaders in to see the president.[101] In May of 1984, Reagan wrote of one such meeting:

> Jay Hair head of 'Wildlife Fed.' came in with Bill Clark & Bill Ruckelshaus. Maybe we're making a little headway with the environmentalists who declared war on me about 3 yrs. ago. I think Jay wants to be fair & heard some things today he hadn't understood before.[102]

The next day, the *Washington Post* reported on the meeting, at least from Hair's point of view, which came "amid an escalation of attacks on Reagan's environmental record from Democratic presidential candidates."[103] Hair concluded that the discussion was "very frank," and that, as the *Post* put it, "Reagan listened attentively," but that he gave "no commitments." That is hardly surprising given Hair's "gift for the president," a book written by "three Washington environmental activists" entitled, *A Season of Spoils: The Story of the Reagan Administration's Attack on the Environment*.[104] Hair's request that Reagan deliver an environmental message because "you haven't talked to any of us" may not have been well received either. The president believed that his views on almost any subject, including natural resources and the environment, had been quite clear for years. As he wrote in early 1981:

> I am surprised at times that there is so much lack of knowl-edge about my positions. For several years except when I was running in '76 and now in the present campaign, I have had five-day-a-week radio commentary on more than 300 stations nationwide. I took up virtually every subject mentionable and stated my views on those subjects, but I guess there were a lot of people who were not listening.[105]

Reagan would soon be confronted by others who were not listening. Less than six weeks after his meeting with Hair, he had "[l]unch in the Roo-sevelt Rm. with leaders of several prominent environmental org's."[106] According to the president,

> They are up in arms over my appointment of Ann[e] Burford to chair the Advisory Committee to Sec. of Commerce on "Oceans & Air." They had to admit our environmental record is great but want me to cancel Ann[e] because their people will take it as a symbol that we are anti-environment. I stayed cool. But I told them Ann[e] had done nothing wrong—she had been railroaded & I owed her something like this to restore her. They were deaf to my suggestion that if they used their publications to tell how good our record is (which they admit) there won't be a fuss over Ann[e]. I spoke to ears that wouldn't hear. They were arrogant & unreasonable.[107]

Obviously Reagan was, as he liked to say, "steamed."[108] He was still steaming a few days later following a "Cabinet Council on Natural Resources." "We have a darn good record on environment," Reagan wrote, "which the environmentalists ignore in their bigotry."[109]

It certainly looked like bigotry because, notwithstanding Clark's outreach and Reagan's interest and availability, environmental groups continued to hit hard. In late June of 1984, six major environmental groups called his environmental record "dismal" and demanded changes in Reagan administration policies, including cut-backs in offshore oil and gas leasing as well as coal leasing and increases in renewable energy funding.[110]

A few days later, Reagan did deliver a major address on the environment. He delivered it, however, not to environmental extremists, who had attacked him for years and opposed his election, but to twenty thousand of his friends at the National Campers and Hikers Association in Bowling Green, Kentucky. There he paid tribute to Theodore Roosevelt, "who for the first time outlined the legitimate role of the Federal Government in protecting our environment," described himself and his administration as inheritors of that great legacy, and discussed the work of his administration in restoring the economy and the environment, including public access to that environment.[111] Said Reagan, "We believe the environment includes people...." He concluded:

> Here in the open, close to the land, we feel refreshed and free. Here we see clearly what is important in life—the liberty our country offers, the love of our families and friends. And here it is that we're given a strong sense of the majesty of our Creator. I just have to believe that with love for our natural heritage and a firm resolve to preserve it with wisdom and care, we can and will give the American land to our children, not impaired, but enhanced. And in doing this, we'll honor the great and loving God who gave us this land in the first place. I thank all of you for what you're doing. And God bless you all. And God bless America.[112]

Neither environmental groups nor the national media remarked on the address.[113] Reagan recorded in his diary, "Of course, the press had one thing on their minds.... [I]t was Mondale's announcement that he had chosen Mrs. Ferraro as his VP choice."[114]

Perhaps the unkindest cut of all came from close to home. Reagan records an October 10, 1988, Columbus Day "call from [his son] Ron.

I don't know who he's been talking to but we had a debate. He's convinced I'm not protecting the environment."[115]

Reagan no doubt took heart that his administration had accomplished what some might have regarded, before he arrived in Washington, D.C., as impossible.[116] He recognized that "people are ecology too," so he put them back into the environmental equation. As one scholar expressed it, he transformed the debate over federal lands management from "an ecological/preservationist perspective to a human-centered/development orientation."[117]

In fact, installing a "human-centered management philosophy" with people at the top of the resource-use hierarchy was the "single most revolutionary change" made at the Interior Department under Reagan.[118] The change allowed the American people, for the first time since the beginning of the environmental juggernaut in the 1960s, to be accorded the right to choose between two competing visions of the future: one in which the federal lands continue to serve as an "economic Eden, in the tradition of a 'Manifest Destiny,'" the other in which America acknowledges "an age of limits [and] preserve[s] the shrinking wilderness for its inherent values."[119] Although this "great dilemma" remains to this day, thanks to Ronald Reagan there is such a dilemma with the choice involving the needs of mankind perhaps as valid, if not more so, than the one that emphasizes nature.[120]

What Do They Want Anyway?[121]

Environmental groups have changed dramatically since the early 1960s.[122] They embrace a paradigm of man and his relationship to the earth and his ability to prosper, preserve, and prevail over a hostile world that differs markedly from that of their forebears and from most of their fellow citizens. While most Americans have great confidence in the ability of the human mind, the ultimate resource, to improve the lot of all while protecting the environment and preserving beautiful places, environmental groups have no such confidence. They believe that only government can perform that function, in a manner in which the misery will be spread around. Environmentalists see a dark future of privation and believe the only solution is government coercion, mandated scarcity, and loss of personal freedom.[123]

Today environmental groups oppose offshore oil and gas exploration and development, as well as onshore drilling. They lie about the most remarkable technological accomplishment in the oil patch since drilling mud, hydraulic fracturing. They oppose nuclear power, as they have since Reagan's days in California, and have all but killed coal, the most abundant energy resource in the country. They say they support gas but only as a "transition" to something like wind, which they support, unless it kills birds, and solar, which they support, unless it interferes with tortoises. Neither wind nor solar, of course, is as cheap, efficient, or reliable as any of the fossil fuel energy sources America has in great abundance. That is just where environmental groups stand on energy; they are likewise positioned on nearly every other issue.

———

Ronald Reagan was right. Perhaps the day will come when the American people will transcend environmental groups as we get on about preserving freedom, building prosperity, and protecting our environment and its truly special places. Perhaps at that time, Congress will address the most nettlesome environmental statute ever written, the Endangered Species Act.

CHAPTER SIX

THE PIT BULL OF ENVIRONMENTAL LAWS

"How much do you miss Dinosaurs? Would your life
be richer if those giant pre-historic flying lizards
occasionally settled on your front lawn?"
—RONALD REAGAN, JULY 6, 1977[1]

"Whatever the Cost"

"Since the beginning of life on this planet thousands of species (plant and animal) have disappeared every century as part of the evolutionary process in an ever changing world," Governor Reagan began a radio address on endangered species. Human beings forget this, he said, because we feel guilty knowing that, as our population increases, we contribute to the "disappearance of some species by destroying their habitat or hunting them down for food, fun and feathers."[2] Therefore, we "identified endangered species and passed laws preventing any act by man which might reduce their numbers. And I'm sure there is general agreement with this policy. But shouldn't we now and then remember nature's part in the elimination of some species and separate the serious from the silly in our own policy?"[3]

Reagan was concerned about the Endangered Species Act of 1973 (ESA) and its impact on two huge power projects in the eastern United States. First up was the "$1.3 billion Dickey-Lincoln generating facility" on the St. John River in Maine, which was halted—"stopped dead in its tracks"—said Reagan, after the discovery of a "species of snapdragon, thought to be extinct, called the Furbish lousewort." Second was the Tennessee Valley Authority's Tellico Dam on the Little Tennessee River, which would "produce electricity for about 200,000 homes and I don't know how many industries providing jobs for people in those homes," reported Reagan. Although "the huge Tellico Dam is 95% complete[,] [a]pparently that's as far as it will get ... because a school of 3 inch fish called the snail darter has been found to spawn in the waters of the Little Tennessee river."[4]

The problem, however, extended beyond these two projects:

> To date more than 200 projects have been halted to protect among other things an inedible clam, some crayfish, freshwater snails etc. And the Fish & Wildlife Service announces it is now going to classify as "endangered" some 1700 species of plants. It is time to ask if some environmentalists, and I do mean *some*, aren't using the Endangered Species Act of 1973 simply to halt construction of projects they don't like.[5]

Before Reagan or anyone else had the opportunity to ask "some environmentalists" that question, the Supreme Court of the United States had its say about Tellico Dam and the snail darter in *Tennessee Valley Authority v. Hill*.[6] Over the dissent of three justices, the Court held that Congress intended the ESA to be applied strictly, that Congress's appropriation of funds over many years to build the dam to its near completion did not implicitly repeal the ESA for that project, and that the "plain intent of Congress in enacting this statute was to halt and reverse the trend toward species extinction, whatever the cost."[7] In fact, the Court ruled, "the plain language of the Act, buttressed by its legislative history, shows clearly that Congress viewed the value of endangered species as 'incalculable.'"[8]

The Supreme Court may not have been completely serious except in its intention to hoist Congress on its own petard.[9] If Congress wrote legislation that permitted a multi-million dollar federal project to be killed by a three-inch fish, then the Court would not bail it out.[10] Congress itself would have to fix the Endangered Species Act. In his dissent, Justice Lewis F. Powell expressed "little doubt" that Congress would do so "to prevent the grave consequences made possible by today's decision,"[11] in light of the fact that the "prospects for such disasters are breathtaking:"

> The act covers every animal and plant species, subspecies, and population in the world needing protection. There are approximately 1.4 million full species of animals and 600,000 full species of plants in the world. Various authorities calculate as many as 10% of them—some 200,000—may need to be listed as Endangered or Threatened. When one counts in subspecies, not to mention individual populations, the total could increase to three to five times that number.[12]

Congress did act quickly, but instead of performing major surgery in response to Powell's warning, it administered a little first aid.[13] In fact, Congress did what it does so often in these situations. It created a panel—"the God Squad"—to resolve the Tellico Dam problem and future difficult ESA cases.[14] After that panel, headed by Carter's Interior secretary, Cecil Andrus, sided with the snail darter, Congress voted to complete the Tellico Dam anyway by attaching a rider to the Energy and Water Development Appropriations Act of 1980.[15] Carter signed the appropriations bill "with regret."[16] Tellico Dam was built.

How Did We Get Here Anyway?

The ESA of 1973 was not the first federal law to address the issue of disappearing species.[17] In 1966, Congress adopted the Endangered Species Preservation Act, which authorized the secretary of the interior to protect habitat by using existing legal authority under the Land and

Water Conservation Fund. The power to limit the taking of species, a term later defined broadly by the ESA to include almost any adverse impact on species, however, remained with the states.[18] Then, in 1969, Congress passed the Endangered Species Conservation Act, which introduced the concept of listing wildlife threatened with worldwide extinction and directed the secretary of the interior to take affirmative steps to develop a coordinated international effort.[19]

In 1973, the House Committee on Merchant Marine and Fisheries declared:

> There is presently in effect a series of Federal laws designed to protect species of fish and wildlife which may face extinction without that protection.... [A]t the time [these laws] were enacted, they were adequate to meet the demands as they then existed. Subsequent events, however, have demonstrated the need for greater flexibility in endangered species legislation, more closely designed to meet their needs.[20]

The Senate report concluded:

> It has become increasingly apparent that some sort of protective measures must be taken to prevent the further extinction of many of the world's animal species. [Today], the rate of extinction has increased to where on the average, one species disappears per year.[21]

How many species were in trouble? While the numbers varied, by most accounts they were relatively small and seemingly easy to address. The Merchant Marine and Fisheries Committee reported that "100 species of fish and wildlife" in the United States were "threatened with extinction."[22] Internationally, the numbers were more startling: "375 species of animals [are] imminently threatened with extinction throughout the world and another 239 species of animals [are] not as yet threatened with extinction but require ... additional controls over their trade."[23] Senator Ted Stevens, a Republican from Alaska and one of the five Senate managers of the conference bill that became law, noted that "109 species and subspecies of wildlife—14 mammals, 50 birds, 7 reptiles, and 30 fish species—[were] threatened with extinction" and advised his colleagues that the list included "such animals as the black-footed ferret, the whooping crane, the eastern timber wolf, the masked bobwhite, the ivory-billed woodpecker, and peregrine falcons."[24]

Support for the ESA was strongly bipartisan. The Senate passed it with only eight "no" votes, the House of Representatives with only four.[25] Surely some of the other ninety-one senators voting for the ESA—including conservatives like Clifford Hansen of Wyoming, Jesse Helms of North Carolina, and Roman Hruska of Nebraska, and liberals like Philip Hart of Michigan, Vance Hartke of Indiana, and Hubert Humphrey of Minnesota—might have foreseen problems with the law, despite the apple-pie-and-motherhood tone of the debate.[26]

Apparently they did not, but there were warning signs. For example, Senator Gaylord Nelson, a Democrat from Wisconsin, one of the Senate's leading environmentalists (and later counselor of the Wilderness Society), spoke of "another danger to our wildlife, a threat that is unavoidable: the expansion of our cities and industries."[27] Nelson had a solution: "Habitat acquisition ... [to provide] a base for the construction of true sanctuaries, preserves free from harmful human intrusion."[28] Another warning sign was the deceptively simple statement of Senator Harrison Williams, a Democrat from New Jersey, that "[c]itizen suits are also permitted...."[29] Finally, although it did not come in time for the vote, it was soon apparent that the ESA was not just about furry or feathered friends like ferrets, foxes, and falcons, but also snap dragons, salamanders, and snail darters; after all, the first uses of the ESA to stop federal projects were to save such obscure species.

Full recognition of what Congress had wrought would come later when the species for whose sake projects were stopped, property seized, and progress stymied began to shift, in Robert Gordon's pithy phrase, from the "warm and fuzzies to the cold and slimies."[30] The outrage and conflict spawned by the ESA eventually produced such massive gridlock in Congress that it failed to reauthorize the statute. The law was kept alive instead by a year-to-year annual appropriation.[31] Finally, reality would hit the American people full in the face as environmental groups filed petitions to list species, then lawsuits demanding that the species be named threatened or endangered, and finally consent decrees ordering the Fish and Wildlife Service (FWS) to protect species, proclaim critical habitat, and pay attorneys' fees and costs.[32]

All that would come later. Meanwhile, environmental groups were still reeling from their narrow escape over the Tellico Dam. The ESA had come within a single vote on the Supreme Court of being eviscerated. The environmental lobby did not want to run the risk of another high-profile, job-killing, revenue-sapping ESA lawsuit that would infuriate the public, inspire opponents, and incite Congress, especially with a newly elected Republican-controlled Senate and the Reagan administration coming into town.[33]

The Reagan Administration Protects Species

Under Reagan, the Interior Department recognized the problem that he had discussed in 1977. Nothing had taken place in four years to lessen concern over the potential impact of the ESA on an economy crippled by high inflation, interest rates, and unemployment. A new Republican majority in the Senate might have a mind to amend the ESA, but no such legislation would get through the House. Major reform was out of the question, although some helpful, but relatively minor amendments might be enacted. Meanwhile, Interior would do what it could to lessen the threat. Under Carter, the department had aggressively listed threatened or endangered species, but generally eschewed recovery plans that sought to achieve the congressional objective of ensuring the long-term survival of threatened or endangered wildlife and plant species. The Reagan administration reversed that ratio, from 1981 through 1983, for example, it adopted fifty-five recovery plans and developed an additional 261— more than double the rate of the Carter administration (thirty-five adopted, ninety-eight developed).[34] This recovery work included:

- A joint effort with the U.S. Forest Service and the states of Idaho, Montana, and Wyoming to create a cooperative

Federal-State Interagency Grizzly Bear Committee to protect and recover grizzly bears within the lower forty-eight states where they are endangered;[35]

- Acquisition, in a single year, of thousands of acres of habitat to protect and recover nine endangered species, including the California condor, bald eagle, Mississippi sandhill crane, Florida manatee, blunt-nosed leopard lizard, Kirtland's warbler, American crocodile, Plymouth red-bellied turtle, and the moapa dace (a fish);[36]

- Atlantic salmon restoration in New England, where adult Atlantic salmon made their first return runs in modern times to the Merrimack River and the Pawcatuck River, and completion of a fish-way at Bellows Falls on the Connecticut River permitting salmon to enter the White River System; the result: one hundred miles of new Atlantic salmon fishing areas and spawning habitat;[37]

- An international bald eagle restoration effort, in cooperation with the Canadian Wildlife Service and the provincial governments of Manitoba, Nova Scotia, and Saskatchewan, which brought twenty-three bald eagles from Canada for suitable nests in Massachusetts, New York, Pennsylvania, and New Jersey;[38]

- Cooperative development, with the state of New York and the province of Ontario, of formal plans to restore lake trout in Lake Ontario;[39]

- The largest captive colony of breeding bald eagles in the world at the Patuxent Wildlife Research Center in Maryland, where bald eagle chicks are produced, raised, and then released to the wild in states where eagle numbers are still low, delivering thirteen eagles to eight states; private corporations and conservation provided support for the unique program;[40]

- A revised fisheries policy establishing agency responsibilities, including: restore depleted and nationally significant fishers, manage fisheries on federal and Indian tribal lands, mitigate fisheries impaired due to federal water development projects, and provide federal leadership in scientifically based management of national fisheries resources;[41]

- A cooperative program with Maryland and Virginia to restock hatchery-reared striped bass as part of a Chesapeake Bay wide recovery program;[42]
- Captive breeding-and-release programs that benefit a number of species, including the peregrine falcon, which now nest in significant numbers in the Eastern, Rocky Mountain, and Pacific regions where none nested for thirty years; the brown pelican, which has recovered to the degree that it was removed from ESA protection in Florida and along the Atlantic Coast; and the whooping crane population, which, in 1941 had dropped to only fifteen in existence, but now number one hundred whooping cranes in the wild with a breeding flock at the federal research center.[43]

One effort by the Interior Department to recover species permanently and to remove them from federal protection bears special mention. The Fish and Wildlife Service abandoned its efforts to recover the California condor in the wild and admitted the superior expertise of the private sector by capturing the last wild condor in 1987 and placing all twenty-seven condors in a captive breeding program managed by the world famous San Diego and Los Angeles zoos. Thriving today, with over 400 condors now alive, over half of those back in the wild, it is unlikely the condor would have survived had not Reagan's Interior Department taken this unprecedented action. In addition, the department acquired an 11,360-acre ranch as the nucleus for the condor's future home: the Bitter Creek National Wildlife Refuge.[44]

Despite its emphasis on recovery, Interior did not neglect its statutory responsibility to list species when merited by the best available data.[45] For example, it listed the southern Selkirk Mountain herd of caribou—the last herd of woodland caribou in the United States outside Alaska—and developed a recovery plan for the herd.[46] The FWS also reclassified the Arctic peregrine falcon and Utah prairie dog from "endangered" to "threatened."[47] By 1988, Interior had added 199 wildlife and plant species to the list of threatened and endangered species.[48] In addition, the FWS engaged in aggressive enforcement of federal laws enacted to protect species, including:

- An investigation into the illegal killing and marketing of bald eagles and other federally-protected birds, resulting in the arrest of fifty people in eight states and revealing that more than three hundred bald eagles had been killed to supply a black-market trade in Native American artifacts;
- A six-month undercover investigation by FWS and state wildlife law enforcement officers, resulting in the arrest of more than forty persons and disclosing a massive illegal trade in game fish poached from public waters in Oklahoma and illegally marketed throughout the Midwest.[49]

In 1982, Congress again amended the ESA with the direct involvement and full support of the Reagan administration. In fact, Interior's active participation in the legislative process ensured the enactment of statutory provisions that provided the FWS with new, crucially important flexibility. Specifically, Congress separated listing from critical-habitat designation, sought to speed up the listing process, established the habitat conservation program (which came into full use years later), allowed for experimental populations to recover species, and addressed concerns regarding species on private property by authorizing incidental take permits.[50] The FWS sought to address this issue by narrowing the definition of "harm" to include only action that "kills or injures wildlife." In addition, Reagan, out of concern for the impact of federal regulations, such as those issued by the FWS, on private property, signed an executive order in 1988 that required federal agencies to limit the impact of their regulations on private property.[51]

In 1988, Congress again amended the ESA, with the support of the Reagan administration, by requiring the monitoring of candidate species, mandating the use of emergency listing powers to protect candidate species at "significant risk" and beefing up recovery plan requirements, including barring the secretary of the interior from moving a species to the head of the recovery plan line because of its popularity or familiarity.[52]

Then, in mid-1988, the landscape regarding the ESA changed forever. Environmental groups overcame the reluctance inspired by the Tellico Dam about filing federal lawsuits alleging ESA violations and sued to end timber harvesting in the Pacific Northwest.[53] The groups won ruling after ruling, shut down the timber industry in Washington, Oregon, and Northern California at a cost of thousands of jobs, and devastated tiny timber-producing communities.

Unfortunately, as NBC's Roger O'Neil, reported, "the politics of environmentalism got in the way of careful science" as environmentalists pursued their "bigger strategy" of ending "the cutting of big old trees in the national forests."[54] Today, the American people know logging was not the problem. Although the FWS maintains the northern spotted owl is still in trouble, the problem is not mankind, but another owl: the barred owl, which the FWS is proposing to kill to save the northern spotted owl.[55] Their experience in the Pacific Northwest taught environmentalists an important lesson: "We're crazy to sit in trees when there's this incredible law where we can make people do whatever we want."[56]

Litigation Is Their Business, and Business Is Good

The story of the ESA today, forty years after its enactment, is the litigation filed almost daily by scores of environmental groups from coast to coast and border to border, demanding the listing of species, the designation of critical habitat, and the payment of attorneys' fees and costs.[57] From the northern spotted owl in the Pacific Northwest[58] to the dunes sagebrush lizard in Texas,[59] from the delta smelt in the San Joaquin Valley of California[60] to the Puritan tiger beetle in Maryland,[61] no one, it seems, is beyond the reach of the FWS and its co-conspirators in the environmental movement.[62]"

In light of these abuses, Congress has refused to reauthorize the ESA since 1992, grudgingly appropriating funds annually for its implementation.

Moreover, when matters get totally out of hand and the opportunity presents itself, Congress steps in with an ESA amendment as a rider in an annual appropriations bill similar to the one that saved the Tellico Dam.[63] Notwithstanding Congress's objections, experts say the law, as written, is excellent. What is wrong is how it has been implemented by the FWS, enforced by environmental groups, and interpreted by federal courts.

The biological definition of "species" is "reproductively isolated" and "genetically distinctive" "natural populations of animals," says Dr. J. Gordon Edwards. "[T]he political definition [of species] omits the requirements of the legitimate scientific definition of 'species' [in that it] considers ANY loose assortments of similar individuals to be so-called species."[64] Sometimes, it is not a "political definition" but a moral one that governs decision making. Former U.S. Forest Service chief Jack Ward Thomas, a northern spotted owl expert, opined, "There isn't a magic number [of owls] that's enough as far as I know in science. All of these decisions ... turn out to be moral decisions...."[65]

The subjectivity of the FWS's decisions, whether "political" or "moral," is the source of the problem, says Dr. Rob Roy Ramey, the wildlife biologist who blew the whistle on the junk science used to list what he calls "the so-called Preble's Meadow Jumping Mouse (PMJM)." The problems begin for the ESA when the wildlife service defines a "species," "subspecies," or "distinct population segment," because the FWS "has no consistent thresholds; as a result, its listing decisions are highly subjective." For example, the "so-called PMJM" did not qualify for listing, Dr. Ramey argues, because "the degree of measured difference between it and other purported subspecies of meadow jumping mice is less than that among mouse populations of the same subspecies." By comparison, Dr. Ramey argues, applying the FWS's approach to *Homo sapiens* yields numerous subspecies and distinct population segments of mankind.

Matters get worse, he says, because the FWS and environmental groups label a species "imperiled" in one location despite its vitality elsewhere and make the same argument for "peripheral populations" of species that are naturally at risk because they colonized historically inhospitable areas, perhaps during unique climatic conditions. Finally, the FWS and environmental groups use national boundaries to create pockets of "imperiled" species that thrive just across the border.

Moreover, "scientific findings" historically meant "reproducible" findings, but not for the FWS, which uses models to predict conditions thirty to one hundred years in the future. The FWS increasingly relies, moreover, on published studies that are incestuous or self-serving (for example, those posted online by environmental groups) and for which underlying data are never made public.[66] The FWS's greatest deficiency, says Dr. Ramey, is conflict of interest. Its work is the product of "species cartels" afflicted with group think, confirmation bias, and a common desire to preserve the prestige, power, and appropriations of the agency that pays or employs them. For example, in a recent sage-grouse monograph, 41 percent of the authors were federal workers, and the editor, a federal bureaucrat, had authored one-third of the papers.[67]

Today, lawsuits by environmental groups are driving nearly everything the FWS does regarding the ESA. Whether due to incompetence, complicity, or slothfulness, the documents prepared by the FWS and their timeliness, or lack of it, expose the FWS to slam-dunk litigation for missed deadlines or arbitrary and capricious decisions. Over the past few years, the U.S. Department of Justice, as attorney for the FWS, has settled scores of cases resulting in the listing of hundreds of species and the payment of millions of dollars in attorneys' fees and costs to litigious environmental groups.[68]

The ESA requires the use of "best scientific and commercial data available," but the FWS relies on its own "professional judgment."[69] Even worse, in its "jeopardy opinions," the FWS refuses to engage in active consultation with the federal land management agency (such as the BLM or the U.S. Forest Service), as directed by the ESA, but instead uses boilerplate for its list of threats facing the species in question.[70] Finally, the FWS fails to require environmental groups that file listing petitions to comply with ESA requirements, such as the "one species per petition" limitation and the demand for "substantial scientific or commercial information" to support listing.[71]

Given the way the ESA has been used since Reagan left office, we can answer the question he asked a few decades ago. Environmentalists are "using the Endangered Species Act of 1973 simply to halt [everything] they don't like."[72] Maybe the time has come to do something about it.[73]

———

Some species may indeed be threatened or endangered, although many are not. What is truly rare is the presence of strategic and critical minerals—minerals essential to the American way of life and national defense—in commercial quantities within the nation's borders.

CHAPTER SEVEN

IF IT CAN'T BE GROWN, IT HAS TO BE MINED

"One wonders if the Secretary of State or the President for that matter sees any threatening pattern in the Soviet presence by way of Cuban proxies in so much of Africa, which is the source of minerals absolutely essential to industry in Japan, Western Europe, and the U.S. We are self sufficient in only five of the 27 minerals important to us industrially and strategically."
—RONALD REAGAN, AUGUST 18, 1980[1]

Out of Africa

In January of 1980, Congressman James D. Santini, a Democrat from Nevada, returned from a fact-finding tour of southern Africa conducted during the Christmas recess. The chairman of the Mines and Mining Subcommittee of the House Interior and Insular Affairs Committee, Santini took along his small subcommittee staff, a staffer from the Foreign Relations Committee, and an enlisted military escort. Only one other member of Congress accompanied him; many of the rest were with their spouses and top Department of Defense officials and officers on shopping and sightseeing tours in London, Paris, and Vienna.[2] Santini, however, used to searching the Nevada desert for arrowheads and other American Indian artifacts, visited mines in Rhodesia, South Africa, and Zaire.[3] When he returned, as the nation worried over energy supplies, gasoline prices, and OPEC, Santini brought home a new concern: the possible interruption of the supply of the strategic and critical minerals that are the building blocks of modern American civilization.[4]

The United States could be "brought to its knees," warned Santini, more quickly by a loss of essential mineral supplies than by a cutoff of oil supplies. "Africa is the Persian Gulf of minerals," he declared, the source of the "cobalt, chrome and manganese, which are absolutely essential to industry and to the defense of our country." "We are heavily dependent on southern Africa—Rhodesia, South Africa, and Zaire—and on the Soviet Union for these minerals," he continued. "A chrome embargo by Russia and Rhodesia would bring the entire industrial world to its knees in just six months." Echoing remarks on the subject by Ronald Reagan,[5] Santini decried the trade embargo on Rhodesia—3.6 billion tons of the world's 3.7 billion tons of known chromium reserves are in South Africa and Rhodesia—because it increased America's dependence on Russia. Confirming Reagan's concerns regarding Zaire's Shaba province, Santini called the area, after his visit to the mines there, "one of the most politically and socially unstable parts of the world," but vitally important because it produces 65 percent of the Western world's supply of cobalt, which is critical to the manufacture of jet aircraft engines.[6]

Decrying the absence of a "national minerals policy," Santini noted that "[w]e still have time to get our act together on minerals and the American people, the administration and the Congress ought to be doing something about it now." He had concerns, however, about a bureaucratic "Catch-22" uncovered by his congressional hearings:

> The Department of Defense, one of our most influential and powerful government agencies, testified it does not get involved in minerals needs; that's handled by the Department of the Interior. [Meanwhile,] Interior's assistant secretary of

energy and minerals told the committee it was not the role of [Interior] agencies to become involved in the minerals policy of defense agencies.[7]

Later that year, the Carter administration's "flaccid" approach to the threat of a "resource war" caught the attention of those preparing the Heritage Foundation's *Mandate for Leadership*, which addressed the "absence of an administration advocate to promote and facilitate the orderly development of domestic mineral resources."[8] Most disturbingly, the "atrophy visible within [Interior's] energy and minerals function" occurs when

> ... the U.S. finds itself confronting an impending minerals crisis—a crisis potentially more destructive to this country's national security than our excessive dependence upon foreign oil imports. America is now 50 percent or more dependent on foreign sources for 24 of the 32 strategic and critical minerals essential to our national survival.[9]

Noting the degree to which the National Environmental Policy Act (NEPA) had consumed enormous amounts of time and energy in the Interior Department for over a decade—as seen, for example, in its attempt to prepare a federal coal leasing program acceptable to environmental groups and the judges to whom they retreated when displeased with Interior's proposals—*Mandate* expressed dismay that Interior had not put similar effort into breathing life into the Mining and Minerals Policy Act of 1970:[10]

> Thus, while driving NEPA to the limits of interpretation, while urging the Solicitor to untenable assertions of Secretarial power and prerogative, while participating in the development (out of the preamble phrase "protect and enhance") of an entire court-ordered and administratively argued concept of Prevention of Significant Deterioration, the Secretary

and Assistant Secretary have declared the Mining and Minerals Policy Act to have little force or effect.[11]

Mandate urged "[a] clear and unequivocal commitment to minerals
advocacy by the incoming Secretary ... to restore balance to Departmental policy making and to review unnecessarily restrictive policies affecting
mineral development."[12] Noting the expertise available in the U.S. Bureau
of Mines and the U.S. Geological Survey, *Mandate* urged Interior to use
that expertise to provide advice "regarding mineral resources decisions"
for "other Executive Branch agencies with surface land management
responsibilities and [for] the Executive Office of the President[,] and,
indeed, for the President."[13]

Mandate called the strategic and critical minerals issue "an impending
minerals crisis" and urged "the formulation and implementation of a
nonfuel mineral policy" that would address: the inability of the American
people to explore on "mineral rich federal lands," "ambiguous governmental policies," the wrong-headed governmental advocacy that industry
develop minerals abroad at a time of "increasing international tension,"
and the ill-considered "[i]solated actions of government agencies" that
adversely affect the ability of the United States to develop domestically
available minerals.[14]

Essential Building Blocks of Civilization

In November of 1980, shortly after Reagan's election as president,
Santini's Mines and Mining Subcommittee issued *U.S. Minerals Vulnerability: National Policy Implications.*[15] "[T]racing the connection between
civilization and minerals," the report concluded that the critical need of
minerals for "every facet of modern existence" is self-evident:[16]

Never in the history of mankind have mineral resources of the
earth been so essential to human existence as they are today;
nor has proof of their influence upon man's progress and
destiny been so obvious.[17]

Likewise apparent was the strategic importance of nonfuel minerals:

> [O]ur survival as a leading nation depends on our mineral supplies. The close relation between minerals and our national security is too apparent to require detailed explanation.[18]

Nonetheless, concluded the report, the "vast majority" of Americans fail to realize "the role of minerals in the human environment" or that "each American man, woman and child require[s] the annual mining of about 21,000 pounds of nonfuel minerals."[19] Oddly, the more U.S. "dependence on minerals has grown, the less the significance of that dependence is perceived and the less the processes needed to make minerals available are understood."

> We are, as a Nation, so far removed from our extractive industries that we no longer are conscious of the fact that the car we drive originated not in Detroit but in a Michigan iron mine, an Ohio limestone mine, a West Virginia coking coal mine, an Arizona copper mine, a Colorado molybdenum mine, a Missouri lead mine, a Tennessee zinc mine, and many others within and outside our borders. America has developed a store-shelf mentality, expecting all of what it needs to appear somehow in the quantity and quality necessary, at the time and place of demand. Meanwhile we are swept along by loud advocates of policies that not only reduce our productive capacity but [also] increase our reliance on others.[20]

It is one thing, concluded the report, for the average American to be ignorant of these realities, especially when unawareness poses such grave consequences, akin to or worse than those experienced regarding fuel minerals. It is quite another matter for the nation's leaders to ignore the facts regarding the strategic and critical nature of nonfuel minerals. Indeed, it must be willful ignorance. After all, beginning in 1909 with President Theodore Roosevelt's first national commission on the subject, continuing through World War II, resuming with America's entry into the Korean War, and continuing for years after, "it became increasingly clear that a sustained policy on minerals was imperative."[21] Moreover, "[t]he urgency and the complexities of a national minerals policy were readily apparent to [the] government officials who had firsthand knowledge of the serious supply problems [they] experienced during World War II," given the plethora of nonfuel minerals studies over the decades, such that no responsible government official could plead ignorance on the issue.[22]

In fact, the report cites to "no less than 20 mineral or material policy studies," which "[a]ll agree ... that foreign imports provide least-cost benefits to the consumer," but "most see the pitfalls of import dependency and how such dependency forfeits freedom to make political, economic, and defense decisions."[23] Furthermore, "[a]ll strongly urge ... improved means of ... portraying the synergistic impacts of governmental policies or actions upon [the minerals] industry and, beyond that, the broad national interest."[24] Therefore, warns the report,

> whether in the pursuit of improvements in the quality of the environment, assistance for developing countries in their attaining larger shares of the earth's resources, or achievement of no growth or a lower living standard for the United States, any group of actions that by cumulative impact weaken[s] America's ability to produce its minerals will exact a price that the citizens of this country may well not want to pay. In the case of energy, Americans have already learned the cost of subordinating U.S. interests to those of others and have concluded that the cost is too great. It is likely that, should the past for energy prove to be a prologue for nonfuel minerals, United States citizens will reach that same conclusion once again. The question remains—will [their] government?[25]

The Santini report argues that all of the reports on nonfuel minerals over almost three quarters of a century reached their "most obvious conclusion" with the Mining and Minerals Policy Act of 1970, which placed in the hands of the secretary of the interior "full responsibility for understanding the nature and state of the mining and minerals industry and for its promotion and encouragement through liaison with other Federal agencies."[26] The failure of that statute to achieve its objective, concluded the report, was not due to "the law's lack of specificity, but rather a deficiency on the part of those [in Interior] who have failed to understand its importance."[27] Although the report faulted the secretary and other Interior officials,[28] it concluded, "Congress too has played a role in the decline of America's mineral capability." For example, Congress failed: to fulfill its oversight role, to inform itself regarding the impact of legislation on minerals production, and to check the executive's embrace of policies that conflict with adequate mineral supplies.[29] Finally, the executive, notwithstanding decades of mining and minerals policy reports, many at its initiative, "has given little or no priority to the Nation's minerals."[30]

The Federal Lands and Minerals

According to the Santini report, "[e]very national commission that has made a comprehensive study of domestic minerals policy or public land management has called for encouraging mineral production from federal lands."[31] In fact, the most thorough study of public land issues was completed just a decade earlier at Congress's direction by the Public Land Law Review Commission and concluded:

> [I]t is in the public interest to acknowledge and recognize the importance of mineral exploration and development in public land legislation. Also, a decision to exclude mineral activity from any public land area should never be made casually or without adequate information concerning the mineral potential. Mineral exploration and development should have a preference over some or all other uses on much of our public lands.... *Mineral deposits of economic value are relatively rare* and, therefore, there is little opportunity to choose between available sites for mineral production.... Also, *development*

*of a productive mineral deposit is ordinarily the highest eco-
nomic use of land.*[32]

Nonetheless, concluded the Santini report, "[o]ver the last 10 years
the United States has made grave, fundamental errors in administering
the public lands with respect to minerals [such that the] existing body of
public land law is being rapidly subsumed into an ever-expanding body
of environmental law."[33] In fact, a 1977 report, the "best study of public
lands removed from mineral development," found that 42 percent of
federal land is closed to hard rock mineral activity, 16 percent is severely
restricted, and 10 percent is moderately restricted. The Santini report
found, however, that because of recent actions, the total lands closed or
restricted had increased by 10 to 15 percent.[34] The Santini report also
expressed fears for the future given that it is "impossible to predict" the
amount of federal land likely to be "severely restricted or effectively
withdrawn" due to wilderness legislation,[35] newly created "Areas of
Critical Environmental Concern,"[36] and "other restrictions, withdrawals,
classifications, and designations yet to be developed."[37] Furthermore,
according to the General Accounting Office, "there is no single source of
cumulative withdrawal statistics," nor is there a "single public document
from which withdrawal statistics can be derived."[38] Nonetheless, concluded the Santini report, Carter's Interior Department showed absolutely
no interest in learning how much federal land was off-limits to mineral
exploration and development.[39]

The "most deplorable aspect of this shortsightedness," argued the
Santini report, was that "the U.S. still knows little about the total mineral
resource potential of its land."[40] In fact, "[t]he U.S. remains a mineral-rich
country," which is why Congress, in the Federal Land Policy and Management Act of 1976, provided for "multiple use and sustained yield"
and ensured that mineral exploration and development would continue
on lands being considered for wilderness designation.[41] Moreover,
"sophisticated exploration techniques, new geologic concepts, and refine-
ments in geochemistry and geophysics" generated remarkable recent
discoveries not only throughout the American West and Alaska, but also
in Maine, Tennessee, Missouri, and Wisconsin. The future, concluded

the Santini report, likely holds more discoveries of strategic and critical minerals, but only if federal lands remain open to mineral exploration and development.[42] Unfortunately, land access restrictions are a greater burden to "small and independent prospectors and miners, who historically have played a key role in the discovery of new mining properties,"[43] than they are to major mining companies. Nonetheless, the Carter administration took no interest in the subject, contending that it lacked "effective tools," because of "[i]nadequate mineral information, insufficient analytical capability and lack of appropriate legal authority and policy guidance...."[44] Worse yet, when land use disputes regarding world-class deposits of strategically critical minerals arose, Carter's Interior Department either remained silent or suppressed the information.[45]

The Reagan Administration Addresses Minerals Policy

To his credit, President Carter initiated, in December of 1977, a cabinet-level Nonfuel Minerals Policy Review, in response to a request from forty-three members of the House of Representatives, under the chairmanship of the secretary of the interior; however, the review was doomed from the beginning.[46] It was given no priority, and many issues that affected access to minerals were excluded from the review because "positions had been developed" on those matters already, including mineral lands in Alaska, the General Mining Law of 1872, and deep seabed mining legislation.[47] After nearly two years—which included seven days of technical forums with reports from fifty-six experts, three days of hearings with testimony from forty-two industry, university, and environmental representatives, and the expenditure of $3.5 million and thirteen thousand federal employee days, "the entire effort was a tragic waste...." Among its shortcomings were failure to "come to grips with the need for hard decisions," refusal to "acknowledge that government has a unique role to play" on minerals issues, absolution of the "government of its adverse influence on domestic minerals development,"[48] failure to "examine mineral land issues," and omission of "the national security aspects of ... increased foreign [mineral] dependence."[49] The

Santini report lauded Carter's "willingness to initiate" the review but concluded that his "unwillingness or inability to give the review the direction and priority necessary for its satisfactory completion was in the end its downfall."[50]

The call by the Santini report for a "serious commitment on the part of the President and his highest appointees"[51] was met by President Reagan in his very first meeting with Watt when he urged a renewed focus on the issue of strategic and critical minerals.[52] Therefore, in answer to the complaint of the Santini report that, during the Carter administration, "there is absolutely no Federal policy-level advocate for minerals," the Reagan administration made the secretary of the interior that advocate.[53] With his charge to Watt and his designation of the secretary of the interior as chairman of the Cabinet Council on Natural Resources and Environment, President Reagan had his advocate for minerals policy, but in April of 1982, he went further by formalizing his decision with an official report to Congress.[54]

Reagan's plan emphasized ensuring the availability of federally owned land for mineral prospecting and development so as to "achieve a proper balance between wilderness and mineral needs of the American people."[55] Reagan declared, in part, that his plan recognized not only "the critical role of minerals to our economy, national defense, and standard of living," but also "the vast, unknown and untapped mineral wealth of America and the need to keep the public's land open to appropriate mineral exploration and development."[56] In July of 1982, Reagan announced that the United States would not sign the Law of the Sea Treaty in part because its seabed mining provisions did not protect American economic and security interests.[57] Finally, less than a year later, he issued the Exclusive Economic Zone proclamation to ensure that deep seabed minerals within the territorial waters of the United States would be available.[58]

The Interior Department, meanwhile, reversed Carter's position on the General Mining Law of 1872. Secretary Andrus had urged that it be revised substantially, while Secretary Watt—with bipartisan support from Western congressional delegations—opposed its revision.[59] The department demonstrated its support of the General Mining Law by promptly process-ing mineral patent applications as intended by Congress.[60]

Unique among modern federal land laws, the General Mining Law permits the individual citizen to initiate a search for minerals on federal lands open for such exploration and, upon discovery, to lay claim to a valuable mineral deposit.[61] In contrast to the bureaucratic inertia against the leasing of federal lands for energy development (which requires sec-retarial action), the aggressive opposition of environmental groups to proposed energy leasing, and the unfortunate willingness of federal courts to substitute their judgment for that of the secretary, the "self-initiation" provision of the General Mining Law ensures that the search for valuable minerals will continue. That is as it should be "given the nature of hard rock minerals—their rarity, their relative obscurity, and the unique and even bizarre clues that reveal their location."[62]

Unlike the Carter administration, the Reagan administration took Congress at its word regarding the search for minerals on lands classified as wilderness until 1984,[63] as well as on lands eligible for future inclusion in the National Wilderness Preservation System, at least in the same "manner and degree" as before the initiation of the review process that might lead to congressional action.[64] In passing the Wilderness Act in 1964, which allowed exploration to continue until 1984, and in enacting the Federal Land Policy and Management Act of 1976, which mandated federal review of lands suitable for designation by Congress as wilder-ness, Congress provided specifically for continued exploration. In fact, Congress mandated that wilderness areas be surveyed to determine the presence of mineral values.[65]

Congress recognized that the rarity of mineral deposits made mineral development the most economically important land use and that the discovery of valuable mineral deposits on federal land would help inform federal decision making regarding which federal lands should be closed to all future economic activity. Moreover, as recently as 1978, in passing the Absaroka-Beartooth Wilderness Act, Congress excluded an area that had been subject to mining for over one hundred years given its rich geology, which includes gold, silver, and copper.[66] Even more recently,

Congress excluded a rich cobalt deposit, the nation's sole potential source of the strategically important mineral, from the Central Idaho Wilderness Act of 1980.[67] Nonetheless, environmental groups opposed those provisions and were joined in their attacks on Reagan and his interior secretaries by senators and congressmen. Congress, however, did not speak with one voice on the subject. In fact, various senators and representatives fully supported the laws as enacted, and some even desired to go further by extending the mining deadline and opening up wilderness lands to the search for strategic and critical minerals, or at the very least, recognizing the rarity of their occurrence in nature and their importance to the nation.[68]

Reagan's Interior Department was more than just a spokesman for the nonfuel minerals policy announced by the president and an advocate for development of minerals important to the country's struggling economy and security. It sought to improve coordination with other federal agencies, to increase the availability of federal lands for mineral exploration and development, and to ensure that the best scientific information regarding the mineral potential of federal lands was made available to the public and to Congress. Specifically, the Department of the Interior:

- Developed and published a "Minerals Data Source Directory" describing in detail 450 sources of minerals data in thirty-two different federal agencies;
- Developed, in cooperation with the Department of State, a process for selecting, training, and evaluating the State Department's regional resources officers to ensure comprehensive, timely, and accurate reports from American embassies regarding foreign minerals;
- Developed, with the Federal Emergency Management Agency, and helped execute an Annual Materials Plan to improve the stockpiling of minerals pursuant to the Strategic and Critical Materials Stock Piling Act of 1979;
- Performed minerals resource assessments on more than 2.8 million acres of Forest Service and Bureau of Land Management lands being considered for wilderness

designation—double the assessments conducted from 1977 through 1980—bringing to more than forty-five million acres of wilderness study lands reviewed for mineral potential, and reported to Congress evidence of mineralization in 60 to 65 percent of the areas examined;

- Revoked outdated withdrawals of 1.7 million acres of federal multiple-use lands in 1983 alone, restoring them to operation of the General Mining Law of 1872, as well as the Mineral Leasing Act of 1910; since 1981, nearly eighteen million acres were restored to multiple-use, whereas during the four previous years, only 1.6 million acres were restored to multiple-use;

- Removed overly restrictive land "classifications," developed in the 1960s, on 7.6 million acres of public lands in 1983 alone; since 1981, nearly 105 million acres of public land were declassified as opposed to a mere eighty thousand acres restored to multiple-use in the previous four years;

- Participated in an international feasibility study to develop a worldwide strategic minerals inventory with data regarding chromium, nickel, manganese, and phosphate at major mines, and published comprehensive reports on the availability of copper and phosphate;

- Increased basic research in critical and strategic minerals processing and recycling technologies to reduce import vulnerability, including innovative processes for extracting cobalt, platinum-group metals, fluorspar, titanium, and phosphate from low-grade domestic resources;[69]

- Modernized "civilian mapping capabilities to produce graphic and digital cartographic data" efficiently and cost effectively to provide emergency support to the Department of Defense and others;[70]

- Focused mineral research programs, especially relating to strategic and critical minerals, on analyzing the benefits of regulations as balanced with their costs and on assisting

the domestic mining and minerals industry in complying
with environmental regulations.[71]

Not surprisingly, given the importance President Reagan assigned to
domestically available minerals, the only two wilderness bills that he
vetoed were rejected because of mineral issues, and he acted on the advice
of his secretaries of the interior. In 1983, he vetoed legislation to create
eight Florida wilderness areas because the portion involving the Osceola
National Forest would have seized mineral rights at a cost to the American people of over $200 million.[72] In 1988, he vetoed a Montana wilder-
ness bill involving 1.4 million acres because of its adverse effect on "vast
mineral development opportunities."[73]

Except for the harsh rhetoric from environmental groups and their
allies in Congress, Reagan's strong views on the importance of strategic
and critical minerals did not provoke a major public policy confrontation.
Supplies from southern Africa were not disrupted, and the Soviet Union
was too much on the defensive to engage in the "resource war" feared in
the early 1980s. Nonetheless, Reagan's strength on the issue provided an
important break with the bipartisan past, a past that was unconcerned
with the essential building blocks of Western civilization. Reagan demonstrated that America's need for strategic and critical minerals, just like
its need for energy, required thoughtful consideration in making public
policy. Such leadership, unfortunately, was not to last.

We Can't Have Mines Everywhere

The sustained growth produced by Reagan's policies allowed President Bill Clinton to conclude that the United States could afford to spend
hundreds of millions of dollars to buy up the mineral rights of a hundred-
year-old mining district—one that Congress had excluded from wilderness legislation so that the ore body could be developed—and to kill a
world-class mine that would have employed hundreds of highly paid
workers, yielded tens of millions of dollars, and cleaned up the mining
activities of the distant past.[74] Later, when President Clinton killed

another mine—this one for coal, not for gold—he declared, "We can't have mines everywhere."[75] Not even, apparently, at the site of a deposit.

Thanks in part to Clinton's economic policies and those of his successors, America's prosperity has evaporated. It can no longer afford to make land-use and environmental policy decisions without considering the effect of those decisions upon the economy, let alone the availability of important minerals, if, indeed, it ever could. We can no longer afford to leave valuable, world-class deposits, capable of generating hundreds of millions in payrolls, revenues, and taxes, in the ground, locked up, and off limits.

The challenges presented by strategic and critical minerals have not gone away. The minerals of concern today include not only cobalt, chromium, manganese, platinum, and titanium, but also rare earth elements such as dysprosium, praseodymium, terbium, europium, and yttrium. The concern is less with Russia and southern Africa than with China, the source of over 95 percent of the global supply of rare earth elements.[76] Although most Americans have never heard of these elements, they are essential—indeed critical—to today's high-technology and transportation industries, all telecommunications, the efficient functioning of America's military, and the rollout of future clean energy technology including wind and solar. Unfortunately, the world has yet to come to grips with the statement of former Chinese premier Deng Ziaoping, who said, "The Middle East has oil; China has rare earths."[77] His unspoken threat to use these minerals as a powerful geopolitical weapon was quite clear. Today, almost none are produced in the United States, although there are rich deposits, particularly in Wyoming and California.[78] Developing both deposits requires lengthy federal approvals and must overcome the aggressive opposition of environmental groups, which is no small task. The United States is tied for last place (with Papua New Guinea) in the time it takes to permit a new mine—seven to ten years.[79]

In the 1980s, the reliability of the supply of cobalt from Zaire's Shaba Province came into question. As the price of cobalt soared, attention turned to Idaho's cobalt deposit, but environmental groups, their congressional allies, and complicit staff tried to kill its development. That deposit, which was thought to be crucial to America's military might, is still around. Times have changed but not the need for cobalt. Today that deposit might be brought into production for uses both old and new. The United States uses 60 percent of the world's cobalt supply but produces none of its own. The mineral is used in superalloys for jet engines and natural gas-powered turbines. It is an essential component of lithium-ion batteries in small electronics, of the nickel metal hydride batteries of the Toyota Prius (one quarter of the world's cobalt supply goes into batteries), and of the catalysts that remove sulfur from petroleum fuel. Combined with the rare earth mineral samarium, cobalt is an essential piece of the permanent magnets used in battlefield tank navigation systems.[80]

If Ronald Reagan were addressing America today, he would likely write about the danger of relying on the country that holds most of our growing $16 trillion national debt for our supply of aptly named rare earth minerals.

———————

President Reagan was the first leader in decades to recognize the vital importance of strategic and critical minerals and to face the issue head on. Likewise, he took a fresh look at America's crown jewels, its premier national parks, set a record in designating new wilderness areas, and dramatically increased and improved wildlife refuges.

CHAPTER EIGHT

GOVERNMENT'S INSATIABLE HUNGER FOR LAND[1]

"The excuse for enlarging the national park is that a buffer
zone ... must be provided to protect the present park boundaries.
But if a buffer zone is added to the park won't that call
for another buffer zone to protect the buffer zone and
that can go on until you run out of [land]."
—RONALD REAGAN, APRIL 13, 1977[2]

Secret Scandalous Landgrabs

I n March of 1978, Ronald Reagan began a radio broadcast with the question "Are we justified in a suspicion that the federal government has quietly and without notice to the people embarked on a policy of land hoarding and perhaps even land grabbing?"[3] The reason for his question and the tale he told his listeners involved "Mineral King," an area in the Sequoia National Forest, in central California near Sequoia National Park, and plans that began in 1965 with a "mandate from Congress and at the direction of President Johnson" to develop the area as a ski and winter sports resort. Presidents Johnson, Nixon, and Ford approved; Governor Reagan and his predecessor approved; California's legislature and the Tulare County Board of Supervisors approved; and why not? asked Reagan. After all, "development of this portion of the National Forest was badly needed and in the public interest."[4]

> Only 15,000 acres of public land in all of California [out of "50 million acres"] is designated for this purpose. Mineral King is the only area in southern California offering a suitable site and there are one million skiers in southern California. It would retain its natural beauty and give 600 permanent jobs in an economically disadvantaged area.[5]

Nevertheless, though "[w]ithin a 100 mile radius of Mineral King there are over 2½ million acres of classified wilderness or roadless areas—national parks and monuments for nature lovers," a "special interest group" of "ardent preservationists" raised enough of a "hue and cry" to kill the project.[6] "In late January [1978]," reported Reagan, "the [Carter] White House asked the Congress to support a bill including Mineral King in the Sequoia National Park." In October of 1978, Carter signed the law that transferred Mineral King from the Forest Service to the National Park Service (NPS). Reagan concluded, "Is the public land really for the public or for an elite few who want to keep it for their own use?"[7]

Reagan objected to "the federal government's determination to acquire even more land than it already owns."[8] The federal government, he thought, owned enough of the nation's land, especially in the West. He also had concerns about the manner in which Congress and the federal agencies it empowered went about seizing "private property" "for public use without just compensation"[9] and the possibility that, by an act of Congress, the "government will be able to keep private [land] owners from using their land...."[10]

Others shared Reagan's concern. From May of 1978 to May of 1981, the General Accounting Office (GAO), as it was then known, issued a series of reports on federal land-acquisition policies and practices.[11] The GAO criticized the federal government, especially the NPS, and urged specific reforms.[12] In 1979, the NPS announced a "revised land acquisition policy," but little changed.[13] Meanwhile, from 1979 through 1982, two independent filmmakers were in northeastern Ohio documenting the effect on local residents of the decision by Congress to create a National Recreation Area (NRA), a unit of the NPS, out of private property in a rural community. When Congress created the Cuyahoga Valley NRA between Akron and Cleveland in 1971, it pledged that the community would be preserved, rejected condemnation and federal land acquisition, and urged the NPS to use scenic easements. By the early 1980s, however, as the Public Broadcasting Service revealed in "For the Good of All," the NPS had bulldozed or burned to the ground hundreds of private residences.[14] "Unfortunately," said *Frontline* host Jessica Savitch, "what happened here with this park is not an isolated case. During the period when this film was shot—1979 through 1982—thousands of families across this country had their houses and their property turned into parklands."[15] The film aired in 1983, but Reagan administration officials did not need a PBS documentary to know the dreadful state of federal land acquisition policies.[16]

Frontline documented the personal costs in human misery of the federal government's pell-mell acquisition of land, but there was also a financial cost to American taxpayers. The land always costs more than the agencies estimated or than Congress envisioned:

- For land acquisition within the Cuyahoga Valley NRA, Congress had authorized $35 million, but, by 1980, the NPS had spent over $42 million to buy but 60 percent of the land and 306 of the 750 homes; by 1984, the NPS had spent $78 million and planned to buy another three thousand acres.[17]
- In 1968, when Congress created Lake Chelan NRA in Washington State, it intended that land acquisition costs would be minimal; however, as of 1980, the NPS had spent $2.4 million and planned to spend yet another $3 million acquiring land that, according to the GAO, it did not need.[18]
- Those miscalculations are nothing compared with the NPS's misrepresentation on the expansion of the Redwood

National Park in California; in 1978, the NPS estimated the cost of land acquisition to be $359 million, but, as of 1994, the cost exceeded $1.4 billion, a 417-percent increase.[19]

During the mid- and late-1980s, the NPS found a method by which it did not have to purchase private property itself, as it did in Ohio, Washington, and California; the NPS made use of nonprofit organizations. For example, when Congress had not authorized the federal agency to buy the land in question or had not appropriated the funds to do so, the NPS would make a list of the most desired land purchases, to be acquired over a three-year period, and would provide it to a nonprofit group so it could buy the land and hold it until the NPS had the funds to buy it.[20] The nonprofit entity bought the land at a reduced price—the landowner took a charitable deduction for the difference between fair market value and the price received—and then the nonprofit organization sold it to the federal government at or even above the fair market value.[21]

Federal land acquisition by means of nonprofit groups in this manner imposes a number of costs on American taxpayers. First, there is the property owner's tax deduction. Second, the nonprofit sells the land to the government at a potentially inflated fair market value. Third, the nonprofit, with its cozy relationship with the bureaucrats who want the land, is paid for its costs and expenses, which may be excessive, unnecessary, or even illegal. Fourth, the nonprofit pays no taxes on its multimillion-dollar enterprise.[22] Fifth, the lands, now in the hands of the federal government, are off the tax rolls of the typically hard-pressed local government. Sixth, the purchased lands, that were once in productive use and generating income (multiplied through the local economy), now lie fallow. Seventh, the federal government will be asked to make "payments in lieu of taxes" to local governments as a small recompense for the loss of job-creating, income-producing, and tax-generating private property.[23] Eighth, the federal government is responsible for management of the lands, which may include expensive clean-up and restoration costs.

Furthermore, nonprofit, land-acquisition entities often act in the absence of a request from a federal agency or even a stated or anticipated need by the agency. In fact, the nonprofit may purchase property not desired by the agency because the agency has other priorities. The property may be unnecessary to fulfill the agency's mission, or it may be too expensive. Too often—to the detriment of the agency, the federal budget, and the American taxpayers—nonprofit, land-acquisition entities, environmental groups, and their allies in Congress will not take the agency's "no" for an answer. They will "buy a piece of land and then create a political climate by public agitation for federal purchase."[24]

In 1981, Congress, the NPS, and the American people found themselves in the midst of a growing controversy over parks, people, and private property due to the remarkable transformation from 1960 to 1980 of the National Park System.[25] Elizabeth Drew, writing in the *New Yorker*, put it this way, "Congress has got in the habit in recent years of authorizing the purchase of parks that could not be described as 'national jewels'.... [A] bit of pork barreling was going on."[26]

In 1916, when the NPS was created, there were already national parks, such as Yellowstone, the first and largest national park. Others followed quickly.[27] Although these parks were created from the expansive public domain across the West, by then there were "private holdings," such as homesteads, mining claims, or visitors' sites—that came to be known as "inholdings"—inside the park boundaries. New parks were added in the 1920s and 1930s, and because some of these new parks were in long-settled areas, more such "inholders" found themselves inside federal enclaves.

In 1933, battlefields and historic places were added to Interior's portfolio, and with them came the people who had lived in the areas for generations. In 1959 and 1961, however, with congressional authorization of the Minuteman National Historic Park and the Cape Cod National Seashore, the situation was turned around: most of the land meant to be part of these public places was privately owned. Congress repeated the process with the authorization of three national seashores: Padre Island (1962), Point Reyes (1962), and Assateague Island (1965). To finish off the decade, Redwood National Park became the first park made up principally of privately owned property. Then, in the 1970s, to "bring parks to the people," a series of national recreation areas, including urban parks, were established from coast to coast.[28]

The growth of the National Park System over those two decades was stunning. In 1960, the system comprised 185 units totaling 25.1 million acres; by 1980, there were 319 units (a 72-percent increase) encompassing seventy-seven million acres (a 207-percent increase). NPS staff increased from 4,036 to 15,349 in the same period.[29] Meanwhile, in 1964, Congress established the Land and Water Conservation Fund to provide money for federal and state acquisition of private property.[30] The NPS used that money—in the case of the Cuyahoga Valley NRA, for example—in its aggressive and often abusive pursuit of "fee simple" ownership of inholdings.[31]

Furthermore, the contradictory aims of the National Park System remained unresolved. Were these lands set "apart as a public park or pleasuring-ground for the benefit and enjoyment of the people," or were they to be "preserve[ed] from injury or spoliation, [including] all timber, mineral deposits, natural curiosities, or wonders ... and [retained] in their natural condition"?[32] The system's split personality was apparent in the early days of the conservation movement. Then it surfaced publicly when President Eisenhower constructed and improved visitor facilities in national parks that he viewed as beautiful destinations for Americans traveling his interstate highway system.[33] Finally it was the reason for the inflammatory rhetoric in 1981 when President Reagan sought to restore parks for the use of American people.

Reagan Restores Parks for People

Ronald Reagan's view of the NPS's land acquisition program was shaped by his understanding that he had "inherit[ed] the most dangerous economic crisis since Franklin D. Roosevelt took office 48 years ago."[34] Obviously cuts in the federal budget had to be made, and Reagan's Interior Department intended to make them. After the NPS shopping spree of the previous twenty years, especially under Carter, Reagan's Interior Department had a number of specific concerns:

- Why is the federal government increasing the size of the federal estate, not just in the West, but also throughout the country?

- Why is the federal government buying expensive land for urban parks that are of more local than national concern?[35]
- Why do environmental extremists determine whether federal land is open to and available for use by the American people?
- Why is the National Park Service ejecting people from their homes and using its power of eminent domain to seize property?
- Why is the federal government spending hundreds of millions of taxpayer dollars to acquire land?

Therefore, it is hardly surprising that President Reagan changed course. In fact, it would have been surprising if he had not done so, given his knowledge of park issues.

An additional problem required a change in NPS's budgetary focus. In October of 1980, the GAO reported that many NPS facilities "did not meet health and safety standards."[36] The NPS's response "ranged from immediate closure of facilities to doing little." To correct the problems, the GAO concluded, "the Park Service will have to spend about $1.6 billion."[37]

In March of 1981, Reagan announced, as part of his economic recovery plan, a moratorium on federal land acquisition. He proposed instead using $105 million from the Land and Water Conservation Fund to improve existing parks.[38] Secretary Watt suspended all federal land purchases until further notice, and the Office of Management and Budget asked Congress to rescind the $104 million available for federal land acquisition in the remainder of that fiscal year. Congress rescinded $35 million of that amount in June.[39] Unfortunately, its refusal to comply fully with OMB's request was bipartisan. Few politicians can resist the temptation to bring a park to their state or district or expand an existing one.

Reagan's Interior Department developed a four-year, billion-dollar program of restoring the premier national parks.[40] In 1981–1982, the national park restoration and improvement budget more than doubled over the last year of the Carter administration to $165.8 million. It jumped to $268.5 million in 1982–1983, and increased again in 1983–1984 to $302.4 million, nearly quadruple the 1980–1981 expenditure. In 1984–1985, the department spent the remainder of the billion dollars.[41] It was the most comprehensive rehabilitation effort ever undertaken in the National Park System.[42]

One example of how those funds were expended took place in the Redwood National Park where, beginning in 1981, the NPS engaged in the "complete restoration, reforestation and rehabilitation of the upper watershed area."[43] At an annual cost of $2 million, forty miles of abandoned logging roads were rehabilitated, the natural drainage channels of major watersheds were restored, and over 400,000 trees and shrubs were planted; all totaled, it was "the most extensive single natural resource restoration/reclamation project ever undertaken by the National Park Service."[44] In yet another example, on the other side of the country, the NPS, at a cost of $12 million, restored the Sandy Hook Beach, which had been eroded badly by storms, at Gateway National Recreation Area in New Jersey; the site hosts 2.5 million visitors annually.[45]

The Interior Department also addressed the health and safety problems that the GAO had brought to light:

- The NPS established the "Visitor Facilities Fund," a six-year, $36 million effort to improve federally owned but privately operated overnight public accommodations and support facilities by providing that concessioners' franchise fees be sent directly to the NPS; previously, those funds were deposited as "miscellaneous revenues" in the Treasury.[46]
- The NPS initiated a "Building Inventory/Inspection Program" to document the repairs needed to bring park facilities up to code. The NPS identified fire and life safety, electrical, mechanical, and structural, public health and safety, and handicapped accessibility issues.[47]
- Tens of thousands of Americans volunteered "time, talents, and goods" to help the Interior Department manage parks and refuges.[48]

- The NPS provided $80 million in grants to state and local governments for rehabilitation and construction of parks and recreation facilities and awarded $40 million in grants for Urban Park and Recreation Recovery, both pursuant to Reagan's Emergency Jobs Act.[49]

The Reagan administration did not focus exclusively on visitor-related issues, of course. The NPS worked to preserve those aspects of the national parks that made them unique and worthy of preservation. The NPS:

- Initiated a $7 million program to address "high priority natural resource" issues in sixty-five units of the National Park System;[50]
- Developed a comprehensive air quality monitoring program in forty units of the National Park System;[51]
- Instituted the first NPS resource assessment program to protect natural and cultural resources;[52]
- Implemented a five-year, million-dollar program to reclaim lands within park boundaries that had been mined for coal and abandoned before creation of various parks;[53]
- Increased research, interpretative activities, accommodation maintenance, and natural resources protection in the national parks through increased recreation fees, most of which were returned directly to national parks.[54]

In response to the various GAO reports,[55] Reagan's Interior Department adopted a policy for using the federal portion of the Land and Water Conservation Fund. It directed its agencies to write resource protection plans to ensure the use of "cost-effective alternatives to direct Federal purchase of private lands and, when acquisition is necessary, [to] acquire or retain only the minimum interests necessary" to meet not only agency objectives but also to serve the purposes for which the federal land was set aside.[56] The policy was then applied throughout Interior—to the NPS, the Fish and Wildlife Service, and the Bureau of Land Management.[57]

This new land-acquisition policy came too late to help those in the Cuyahoga Valley NRA, but it ensured a higher level of protection for other inholders, not to mention taxpayers.

Meanwhile, the park restoration effort continued. One of the park visitors who enjoyed the results was President Reagan himself, who in July 1984 spoke at Mammoth Cave National Park near Bowling Green, Kentucky. He liked what he saw, as he recorded later in his diary:

> Seeing the cave for the first time was an experience made more enjoyable by the high morale of the Park [Service] Rangers. Our billion dollar refurbishing of the parks was needed and has done a great deal for them. Of course, the press had one thing on their minds and it wasn't a cave—it was Mondale's announcement that he had chosen Mrs. Ferraro as his vice president choice.[58]

Supporting Parks, Refuges, and Wilderness Areas

Reagan's Interior Department had not turned its back on acquiring private lands when necessary for the mission of the national parks and national refuges. Rather, the department required that acquisitions be prudent, restrained, and frugal; that they serve national and not solely local interests; and that they not be made simply because the land was available for purchase or for narrow political purposes. Following these guidelines, the department set historical records with its land acquisitions. For example, from 1981 through 1983, 474,700 acres of parkland entered the federal estate, much of that through trades and donations, but all consistent with the new resource protection plans. In 1983 alone, Reagan's Interior Department acquired 375,500 parkland acres, more than was acquired in any single year of the Carter administration:[59]

- Gates of the Arctic National Park and Preserve—102,000 acres around spectacular Chandler Lake were added thanks to a land exchange with the Arctic Slope Regional

Native Corporation. The added lands included hiking routes to adjoining scenic wild lands and improved protection of Dall sheep habitat, park watersheds, and caribou migration routes;

- Wrangell-St. Elias National Park and Preserve—10,000 acres in the heart of the park and preserve unit, an area prized for its scenic values, were added thanks to the donation of mining claims from Cooper Industries of Texas— the largest such donation in NPS history;
- Great Smoky Mountains National Park—2,343 acres of privately-owned lands within a designated wilderness— the park's largest remaining inholding—was purchased from Cities Service Company for $1.1 million, ending forty-three years of futile efforts by the NPS; and
- Grand Teton National Park—1,221 acres went into the federal estate and out of private hands in a complex land exchange thanks to a purchase by Rocky Mountain Energy Company of the inholding for $9.8 million and an exchange by the company for 1,190 acres of public land in Wyoming's Carbon County. (Because the federal land was appraised at $11.3 million, the company paid the $1.5 million difference to the United States).[60]

Meanwhile, Reagan supported legislation that added new units to the National Park System, including the first new national park since 1972—the first and only national park in Nevada[61]—and additions to the National Trails System.[62] The NPS designated five new national natural landmarks due to important biological and geological features,[63] designated three areas as world heritage sites because of their "universal significance to mankind,"[64] designated national historic landmarks,[65] and established three historic areas earlier authorized to become part of the National Park System.[66] The Interior Department did not shortchange urban areas, revitalizing historical and cultural protection programs. The Reagan administration:

- Provided powerful free-market incentives, specifically enactment of Reagan's Economic Recovery Tax Act of 1981,[67] that allowed citizens to make an economic choice to preserve nationally historic structures, which caused the private sector to invest more than $12 billion in some 18,000 historic rehabilitation projects;[68]
- Increased approval of historical rehabilitation projects from the 1977 to the 1980 level of 1,761 projects (representing $786 million in investment) to 5,177 projects (representing $3.8 billion in private investment) from 1981 through 1983; in 1983 alone, two thousand projects (representing nearly $2 billion in private investment) were approved, which created almost eight thousand new housing units, including five thousand low- and moderate-income housing units;[69]
- Targeted $25 million from Reagan's 1983 Emergency Jobs Act to the Historic Preservation Fund for work on historic properties, creating thousands of new jobs on some 1,200 historic preservation projects;[70]
- Added 5,200 districts, sites, buildings, structures, and objects, in 1983 alone, to the National Register of Historic Places;[71] and,
- Published the first "Standards and Guidelines for Archeology and Historic Preservation," which set forth technical advice on archeological and historic preservation activities and methods.[72]

The Reagan administration's record regarding land acquisition is even more impressive when considering not only additions to units of the National Park System, but also acquisitions for the National Wildlife Refuge System (NWRS), which is managed, not by the NPS but by the Fish and Wildlife Service.[73] The 150 million acres of the NWRS boast wild lands and accompanying wildlife that are the equal of many, if not most, national parks, but hunting is permitted on NWRS lands. When considering lands brought into the federal estate, it seems only fair to include lands added to the NWRS, especially because use of the Land and Water Conservation Fund is authorized not just to acquire parklands but also for additions to the NWRS.[74]

From 1981 through 1983, the Interior Department acquired over 1.6 million acres for the federal park and wildlife estate. In 1983 alone, using trades, donations, and purchases, it added more new park and wildlife land to the federal estate than had been added since Alaska was purchased in 1867.[75] Notwithstanding the amount of land involved, each acquisition met the new high standards for bringing land into the federal estate. "Neither Teddy Roosevelt, nor Franklin Roosevelt, nor Lyndon Johnson, nor Jimmy Carter matched our 1983 record of federal park and wildlife land acquisition in a single year," boasted a report delivered to the president in late 1983.[76]

Meanwhile, Interior dramatically increased funding for its wildlife refuge management programs. In fiscal year 1984, for example, the $16.6 million budget for the Fish and Wildlife Service's Accelerated Refuge Maintenance and Management Program was the NWRS's largest increase in maintenance funding ever.[77] Reagan supported the Coastal Barrier Resources Act, which bars any federal permitting (except for national defense) or use of federal loans, grants, and subsidies to develop projects in the delicate undeveloped coastal barrier ecosystem.[78] Not only did these efforts protect sensitive ecosystems, they also protected taxpayers from paying large insurance claims for structures on unstable coastal lands that were damaged or destroyed. In addition, during Reagan's term, thirty-six refuges were added to the National Wildlife Refuge System.[79]

The Reagan administration disagreed with some members of Congress and virtually all environmental groups about how many of the lands within the Wilderness Preservation System should be managed or about the proper approach to federal lands being studied for designation by Congress as wilderness areas.[80] The administration believed that Congress meant what it said when it left wilderness areas open to natural resources development, including energy and nonfuel minerals, until 1984 and operated accordingly. It was Congress's prerogative to change its mind,[81] but Reagan's Interior Department sought to provide Congress the information necessary to make decisions over what federal lands should be "locked-up" and what land might remain available to meet the nation's need for energy as well as for strategic and critical minerals.

By late 1983, the Interior Department had completed studies on 6.4 million acres of potential wilderness in designated wilderness study areas, including half of the 780 areas on lands managed by the Bureau of Land Management.[82] By October of 1984, 90 percent of the prospective wilderness acreage had been studied.[83] The department recommended or supported various additions to the National Wilderness Preservation System (NWPS) in the lower forty-eight states totaling 1,820,098 acres—twice that recommended (881,577 acres) from 1977 through 1980. Of that, 1.5 million acres within units of the National Park System became part of the NWPS:

- Cumberland Island National Seashore, Georgia;
- Sequoia/Kings Canyon and Yosemite National Parks, California; and
- Sleeping Bear Dunes National Lakeshore, Michigan.

The remaining 301,670 acres covered Bureau of Land Management Land property now included in the NWPS:

- Bear Trap, Montana;
- Aravaipa Canyon and Arizona Strip, Arizona; and
- Bisti Badlands, New Mexico.[84]

Reagan signed wilderness legislation recommended or supported by the Department of Agriculture's U.S. Forest Service as a result of bipartisan agreements among the congressional delegations of the states in which the federal lands were located. In fact, Reagan signed nearly forty bills designating over ten million acres of wilderness areas, accounting for almost 10 percent of the NWPS lands then in existence—more than any other president since the Wilderness Act of 1964 was signed into law.[85] Reagan also vetoed two wilderness proposals that were too costly, too one-sided, or lacked bipartisan support.[86]

The Reagan Record on Fish, Wildlife, and Parks

Reagan was happy with the Interior Department's report of October 1983, and shared it with the American people. The first section of the report addressed the part of the department known as "Fish, Wildlife, and Parks," and its accomplishments are impressive. That summary and Reagan's knowledge of those efforts—through meetings of the Cabinet Council on Natural Resources and Environment, sessions with his secretaries of the interior, and preparations for speeches, such as the one he delivered at the Mammoth Cave National Park in 1984—led him to reject out of hand the condemnation of most environmental groups and their allies in Congress. Interior did what the president wanted. It decreased federal expenditures, restored the health and safety of the national parks, ensured open access to the public's land, and controlled the federal government's insatiable hunger for private property. It was a record well worth emulating.[87]

That Was Then; This Is Today

In 1991, officials from the National Park Service and their allies gathered in Vail, Colorado, to discuss the future of the National Park System. What emerged is referred to as "The Vail Agenda:"

> While public access and enjoyment are essential elements of the purpose of the park system, it should not be the goal of the National Park Service to provide visitors with mere entertainment and recreation. Rather, the objective should be to provide the public with enjoyment and enlightenment attendant to those park attributes that constitute each unit's special meaning and contribution to the national character. This is use and enjoyment on the *park's* terms. It is entertainment, education, and recreation *with meaning*.[88]

Without Reagan's guidance, the NPS reverted to the position it had embraced for decades—parks are not for people but for NPS-inspired

Land and Water Conservation Fund
Annual Appropriations; FY1977–FY2012
(Millions of Dollars)

Fiscal Year	Land Acquisition	State Grants	Other Programs	Total
1977	$356	$182	$0	$538
1978	$491	$314	$0	$805
1979	$361	$376	$0	$737
1980	$202	$307	$0	$509
1981	$108	$180	$0	$288
1982	$176	$4	$0	$180
1983	$220	$115	$0	$335
1984	$227	$75	$0	$302
1985	$213	$74	$0	$287
1986	$121	$47	$0	$168
1987	$176	$35	$0	$211
1988	$150	$20	$0	$170
1989	$186	$20	$0	$206
1990	$212	$20	$0	$232
1991	$309	$33	$0	$342
1992	$294	$23	$0	$317
1993	$256	$28	$0	$284
1994	$228	$28	$0	$256
1995	$189	$28	$0	$217
1996	$137	$1	$0	$138
1997	$158	$1	$0	$159
1998	$896	$1	$72	$969
1999	$328	$0	$0	$328
2000	$406	$41	$20	$467
2001	$449	$90	$456	$995
2002	$429	$144	$105	$677
2003	$316	$97	$116	$529
2004	$165	$94	$230	$488
2005	$164	$91	$204	$459
2006	$119	$30	$213	$362
2007	$120	$30	$216	$366
2008	$129	$25	$101	$255
2009	$152	$19	$104	$275
2010	$278	$40	$133	$450
2011	$177	$40	$84	$301
2012	$199	$45	$83	$327

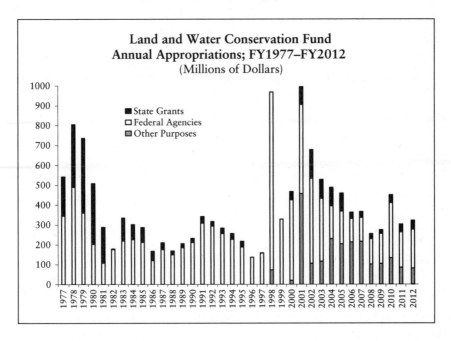

Land and Water Conservation Fund
Annual Appropriations; FY1977–FY2012
(Millions of Dollars)

■ State Grants
□ Federal Agencies
▣ Other Purposes

"meaning."[89] As Reagan had feared, the NPS's restrictive viewpoint extends well beyond any park boundary. In 1994, the superintendent of Yosemite National Park in California declared that no tourist facilities should be constructed near the park:

> It is not our intent to adversely affect local economies. Rather, it is to inform you that the National Park Service is no longer seeking development of outside accommodations to support park visitors. We cannot be responsible for economic disloca-tion resulting from future expansion and marketing of Yosem-ite based tourism knowing that a limit on park visitation to protect park resources will be implemented in the near future.[90]

The author of that letter later became superintendent of Yellowstone National Park, from which position he declared, "I believe the only way we can protect a national park in today's environment is to work beyond park boundaries—work with our neighbors and look at the larger pic-ture."[91] That is what President Clinton did when a mining company discovered a world-class deposit outside Yellowstone in an area that had been mined for decades. On the eve of the 1996 Republican National Convention, Clinton announced a multi-million-dollar deal, using money from the Land and Water Conservation Fund and other federal lands, to kill a world-class mine and with it thousands of jobs, millions of dollars in taxes, and tens of millions of dollars of revenues.[92] Just as Governor Reagan feared, government's insatiable hunger for land leads to buffer zone after buffer zone after buffer zone. It is not enough for national park officials and environmental extremists that an activity beyond park boundaries is legal, produces jobs, revenues, and taxes, and is environmentally sound. Unfortunately, when politicians lack the courage of Ronald Reagan, covetous bureaucrats and environmental groups get their way.[93]

In spite of all the attacks on Reagan by environmental extremists, it was Bill Clinton's federal lands policies that were lawless, unilateral, and partisan. When Western states refused to pass wilderness legislation favored by environmental groups, Clinton dusted off the Antiquities Act of 1906 to declare millions of acres across the West off-limits to economic activity. In the most infamous case, Clinton faced the media at the edge of the Grand Canyon in Arizona to announce creation of a national monument hundreds of miles away in Utah to kill a vast coal mine—along with hundreds of jobs, millions of dollars in taxes, tens of millions of dollars in revenues, and more low-cost electricity for southern California.[94]

Clinton decreed yet another national monument in 2000, over the objections of Tulare County, carving the Giant Sequoia National Monument—just as had been done over Reagan's objections with the Mineral King location twenty-two years earlier—from the Sequoia National Forest.[95] Reagan's words echoed with new meaning, "Is the public land really for the public or for an elite few who want to keep it for their own use?"[96]

————

An old-line agency like the National Park Service often has a will of its own, but during his tenure as president, Reagan and his secretaries of the interior brought it to heel, making it conform to its statutory mandate, the rule of law, and the Constitution. Just how was that possible?

CHAPTER NINE

INSIDE THE BELTWAY: TAMING THE BUREAUCRACY— TEAMING WITH CONGRESS

*"And every once in a while, somebody has to get
the bureaucracy by the neck and shake it loose and say,
'Stop doing what you're doing.'"*
—RONALD REAGAN, FEBRUARY 27, 1975[1]

Warning: "No Major Shifts" at Interior

Two weeks, to the day, after Election Day 1980, the *New York Times* ran a story about outgoing Secretary of the Interior Cecil Andrus. He was unfazed by the Reagan landslide and the likelihood that a Sagebrush Rebel like the newly elected president would take Andrus's place at Interior. The way the *Times* described it, Andrus "is certain that the incoming Reagan administration will be able to make few, if any, major changes in the next four years in the slow, cumbersome way the nation's natural resources are developed and regulated." Andrus warned, "My successor will have to pick his way through these legal and bureaucratic minefields."[2]

Doug Baldwin, James Watt's Wyoming friend and colleague from his days campaigning and working for Senator Milward Simpson, clipped the article at his desk at the Interstate Commerce Commission in Washington and mailed it to Watt. When Watt read it the next week, he "agreed with it" and affixed the clipping to his refrigerator door to remind him and his wife to "pray for the man who will have to face this frustrating job."[3] At the time, of course, Watt thought that man was Clifford P. Hansen. After all, how does any one person effectively manage a vast federal department with nearly eighty thousand employees across the country and deep into the Pacific Ocean, in scores of bureaus and agencies, each assigned a host of conflicting, confusing, and contradictory statutory and regulatory responsibilities?

Hitting the Ground Running

President Reagan was able to "get the bureaucracy by the neck" for three reasons. First, he entered office armed with "a remarkably coherent agenda and set of policy priorities,"[4] especially for the Interior Department. He had vast experience with the department as governor of California, and as he prepared to run for president, he read, researched, and spoke about the department, its agencies, and its activities during the Carter administration.[5] Moreover, Interior was a particular focus of his plans to "cut spending on virtually all domestic policy areas."[6]

Second, Reagan's primary criterion for appointees was "[p]ersonal and ideological loyalty." That approach gave him three secretaries of the interior who were fiercely loyal to him—leaders of the "let Reagan be Reagan" crowd.[7] In Reagan's first meeting with Watt, he quickly saw that this Westerner with a wealth of experience at Interior was fully in line with his views on what needed to be done, as well as when, where, and why.

Finally, in the earliest days of the administration, when it mattered most, Reagan had a strong White House staff led by Edwin Meese III, counselor to the president, James A. Baker III, chief of staff, and Michael Deaver, deputy chief of staff.[8] That staff, along with the broader White House leadership team, was put to early use. For example, to ensure control of the administration's policy and legislative agenda and especially its budget process, the president, Meese, Baker, David Stockman, the director of the Office of Management and Budget, and Martin Anderson, the chief domestic policy advisor, huddled in late December and early January with newly designated secretaries who did not yet have their management teams together.[9] There was one objective, said Stockman: to "brow-beat ... the cabinet, one-by-one, into accepting the cuts. It was divide-and-conquer, not roundtabling."[10]

There was one cabinet member who was not subjected to such treatment: James Watt, who had met and worked with Meese on various projects when they were in the nonprofit world. Stockman talked to Watt in late December about the need to slash the budget, and Anderson quickly recognized Watt as an advocate from outside the White House who agreed with Reagan's domestic policies and budget priorities. Watt's special treatment was something of a surprise, for he had been excluded from unofficial and official Reagan transition planning.

In preparing to assume power, Reagan began "earlier and conducted a more elaborate operation than any other president in history."[11] An April of 1980 meeting yielded two major efforts, one led by Richard Allen, who headed "132 people divided into 25 working groups" to address foreign policy, the other led by Martin Anderson, who headed "329 people in 23 issue-area groups" to consider domestic policy. Meese presided over "several low-visibility planning operations including a personnel operation headed by E. Pendleton James."[12] After the election, an executive committee composed of William Casey, Anne Armstrong, Paul Laxalt, Casper Weinberger, and Meese presided over seven deputy directors, including an operations section led by William Timmons with "100 transition teams that spread throughout the government immediately after the election [to report on] the status of agency operations and policy and prepare briefing books for appointees to the agencies."[13] In the interim, "while all eyes were fixed on the Presidential campaign," scores of experts were working on the Heritage Foundation's blueprint for the new administration, *Mandate for Leadership.*[14]

Watt flew to Washington in the summer of 1980 to meet with the Capitol Hill staffers and downtown lawyers who were drafting *Mandate*'s chapter on the Department of the Interior. Because of his years of experience with the department, he was handed the gavel. Although Watt knew what Interior was up to out West, his knowledge of policy and personnel at headquarters was six years out of date, and he soon relinquished the leadership of that effort.[15] After the election, Watt inquired about joining the Interior transition team, but word came back that he was "too conservative."[16]

After Watt met with Reagan, he began to put together his own transition team.[17] He knew that the official transition team would produce lists of candidates ("Pick One!") for top presidential appointments such as the various assistant secretaries, but Watt had a relatively free hand in selecting his deputies.[18] That was exactly what he wanted. Watt believed in deputies, had been one himself, and knew that, while their bosses—the presidential appointees—were testifying, speaking, and attending high-level meetings, deputies were dotting the i's crossing the t's and making things happen.[19]

Before appointing deputies, however, Watt prepared for his own confirmation, bringing in a team of current and former colleagues and friends.[20] After the hearings, Watt insisted on his choice for undersecretary, the department's chief operating officer—his former colleague Donald Paul Hodel, whose Republican credentials and political support assured quick White House approval.[21] White House Personnel, on its own or in cooperation with Republican officials in Washington or the states, offered up various potential presidential nominees from whom Watt selected Interior's top officials,[22] including a selection from the Reagan Interior transition team.[23] There were two presidential appointments for which Watt demanded and received the right to recommend career civil servants—the heads of the U.S. Geological Survey and the National Park Service.[24] As the presidential appointees awaited clearance, congressional hearings, and confirmations, Watt appointed knowledgeable political deputies who were aligned with Reagan's philosophy[25] (with a few notable exceptions[26]) to begin work immediately on accomplishing the president's agenda.[27]

Getting the Bureaucracy by the Neck

That work began on Monday, January 26, when Watt addressed the career employees, seven hundred at a time, in a series of seven meetings, regarding what they were to expect during the administration of Ronald Reagan.[28] First, he assured them that Reagan was personally knowledgeable about and interested in what they did:

> When he interviewed me for this job, President Reagan used our jargon and talked about the USGS, BLM, the Endangered Species Act, and the Bureau of Reclamation—he, too, has not learned the new name [Water and Power Service]. And so we have the privilege of working with a man who has been involved in public land issues, a man who cares and who has some ideas about what we ought to be doing.[29]

Further, Watt reminded them of the significance of the presidential election:

> On November 4, the people of America spoke with great clarity. They called for a dramatic new beginning and a change in our course of government. It will come as no great surprise, I am sure, that I am hereby accepting the resignations of all appointees of the Carter administration. The fact is that you were terminated on November 4, and I am simply putting the decision of the American people into effect. I expect you to be prepared to depart at the end of work today.[30]

Next, Watt explained Reagan's vision of the Interior Department's role, a vision that was in keeping with its long tradition:

> The changes President Reagan has commanded me to bring to the management of our environment and our resources will be exciting[:]

- For those of you committed to the multiple use of our lands,
- For those of you committed to preserving the best values of our natural and cultural heritages, and
- For those of you committed to using the lands for people of this generation and future generations.
- To those of you who do not share this commitment, you will be happier if you seek employment opportunities elsewhere.[31]

In addition, the new secretary assured Interior's career employees that he trusted and valued them, that political leadership, not professional employees, was at fault for past failures, and that he intended to rely on the professional employees:

> My experience in the past here in the Department has been that when there have been foul-ups or failures, it has been because of inept direction and leadership from the political side, not the career side. I will rely upon the professionalism which is in the bureaus and is the strength of the Department. This is where the people are located who really understand the mission and the resource base we are charged with managing.[32]

Finally, Watt summarized the aims of Reagan's Interior: balance economic use and preservation of public lands; develop energy resources in an environmentally sound manner; remove excess regulations; institute a Good Neighbor policy with the states; develop a strategic minerals policy; seek self-determination and economic development for American Indians; protect and preserve wildlife habitat, parks, recreation areas, and refuge lands by improving existing facilities; and develop water resources for agricultural, industrial, and domestic use.[33]

The following Monday, and every working Monday thereafter, Watt met with Interior's political appointees. He brought them news from his sessions at the White House, from his meetings with heads of other departments and agencies, and from his discussions with others in Interior and its various bureaus by which he sought both to inform and inspire. After the expiration of his six-month ban on travel by all political appointees until progress had been made in taking control of the bureaucracy and implementing the president's policies, he related significant events from his travels.

The tales Watt told were never self-aggrandizing; in fact, they were often self-deprecating.[34] Watt, who left no doubt of his admiration for President Reagan, often related something the president had said or done that revealed his courageous commitment to principle. He welcomed comments in these Monday meetings from the political appointees, whether presidential or secretarial. Often he asked someone to relate a recent experience, encounter, or event of which Watt had been informed already, as a teaching opportunity for everyone else. Whether he concluded a meeting with "Do the needful." ("I trust you and your willingness and your ability to do the right thing when it needs doing.") or not, Watt communicated that message as the one-hour gathering came to an end.[35]

The following Tuesday, and every working Tuesday thereafter, Watt met with the political appointees, as well as nonpartisan bureau heads and deputies. Watt was no less candid during these meetings; however, whereas the appointees' meeting had covered both substantive and political matters, the "Bureau Heads' Meeting" was all business. Watt continued to speak about the president, but here he revealed the president's support for Interior's efforts while remaining sensitive to the fact that many of these people were career employees and not political appointees, and thus they had no desire to be brought into political controversies. Nonetheless, the trust remained. In Watt's view, if someone were in the room, he was part of the team and had earned Watt's full trust and confidence.[36]

In March of 1981, Watt, Hodel, all the assistant secretaries-designate, and a handful of other top appointees and personal aides gathered for a daylong session to develop a sophisticated management-by-objective (MBO) program,[37] which began with a mission statement:

The mission of the Department of the Interior is to manage
properly the trust responsibilities of the United States and to
encourage and provide for the preservation, development and
management of the natural resources of the United States for
the use, enjoyment and security of its people, now and in the
future.[38]

Then Watt and the others defined goals consistent with that mission
statement:

It is a goal of the Department of the Interior to act with
common sense and environmental sensitivity to:

1. Open federal lands to public access for appropriate use or
   users.
2. Manage, preserve, and restore our National Park System
   for the benefit and use of people.
3. Increase domestic production of energy and mineral
   resources.
4. Increase the supply of quality water in cooperation with
   user groups.
5. Promote the development of economic and social resources
   of Indian tribes and trust territories.
6. Create balanced ecosystems through proper management
   of wild plants and animals.
7. Establish and implement sound management concepts and
   practices.[39]

Later, the assistant secretaries and their deputies, together with their
bureau heads and their deputies, defined objectives for their segments of
the department and assigned tasks and subtasks, which, on occasion,
were extended to the field office level, along with dates by which each
listed item was to be accomplished. In this way, Watt and Hodel held
political appointees accountable, and those appointees in turn, using a
detailed computerized management information system, tracked the

status of each important management objective to identify quickly and efficiently what tasks needed to be completed and who was responsible.[40]

Watt had generally described to the career employees President Reagan's vision for the Department of the Interior and how he intended to fulfill that vision. The MBO program put flesh on the bare bones of that vision with a mission, goals, objectives, tasks, and subtasks, along with deadlines and specifications regarding who was responsible and would be held accountable. Interior and its employees now knew what President Reagan expected of the department, what Watt intended to do, and how they were going to help him do it. Watt, however, did not leave it at that; he established personal, routine contact with every senior manager in the department through regular meetings:[41]

- Each Monday, after the meeting with the political appointees, Watt and Hodel met with a handful of political appointees and forty to fifty career employees at one of Interior's bureaus to discuss tasks, duties, problems, and solutions, and to answer questions from anyone present. After forty-five minutes, Watt and Hodel traveled with the assistant secretary and his deputies to another bureau for a similar meeting. The following Monday, Watt and Hodel met another assistant secretary to repeat the process.[42]

- Each Tuesday, after the Bureau Heads' meeting, Watt and Hodel joined with one of the six assistant secretary-level appointees and his deputies at their offices, along with the bureau heads and their deputies, to receive a status report and discuss objectives, tasks, and subtasks. As time went on, however, with the MBO program established and policies decided, Watt spent less time in MBO meetings; implementation had become ministerial. Moreover, Watt's presence often was required elsewhere.

- Every afternoon that Watt was in the department, he scheduled open time, during which any senior manager, presidential appointee, Schedule C, or career employee,

could come in with "a problem, an idea, or just to shoot
the breeze, to get the Secretary's full attention in a small
group setting with no agenda."[43]

- Every Friday afternoon, Watt held an assistant secretary-
level meeting with the top presidential appointees, along
with Watt's top aides.[44]

By developing and implementing an MBO program, that is, by creating a mission statement for the Interior Department, Watt, Hodel, and
the other political appointees—with the direct involvement of career
professionals—provided a blueprint to realize the Reagan Revolution.[45]
They sought to avoid being captured by the bureaucracy, which continued
its relentless march out of inertia or because of outside influence. Watt
was wary of being distracted by the media, including inflammatory
headlines and stories in the *Washington Post*, and of being overwhelmed
by the paperwork and meetings[46] and the monotonous grind of running
a bureaucracy. He was determined not to provide the "inept direction
and leadership" of which he accused previous administrations.

Finally, Watt had an advantage over some of his cabinet colleagues;
he chose the key members of his team. Therefore, he did not need to
worry whether they were going to carry out the president's and his directives, which allowed him to deal with the external aspects of his job. He
knew the department was on the right track because his team would see
to it. Nonetheless, he reminded everyone on a weekly basis why they were
there and what they wanted to accomplish. This mission-oriented focus
allowed his team to handle unexpected problems without checking with
"the boss." In other words, they could "do the needful."

The Reagan Agenda at Interior

In his first inaugural address, Ronald Reagan promised to reduce the
"unnecessary and excessive growth of government," "curb the size and
influence of government," "remove the roadblocks that have slowed our
economy and reduced productivity," and "demand recognition of the

distinction between the powers granted to the Federal Government and those reserved to the States or to the people."[47]

The first three-part order of business, therefore, at the Interior Department included reducing spending, shrinking the bureaucracy, and eliminating red tape.[48] Reducing spending was first because the fiscal year 1982 budget had to be addressed in time for the president's mid-February 1981 announcement.[49] Watt's early discussions with Stockman demonstrated that Watt needed no encouragement to cut Interior's budget and developed a relationship between the two that ensured a creative approach to cutting spending for federal programs while strengthening conservative, free-market principles.[50] One example was Watt's approach to parkland acquisition.

Watt had been given the General Accounting Office report decrying the sorry condition of the national parks and the need to spend more than a billion dollars to restore them.[51] The report put him in mind of a luncheon he had attended years earlier as a high school student with his father, a lawyer and chairman of the Platte County Republican Party, and Governor Milward Simpson. The governor talked about the deteriorated condition of Yellowstone National Park and a letter he had written to President Eisenhower on the subject. The letter resulted in Eisenhower's highly praised "Project 66" to build and restore public facilities in the national parks to ensure their use by the American people.[52] Watt saw an opportunity for President Reagan to undertake a similarly bold effort. At the same time, Watt sought to reduce dramatically if not eliminate totally massive federal expenditures (almost a billion a year) from the Land and Water Conservation Fund,[53] to respond to public and professional outcry over abusive NPS land acquisition practices,[54] and to curtail purchases of expensive property for urban parks that were of local interest only.

A quick call from Watt to Stockman gained the OMB director's support for spending $250 million annually over four years to restore parks while cutting $900 million annually in land acquisition expenditures.[55] Cutting spending was not an end in itself, but it provided a mechanism for changing priorities and policy, without any request to Congress for additional statutory authority.[56]

Another projected cut in federal spending entailed regulatory relief in response to a battle in Carter's War on the West and his attack on Eastern coal mining. Congress wrote the Surface Mining Control and Reclamation Act (SMCRA) to provide states the authority to run their coal reclamation and enforcement programs ("primacy"), but the SMCRA regulations written by Carter's Interior Department all but barred the states from obtaining primacy. Watt pledged to rewrite the program to allow states to do as Congress intended, brought in a team of former state officials to do so, and projected a 27-percent savings for the federal Office of Surface Mining.[57]

Some of the cuts in federal expenditures had more prosaic origins. Early on, Watt and Hodel, along with the assistant secretary-designate and his deputies, met with career employees of various bureaus. Near the end of one meeting, a career official from the Heritage Conservation and Recreation Service (HCRS)—the organization once headed by Watt when it was the Bureau of Outdoor Recreation—asked, "Mr. Secretary, do you plan to abolish the HCRS?" Without hesitating, Watt replied, "Yes." The official said nothing and the meeting soon ended. Afterward, as Watt and Hodel strode down the hallway, Hodel asked, "Jim, when did you decide to abolish HCRS?" "I decided to do it as soon as he asked the question," said Watt. "If an official asks if his agency is going to be abolished, then he knows the answer already."[58] The HCRS was absorbed by the National Park Service.[59]

All told, the Interior Department requested a 15.3-percent cut in funding for fiscal year 1982, which began October 1, 1982.[60] Unfortunately, Congress added funds that the department had not requested and continued to do so for the remainder of Reagan's presidency to the tune of four billion dollars, despite the determined efforts of his interior secretaries, Watt, Clark, and Hodel.[61] Meanwhile, largely through attrition, the department cut the number of employees, reducing full-time personnel by seven percent from 1981 to 1984, with limited use of reductions-in-force.[62] Over eight years, Reagan's Interior Department reduced its personnel ceiling by 11 percent.[63]

Reagan initiated a number of efforts to improve the management of the federal bureaucracy.[64] Chief among them was one that he discussed in his radio address of July 30, 1983—Reform 88:

[A]n ambitious program to upgrade management of the Federal Government [whose] long-range goal is to overhaul the entire administrative system, which [includes] 330 differing financial systems, and 200 payroll systems.... [T]here's never been an effective effort to manage this growing administrative monster. Each year we've fallen behind the private sector in management techniques.... The greatest nation in the world deserves the best government, and with your support, we'll have it.[65]

Reagan's goal was simply to "get this government running as honestly and efficiently as any successful American business."[66] Needless to say, there had been scores of similar, "centrally directed federal management improvement initiatives" in past administrations, but the results had been "dismal and somewhat disappointing."[67] Reagan's initiative, however, unlike those of his predecessors, was not viewed by the political appointees, career employees, or the vast bureaucracy as "a frontal attack on the political system" or an effort to "redefine organizational relationships, alter program outcomes, or disturb the budget process."[68] Reagan's Reform 88:

... focused instead on the general upgrading of agency management systems in the areas of personnel, finance, communications, facility utilization, and procurement. They included several innocuous efforts such as the establishment of an electronic mail system between the Executive Office and the agencies, an overhaul of debt collection procedures, new cash management policies, and the standardization of financial bases. Other initiatives [sought] to increase standardization, compatibility, and automation of administrative systems....[69]

In other words, as Meese put it, Reform 88 concentrated not on "doing different things, but on doing things differently and doing them better."[70] Reform 88 was more flexible than earlier efforts. In fact, much of the planning and implementation was to be done by career federal employees, who knew the problems and had to live with their solutions.[71] The results in the Interior Department were impressive. Project 88:

- Reduced, initially, Interior's payroll systems by 50 percent, and then, in 1984 converted to a single system for an annual savings of two million dollars;[72]
- Implemented cash management initiatives on a department-wide basis resulting in cost savings in excess of $25 million;[73]
- Expanded the role of the Bureau of Reclamation's Denver Cooperative Administrative Support Unit, to provide services to twenty-six federal agencies, which employ 9,318 full-time federal employees at the Federal Center and in downtown Denver;[74]
- Slashed by two million hours (over 19 percent) the time needed by the public to prepare information for submission to Interior;[75]
- Implemented Interior's first mineral royalty audit program and collected, in fiscal years 1981 through 1983 $84 million in unpaid or underpaid royalties—triple the $28 million collected from 1977 through 1980;[76]
- Strengthened internal controls, conducted 1,240 vulnerability assessments, completed 280 evaluations of major Interior activities and reported to the president and Congress on the evaluation results;[77]
- Developed a program to bring injured employees back to work, reducing workers' compensation costs, which reduced annual costs by $750,000 with future actuarial savings of $12.7 million;[78]
- Set up an Interior-wide, unified electronic mail system;[79]
- Mandated payment of mineral royalties by electronic funds transfer, saving $1.1 million in annual interest costs;[80]
- Instituted an energy conservation program, which achieved a 20-percent reduction in energy usage;[81]

- Developed the Quarters Management Inventory System to appraise, simply and economically, over ten thousand Interior-owned homes, which reduced the cost from $1,100 per unit to under $18 per unit.[82]

Another Reagan "good government" initiative, Executive Order 12615, required all agencies to accelerate reviews of activities that could be performed by the private sector to permit federal employees to perform functions that are inherently governmental.[83] The Interior Department's response put it in the top five agencies.[84] The department:

- Sold 95 percent of the Bureau of Reclamation's small loan portfolio to private loan contractors at discounted rates, which exceeded the sales target set by Congress ($230 million) by $62 million, at a cost of less than one quarter of one percent of the principal amount realized by the program;[85]
- Contracted with a private company for all travel services provided at headquarters;[86]
- Referred over $169 million in accounts and loans receivable to private collection agencies, offset salary owed to collect delinquent debt from employees, referred 662 cases, representing $654,000, to the Internal Revenue Service for offset against taxpayer's federal tax refunds, and wrote off over $85 million as delinquent, uncollectible debt;[87]
- Contracted for unemployment compensation services for all Interior bureaus to "strengthen internal control, improve management, and reduce costs," which resulted in a savings of $5 million;[88]
- Issued a contract to purchase an off-the-shelf financial management software package to improve and consolidate ten bureau accounting and payment systems and to reduce the number of data processing sites from thirty to two.[89]

The Interior Department's efforts to implement Executive Order 12615 more aggressively were stymied, unfortunately, by limits imposed by Congress.[90]

Eliminating Red Tape and Charting a New Course

In February of 1981, President Reagan issued Executive Order 12291 on federal regulation, the purpose of which was to

> reduce the burdens of existing and future regulations, increase agency accountability for regulatory actions, provide for presidential oversight of the regulatory process, minimize duplication and conflict of regulations, and insure well-reasoned regulations....[91]

Earlier, the president had created the Task Force on Regulatory Relief, chaired by Vice President Bush, to "cut away the thicket of irrational and senseless regulations...."[92] In light of Reagan's promise to increase production of energy and minerals from federal lands and the commitment of his interior secretary to a good neighbor policy, much of the Interior Department's early regulatory reform efforts were devoted to Outer Continental Shelf oil and gas leasing, onshore oil and gas leasing, coal leasing, and return of authority to regulate coal mining reclamation to the states.[93] The review, however, extended beyond these vast sets of regulations[94] to every "major rule," defined as any regulation that results in:

1. An annual effect on the economy of $100 million or more;
2. A major increase in costs or prices for consumers, individual industries, Federal, State, or local government agencies, or geographic regions; or
3. Significant adverse effects on competition, employment, investment, productivity, innovation, or on the ability of United States–based enterprises to compete with foreign-based enterprises in domestic or export markets.[95]

Nonetheless, by late 1983, the Interior Department had completed action on fifty of the fifty-five rules targeted for revocation or revision as part of Reagan's major regulatory reform effort.[96] At the close of the administration, the department reported that it had completed action on fifty-three of fifty-five areas identified shortly after the president issued his executive order.[97] Specifically, Interior had "removed unnecessary rules, remedied regulations with unanticipated consequences, and reduced the public's paperwork burden," so much so that Interior's portion of the *Federal Register* decreased by 48 percent between 1982 and 1987.[98] Moreover, the department reduced the number of rules subject to White House review and subsequent publication in a volume of the federal government's most important rules from forty-five in 1985 to twenty-nine in late 1988.[99]

The speaker of the House, Thomas "Tip" O'Neill, viewed the Reagan Revolution with hostility. It challenged everything that the Massachusetts liberal stood for during his long tenure in Congress.[100] Although Reagan had a legislative agenda that required congressional action, he believed that he could accomplish most of his desired reforms administratively, that is, with the powers entrusted to the president of the United States.[101] Watt shared that view, especially given the make-up of the House committees with jurisdiction over his department.[102]

Of course, one administrative tool was revision of the department's budget, which Watt had used to great effect in the unprecedented revision of the lame-duck Carter administration's fiscal year 1982 budget. Another one, used by every new administration, was the selection of personnel. Reagan's White House had carefully selected its presidential appointments,[103] and the Interior Department did the same with Schedule C and secretarial appointments. Regulatory reform was yet another tool, and the entire Reagan administration seized it as quickly as Interior did. Although the administration can remove and revise unduly burdensome regulations, it still may fail in charting a totally new course, which was what Reagan had promised.

As Reagan knew from his years of dealing with Interior and its agencies, the plethora of statutes pursuant to which the secretary operates leaves much to his discretion.[104] The difficulty, however, is that charting a totally new course, as Watt did, for example, with the Outer Continental Shelf (OCS) oil and gas leasing program, is incredibly complex. Fortunately, Watt had the energy, intellect, enthusiasm, experience, and intrepidity to accomplish what might have been impossible for almost anyone else.[105] Watt knew that he had the discretion to accomplish exactly what Reagan asked of him and that he did not need any new legislative authority from Congress.[106]

What Watt needed, though, was the support of the men and women at Interior—not just political appointees, but the career employees and professionals who did most of the mind-numbing paperwork. Revising the OCS oil and gas leasing program, for example, required thousands and thousands of hours of work by hundreds of Interior employees from every bureau and agency. In decision meetings—standing-room-only sessions filled with political appointees and career employees—Watt was engaged, informed, but always in pursuit of additional, if relevant, information, and nonetheless, ready and willing to make a decision.[107] If he had a question, he went to the source, not the assistant secretary, or his deputy, a bureau head, or his deputy, but to the one who wrote the document. If that person were not in the room, Watt would dig for more information from the source. Then he made his decision, marked the document, signed his name, explained his decision, and thanked everyone.[108] From that point on, however, it was his decision and his alone. He took full responsibility.

Several aspects of Watt's leadership on behalf of the president are worthy of note. First, Watt enthusiastically engaged federal employees in the work of the agency by which they were employed. If they supported that agency's mission, they could not help but be encouraged.[109] Second, he eagerly made decisions, and in making those decisions he earnestly sought the advice of federal employees who knew their subject. In a federal bureaucracy as hidebound and ponderous as Interior, the willingness of its top official to seek advice and to make a timely and even speedy decision cannot be overvalued. Third, Watt had not surrounded himself with "special assistants" who ran the department. That was done by the assistant secretaries and their deputies, and when there was a dispute among them, the secretary resolved it with all the parties in the room.[110]

Fourth, Watt was gracious in crediting those who paved the way with endless amounts of paperwork for him to mark a box and sign his name, but he guarded their careers by taking full responsibility for the result, whether within the department or in congressional testimony. Fifth, Watt mastered the decision documents prepared for him and used that information effectively in Capitol Hill hearings, media events, and public appearances. Nothing is more disappointing to a career bureaucrat or political appointee, sitting in the fourth row at a congressional hearing, than hearing his boss muff a question; it usually yields a palm slap to the forehead and a whispered, "That was in his briefing book." In that regard, Watt never disappointed. If it was in the briefing book or the decision document, it was in his head, on his tongue, and on the record.[111]

Watt may have seized Interior "by the neck," as President Reagan had urged, but there was a much larger federal bureaucracy beyond his department, including the Office of Management and Budget, the Department of Justice, and the Forest Service, to name a few. Watt prevailed more often than most cabinet secretaries in his efforts to fulfill the president's directives. But there were some stalemates that affected the department.

When Clark arrived at Interior, his commitment to Reagan's policies and his unique position as the president's top hand won him the president's assistance in seizing the remainder of the bureaucracy by the neck. Three important issues stand out. The first was the unresolved financing of Western water projects. The sharp-pencil types at OMB and the privatization advocates who had created such a ruckus over the ill-fated Asset Management Program insisted on a cost-benefit calculation and a cost-sharing formula that would have prevented improvements to long-standing Bureau of Reclamation projects and would have killed any new ones that might be justified and desired by state and local governments. Clark cut through the red tape and forced a resolution that placated—if it did not please—the OMB's bean-counters while making great sense to Westerners.[112]

Another long-running battle with the persnickety analysts and privatization advocates at OMB concerned the fees charged to Western ranchers for letting their cattle graze on federal land, including lands managed by the Bureau of Land Management and the U.S. Forest Service. Grazing leases on privately owned land are dramatically different from grazing permits on federal land. Unlike a private landowner, the federal government has thousands of environmental group members staring over its shoulder with lawsuits at the ready.[113] Reagan, Watt, and Clark understood this difference, but the OMB staffers did not. They developed a scheme that would have made grazing fees so onerous that they would have driven many ranchers off their allotments. Fees would have differed from state to state across the West and even from grazing district to grazing district. After months of futile negotiation among the various agencies, Clark called for a status report. Told by a political appointee that OMB was immovable and that reasonable grazing fees would come only through an executive order, Clark hung up. A short time later a high-ranking OMB official called the appointee, "Secretary Clark advised me that you have an Executive Order on grazing fees for the President's signature." The executive order was delivered within the hour and signed by President Reagan the next day.[114]

Finally, although Watt had ordered the Interior Department's solicitor to revoke an opinion issued by the Carter administration claiming a "non-reserved" water right that preempted state authority over Western water—a new opinion was issued restoring the primacy of Western states over their water—it appeared that career attorneys in the Department of Justice had not gotten the word, at least as it related to on-going litigation involving wilderness areas. Clark learned of the foot-dragging, asked for a "one-pager" on the subject, and then headed to the White House for a meeting with President Reagan and the Cabinet Council on Natural Resources and the Environment.[115] The president directed the federal government to argue that state law controlled the creation of water rights in Western states and that congressional designation of federal lands as wilderness did not create a new federal water right.[116]

Congressional critics, environmental extremists, and the compliant and clueless media complained that the Interior Department had breached a long-standing consensus on natural resources and environmental issues, which could be changed only through legislation.[117] In fact, there was no such consensus. The congressional record on these issues was positively schizophrenic. Congress, for example, had designated federal land as wilderness areas, but allowed mineral entry, exploration, and even development in those same areas, at least until 1984. Congress had the ability to change its mind, even if doing so seemed hypocritical, but there was no basis for opponents of the Reagan administration—either members of Congress or radical environmental groups—to contend that Interior lacked legal authority to proceed administratively.

The Administrative Presidency Seeks Legislative Authority

The Interior Department had a legislative agenda of one item: reform of the Reclamation Act of 1902.[118] Nearly eighty years after passage of the landmark legislation, the West—what early maps had described as the "Great American Desert"—was one of the world's leading producers of agricultural products and home to millions.[119] Indeed, the legislation had lived up to its early billing "by the most enthusiastic irrigation experts" as the federal mechanism by which "[m]illions of acres of arid land in the West will be thrown open to the farmer through irrigation [and] open the way for the mightiest Anglo-Saxon civilization the world has ever known."[120] Briefly summarized:

> The work which the government is executing in constructing great storage and diversion dams and in building canals, laterals, and headgates is the largest undertaking of the kind in the history of the United States. The individual projects ... are so vast in scope and their execution is so expensive as absolutely to prohibit their undertaking by private capital.[121]

The Reclamation Act of 1902, signed into law by President Theodore Roosevelt, fulfilled the vision of the great Western explorer John Wesley Powell, who noted that the American West had an abundance of snowfall, which, after melting in the summer, rushed to the ocean, leaving the West barren and all but uninhabitable.[122] The Bureau of Reclamation, which since 1907 is the Interior bureau responsible for the Act, is well known for its six hundred dams and reservoirs, power plants, and canals in seventeen Western states, among them the Hoover Dam on the Colorado River and Grand Coulee on the Columbia River. The bureau is both the biggest wholesaler of water in the nation—delivering water to thirty-one million people, including one out of every five Western farmers irrigating ten million acres of farmland that produce 60 percent of America's vegetables and 25 percent of its fruit and nuts—and America's second-largest provider of hydroelectric power. Its fifty-eight power plants serve the electricity needs of 3.5 million families.[123]

The Interior Department recognized the need to modernize the law by addressing antiquated acreage limitations that no longer allowed an economic operation. The requirement of residency on irrigated land needed to be eliminated and cost recovery on large-scale commercial operations needed to be permitted.[124] The department also sought an increase in the acreage limitation from 160 to 960. Watt and his officials sent a bill to Capitol Hill and the director of the Bureau of Reclamation testified in favor of the legislation, which Congress passed.[125] The president declared, "While preserving the basic objectives of the original program, this legislation provides a new direction for the federal role in Reclamation—one that will, I believe, prove to be a significant step forward on our road to economic recovery in the 1980s."[126] Reagan also videotaped a message that was greeted with applause by agricultural groups across the West.

In January of 1982, Watt received the final report from a commission that he had established six months earlier to respond to "serious allegations of massive irregularities in royalty payments due the Federal government, Indian tribes, and States; and the allegations of theft of oil from Federal and Indian lands."[127] In response to media reports in the spring of 1981[128] and to recommendations made by the General Accounting Office during the Carter administration, Watt quickly assembled a Commission on Fiscal Accountability of the Nation's Energy Resources to ascertain the facts and make recommendations.[129]

The Commission reported "the problems in collecting royalties and preventing theft ... have been outstanding for more than 20 years"[130] and made numerous recommendations. In March of 1982, the Interior

Department asked Congress to adopt the recommendations, including the prosecution of those who removed oil from federal or Indian lands without documentation and civil penalties in cases of inadequate protection on federal and Indian leases to prevent theft.[131] Watt did not wait for Congress, however. He removed from the U.S. Geological Survey its Conservation Division, which had been charged with post-leasing activities, including royalty collection, and created the Minerals Management Service.[132] He ordered "look-back" audits to ensure that all royalties owed had been paid.[133] As the legislation progressed through Congress, Representative Sidney R. Yates, the Democrat from Illinois—who chaired the subcommittee responsible for Interior's appropriation and no fan of Reagan's interior secretaries, said that previous interior secretaries "did not have [Watt's] political courage to move forward" on the issue of royalty collection.[134]

The Senate Energy and Natural Resources Committee devoted every business meeting from May 3 to July 27, 1982, to Watt's proposal.[135] The legislation passed both houses of Congress by voice vote and, on January 12, 1983, less than one year after the commission delivered its report, President Reagan signed the Federal Oil and Gas Royalty and Management Act,[136] declaring:

> [Congress] met our call for quick and strong legislation with a true bipartisan commitment to enact this bill[,] a great achievement for this administration. [T]he royalty management system has been plagued with problems for well over 30 years. We are the first administration to acknowledge those problems and to tackle them head-on. Secretary Watt has worked hard to improve a system that provides a major source of revenues for the United States. With the authority granted to the Secretary … I believe that we can have a strong and sound Federal royalty management program.[137]

Carter's Interior Department had issued oil and gas leases on federal lands within Fort Chaffee, a military reservation in northwestern Arkansas near Fort Smith, in 1979.[138] Because the land was unavailable for oil and gas leasing until 1976, the Bureau of Land Management concluded it was not within a "Known Geological Structure" (KGS)[139] and issued the leases noncompetitively, that is, under Interior's lottery system.[140] Thirty-three thousand acres were sold for one dollar an acre.[141] The next year, Carter's Interior Department issued federal oil and gas leases on tracts adjoining the previous year's Fort Chaffee leases. This time, however, the Bureau of Land Management said the lands were within a KGS, leased them competitively, and received $1,705 an acre for a total of $43 million; $21.5 million was paid to Arkansas.[142]

Meanwhile, litigation followed involving successful and unsuccessful bidders, the state of Arkansas, and Secretary Andrus. Reagan's Interior Department inherited the lawsuit, which was not resolved until 1984, when a court of appeals held that the KGS designation was "arbitrary" and that the leases were invalid.[143] The court said simply, "the Department did not do its homework...."[144] The Fort Chaffee controversy demonstrated the danger of withholding federal land from energy exploration, the deficiencies of a leasing program so limited as to deprive the federal government of basic knowledge about the value of the land it holds in trust for the American people, and the defects of the bureaucratic process for KGS designations.

Another similar controversy arose in 1983 in northeastern Wyoming when noncompetitive leases were issued on tracts that were thought to encompass four separate KGSs. In fact, there was one large, common formation beneath the four KGSs and the fourteen newly issued noncompetitive leases.[145] The Interior Department reformed the procedures for designating KGSs, amended the process for reviewing lands prior to oil and gas leasing, and assigned more employees to the task of designating KGSs.[146] To discourage fraud and speculation, it increased the filing fee in 1982 for participation in the noncompetitive program from twenty-five dollars to seventy-five dollars. In October of 1983 it suspended the lottery program, and in 1984, it required payment of rentals in advance.[147] The department also issued three new instructional manuals to ensure the accuracy of KGS designations.[148] At the same time, it aggressively litigated demands by potential lessees that they be issued noncompetitive leases in undesignated KGSs.[149] As a result, the onshore oil and gas leasing program was neither predictable nor stable.[150]

Legislative remedies had been attempted in past years and began in earnest in 1981, but Congress was not able to agree on the best approach.[151] In 1985, the Interior Department urged a market-oriented, two-tiered system.[152] In congressional testimony in 1987, Reagan officials argued that the two-tiered approach brought stability and predictability to the federal oil and gas leasing program and recognized the depressed conditions in "the oil patch" as well as continuing threats to national security.[153] On December 22, 1987, with the support of the Reagan administration, Congress agreed on a two-tier competitive and noncompetitive leasing system with minimum required bids[154] and passed the Federal Onshore Oil and Gas Leasing Reform Act of 1987.

Although the Interior Department accomplished as much as it could administratively, when circumstances and the national interest demanded a legislative solution, Watt, Clark, and Hodel worked with Congress to enact reasonable and balanced federal laws.[155]

Cabinet Council on Natural Resources and Environment

Early in 1981, Watt called me to his office to advise me of a meeting on the Law of the Sea Treaty that afternoon a few block away at the State Department's "Foggy Bottom" headquarters. "You're the only one around here who knows anything about it, so I'm sending you," Watt only half joked. It was not much of a compliment: a handful of the deputies and personal aides had been sworn in, and the presidential appointees would not be nominated for weeks or confirmed for months. When I was the lawyer for the House Mines and Mining Subcommittee, I had followed the issue, and I had "spent a week one afternoon" at the United Nations listening over headphones to the translations of debates on the deep seabed mining provisions of the treaty. I was also responsible for two bureaus, the U.S. Geological Survey and the Bureau of Mines, which had researched various mining and metallurgical issues pertaining to the treaty. Moreover, Alexander F. Holser, a physicist, research engineer, and former CIA scientist, worked for me on Law of the Sea issues, and his office was right across the hall from mine.

Later, after a quick briefing from Holser, I arrived at the State Department, dashed to the secretary's conference room, and found a seat at the far end of the table. My choice of seating, it turned out, was fortunate. William Clark, then the deputy secretary of state, entered the room in the company of someone I assumed to be an aide, and then sat down opposite me. I had never met Clark and would not see him again until he took over for Watt two years and nine months later, so I knew only two things about him: he was a long-time professional and personal friend of President Reagan and he had taken a terrible public beating during his confirmation hearing. I was struck by his diffidence in presiding over the meeting, which I attributed to that confirmation experience.

Clark announced the purpose of the meeting—to provide instructions for the Law of the Sea Treaty negotiators who were headed to New York the next day—and then turned the meeting over to the aide, who turned out to be a career foreign service officer (FSO) and a member of the delegation. He discussed the decision document I had received by fax before leaving my office, which set out a typical bureaucratic choice: (1) abandon the negotiations now, (2) sign the treaty as written, or (3) send the delegation to New York without any instructions other than maximum flexibility to get the best deal possible. I had fumed about it on my walk over and thus could not believe, when the vote began down the left side of the table from Clark, that each departmental representative voted for the third option.

"Mr. Secretary," I began when the voting reached me, "Interior opposes each one of these options and instead favors a new option, option number four, which orders the delegation to defend principles enunciated by President Reagan." Then, I laid out three or four of those principles. To my amazement, as the voting proceeded up the table to my left, each one voted for the new option. I did not believe it was my powers of persuasion that turned the tide; instead, I concluded that those on Clark's left were Carter career hold-overs and those on his right were the Reaganites. Whatever it was, when the vote reached Clark, he paused for but a moment and then

Ronald Reagan

James G. Watt

William P. Clark

Donald Paul Hodel

President Reagan, joined by Secretary Hodel, Lou Gossett Jr., and Clint Eastwood, announces "Take Pride in America." *White House Rose Garden—July 21, 1987*

Three Fighting Men and the American Flag at the Vietnam Veterans Memorial

MOUNT WATTMORE NATIONAL PARK

Washington, D.C.

"BATTING FOR WATT AND PLAYING RIGHT FIELD...."

TO SEC. HODEL, WITH LOVE

intoned quietly that it was number four. The FSO responded without hesitating. "Mr. Secretary, I will prepare the document."

"Mr. Secretary," I interrupted as the FSO rose to his feet. "I believe we would all like to review that document. I am prepared to stay at my office for whatever length of time is required to be able to respond in a timely fashion." I looked up and down the table for nods of agreement; there were a few. The FSO did not wait to be instructed. "Mr. Secretary, I will prepare the document and circulate it for approval." Then he left.

Holser and I stayed late that night—until nearly ten, if I recall correctly—and I was told when Holser handed me what became the final version that Interior was the last one to sign off. I wanted to make sure it was right. I do not think my fly-specking and word-smithing caused the Law of the Sea Treaty negotiations to crash and burn; that was done by people way above my pay grade and no doubt by someone in the Oval Office or nearby.[156] I do think the instructions with which we sent the delegation north, however, ensured that the team could not announce some ephemeral "progress" that might have made it publicly difficult to scuttle the talks. I did learn the necessity of speaking up, not once but consistently, and of attempting to control the document.[157]

Some months later, Ambassador Theodore G. Kronmiller, a deputy assistant secretary of state, came to my office at Interior. He out-ranked me and could have asked that I come to him, and I would have been honored to do so; however, he insisted on my office because the matter was sensitive.

"Now that we've killed the Law of the Sea Treaty," he began, "it is time to put the last nail in the coffin."

"What would that be?" I asked.

"President Reagan will issue an Exclusive Economic Zone [EEZ] proclamation to claim jurisdiction beyond the Outer Continental Shelf over territory that the treaty purportedly grants us but that we still have to defend with our navy. I can't do it at State, but you can do it from here. After all, the Outer Continental Shelf proclamation that Truman issued was crafted right here at Interior by Ickes."

"I'll brief Jim [Watt] and run it through a senior interagency group [SIG] and up through the Cabinet Council on Natural Resources and Environment," I said. "What about State?"

"They will object, but what are they going to do?" Kronmiller said rising from the couch. "It will be fun to watch."

I briefed Watt, got his agreement to the proposal, and sent out documents to gather the group and draft an EEZ proclamation. There were few objections, except from one of the State Department representatives, but then State stopped attending and we voted the proclamation out and on its way to Watt's Cabinet Council.

There was only one hitch. One day Watt called me. "I just got a call from Ed Meese. He wants to know what you're doing with the EEZ proclamation. I told him you were following my orders." Watt paused. "Tell me again what we're up to." So I did.

After the Cabinet Council on Natural Resources and Environment's EEZ proclamation reached the White House, I got a call from Kronmiller. "They're going nuts over here," he said. "They are sending over an ocean's policy to accompany your EEZ proclamation."

"I thought they opposed it?" I asked.

"They do but now they know it is a done deal awaiting the President's signature and they want to tidy up some issues. Dotting the i's and crossing the t's is all. Congratulations."

On March 10, 1983, "to promote and protect the oceans interests of the United States,"[158] the president issued his EEZ proclamation:

[T]he United States will exercise sovereign rights in living and nonliving resources within 200 nautical miles of its coast. This will provide United States jurisdiction for mineral resources out to 200 nautical miles that are not on the continental shelf. Recently discovered deposits there could be an important future source of strategic minerals.[159]

President Reagan, who had used cabinet government effectively as governor of California, intended to do the same in Washington, with some minor changes.[160] During his first term, the cabinet council system,

including the Cabinet Council on Natural Resources and Environment, chaired by Watt and, later, Clark, functioned exceedingly well.[161] In the second term, however, the seven cabinet councils were replaced by two major councils, the Domestic Policy Council and the Economic Policy Council.[162] The result, unfortunately, was that "major presidential aides could ignore or end-run the system."[163] That is what occurred when, for the only time in the Reagan administration, a natural resources policy apparently in direct conflict with the president's views was presented to him in a one-on-one meeting with no opportunity for opposing views. Reagan was ill-served in the process.

The occasion for this misstep was the Montreal Protocol, a treaty to limit chlorofluorocarbons (CFCs) that were thought to deplete and modify the ozone, harming human health and the environment. In late May of 1987, the Domestic Policy Council took up the issue. As always, Reagan expressed concern over proposed regulations. Secretary Hodel, who believed that the president deserved a number of policy options, echoed those concerns. Unfortunately, White House aides and officials at the Environmental Protection Agency (EPA) concluded that Hodel was out of step with environmental orthodoxy and leaked an inaccurate and insulting version of Hodel's comments. They falsely alleged that Hodel had urged that the American people be instructed to don hats, wear sunglasses, and apply sunscreen.[164] The newspaper stories provided the EPA with an opportunity to denounce Hodel and his "proposal," to proclaim the treaty as the only option, and to declare that the danger posed was scientifically unquestioned—and in fact, unquestionable.

The story made headlines. Environmentalists mocked the secretary of the interior and demanded his resignation.[165] Two weeks later, in another Domestic Policy Council meeting, Hodel again raised questions about the science and the cost. Afterward, Reagan wrote, "I'm faced with making a decision on instructions to our team on what we seek world wide in reduction of Fluorocarbons that are destroying the Ozone layer. Right now I don't have the answers."[166]

White House aides and the EPA had the answer. Hodel was *persona non grata* regarding the Montreal Protocol. In September of 1987, EPA administrator Lee Thomas was ushered into the Oval

Office for a one-on-one with the president. Later Reagan wrote of the meeting, "This is an historic agreement."[167] In December of 1987, he signed the treaty and forwarded it to the Senate for ratification.[168]

Those who generally oppose Ronald Reagan's environmental policy praise him for signing the Montreal Protocol and for nothing else, but recent research shows that, as with most matters, Reagan's instincts were right.[169] Moreover, Hodel was right as well in his attempt to "let Reagan be Reagan."

═══════════

The president, who had campaigned on the need to develop domestic energy resources, especially on federal lands, was interested in more than just oil and natural gas. He sought to develop the nation's rich coal deposits and, in the process, to get the federal government off the backs of state officials trying to comply with federal law and mine coal.

CHAPTER TEN

AMERICA: THE SAUDI ARABIA OF COAL

"We have an estimated one-half of all the known coal reserves in the world.... [W]hy aren't we mining more? We are producing about 150 million tons a year—below our capacity to produce."
—RONALD REAGAN, OCTOBER 2, 1979[1]

Coal–America's Most Abundant Energy Source

There is a reason why, in the earliest days of his administration, President Carter announced plans to double the nation's production of coal by 1985: it is America's most plentiful energy resource and is found in great abundance in states as diverse as Kentucky and West Virginia, Illinois and Indiana, Montana and Wyoming.[2] America, it is often said, is the "Saudi Arabia of coal."[3]

Ronald Reagan asked exactly the right question in a radio address in 1979: "Why aren't we mining more [coal]?" The answer was Carter was positively schizophrenic on the subject. He wanted to increase coal production, but he also embraced draconian environmental laws and regulations that hampered the mining of that coal. For example, Carter supported a provision in the Clean Air Act Amendments of 1977 that barred the importation of Western coal into the Midwest and Appalachian states.[4] Moreover, members of environmental groups that supported Carter when he ran for president in 1976 filled key spots in his administration, and they pushed an array of legislative items, some of which President Ford had vetoed, that Carter readily signed and that they then implemented with a vengeance.

These laws and regulations affected coal-mining states differently. For Eastern states, their inability to mine coal, let alone mine more coal economically, was the result of a new federal law mandating reclamation of coal lands, prohibiting certain mining techniques, and barring mining of some lands. For Western states—because coal there was owned by the federal government—their challenge in being able to mine more coal was due to a long-running moratorium on the leasing of federal coal, relentless litigation by environmental groups, and ever-changing federal laws regarding the leasing and mining of federal coal.

In Reagan's view, Carter's policies violated two core values. The first was federalism—the principle that states are sovereign and should be allowed to run their own affairs, especially when Congress mandates that result. The second was respect for the marketplace. The United States, as a landowner, should not act as a monopolist, Reagan believed, but must make its rich resources available to the American public. Restoring those values was a high priority of the Reagan administration.

States Will Run Their Own Programs

In 1972, Congress began debating the merits of legislation that came to be known as the Surface Mining Control and Reclamation Act (SMCRA), which President Carter signed into law on August 3, 1977.[5] Like the Clean Air Act before it,[6] SMCRA provided for minimum national standards that Interior Department regulations would implement.[7] The act got through Congress because of the promise that states, after meeting SMCRA's minimum requirements, would retain primary regulatory authority or "primacy."[8]

Often hailed as an example of "cooperative federalism,"[9] SMCRA does not provide for shared regulation of the environmental effects of coal mining. It mandates either a federal program or a state program but not both, requiring, as a federal court of appeals put it, "extraordinary deference to the States."[10] Congress may have adopted minimal national standards, but it intended that each state run its own program. By so doing, Congress, at least to some degree, preserved federalism.

The Carter administration took a different view of coal-mining regulation. It turned SMCRA into a recipe book for top-down command and control. In March of 1979, after the receipt of thousands of pages of comments from hundreds of sources and testimony from nearly two hundred witnesses, Carter's Office of Surface Mining (OSM) published five hundred pages of regulations that left little flexibility for the states to develop regulatory programs that reflected "the diversity in terrain, climate, biologic, chemical, and other physical conditions in areas subject to mining operations," as intended by Congress.[11] Although some coal mining states were granted primacy, the major ones were unwilling to impose the OSM's onerous program mandates without tailoring them to their own climate, geology, and topography. By January of 1981, 89 percent of the coal mines in the country remained under federal regulatory control.[12]

Ronald Reagan called America "a nation unique in all the world" because its government is a "federation of Sovereign States," which "is probably our greatest guarantee against tyranny by a centralized national government."[13] A former governor, he believed in the Founding Fathers' vision of the role of the states in the federal system, and as president he pressed for true federalism. Reagan's insistence that the federal government be a "good neighbor," Watt concluded, applied to the OSM.

To accomplish that objective, he called on three officials from major Eastern coal-mining states who were involved in their states' regulatory programs to join the Interior Department to reform OSM's regulatory regime. Richard Harris of Indiana, J. Steven Griles of Virginia, and Dean Hunt of Kentucky set to work rewriting the hundreds of pages of regulations.[14] That is not to say that Western elected officials were happy with the OSM. In fact, they were livid over the Carter era regulations, which Governor Herschler of Wyoming called "overkill" and "a lawyer's maze, designed to confuse and harass an adversary."[15]

By January of 1982, the OSM had established a regulatory reform task force, which nine months later had rewritten 91 percent of the permanent regulations, permitting states to assume responsibility for surface mining reclamation in accordance with each state's geology, topography, and climate.[16] OSM eliminated Carter's paint-by-numbers approach and adopted performance standards, based on the expert advice of engineers, geologists, state regulators, and conservationists, each with many years of experience controlling the adverse effects of surface coal mining. By establishing measureable performance standards rather than mandating specific techniques, the new regulations allowed states to develop their own creative approaches to mining techniques and environmental controls. By 1983, all twenty-four major coal-producing states had primacy and 99 percent of the operating coal mines in the country were under state regulatory control, as envisioned by Congress when it enacted SMCRA.[17]

OSM also reached agreement with American Indian tribes regarding the regulation of coal mining on their reservations.[18] Meanwhile, it reorganized to reflect its changed role from direct regulation to oversight:[19] technical centers were established in Denver and Pittsburgh, thirteen field offices and six area offices were created and the number of field locations was reduced from forty-two to twenty-two.[20] Nonetheless, OSM continued its role as set forth in SMCRA,[21] and developed new initiatives and national incentives.[22]

SMCRA also established the Abandoned Mine Land (AML) program to reclaim mined lands across the country and a fund to restore those lands.[23] In the first three years of the Reagan administration, OSM approved twenty-two of the twenty-five coal-mining states' AML programs and one was added later. Prior to 1981, only two state AML programs had been approved.[24]

The Interior Department's implementation and enforcement of SMCRA under Reagan was not without controversy. Environmental groups, as well as coal mine operators and their trade associations, frequently filed litigation.[25] The administration, however, did just what the law anticipated—the states operated the regulatory programs and the OSM provided oversight.

Federal Coal Leasing and the Carter Approach

In 1920, Congress enacted the Mineral Leasing Act, which placed coal, as well as oil and gas and other hydrocarbons, within the discretionary leasing authority of the secretary of the interior through, after its creation in 1946, the Bureau of Land Management.[26] Under the Mineral Leasing Act, the BLM leased coal competitively in areas where coal was known to exist and non-competitively outside of those areas. For areas where coal was not known to exist, the BLM issued prospecting permits; if the holder of the permit discovered coal in commercial quantities he was entitled to a preference right lease to mine the deposit.

In 1971, the BLM concluded that, because the Mineral Leasing Act contained no requirement for diligent development, coal leasing had increased dramatically from 1945 to 1970, but coal production had fallen. Therefore, the BLM declared a moratorium on coal leasing and commenced development of a new coal leasing program, which was introduced in 1974. In the meantime, however, the National Environmental Policy Act (NEPA) was in its ascendancy. NEPA increased paperwork for agencies required to perform its mandated analysis, leading to lawsuits by environmental groups unhappy with the depth of that analysis. That litigation in turn led to judicial interpretations of the proper level of analysis required by NEPA, which led to more paperwork by federal bureaucrats, and on the circle went, endlessly it seemed.[27] The BLM's new coal leasing program fell prey to the vicissitudes of NEPA and its cycle of litigation and new rulemaking.

In June of 1976, the Ford administration prevailed in a critical NEPA challenge before the Supreme Court of the United States, which sustained the administration's more limited view of NEPA's requirements as it prepared for coal leasing in Montana and Wyoming's Powder River

Basin.[28] In 1977, however, the Carter administration lost before a federal district court in an environmental group's NEPA challenge to the coal leasing program.[29] Lacking any enthusiasm for coal leasing, the Carter administration declined to appeal the ruling and embarked on the central planning mandated by the federal judge, an approach that found much support in the administration. In fact, as an indication of its mindset, one Interior agency "toyed with the idea of hiring a U.S. specialist in Soviet economic planning to look at the federal [coal] leasing program," which was rejected ultimately as "politically too risky."[30] Nonetheless, Carter's Interior Department spent the rest of the decade attempting to impose the vague, vaporous visions of central planners on America's federal coal leasing program.[31]

Congress, meanwhile, under heavy pressure from environmentalists, was busy changing the ground rules. In 1976, Congress passed the Federal Coal Leasing Amendment Act, which amended the Mineral Leasing Act by eliminating new non-competitive coal leasing, requiring diligent development and continued operations on coal leases, mandating receipt of fair market value for leases sold, and directing the BLM to assure maximum economic recovery.[32] That same year, Congress passed the Federal Land Policy and Management Act (FLPMA) requiring that the BLM assure public participation in its land use planning regarding the multiple use of its resources and reinforcing the BLM's procedural duties under NEPA.[33] Finally, in 1977, Congress passed SMCRA, which included standards for permitting surface coal mining on federal leases and criteria for designating federal land as "unsuitable" for coal mining.[34] Pursuant to those laws and consistent with the demands of the environmental groups and a federal court, Carter's Interior Department in 1979 adopted a new BLM coal leasing program.

In their response to Carter's federal coal leasing program, the authors of *Mandate for Leadership* did not pull any punches:

> The moratorium on new coal leases initiated in 1971 continues in force today, nearly a decade later. While that moratorium could well have ended in mid-1978 or early 1979 with a favorable ruling from the U.S. Supreme Court followed by

lease sales in mid-1979, the Carter Administration refused to appeal and condemned the nation to nearly four years of more studies, reviews and statements. That lengthy process will finally end in early 1981 with the first scheduled lease sale.[35]

Nonetheless, *Mandate* concluded, "America's need for development of its coal resources clearly outweighs the administrative and regulatory deficiencies of the Carter Administration's coal program."[36] Therefore, "the new Administration must permit the 1981 coal lease sale to take place...."

Reagan's Interior Department Leases Federal Coal

The Reagan administration, recognizing that "[l]ess than 1% of federal coal lands were under lease and new leasing had been at a virtual standstill since 1971" and that "35% of the coal ... will come from public lands," moved to implement the Carter coal leasing program.[37] From January of 1981 to October of 1983, the Interior Department leased 2.5 billion tons of federal coal, which netted $128.6 million in bonuses, including 1.5 billion tons of coal beneath 32,000 acres in Montana and Wyoming. By comparison, from 1973 through 1980, only 387 million tons of federal coal were leased and netted bonuses of only $2 million, that is, a tenth of the price per ton netted during the early years of the Reagan administration. In 1983 alone, the department leased 800 million tons of coal beneath 18,609 acres, which translates into 3.2 tons for each American citizen.[38]

In July of 1983, however, Congress once again involved itself in the federal coal leasing program, this time by passing a law, which Reagan signed, requiring the secretary of the interior to appoint a commission to review coal leasing procedures and to report to Congress by January of 1984 on methods to ensure the receipt of fair market value for leases.[39] Federal coal leasing was suspended, after resolution of a short-lived but still surviving constitutional challenge, to await the results of what became known as the Linowes (II) Commission.[40]

After receipt of the Linowes Commission's report in February of 1984, the Interior Department began preparing a new "Federal Coal Management Program" to implement the commission's recommendations. In October of 1985, a Final Environmental Impact Statement, as required by NEPA, was released, which permitted continuation of the federal coal leasing program.[41] Under the revised program, federal coal leasing was modified to enhance its flexibility; to be orderly and predictable for state and local governments and for industry; to promote competition, assure fair market value, ensure adequate data, and clarify surface owner consent; and to establish standards for inspection, production verification, maximum economic recovery, logical mining units, and diligence. The new program also mandated the resolution of non-competitive coal leases within two years and established the lease by application (LBA) process.[42] Thus, the Reagan administration, given the opportunity that resulted from the controversy with regard to fair market value, did exactly what *Mandate for Leadership* recommended—it reformed the coal leasing program.[43]

Furthermore, although no additional formal federal coal leases were issued during the Reagan Administration, a substantial amount of federal coal was leased by means of the emergency and LBA process. Then, in January of 1990, in accordance with the federal coal leasing program, the Powder River Basin region was decertified to allow leasing through the LBA process to permit mines to maintain production.[44] Also thanks in part to federal coal leases issued by the Reagan administration, Wyoming is now the nation's leading coal producer. Wyoming's production, mostly from the Powder River Basin, exceeds that of the next top six coal-producing states combined.[45]

The Interior Department attempted to lease coal in another region of the Mountain West, the San Juan Basin in the northwestern corner of New Mexico, which comprises some 1.9 million acres of land and minerals in an area commonly known as "checkerboard lands."[46] Within the area lay 75,000 acres of noncompetitively leased coal in private hands (Preference Right Lease Applications or PRLAs), as well as twenty-four federally owned tracts with as much as 1.32 billion tons of coal.[47] Coal leasing advocates believed mining of the coal over a forty-year period

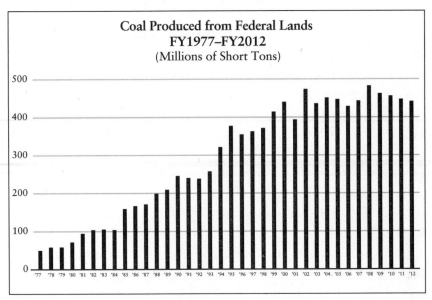

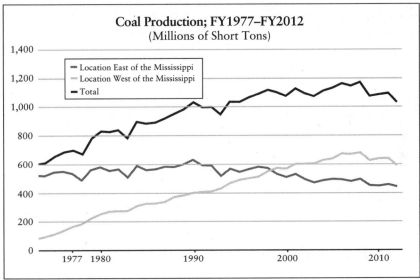

would generate two thousand high-paying jobs with an annual income of $45 million to the local economy, plus up to $288 million in severance taxes, and $700 million in royalties to be shared equally by New Mexico and the federal government.[48]

Developing the coal reserves was problematic, however, because of three wilderness study areas (WSAs) and unresolved land claims by the

Hopi and the Navajo. In time, an intrastate battle erupted among a Democrat governor, a deeply divided (along party lines) congressional delegation, American Indians seeking to vindicate their claims, and environmental groups bent on savaging the Interior Department and its officials.[49] The leasing of federal coal lands stalled, therefore, and development of the PRLAs was subjected to months of environmental studies after earlier litigation victories by environmental groups. New Mexico ultimately developed a compromise that resulted in the designation of two new wilderness areas in the San Juan Basin—the Bisti and the De-na-zin—and continuation of one area as a WSA, legislation that President Reagan signed.[50] Ironically, the Navajo obtained rights to the coal beneath the WSA and an additional 29,000 acres. It would fall to future administrations, if any supported developing America's rich coal reserves, to untie this Gordian knot.

Although it was Carter who set the goal of a billion tons of coal, it was Reagan who achieved it. In 1990, the United States produced more than a billion tons of coal, much of it from federal leases in the West, but the majority of it from mines in states east of the Mississippi now in charge of their own reclamation programs.[51]

Ironically, given the abuse heaped upon the Reagan administration for its Powder River Basin coal leases, environmental groups and leftist politicians continue to hammer away at the alleged "give away" involved in leasing federal coal, even when the ones doing the leasing are part of the Obama administration.[52] Recently, a coal lease sale in Wyoming's Powder River Basin was condemned by a Massachusetts think-tank, which asserted that it was a "wake up call."[53] It seems the drumbeat against developing the country's federally owned energy resources never ends.

The Obama Administration's War on Coal

It is one thing when extremist environmental groups attack every energy-producing, job-creating, revenue-generating proposal for developing the nation's natural resources;[54] it is quite another when the president of the United States and his highest officials declare war on a specific energy resource, the hard-working men and women who produce it, and the states and communities that depend on it for jobs, revenue, and their way of life.

Unfortunately, that is just what the Obama administration is doing with its "War on Coal." Where to begin? Perhaps with the words of Senator Obama himself, "[I]f somebody wants to build a coal-powered plant, they can; it's just that it will bankrupt them. ..."[55] Senator Obama intended to bankrupt them by means of cap and trade federal legislation, which died in the Senate.[56] Not to be denied, the Environmental Protection Agency embarked upon an administrative cap and trade plan starting with a finding in December of 2009 that greenhouse gases "threaten the public health and welfare of current and future generations," the first step in regulating them.[57]

Then in an unprecedented action, the EPA challenged a permit issued by the U.S. Army Corps of Engineers for the Mingo Logan Mine in Logan County, West Virginia. The permit had been granted after seven years of study and thousands of pages of documentation—the most thoroughly studied proposed mine in American history.[58] Meanwhile, the EPA fell into frenzied rule-making under the Clean Air Act. One set of rules, the EPA acknowledged, could be complied with only by abandoning coal and shifting to natural gas.[59] Another rule allegedly targets mercury—that is solely the public relations cover for it—by assuming a "Frankenplant" that can achieve emission goals as to all pollutants, which have been achieved only by separate plants targeting each separate pollutant.[60] It is not just the EPA; the OSM moved to overturn a stream protection rule, five years and 40,000 comments in the making, by prohibiting the disturbance of any stream with a "biological community," whatever that term means, including ephemeral streams that are dry most of the year.[61] OSM's plan will impact dramatically longstanding, accepted mining practices throughout the country, with "devastating" economic impacts in West Virginia.[62] Across the Appalachian region, as many as 220,000 jobs and $14 to $20 billion in coal production would be lost.[63] And the list goes on and on.

Layoffs in coal country have begun. That may be of little interest in San Francisco, where Obama coyly disclosed his plans to "bankrupt them," but one can rest assured how Ronald Reagan would respond.

———————

Oil and gas on federal lands across the country; rich energy resources beneath the ocean; nearly a third of the continent devoted to economic activity and recreation; parks, refuges, and wilderness areas that are the envy of the world; untold riches in strategic and critical minerals; and tons of coal to burn—all controlled by a federal department little known to most Americans. Yet there is even more in the department of "everything else."

CHAPTER ELEVEN

A DEPARTMENT OF MISCELLANY[1]

"I'm sure you remember Vietnam—there was a war there once. Finally history is catching up with what has to be our most lied about war.... Do you have the feeling we should apologize to those young men of ours who fought [there] so bravely under so many handicaps and with so little appreciation?"
—RONALD REAGAN, FEBRUARY 1978[2]

Volunteerism–Coast to Coast

In May of 1982, President Reagan announced the creation of the Statue of Liberty–Ellis Island Centennial Commission, chaired by Lee Iacocca, to prepare the neoclassical sculpture, designed by Frederic Bartholdi and a gift from France, on Liberty Island in the New York Harbor for the 1986 centennial celebration.[3] The commission became the most successful public-private partnership in history; it was the Reagan administration's marquee project to restore and protect public facilities without spending tax dollars.

The National Park Service, which has administered the Statue of Liberty since 1933 and nearby Ellis Island since 1965, had discovered that the colossal Roman goddess of freedom was in need of substantial restoration. With the NPS as its public partner, the nonprofit Statue of Liberty–Ellis Island Foundation raised hundreds of millions of dollars and employed "[a]n army of architects, historians, engineers, and almost 1,000 laborers" to restore Lady Liberty.[4] After the statue was closed in 1984, the NPS supervised the project.[5] On July 4, 1986, President Reagan, accompanied by French President François Mitterrand, presided over the rededication—the high point of Liberty Weekend, which ran from July 4 through 6. The celebration, in which fireworks filled the skies and tall ships the harbor, was broadcast to 1.5 billion people in fifty-one countries.[6]

After the restoration of the Statue of Liberty, the Interior Department, the NPS, and the private foundation began work on Ellis Island, "the largest historical restoration in the history of the United States."[7] By the end of the Reagan administration, over $300 million had been raised for the Ellis Island Immigration Museum, which included "theaters, libraries, an oral history recording studio, and exhibits on the immigration experience," as well as rooms restored to appear as they did at the height of immigrant transit through Ellis Island.[8] Remarkably, the work was completed two years ahead of schedule, a mere two years after Reagan left office.[9]

Since then, more historic buildings on Ellis Island have been restored, the museum library and oral history studio have been expanded and upgraded, and the Children's Orientation Center and the Ellis Island Living Theatre have been added. The foundation that the Reagan Interior Department established has raised over $600 million in private funds, contributed generously, and ensured a welcoming experience for forty million visitors since the site opened in 1990.[10]

A few days after the rededication of the Statue of Liberty, President Reagan spoke in the Rose Garden to honor nearly a hundred individuals and organizations for their personal commitment to America's natural and cultural resources as part of the "Take Pride in America" campaign:

Our beautiful land is blessed from sea to shining sea with bountiful natural and cultural resources on federal, state and local lands. We are also blessed that the American people possess a unique volunteer spirit rooted in our frontier tradition.... Through our stewardship of these natural wonders and great monuments of history, we can express our love for our country, our pride in America, and our desire to preserve our resources and heritage for the future![11]

President Reagan had launched the campaign, in response to a request from the secretary of the interior, in his 1986 state of the union address, to encourage a sense of stewardship for public lands and resources and to promote the participation of private citizens and organizations in their care.[12] A partnership of federal agencies, states, and private groups, the campaign grew out of the recognition that the care of public lands and resources is too big a job for federal employees if "Americans did not care about those lands."[13] Take Pride in America included a public service advertising campaign and provided recognition to "outstanding stewardship activities."[14]

The public service campaign featured "good guys"—Clint Eastwood, Charles Bronson, and Louis Gossett, Jr.—in public service announcements (PSAs) that were distributed to nine hundred television stations, four hundred cable outlets, eight thousand newspapers, and six thousand radio stations. Ten thousand radio PSAs featuring Reagan administration cabinet officers were released, and Jack Elrod's *Mark Trail*, the nationally syndicated comic strip, highlighted the "Take Pride in America" campaign. The private sector volunteered its time and services, valued at well over $50 million, in producing, printing, and airing the PSAs.[15] The next year there were over five hundred nominations for the "Take Pride in America" awards. The ninety projects that were honored represented the involvement of more than 260,000 individuals.[16] The program was codified by Congress in 1990 and today operates, as it began, out of the Interior Department with the slogan "It's Your Land, Lend A Hand."[17]

Reagan, American Indians, and Self-Determination

Governor Ronald Reagan burnished his environmental credentials in 1972 when he opposed construction of a federally approved dam at Dos Rios, California, which would have flooded lands occupied by the Yuki tribe.[18] He also secured his reputation as a defender of private property rights and the sanctity of contracts into which the federal government enters—in that case, a treaty with American Indians. "It's about time we lived up to treaties," he declared, "We're not going to flood them out."[19] Then, in 1978, as he prepared for his presidential run, Reagan sided with an American Indian in a radio address chiding President Carter for his refusal to accept the gift of a ceremonial headdress from Chief Redbird of the Cherokee Nation, breaking the chief's spirit and a tradition going back to President Woodrow Wilson. The governor concluded, "Yes [Chief Redbird] is despondent—he must also be somewhat bewildered by the ways of the white man."[20]

In 1980, Reagan intended to leave no confusion as to where he stood on issues important to American Indians. "I believe deeply in the rule of law[,] adherence to treaties and court decisions[, and] Indian tribal government through the fulfillment of treaty obligations."[21] He vowed to consult with American Indians and said he supported tribal self-determination. Reagan favored continuation of the federal-tribal trust relationship and opposed the policy of termination, which was designed to assimilate Indians into "mainstream society," as socially "devastating," "greatly discredited," and "morally and legally unacceptable."[22]

The implementation of Reagan's policy of a "government-to-government" relationship between the United States and over 550 tribal governments and nearly two million tribal members—especially the nearly 800,000 American Indians living on fifty million acres of reservation land—fell to the secretary of the interior, the assistant secretary for Indian affairs, and the Bureau of Indian Affairs (BIA), "the oldest federal agency in continuous existence."[23]

When asked at his confirmation hearing if he supported the new president's policy regarding American Indians, Secretary Watt replied, "Without reservation." When his unintended pun brought a wave of laughter, he added, "May we back up on that? I want the Indians to have control of their reservations and I support it enthusiastically—maybe that's better!"[24] Reagan nominated the first American Indian raised on a reservation, Kenneth L. Smith of Oregon's Wasco Tribe, to the position of assistant secretary for Indian affairs, a post that required Senate confirmation, after extensive consultation with elected tribal leaders.[25]

In January of 1983, after instructing the cabinet council working group on Indian policy that "this Administration should strongly reaffirm our Nation's commitment to the government-to-government relationship between the federal government and federally recognized tribes,"[26] Reagan issued "the first major presidential Indian policy statement" in over ten years.[27] The statement affirmed critical conservative principles, including distrust of federal power, confidence in the government closest to the people, and federalism and dual sovereignty, especially Reagan's "New Federalism," his policy of devolving federal programs and authority to states and localities.[28] Most importantly, however, the statement affirmed "the government-to-government relationship" among federal authorities, the states, and federally recognized tribes.[29] Unfortunately, Reagan's powerful support for self-determination and his purposeful abjuration of termination did not receive the media attention it deserved.[30]

What did get media attention, instead, was Watt's statement in a radio interview, "If you want an example of the failure of socialism, don't go to Russia, come to America and go to the Indian reservations." Noting that reservations suffer from high rates of drug abuse, alcoholism, unemployment, divorce, and venereal disease, he observed, "Every social problem is exaggerated because of socialistic government policies."[31] Of course, the media did not cover Watt's conclusion, "We ought to give [American Indians] freedom. We ought to give them liberty. We ought to give them their rights. But we treat them as incompetent wards."[32] The press ignored similar statements by Representative John Patrick Williams, a Democrat from Montana, who referred to reservations as "the worst ghettos in America," and Senator Barry Goldwater, the legendary Arizona Republican and 1964 nominee for president who said reservations feature "people living in just as poor, squalid conditions as you'll find in El Salvador or Ghana."[33] Reagan caused a similar stir a few years later when, on a visit to the Soviet Union, he said that the federal government should not have permitted Indians to retain their "primitive lifestyles" and that they should "join us" and "be citizens along with the rest of us."[34]

Reagan's and Watt's remarks were doubly problematic. First, they were considered insulting to American Indians personally.[35] Yet Watt had attacked failed leadership, specifically the fact that "the Indian people of America have been abused by the U.S. government for too many years."[36] Second, the remarks suggested a policy of termination of the reservations and of the federal government's trust responsibilities.[37] No such retreat was intended or occurred.[38]

Following Reagan's 1983 Indian policy statement, Congress passed laws that reinstated an Oregon tribe that had been terminated as a federally recognized tribe, repudiated a resolution from the 1950s calling for an end to the federal-tribal relationship, and revised the Indian Self-Determination and Educational Assistance Act of 1975 to permit more contracting opportunities for tribes.[39] Earlier, consistent with Reagan's commitment to a government-to-government relationship, Congress passed the Indian Tribal Governmental Tax Status Act, which treats tribal governments equally with state and local governments for some tax purposes,[40] and the Indian Mineral Development Act of 1982, which provides Tribes with flexibility in the development and sale of mineral resources, including joint ventures with mineral developers.[41]

Meanwhile, as the Interior Department worked with tribes to identify mechanisms to improve the economies of reservations, such as tax incentives to stimulate investment and greater federal loans to reservations,[42] the Reagan administration addressed the issue of Indian gaming.[43] Objections to Indian gaming by the states were resolved by the Supreme Court of the United States, which held in a six-to-three ruling that "State regulation would impermissibly infringe on tribal government," citing in support, President Reagan's Indian policy of 1983.[44] In 1987, Reagan signed the Indian Gaming Regulatory Act,[45] which one writer called "a godsend for Indian country."[46] Eight years later, Indian gaming grossed

$5.5 billion; during 2004, Indian gaming grossed $19.4 billion;[47] and in 2011, Indian gaming grossed $27.2 billion.[48]

Hypocrisy and Hetch Hetchy

On April 18, 1906, San Francisco was devastated by an earthquake and fire.[49] Suddenly, its need for a reliable source of fresh water became urgent. The city's picturesque location on a dry, sandy peninsula left it perpetually short of fresh water, but there was a potential source in the Sierra Mountains just 150 miles east, where the Tuolumne River flows rough and deep in the Hetch Hetchy Valley. City engineers had concluded, as far back as 1881, that if the river were dammed, it could generate hydroelectric power. There was one problem. In 1890, Congress had created the Yosemite National Park, putting the Hetch Hetchy Valley off limits to the economic use proposed by San Francisco. After the earthquake, however, the city filed a reservoir site application with the secretary of the interior, and it was granted in May of 1908. A final decision would be made by Congress and President Woodrow Wilson, but not until 1913, and during the interim, the Hetch Hetchy debate would shake the conservation movement as mightily as the earthquake that had rattled San Francisco.

The battle—between conservation ("wise use") and preservation— was a new one. There had never been a nationwide, public dispute about putting nature to productive use. The disagreement, which split two great friends and wild land proponents, Gifford Pinchot and John Muir, was not over whether the interest of nature or the interest of mankind should prevail. It was about which *human need* was paramount. Pinchot thought "the benefits to be derived from [Hetch Hetchy's] use as a reservoir" were superior in importance to preserving "the present swampy floor of the valley...." Muir thought that San Franciscans, "instead of lifting their eyes to the God of the Mountains, lift them to the Almighty Dollar." Muir believed he was doing the Lord's work by preserving His Creation: "Dam Hetch Hetchy! As well dam for water-tanks the people's cathedrals and churches, for no holier temple has ever been consecrated by the heart of man."[50] Others saw God's will differently: "I admire the beauties of nature and deplore the desecration of God's Creation," said one congress-man during the debate, "yet when the two considerations come in conflict the conservation of nature should yield to the conservation of human welfare, health, and life."[51]

Although in the end Muir lost, Hetch Hetchy Valley became a *cause célèbre*, and the conservation movement gained a symbol as powerful as the *Maine* or the Alamo. Three years later, a powerful bureaucratic entity capable of fighting back for individual parks, the National Park Service, was created. The NPS and the movement that gave birth to it were later able to challenge successfully an attempt to construct a dam at Dinosaur National Monument in Utah.[52] Ironically, they were successful in part because they challenged the efficiency and economics of the dam at Echo Park.[53]

Thus the battle lines were drawn between those who rallied to the cry "Hetch Hetchy" and those who did not. Then, nearly seventy-five years later, the lines blurred when Secretary Hodel placed a call to his law school classmate Michael McCloskey, the chairman of the Sierra Club, the old-line environmental organization that had suffered its first major defeat when O'Shaughnessy Dam was built and the Hetch Hetchy Valley was flooded. "Mike," said Hodel, "what would you think if we proposed to restore the Hetch Hetchy Valley?"[54] Then Hodel went public with his idea:

> With few exceptions, the major scenic areas are now protected. What's being considered now are ways to better use existing parkland. Consider the Hetch Hetchy dam in California. The decision to flood that valley would be unthinkable today. Behind my idea to drain the reservoir is the need for additional land in Yosemite to accommodate some of the crowds. You could add a million acres of mountain land there and you wouldn't decrease the crowding in Yosemite Valley. It occurred to me that what you need is a second Yosemite Valley.[55]

San Francisco's mayor, Dianne Feinstein, now a U.S. senator, responded angrily: "I'll do all in my power to fight it." She declared the water from Hetch Hetchy a "birthright" of San Franciscans and the proposal "dumb, dumb, dumb."[56] In October of 1987, Hodel, accompanied by Feinstein and environmental group leaders, stood atop the O'Shaughnessy Dam at mid-span and declared, "The vision of this gorgeous valley being restored is exciting to all of us."[57] The following month, the Interior Department's Bureau of Reclamation released its analysis.[58]

The irony that the City of San Francisco—a hotbed of environmental rectitude, birthplace of the Sierra Club and Friends of the Redwoods—and its political leaders would battle a plan to enhance the environment in their backyard was not lost on others across the country who had been on the receiving end of environmental schemes for decades.[59] The hypocrisy of their position, however, did not give Bay area politicians pause. They continued to assail the Reagan administration on various issues, such as offshore oil and gas development, wilderness designation, and reclamation projects for other communities.[60]

In 2003, Hodel appeared in a video featuring the actor Harrison Ford—"Hetch Hetchy: Yosemite's Lost Valley"—urging continued study of the proposal to drain the reservoir. Then, in 2005, Hodel published a column in the *San Francisco Chronicle* urging the citizens, with their "reputation of high-minded environmentalism," to join in a search for a method of restoring Hetch Hetchy while meeting the city's needs for water, electricity, and revenue. Hodel even cited a success story from the Reagan administration, "the restoration of the Statue of Liberty," which was supported solely by charitable contributions "not with taxpayers' money. And, it was a great project."[61]

Trust Territory of the Pacific Islands

The Trust Territory of the Pacific begins 1,800 miles west of Hawaii and stretches to within five hundred miles of the Philippines.[62] Although this rectangular area—often referred to as Micronesia as it spreads north from the Equator for 1,300 miles—is nearly the size of the continental United States, the 2,100 islands scattered across its three million square miles of open sea total 707 square miles, an area but two-thirds the size of Rhode Island.

These islands, which had been occupied continuously by colonial powers since the sixteenth century, were taken from Germany by Japan during World War I and were established as a Japanese mandate by the League of Nations after that war. They then became household names in World War II as the navy and Marine Corps used them as stepping-stones in the drive across the central Pacific north to Japan: Kwajalein and Eniwetok (Marshalls), Saipan and Tinian (Marianas), and Peleliu (Carolines).[63] Even before the end of the war, the United States made clear that it intended to keep whatever Micronesian bases it believed were necessary to protect its security.[64] In fact, John Foster Dulles went so far as to caution the UN General Assembly that, if the demands of the United States regarding Micronesia were not met, the United States would simply ignore the United Nations and continue its occupation.

In July of 1947, by a joint resolution of Congress, the United States accepted a "strategic trusteeship" over the "former Japanese mandate islands," which, under the terms of the trust agreement between the United States and the UN, gave America the type of control over the islands that was just short of outright annexation. Nonetheless, under the terms of that trust agreement, the United States was required to "promote the development of the inhabitants of the Trust Territory toward self-government or independence as appropriate."[65]

The Trust Territory, which includes the Northern Mariana Islands, the Federated States of Micronesia, the Marshall Islands, and Palau, was first administered by the navy, but in 1951 responsibility was assigned to the Department of the Interior, which negotiated "very cautiously" to protect the United States' "future strategic needs in the area."[66] By the early 1970s, it became apparent that negotiations would proceed along separate tracks as to the Northern Mariana Islands, the Federated States of Micronesia, the Marshall Islands, and Palau.

President Reagan's policy regarding the territories and his instructions to Watt, Clark, and Hodel mirrored his policy regarding American Indians: ensure self-determination and enable economic growth and stability, primarily by rebuilding the private sector.[67] In 1982, the United States entered into a compact of free association with the Federated States of Micronesia (FSM), which includes part of the Caroline Islands. In 1983, the United States and the Marshall Islands entered into a compact of free association. Plebiscites followed in each country, and in early 1986, Congress approved the two compacts.[68] Earlier, the Northern Mariana Islands had entered into a covenant to become a commonwealth of the United States. Although Congress approved the agreement, portions had not gone into effect. Then, in early 1986, the United States and the Republic of Palau also entered into a compact of free association, which was approved by Congress; however, as of 1986, the political status of Palau was yet to be determined. The Interior Department, consistent with the president's instructions, sought to terminate the trusteeship unilaterally, that is, without resort to the UN Security Council. The department insisted that the trusteeship terminated on the date the president declared it at an end. Therefore, in late 1986, the United States advised the United Nations of the status of its agreements with the island countries. Thereupon, in November of 1986, Reagan announced freely associated state status for the FSM and the Marshall Islands as well as commonwealth status for the Northern Mariana Islands, which made its domiciliaries citizens. Reagan declared, "I welcome the Commonwealth of the Northern Mariana Islands into the American family and congratulate our new fellow citizens."[69]

As negotiations led to the independence of the island nations, the Interior Department sought to strengthen the local governments while it reduced its own physical presence. Three and a half decades of trusteeship had cost the United States nearly three billion dollars with no end in sight. Most residents were employed by local governments whose management systems and infrastructure were antiquated, and the private sector lacked an incentive to invest. Governments, consequently, overspent and required a bailout from Congress. With the bipartisan support of Congress, the Interior Department exercised "tough love," aiding the territories' efforts to modernize and helping them to attract investments, but ending their ability to tap into federal funds.[70] The eight years of the Reagan administration saw "the infusion of millions of dollars in capital improvements to set the stage for economic diversification and growth that are critical to … self-sufficiency goals."[71] Finally, "after a massive reduction in the Trust Territory government and federal staff in Saipan, in 1987 the Office of High Commissioner was abolished."[72]

Meanwhile, one Pacific island that had belonged to the United States since it was ceded by Spain in 1898 at the end of the Spanish-American War—Guam—did not come under Interior's supervision until 1950, when Congress made it into a territory.[73] Because it is the largest island in the western Pacific between Hawaii and the Philippines, Guam's economic and political relationship with the United States has turned exclusively on America's military needs in the Pacific.[74] Guam—whose license plates bear the motto "Where America's day begins"—lies 1,550 miles from Tokyo but 3,700 miles from Honolulu. Nonetheless, Guamanians took pride in being "more American than Americans," which they demonstrated by their service in the Vietnam War.[75] Today, their economy depends on tourism and the U.S. military.

Although Guam is governed by an elected government and legislature, it elects only a non-voting delegate to the U.S. House of Representatives, and it has no vote for president in the Electoral College.[76] Guam's future, whether as a commonwealth, a state, a territory with the Northern Mariana Islands, or an independent nation, will eventually be determined by a plebiscite. Unfortunately, Guam law currently restricts voting in the plebiscite to "Chamorro," a racial designation referring to the original inhabitants of Guam and their descendants, who constitute 36 percent of Guam's voting-age population. Excluded are most Caucasian, African-American, Korean, Chinese, and Filipino citizens of the United States living on Guam and registered to vote in elections. Although the U.S. Constitution and federal voting laws apply to Guam, the plebiscite campaign continues unabated.[77] Even worse, it appears to have drawn the financial support of Obama's Interior Department. The Department of Justice's Civil Rights Division, moreover, has turned a blind eye to this abuse.[78] A class action lawsuit has been filed, however, and the issue may ultimately be decided by the Supreme Court of the United States.[79]

Guns on the Mall

In December of 1981, I received a telephone call from my fellow Marine Jim Webb. We did not meet as Marines but as lawyers for House of Representatives committees after publication of Webb's *Fields of Fire*.[80] When I read the lengthy, laudatory write-up of Webb's first novel in, of all places, the "Style" section of the *Washington Post*, I was struck by our similarities: Scots-Irish parents from Kentucky and Arkansas, Marine Corps veterans, law school graduates, attorneys as wives, and now Republican lawyers ("Minority Counsels") on Capitol Hill. Then I read the kicker. The *Post* writer asked Webb his opinion of Jane Fonda. "Jane Fonda can kiss my ass," he replied. I reached for the telephone.

After meeting, we did not see each other often; we had demanding jobs—and he, a "Renaissance Man," had multiple undertakings—but we had a bond that stretched back to Scotland, included the crossing of the Atlantic Ocean, generations of travel down the Appalachian Mountains into the South, and, during the depths of the Great Depression, the emigration of our parents to the West.[81] Most importantly, we were Marines; we knew we could depend on each other. When, sometime in 1981, I learned of Webb's disappointment with the plan for the Vietnam Veterans Memorial, I offered my help.

Vietnam veterans—angry over their mistreatment while in uniform, the lack of honor given them when the war was over for the price they and their brothers paid, and the lies told among America's elite about who they were and what they did[82]—wanted a bit of the respect they never got. They wanted a monument. Webb joined in the effort. They created a foundation, raised funds, convinced Congress to pass legislation, and held a contest to select the design.[83] Along the way, however, they had been persuaded that the winner should not be selected by them; so they turned that decision over to a panel of art and architecture experts, none of whom was a Vietnam veteran.

The veterans were excited. It seemed that their dream of a memorial to honor those they had left behind and those who came back would become a reality. Then, in May of 1981, the winning design was announced. It was a shocker. Two black walls of granite descend into a grave-like depression and meet at an angle, and upon them would be etched the names of the 58,272 who died in Vietnam.[84] At first veterans remained silent, then their fury erupted. It is "abstract, anonymous, inconspicuous, and meaningless [and] so unfulfilling as a lasting memorial that no memorial would be a better alternative," said Scott Brewer.[85]

Tom Carhart saw "a black trench that scars the Mall [with b]lack walls, the universal color of shame and sorrow and degradation."[86] Wrote Webb, it is "a black hole," and "a very strong nihilistic statement regarding the war," a statement that veterans do not believe.[87]

Because the secretary of the interior had to approve the design, I said in my first call to Webb regarding the Vietnam Veterans Memorial, "We can stop it." Then we would demand the changes that he and other veterans wanted. Webb begged off. They were negotiating. I told him to call me if things fell apart. Now, in December, Webb was calling me.

"They're just screwing with us," Webb related. "Can you get to Watt?" "Of course," I replied, but by now weeks had passed.[88] The secretary's failure to object earlier implied consent. I grabbed the most recent story on the memorial in the *Post* and read it carefully. There had been some changes: lights along the top for safety, a path for wheelchair access next to the Wall, and a mechanism for locating the names of loved ones and fallen brothers in arms, which were listed, not alphabetically, but by their dates of death. I reviewed the enabling legislation and concluded an argument could be made that the design was not final and that the clock for the secretary to object had not begun to run. I drafted an opinion and walked down the hall to Solicitor Bill Coldiron, a gray-haired Kentuckian and former army captain who participated in the D-Day landings and the Battle of the Bulge, and who later went west to Montana to teach and practice law. I showed him my draft and asked if he would sign it if need be. "Of course I'll sign it," he said.

I drafted a memorandum to Watt and made my case for why he should become involved and how, at this late date, he could.[89] On New Year's Eve he called me at home. He thanked me for my work during the past year and then asked what I wanted him to do about the memorial. "Stop it by sending a letter saying the design is not final, that you continue to have the right to object, and that you do object."

"I have a better idea," he replied. He usually did, especially in response to my Marine "high diddle diddle, right up the middle" approach. "Draft a letter saying that I am eager to sign off on the design and to advise me when the design is final so that I may approve expeditiously." That is what I wrote, what Watt signed, and what he mailed in early January of 1982.

The response was immediate: all hell broke loose! The park purists, the arts community, and the anti-Vietnam War activists all of whom favored the simple, sheer, stark funerary architecture, objected vociferously.[90] Soon, however, Virginia Senator John Warner, a Republican, agreed to help achieve a compromise, one that included The American Flag, a heroic statue, and an inscription. The flag would stand atop and behind the apex of the Wall, and the statue would be centered between the two walls where the rising ground levels out.[91] We had won. My memorandum to Watt and his response had forced an agreement to include elements to honor Vietnam veterans.

Frederick E. Hart, a remarkably accomplished and largely self-taught sculptor, whose design for the monument ranked third but who had submitted the top-ranking sculpture, was commissioned to produce the statue.[92] Watt and I visited his downtown studio as he created *Three Fighting Men*, using Marines from Quantico, Virginia, as his models. Meanwhile, the attack on the compromise continued. Maya Lin, who designed the Wall, accused Hart of "drawing mustaches on other people's portraits."[93] She was not alone.[94] All of it had its effect. The Commission on Fine Arts rejected the compromise and decreed that the flag and statue be "shunted off out of view" and "in the trees."[95]

Webb and I met with Hart, who agreed that the memorial should be unified according to the original compromise. I asked Watt to meet with Hart alone and make his decision based on Hart's recommendation. Watt refused. He wanted everyone in the room. On the morning of the meeting, I learned that Hart had signed off on a compromise: the flag and *Three Fighting Men* would not be hidden from view nor would they be at the Wall. Instead, they would be situated in a clearing south of the Wall. At the meeting with Watt, the "new compromise" was displayed on a scale model erected at eye level. After a short presentation, all attention turned to Watt, who twice asked where Hart, "the sculptor," wanted the statue placed. Twice Hart stayed with the compromise agreement he had made with the arts community. Watt thanked the participants and left the room. As I followed him into the hallway, he erupted. "You almost had me walk the plank for your Marines." Inside, Webb was furious with Hart. I was too, but later I understood. He was standing with his colleagues in the art community. I was standing with my Marines. Watt signed off, and the memorial was completed as it stands today.[96]

On November 11, 1984, Reagan made his first official appearance at the Vietnam Veterans Memorial when he spoke at the dedication of the *Three Fighting Men*.[97] When he returned to the White House, he wrote in his diary:

> I briefly addressed 100,000 people for the acceptance of the Memorial statue. It was quite an event and I hope it finally makes up for the way the Vietnam [r]eturnees were treated when they came home.[98]

Late on an October afternoon with winter in the air and signs of the shortening of the days about me, I visited the Vietnam Veterans Memorial. I walked down the west wall to see the name of my high school friend, John William Kobelin II—killed in 1969 while I was en route to Marine Corps OCS. I walked back to the *Three Fighting Men* and stared into their bronze faces; then I approached the flag and read anew the inscription that Webb wrote for its base, which bears the seals of the five military services:

> This flag represents the service rendered to our country by the veterans of the Vietnam War. The flag affirms the principles of freedom for which they fought and their pride in having served under difficult circumstances.

Standing beneath the flag as leaves swirled about on the pavement, I looked back at the *Three Fighting Men*, who appear to be staring across the dip in the ground at the Wall beyond, and then I realized that my friend Hart was right.

Webb and the others veterans were right, too. The flag and its inscription belong here, as do these *Three Fighting Men*.[99] In time, all who know the names on the Wall will have passed away and its meaning will have dimmed. In those days, however, the looks on the faces of the *Three*

Fighting Men and the flag above them will remind Americans of who those brave men were and what they did long ago and far away.[100]

Not much remains of what I did down the street at Interior, but perhaps time will bring back the decisions that merit resurrection—and many of them surely do. Whatever happens, this memorial—with the *Three Fighting Men*, the American Flag, and Jim Webb's inscription—still stands. I am thankful I was there to answer the telephone, write a memorandum, and plead a case with a secretary who heard me out, made a courageous decision, and took the action I recommended. It was an action supported fully by the president we both served—as demonstrated by his decision not to appear publicly at the memorial until the *Three Fighting Men* and the American Flag were there to complete it—Ronald Wilson Reagan.

CHAPTER TWELVE

THAT SHINING CITY: AMERICA AS A CHOSEN LAND[1]

*"I've spoken of the shining city all my political life, but
I don't know if I ever quite communicated what I saw when
I said it. But in my mind it was a tall, proud city built on rocks
stronger than oceans, windswept, God-blessed, and teeming
with people of all kinds living in harmony and peace; a city
with free ports that hummed with commerce and creativity."*
—RONALD REAGAN, JANUARY 11, 1989[2]

Things Are Bad

How bad are they? We know, for example, that the United States has a $16 trillion debt, and that the debt accumulated by the American people, which they will pass on to their children and grandchildren, grew more in the last four years than in the previous eight years.[3] What we did not know, at least until two experts pointed it out in the days following the November 2012 election, is that the debt is not $16 trillion but is, in reality, $87 trillion.[4] We are beginning to learn, moreover, that neither Congress nor the White House is serious about the deep, deep hole in which we find ourselves.[5]

When President Reagan took office, he faced the worst economy since the Great Depression.[6] What was the economy like when Barack Obama became president? Was it worse than the one Reagan faced—or not as bad?[7] That is irrelevant. What matters is what each man did and the results. Reagan slashed federal expenditures, cut taxes, and reduced regulation, including opening federal lands to the private sector to discover and develop energy. The economy bloomed. Obama launched a trillion-dollar "stimulus," unleashed federal lawyers and regulators, and increased taxes. The economy bombed.[8]

Meanwhile, in the three decades since Reagan left Washington, four successive presidents, an "environmental president," a president who was a willing tool of the environmental movement, a president distracted by a war on terror, and a president whose first job as a "community organizer" gave him common cause with environmental extremists—each abandoned Reagan's principled and far-sighted approach to management of the third of the country and the more than a billion offshore acres that are all owned by the American people.

It is true that the remarkable economic recovery ensured by Reagan's leadership and policies was in part to blame.[9] With the economy booming, the cost of doing what environmental groups demanded—increasing regulations, barring economic activity, and closing federal lands to public use—seemed to be *de minimis*. Over time, nearly the entire Outer Continental Shelf—that is, federal waters in the Atlantic, the eastern Gulf of Mexico, the Pacific, and adjoining most of Alaska, was placed off-limits to new exploration and production. Only the central and western Gulf of Mexico, where oil and gas drilling has gone on since 1947, remained mostly open. A major gold mine, the value of whose ore exceeded many billions of dollars of potential benefit to the United States, state and local economies, and thousands of workers, was closed off forever. Furthermore, the largest coal deposit in the United States was locked up, also forever, because "we can't have mines everywhere." How many billions of dollars would have surged through the economy had people in rural Utah developed that energy and deliver it to the people of southern California? Meanwhile, the Obama administration refuses to develop federal energy resources while heaping a crushing regulatory burden on the productive sectors of America's economy.[10]

There may have been a time—perhaps it was in the 1990s—when America could afford such myopic management of its resources, but that time has long since passed. Environmentalists like to talk about "sustainability," whatever that means in a fast-paced and technologically advanced country that can quickly and automatically green the economy by substituting, recycling, and conserving—all without federal mandates.[11] In the critically important context of the U.S. economy, however, sustainability has a clear and unequivocal meaning. Sustainable means "survival," as in, unless we stop doing what we are doing, we do not survive—not our economy, not our military, and not us as a free and prosperous people.

A reordering of our natural resources and environmental policies will not solve all of our problems, of course. Reagan recognized that truth, but he also knew that the manner in which the federal government manages its own property sets a tone for the rest of the country and shores up the fundamentals on which our economy is built, including by making use of the public's rich store-house of energy and minerals. Environmental groups will have a conniption fit, as they did three decades ago, but nothing short of admitting our hopeless state and accepting privation will please them.[12] They do not believe in the future where all enjoy abundantly; they believe only in one of shared—except for them—misery. That was basis for their inherent hostility toward Ronald Reagan. Unlike them, he saw a shining city on a hill and a time when America would hum "with commerce and creativity."

Return to the City on a Hill

Ronald Reagan, a devout Christian, was no utopian.[13] He knew this life brings pain and that no system of government, no leader, no special set of rules could guarantee otherwise.[14] He knew there was evil.[15] Throughout his life, therefore, he battled those who, in the name of effecting heaven on earth, denied freedom, subjugated their citizens, and

oppressed the people of the world whom they found in their way. He
focused on the individual—an individual created in the image of God.
As a result, the "hero" of his vision of the "city on a hill" was not the
city itself but each citizen within the city, enabled as a result of freedom
to live out "his story," the one intended by God.[16]

He believed that America, "the city on a hill," was not just a meta-
phor or a hackneyed political slogan, or even a claim of American exceptionalism—and Ronald Reagan believed that, by the grace of God,
America was exceptional—but much more, a "sacramental vision"[17] that
required him to defend the individual, and his God-given liberty. "Hence,
just as communist power represented the external threat, modern government expansion represented the internal threat to America's consecrated
mission of freedom."[18]

Ronald Reagan's battle against outside oppression—in his day, communism, but which he recognized to have come under the name of "Hit-
lerism," "Kaiserism," and "back through the ages in the name of every
conqueror that has ever set up a course of establishing his rule over
mankind"[19]—is well known. ("We win and they lose.") His fight against
internal oppression was no less vigorous; he distrusted the politicians in
Washington as deeply as he distrusted the Politburo in Moscow, but with
a difference:

> By temperament as well as by conviction, Reagan seemed to
> find it difficult to ever think or speak ill of other Ameri-
> cans.... America could make mistakes, but they were the
> mistakes of innocence—trusting others too much, doubting
> itself, forgetting its calling, following false prophets.[20]

Even in the 1960s, challenging supporters of "the liberal welfare
philosophy," Ronald Reagan sounded a deferential but still distrustful
tone:

> The overwhelming majority of our opponents does not know-
> ingly and would not knowingly support a Socialist or Com-
> munist cause. I am convinced that they are patriotic; they are

sincerely dedicated to humanitarian ideals. I think it would be foolish and immoral to infer anything else. At the same time, I think it would be foolish to let them have their way without opposition. If someone is setting fire to the house, it doesn't make much difference whether he is a deliberate arsonist or just a fool playing with matches. Our friends seek the answer to all problems of human need through government. Freedom can be lost inadvertently in this way.[21]

President Reagan did not just preach such forbearance, he practiced it. When the famous photographer Ansel Adams said, "I hate Reagan," the president asked for a meeting. Afterward, Reagan concluded that he had been speaking to ears that could not hear and went about his responsibilities regarding natural resources and environmental issues as he saw them. Meanwhile, he never stopped teaching that America was uniquely endowed by God with a responsibility to the people of the world. He urged the young, "If your parents haven't been teaching you what it means to be an American, let 'em know and nail 'em on it. That would be a very American thing to do."[22]

Whether in the governor's office in Sacramento or in the Oval Office in Washington, Reagan never saw himself as part of the government. Looking back in 1976 on his time as governor, he said, "I never in my life thought of seeking or holding public office and I'm still not quite sure how it all happened. In my own mind, I was a citizen representing my fellow citizens against the institution of government."[23]

Reagan saw himself as a citizen and a leader, and he urged Americans never to forget their high calling to preserve freedom—not for freedom's sake, but for the sake of each individual created in the image of God. Appropriately, he declared in his Farewell Address to the nation:

I know we have [stood for freedom], but in the past few years the world again—and in a way, we ourselves—rediscovered it.... They called it the Reagan revolution. Well, I'll accept that, but for me it always seemed more like the great rediscovery, a rediscovery of our values and our common sense.... But as long as we remember our first principles and believe in ourselves, the future will always be ours. And something else we learned: Once you begin a great movement, there's no telling where it'll end. We meant to change a nation, and instead we changed a world.[24]

With these words Ronald Reagan conveyed three truths about the "shining city on a hill." First, he said it was not about him. Ever self-effacing, even self-deprecating, Reagan had boundless confidence in the American people, as individuals, to achieve great things. A lifelong storyteller, he loved tales of Americans who, against all odds, did something great or wonderful or amazing. Americans did not need to be preached to or poked at or prodded. Left on their own, with the government out of the way, there was no end to the good that American men and women could accomplish, if they did not mind who got the credit.[25] In his last speech as president, Reagan himself did not take the credit. He knew that America would need good leaders in the future, but first it needed citizens who would fight for freedom.

Second, Reagan did not just overcome the Soviet Union. He first overcame the 1960s. That era—its "Blame America first" attitude, its anti-authoritarianism, and its embrace of moral relativism—came and went, but Ronald Reagan remained unchanged. He did as he had always done. He extolled the principles that the Founding Fathers had learned through harsh personal experience.[26] He defended not only individual liberties, but the rule of law. He knew that regulations imposed by unsupervised, unrestrained, and unaccountable bureaucrats lead to tyranny.[27] Reagan believed that America, by the grace of God, embraced values that were unknown in many other parts of the world, and he urged Americans to cling to them.

Finally, Reagan knew that hard times would come, that America would face new challenges to its liberty. The events of his own lifetime had taught him that freedom is only a generation away from extinction and that each generation has an obligation to pass on freedom to the next one. Hard times, however, did not relieve America of its responsibility to the people of the world to serve as "a shining city on a hill." Americans have a moral duty to recognize their country's greatness, to give thanks for it, and to proclaim it to the world as an example to others. Reagan would reject the misguided view that America is no more exceptional than any other country and should join the nations of their world in a sad march toward despotic rule and government-imposed privation.

Ronald Reagan, the oldest president, called out to generations of Americans not yet born and asked that they carry the torch of freedom and that they proceed, confident that America's greatest days lie ahead and that they share the vision he had of America as a beacon to the world—a city God-blessed and free and humming with commerce and creativity. "That's how I saw it," Reagan said, "and see it still."[28]

ACKNOWLEDGMENTS

My greatest debt is to Ronald Wilson Reagan. With each passing day, year, and decade, Americans learn how fortunate our country was to have him as our president at such an important time. We can only pray that we will be blessed with like-minded, far-sighted leaders in our future. I was privileged to serve in his administration.

My thanks goes out as well to the political team at Reagan's Interior Department, including James G. Watt, William P. Clark, and Donald Paul Hodel, as well as Robbie Aiken, Barry Allbright, Douglas P. Baldwin, David S. Brown, Garrey E. Carruthers, Ric Davidge, Emily DeRocco, Frank DuBois, Keith Eastin, Theodore J. Garrish, Alexander Good, J. Steven Griles, Katherine Gwin, William P. Horn, David G. Houston, Stanley W. Hulett, Dean K. Hunt, Bette S. Levin, Richard T. Montoya, Diane Kay Morales, J. Craig Potter, David C. Russell, William H. Satterfield, and Moody R. Tidwell III, for all they did during their service to President Reagan and for their support of my efforts, many suggestions, and steadfast willingness to allow me to interrupt them in their current pursuits. I am especially appreciative of the generous assistance of Messrs. Davidge, Griles, Hodel, Horn, Houston, Montoya, and

Potter in fact-checking, proofreading, and last-minute rescue efforts. Any errors that remain are my responsibility alone.

A portion of this manuscript is based on my personal experiences at Reagan's Interior Department with Watt, Clark, and Hodel, recollections that I refreshed by reviewing various contemporary records, including media reports, and by speaking and corresponding with others who were there with me or after I left the department in early 1984. My account of events to which I was not a party is based upon face-to-face and telephone discussions and electronic mail exchanges with individuals who participated in those events. Those conversations and exchanges took place between August 2012 and May 2013. I am satisfied these narratives are an accurate account of what took place.

President Reagan and his secretaries of the interior were well served by career professionals. I received able assistance from Thomas M. Gernhofer, Anne G. Giesecke, Abraham Haspel, Tom Readinger, and Cathi Townsend.

I am indebted to all those who responded to my pleas for more facts, citations, documents, and photographs as well as quick answers to a host of assorted questions. Those include Ron Arnold, author of *At the Eye of the Storm: James Watt and the Environmentalists*; and C. Brant Short, author of *Ronald Reagan and the Public Lands: America's Conservation Debate, 1979–1984*; as well as J. Christian Adams, David S. Addington, Tom Altmeyer, Martin Anderson, Ernest Angelo Jr., Carolyn Bailey, Andy Berger, Stephen M. Brophy, George Byers, Margaret Byfield, Leslie Coleman, Kay Conrad, Holly Doremus, Robert F. Durant, Jane Fitzgerald, Dan Gerkin, John R. Gibson, Robert Gordon, Cornelia Ilie, Hugh Heclo, Nancy R. Hutchins, John Hutchinson, Scott Johnson, Kerri Jones, Paul G. Kengor, Daniel Kish, Kevin Kookogey, Jeff Kubina, Brent Kunz, Ben Lieberman, Fredde Lieberman, Tom Loranger, Jennifer Mandel, N. A. McMurry, Edwin Meese III, Julie A. MacDonald, Katherine L. Mead, Malina Moore, Wade Myers with the National Park Service, Shelley Nayak, Ann Pendley (no relation), Michael Pinckney with the Ronald Reagan Presidential Library, Rob Roy Ramey II, Richard L. Ranger, Dean A. Rhoads, Kelly Robbins, John W. Robinson, Natalie Russell, James D. Santini, Susan Schrepfer, Lori Schwartz, Hasting Stewart, Katie Sweeney,

Barbara Walz, Rebecca Winkel, Sue Ellen Wooldridge, Ryan Yates, and Brett Young.

I am grateful for the support of my friend Marjory G. Ross, president of Regnery Publishing, Inc., and her outstanding team, including Harry W. Crocker III, Mark Bloomfield, Lauren Chieffo, Amber Colleran, Frank Fochetta, Amanda Larsen, Ryan R. Morden, Henry Pereira, Lindsey Reinstrom, Brittany M. Roh, Alberto G. Rojas, Maria Ruhl, Hannah Sternberg, and Karen Woodard. I am especially gratified by the outstanding and painstaking work performed by Regnery's editor, Thomas Spence, on my manuscript.

President Reagan's message spans generations; that is obvious from the wonderful support I received from two young people who greatly admire him. Matthew D. Skeen Jr., who received his law degree from the University of Colorado in May 2013, and Chelsea Bratten, who will receive her B.A. in politics from Hillsdale College in May 2015, helped me ably. America is in good hands if they are part of its future.

Finally, I am most thankful for the enthusiastic support, diligent assistance, and wise counsel of my wife, friend, and partner-in-law, Lis.

PRESIDENT RONALD REAGAN PROCLAMATION 5030 EXCLUSIVE ECONOMIC ZONE OF THE UNITED STATES OF AMERICA

MARCH 10, 1983

EXCLUSIVE ECONOMIC ZONE OF
THE UNITED STATES OF AMERICA

- - - - - -

BY THE PRESIDENT OF THE UNITED STATES OF AMERICA

A PROCLAMATION

WHEREAS the Government of the United States of America
desires to facilitate the wise development and use of the
oceans consistent with international law;

WHEREAS international law recognizes that, in a zone
beyond its territory and adjacent to its territorial sea,
known as the Exclusive Economic Zone, a coastal State may
assert certain sovereign rights over natural resources and
related jurisdiction; and

WHEREAS the establishment of an Exclusive Economic Zone
by the United States will advance the development of ocean
resources and promote the protection of the marine environment, while not affecting other lawful uses of the zone,
including the freedoms of navigation and overflight, by other
States;

NOW, THEREFORE, I, RONALD REAGAN, by the authority vested
in me as President by the Constitution and laws of the
United States of America, do hereby proclaim the sovereign
rights and jurisdiction of the United States of America and
confirm also the rights and freedoms of all States within an
Exclusive Economic Zone, as described herein.

The Exclusive Economic Zone of the United States is a
zone contiguous to the territorial sea, including zones
contiguous to the territorial sea of the United States, the
Commonwealth of Puerto Rico, the Commonwealth of the Northern
Mariana Islands (to the extent consistent with the Covenant
and the United Nations Trusteeship Agreement), and
United States overseas territories and possessions. The
Exclusive Economic Zone extends to a distance 200 nautical
miles from the baseline from which the breadth of the
territorial sea is measured. In cases where the maritime
boundary with a neighboring State remains to be determined,

2

the boundary of the Exclusive Economic Zone shall be determined by the United States and other State concerned in accordance with equitable principles.

Within the Exclusive Economic Zone, the United States has, to the extent permitted by international law, (a) sovereign rights for the purpose of exploring, exploiting, conserving and managing natural resources, both living and non-living, of the seabed and subsoil and the superjacent waters and with regard to other activities for the economic exploitation and exploration of the zone, such as the production of energy from the water, currents and winds; and (b) jurisdiction with regard to the establishment and use of artificial islands, and installations and structures having economic purposes, and the protection and preservation of the marine environment.

This Proclamation does not change existing United States policies concerning the continental shelf, marine mammals and fisheries, including highly migratory species of tuna which are not subject to United States jurisdiction and require international agreements for effective management.

The United States will exercise these sovereign rights and jurisdiction in accordance with the rules of international law.

Without prejudice to the sovereign rights and jurisdiction of the United States, the Exclusive Economic Zone remains an area beyond the territory and territorial sea of the United States in which all States enjoy the high seas freedoms of navigation, overflight, the laying of submarine cables and pipelines, and other internationally lawful uses of the sea.

IN WITNESS WHEREOF, I have hereunto set my hand this tenth day of March, in the year of our Lord nineteen hundred and eighty-three, and of the Independence of the United States of America the two hundred and seventh.

SECRETARY OF THE INTERIOR WATT FINAL REPORT TO PRESIDENT REAGAN

United States Department of the Interior

OFFICE OF THE SECRETARY
WASHINGTON, D.C. 20240

October 1, 1983

The President
The White House
Washington, D.C. 20500

Dear Mr. President:

This year, 1983, has been marvelously successful. It has been: *A Year of Enrichment—Improving the quality of life for* all *Americans.*

All of the lands (one–third of the Nation) managed by the Department of the Interior are in better condition today than they were three years ago when we took responsibility for them. Because we have cared and exercised stewardship, the parks, refuges, forests, coastal barriers, wetlands and deserts are being better managed. This is also true for the wildlife living on these lands.

Our efforts to bring common sense and balance to the management of our natural resources have been successful, because we have put **people** in the *environmental equation*. People are important; they need jobs, recreation, agricultural products, energy and water, plus all the other values that come from the lands and waters of this country. In addition, they want to be assured that future generations in the 21st Century will enjoy these same benefits. That is why we have worked so hard to bring about the change, progress and enrichment necessary to improve the quality of life for *all* Americans.

Our National Park System is the envy of the world. Unfortunately, funds to restore and improve the parks were cut by over 50 percent from fiscal year 1978 to fiscal year 1981. To reverse that trend, we implemented a $1 billion Park Restoration and Improvement Program. The Reagan program is a great success. In fact, our program is the largest commitment that has ever been made to the National Park System. In 1956, President Eisenhower initiated Project 66, a ten–year effort of $500 million to upgrade the parks. Our program far exceeds even that gallant effort.

In the years ahead, we will be able to purchase the additional parklands needed to round out the federal recreation estate. Unfortunately, by fiscal year 1981, appropriations for parkland acquisitions were cut to one–sixth of what had been appropriated in fiscal year 1978. Because of the economic conditions inherited in 1981, we have not yet been able to increase the appropriation requests for parkland acquisitions. Even at that, because of our commitment to good conservation practices, we have set a remarkable record of increasing protection for the fragile and ecologically important conservation lands of the Nation. In our

three years, we have acquired for the Federal Government more than 1.6 million (1,620,651) acres of land to be managed as national parks and wildlife refuges.

In 1983 alone, we have, through trade, donations and purchase, added more park and wildlife land to the federal estate than any previous Administration added in a single year since Alaska was purchased in 1867. In fact, in this single year, we have added more park and wildlife land to the federal estate than was added from 1977 to 1980. (During that period, management responsibilities for tens of millions of acres were shuffled between various federal bureaucracies, but not as many new acres were added to the federal estate.) Neither Teddy Roosevelt, nor Franklin Roosevelt, nor Lyndon Johnson, nor Jimmy Carter came close to our 1983 record of adding to the federal park and wildlife estate in a single year.

Our stewardship commitment extends to preserving for future generations those historic sites and structures that pay tribute to America's past and the principles upon which our Nation was founded. As a result of the 1981 Economic Recovery Tax Act's 25 percent tax credit for private sector restoration of historic structures, in our three years private investment in historic preservation has increased five–fold over the investment from 1977 to 1980.

Preservation is important in improving the quality of life for all Americans. One of the areas of preservation that has received our special attention is the Endangered Species Program. Congress set-up a program requiring the Department of the Interior to identify those plants and animals that are endangered and then develop plans for their recovery. Because of our concern for and commitment to stewardship, we have accelerated the efforts to bring about the recovery of those endangered plants and animals. By the end of this year, we will have approved or reviewed nearly three times as many recovery plans as were developed in the four–year period 1977 to 1980.

Because we have put people in the environmental equation, we recommended or supported additions to our great wilderness system in the Lower 48 States totaling more than 1.8 million acres. We believe wilderness preservation is one of the legitimate multiple uses of the vast public lands. Not one acre of land has been leased for mining or drilling in the national parks or on the wilderness.

Mr. President, when we took office, I pledged to the Governors of the fifty States that the Department of the Interior would be a "good neighbor" in managing the 750 million acres of land spread throughout the Nation. I told the Governors that we would include them in our land use planning and that we would make available isolated, small tracts of federal lands to communities needing land for hospitals, schools, parks, recreation areas or housing projects.

We also stated that we would sell isolated, small tracts of land to ranchers and farmers so that more efficiency could be realized by both the Federal Government and the individuals in managing these lands. Of course, the national parks, wildlife refuges, wilderness areas and Indian trust lands have never been and are not for sale.

Despite some criticism that we were selling our national heritage, the facts tell a different story. In 1982, we sold 55 tracts of land, the largest one equalling 507 acres. The total sold in 1982 was 1,312 acres. In 1983, we sold 93 tracts totaling 7,981 acres. The largest tract was 640 acres.

Many of the western States were promised title to lands when they joined the Union at Statehood, but, for many years, delivery of those promised lands was "delayed." We promised the Governors that, if they would identify lands they had a right to claim under their Statehood acts, we would make the Federal Government honest. The response from the Governors has been tremendous. As a result, by the end of this year more land will have been delivered by the Reagan Administration to the States to support their school systems than at any time since 1969.

People are important. That is why so much of our effort is on providing for their consumer needs now and into the 21st Century. In order to hold down the cost of housing, we have made changes in the way we manage our forest lands. We want those lands to produce timber in the centuries ahead so that all generations will have an increased sustained yield.

We also have a strong commitment to water resources development. People need water—as a reliable and safe drinking water supply, for irrigation making our Nation the breadbasket of the world, for electric power generation and for enhancement of wildlife habitat.

This year, we have made major strides in implementing a national water policy which reflects State primacy in managing their water resources. We have put in place new Principles and Guidelines for water project planning which remove cumbersome and burdensome regulations, promote flexibility in planning and encourage water project development. In addition, we have proposed to Congress new water projects. Cost–sharing arrangements will be established on a case–by–case basis, according to the non–federal partners' ability to participate and honoring prior commitments made by the Federal Government.

Most of the future energy needed to heat houses, fuel cars and increase the number of jobs for Americans will come from federally controlled lands and offshore areas. With that understanding, we have aggressively moved to increase energy potential for the decades to come. People need energy. Our efforts to increase the supply of energy sources and reduce our dependency on foreign countries have been carried out with more environmental stipulations, conditions and care than ever before. We know that we can have both an increased energy supply for people and an enhanced environment.

For America to be strong domestically and militarily, we had to reverse the policies and programs of the past. During the 1970s, energy production from federal offshore and onshore lands fell, weakening our economy and increasing our dependency on foreign countries. In that period, the Department of the Interior reduced leasing activities. Reduced leasing hurts consumers, because of the long lead time needed to get oil and gas, coal, geothermal and other forms of renewable and non–renewable energy to the people—the consumers.

Our actions to implement proper environmental safeguards and lease federal lands will not benefit American consumers immediately, but will benefit future generations. In three years, we have leased nearly twice as much *onshore* oil and gas land as was leased between 1977 and 1980; we have also leased more than twice the *offshore* lands; and, 3½ times as much coal land.

Mr. President, our excellent record for managing the natural resources of this land is unequalled—because we put **people** in the environmental equation.

This year, 1983, has truly been *A Year of Enrichment— Improving the quality of life for* **all** *Americans.*

Sincerely,

Jim Watt

Secretary

PRESIDENT REAGAN RADIO ADDRESS TO THE NATION ON THE RESIGNATION OF SECRETARY OF THE INTERIOR JAMES G. WATT

NOVEMBER 26, 1983

1

My fellow Americans: There is a change of management over at the Dept. of Interior. James Watt has resigned & I have asked Judge William Clark to take his place.

When Jim became Sec. of Interior he told me of the things that needed doing, the things that had to be set straight. He also told me that if & when he did them he'd probably have to resign in 18 months. Some times the one who straightens out a situation uses up so many brownie points he or she is no longer the best one to carry out the duties of day to day management. Jim understood this but he also realized what had to be done and he did it for more than 30 months – not 18.

It's time to take inventory. The Dept. of Interior has jurisdiction over one third of the land in the United States, some 750 mil. acres. This includes Nat. Parks, wildlife refuges, wilderness lands, wet lands & coastal barriers. Not included in the 750 mil. acres are our OFF SHORE coastal waters – the Continental Shelf which is also Interiors responsibility.

Our Nat. Parks are the envy of the world but in 1981 they were a little frayed at the edges. Beginning in 1978 funds for upkeep & restoration had been cut in half. Jim Watt called for a bil. dollar improvement & restoration program. This was more for one year than had been spent in all the preceding 4 years put together. It was the largest commitment to the Park system that has ever been made.

Appropriations for acquiring additional park land had also been lacking. In 1981 they amounted to only one sixth of what they'd been in 1978. You, of course, remember the ec. crunch we were facing in 1981 yet even so Sec. Watt set out to increase protection for fragile & important conservation lands.

At the end of these 3 yrs. Interior will have acquired more than 1.6 mil. acres of land for parks & wildlife refuges. In this year (1983) alone through trades, donations and purchase we will have added more park & wildlife land than has been added in any single year since the purchase of Alaska in 1867. And it is more than was added in the 4 yrs. from 1977 to 1980 ②

~~Interior~~ also is in charge of preserving historic sites & structures. In the Ec. Recovery program we launched in 1981 we gave a 25% tax credit for ~~historic~~ private sector restoration of historic structures. The result has been private investment in historic preservation 5 times as great as in the preceding 4 years.

~~~~, Preservation of endangered species is ^also a responsibility of the Dept. and ~~by the~~ the approval & review of plans to bring about recovery of endangered plant & animal species has nearly tripled in the 30 months ~~Sec.~~ ^Jim Watt FROM THE VERY FIRST DAY ~~proposed to the~~ Govs. of our 50 states that the dept. would be a good neighbor; that they would be ~~involved~~ in land planning and that small tracts of isolated Fed. lands would be made available to communities needing land for hospitals, schools, parks or housing. He also stated that isolated, small tracts would be sold to farmers & ranchers. An example of what I'm talking about is a strip of land 2 miles long and only 2 ft. wide that was recently ~~sold~~. I think you can imagine how that must have ~~~~ ^raised some problems ~~~~ private land owners ~~~~ ^had with clouded title to their property ~~~~ Of course this was distorted and led to protests that he was

selling ~~the~~ Nat. Parks & ~~the~~ wilderness. ^What he actually did was ~~sell, in 1982~~ ~~~~ 55 tracts that totaled ^ONLY 1300 acres & this year 93 tracts totaling ^a little under 8000 acres. The largest parcel was ~~~~ 640 acres, ^THATS ONE SQ. MILE None of it was Park, wildlife refuge, wilderness or Indian trust lands. They are not for sale.

While all this was going on I've be. recommend that 21,000 acres be added to the wilderness system and endorsed Congressional action to designate an additional 300,000 acres. ^FOR THE SAME PURPOSE NOT ^one acre of Park or ~~wilderness~~ ^LAND was leased for oil drilling or mining contrary to what you may have read or heard. When territories ^were becoming states they were promised title to Fed. lands within their borders. But as more & more western states ~~joined~~ the Union there began TO BE A DELAY, IN FACT A PERMANENT DELAY IN TURNING OVER THESE LANDS.

Jim Watt promised the Governors that if they'd identify lands,

③

they had a right to claim under their statehood acts we'd make the Fed. govt. honest. The Governors responded and as a result, by the end of this year more land will have been delivered to the states to support their school systems then at any time since 1969.

Changes have been made in the management of Forest lands which are eligible for multiple use. Those lands will provide lumber on a sustained yield basis. This will benefit Americans who cherish the dream of owning their own home.

We've made giant strides in implementing a national water policy which recognizes State primacy in managing water resources. People must be a part of our planning & people need a reliable, safe, drinking water supply, water for irrigation, for generating power and for enhancement of wildlife habitat.

Since I've mentioned energy let me touch on that for a minute. It is estimated that 85% of the fuel we need (oil, gas & coal) to keep the wheels of industry turning is on Fed. owned property including the off shore continental shelf. Efforts to increase the supply of energy have been carried out with more environmental stipulations than ever before. We can & will have an increased energy supply with an enhanced environment.

James G. Watt has served this nation well & I'm sure Wm. Clark will do the same.

Until next week - Goodbye & God Bless You.

APPENDIX 4

SECRETARY OF THE INTERIOR CLARK FINAL REPORT TO PRESIDENT REAGAN

26 November 1984

Dear Mr. President:

Thank you, Mr. President, for the trust and confidence you have placed in me the past 14 years. I shall attempt to express some year end observations to you as simply and candidly as I can:

1. <u>Interior</u> The policies begun by Jim Watt are going well and I hope to make them your quiet legacy. I feel deep satisfaction here — it's not unlike running a very large ranch.

6. Finally, Mr. President, your ten foot tall integrity — matching my own father's — is an inspiration to us all — That's what your twenty year mandate has been all about.

Sincerely,
Bill Clark

SECRETARY OF THE INTERIOR HODEL FINAL REPORT TO PRESIDENT REAGAN

THE SECRETARY OF THE INTERIOR
WASHINGTON, D.C.
December 15, 1988

Dear Mr. President:

On a clear hot Washington day in July 1986, you honored nearly one hundred individuals and organizations for their commitment to America's natural and cultural resources. It was a high point in the "Take Pride in America" campaign which we had launched jointly to encourage grassroot support for our common goal--to nourish the lands and resources that belong to all Americans. Literally thousands of Americans heard our message and answered our call. It was the most popular of all our policies and programs.

As you so eloquently stated that day on the White House lawn:

> Our beautiful land is blessed from sea to shining sea with bountiful natural and cultural resources on federal, state and local lands. We are also blessed that the American people possess a unique volunteer spirit rooted in our frontier tradition.

You understood, too, that "through our stewardship of these natural wonders and great monuments of history, we can express our love for our country, our pride in America, and our desire to preserve our resources and heritage for the future."

You have given your Secretaries of the Interior six important charges for the stewardship of the public lands and natural resources which the federal government holds in trust for all Americans. Under your leadership, it has been our highest priority to:

- protect our national park, wilderness and wildlife resources;
- enhance our ability to meet our energy and mineral needs with domestic resources;
- ensure quality water supply;
- improve relations with state and local governments;
- enhance the quality of life for Native Americans and the people of the Island Territories; arid,
- improve the overall management and efficiency of the Department of the Interior.

While the missions and responsibilities of this Department are varied and at times conflicting, we have tried to seek a consensus on these major objectives and then work constructively to resolve differences about program specifics. In so doing, we firmly believe that America does not have to choose between an improving environment, on the one hand, and economic growth, on the other; by identifying common goals and working together toward them, we can have both.

As your tremendously successful eight-year Administration comes to a close, I have the privilege to present to you our record of accomplishments at the Department of the Interior.

Sincerely,

DONALD PAUL HODEL

JIM WATT'S MONDAY MORNING TEAM

BY WILLIAM PERRY PENDLEY

"Put a loyal team together.
Get our people all in place.
Find a room where we can meet.
Set a schedule and a date."

Jim phoned us each from Denver,
Reached us all across the map.
Told us Reagan had called him.
To his shoulder gave a "tap."

Doug and Emily were at ICC.
Perry was on "The Hill."
Hefflefinger was at DOE
And Moody, at Labor still.

Shipley drove in from Denver
The "brown book" to his chest.
Russell was brought from the Senate
And Don from the Pacific Northwest.

In the cold days after Jim's hearing,
In the Department's bitter chill,
We all gathered to study the lists,
Of Republicans—positions to fill.

Ray Arnett was on a list of one
For the traveling hunter's post,
Dick Harris was Lugar's man,
To reform OSM's regulatory host.

But most were called "Mountain Mafia."
By Denver's *Rocky Mountain News*
They came from throughout the West
With conservative, Reagan-like views:

Broadbent was Laxalt's dam builder,
Bob Burford, a cowboy and a miner,
Coldiron was our non-Indian lawyer,
And Hulette, the token 49-er.

DuBois was yet another wrangler,
Barr from the arid southwest,
Jantzen knew girl cats from boys,
And Robin—only his name was "West."

Professors Carruthers and Miller
Both were "Mountain Mafia" men
While Kitty had Helene's endorsement
Unlike the careerist Dickenson.

Jim always believed in deputies
He'd been one once himself.
So he brought in a bunch of doers,
Committed; loyal above all else.

Moody joined with Coldiron.
Emily teamed up with Doug,
Russell and DuBois went to lands,
Potter: to the maker of animal rugs.

John Fritz and Roy Sampsel,
Joined the native born Ken Smith,
Brown and Powell were with Hulette
While Arnett got inholder Davidge.

Steve Griles was our "Johnny Reb," and
Texans Mulberry, Morales, and Mary Lou
Along with Delaware's William Horn
Further rounded out Watt's crew.

There were many others among us,
For whose names I have no rhymes,
Garrish, Sanjuan, Peck and others,
Stanzas for which I had no time.

On Monday mornings we would gather,
Jim was upbeat, even when times were hard,
He'd guide and inspire us each week,
He'd start us up and lead the charge.

We had some exciting adventures,
Each week was challengingly new,
OCS, EEZ, BLM, PRIP, BOR (now gone)
Was all part of our alphabet stew.

We lived together through scandal,
Thanks to the media's outrageous hype,
Through Powder River, Beach Boys,
Christmas parties--you know the type.

But we all knew what was important,
That we accomplished our goal,
Of implementing the Reagan mandate
So that that story could be told.

It's a chance few are given,
To make a difference, or so it seems,
To implement your President's wishes,
As a part of his most loyal team.

Those viewing what we accomplished—
People who've known other Interiors—
Say all else, past and future,
Regardless, will always be inferior.

We've all gone to different places,
For our service, each paid a price,
But ask each one: do it all again?
"Affirmative"—affirmative thrice.

Delivered at Jim Watt's
Monday Morning Team Farewell Party
May 19, 1986—Washington, D.C.

APPENDIX 7

RESEARCH MATERIALS

James G. Watt, Secretary of the Interior, donated his official papers to the American Heritage Center of the University of Wyoming.

Garrey E. Carruthers, Assistant Secretary, Land and Water Resources, U.S. Department of the Interior, donated his official papers to New Mexico State University.

Frank A. DuBois, Deputy Assistant Secretary, Land and Water Resources, U.S. Department of the Interior, donated his official papers to New Mexico State University.

Professor C. Brant Short, Ph.D., author of *Ronald Reagan and the Public Lands: America's Conservation Debate, 1979–1984*, donated the materials he collected on the Sagebrush Rebellion to Utah State University.

William Perry Pendley, Deputy Assistant Secretary, Energy and Minerals, and Acting Director, Minerals Management Service, donated his official papers to the American Heritage Center of the University of Wyoming.

The Ronald Reagan Presidential Foundation & Library is located at 40 Presidential Drive, Simi Valley, California 93065; www.reaganfoundation.org. As a presidential library administered by the National Archives and Records Administration, the Reagan Library, pursuant to the authority of the Presidential Records Act, is the repository of presidential records for President Reagan's administration. Its holdings include fifty million pages of presidential documents, over 1.6 million photographs, a half million feet of motion picture film, and tens of thousands of audio and videotapes.

The Public Papers of President Ronald W. Reagan located in the Ronald Reagan Presidential Library and that contain the statements, speeches, and papers released by the Office of the Press Secretary during the Reagan Presidency are available online here: http://www.reagan.utexas.edu/archives/speeches/publicpapers.html. A small number of documents from the Ronald Reagan Presidential Library are available online at the National Archives and Records Administration's online Archival Research Catalog (ARC): http://www.archives.gov/research/arc/index.html.

NOTES

PROLOGUE

1. Peter D. Hannaford and Charles D. Hobbs, *Remembering Reagan* (Regnery, 2000), 22.
2. Anna Quindlen, "Lights Go On, Bells Ring in Big Cities and Villages," *New York Times*, January 21, 1981, A3.

RONALD REAGAN'S SECRETARIES OF THE INTERIOR

1. James C. Humes, *The Wit & Wisdom of Ronald Reagan* (Regnery, 2007), 50.

PREFACE

1. *Annual Report of the Secretary of the Treasury for* 1848, House Executive Documents, 30th Congress, 2d session (1848–49), Vol. 2, No. 7, 35–37.
2. With these additions, the nation nearly reached its current contiguous United States (CONUS) size; only the Gadsden Purchase of 1853 and resolution of the northwestern boundary dispute with the United Kingdom (Treaty of Washington in 1871) remained.
3. For the history of the U.S. Department of the Interior, see generally, Henry B. Learned, "The Establishment of the Secretaryship of the Interior," *American Historical Review* 16 (1911): 751–53; Norman O. Forness, *The Origins and Early History of the United States Department of the Interior* (Ph.D. dissertation, Pennsylvania State University, 1964, by Forness) 25; and Robert M. Utley and Barry Mackintosh, "The Department of Everything Else: Highlights of Interior History," National Park Service, 1989, http://www.nps.gov/history/history/online_books/utley-mackintosh/index.htm. See generally, Ron Arnold, *At the Eye of the Storm: James Watt and the Environmentalists* (Regnery Gateway, 1982) ix–xii.
4. *Cong. Globe*, 30th Congress, 2d session, 543.
5. Ibid., 680 (March 3, 1849).
6. Ewing was a "Westerner." He was born in what is now West Virginia, moved west to Ohio where he became a "frontier lawyer," and, as an elected official earned the nickname, "Logician of the West," for his mental skills. *Dictionary of American Biography* 6: 237–38; Forness, *The Origins and Early History of the United States Department of the Interior*, chapter 3; Eugene Trani, *The Secretaries and Under Secretaries of the Department of the Interior* (typescript, Department of the Interior Library, 1966), 10–16.

7.   *Cong. Globe*, 30th Congress, 2d session, 673 (March 3, 1849). "There is something ominous in the expression 'the Secretary of the Interior,'" Senator Calhoun declared. Ibid. There is something "ominous" in the expression given that the "interior ministry" of most foreign countries is devoted to policing, national security, and immigration. http://en.wikipedia.org/wiki/Interior_ministry. As Under Secretary, Hodel met with a visiting official from a foreign Interior Ministry and hence a member of the country's secret police. On learning from Hodel of the mundane tasks assigned Interior, he beat a hasty retreat.

8.   Quoted in Horace S. Merrill, *William Freeman Vilas, Doctrinaire Democrat* (Madison, Wisconsin, 1954), 134, 139.

9.   Utley and Mackintosh, "Nationwide Concerns."

10.   The functions and organizations of the department from its inception are described in "Secretary of the Interior: Activities and Duties, 1849–1949," in the Department of the Interior Library. This consists of three loose-leaf binders containing the same data differently arranged: Vol. I, chronologically, Vol. II, by subject classification, and Vol. III, alphabetically by original designation. The call number is J84/A44. In addition to its "responsibilities for Indians, public lands, patents, and pensions," during the last half of the nineteenth century, the department was charged with tasks that "ranged from the conduct of the decennial census to the colonization of freed slaves in Haiti, from the exploration of western wilderness to oversight of the District of Columbia jail, from the regulation of territorial governments to construction of the national capital's water system, from management of hospitals and universities to maintenance of public parks." Utley and Mackintosh, "Getting Organized."

11.   The Department of the Interior also had a special relationship, thanks to Congress, with the District of Columbia, which included responsibility for its public buildings (1849–1867 and 1933–1939), its parks (1849–1867 and from 1933 to date, as, currently, National Mall and Memorial Parks of the National Park Service), its police (1849–1873), its jail (1849–1872), a railway linking Washington and Georgetown (1862–1910), a railroad bridge that crossed the Potomac River (1863–1867), and operation of its water supply (1859-1867). The secretary of the interior had oversight of the Columbia Institution for the Instruction of the Deaf and Dumb (1857–1940) (now Gallaudet College); the Columbia Hospital for Women (1866–1881); Freedmen's Hospital (1874–1940); the National Hospital for the Insane (St. Elizabeth's Hospital) (1852–1940); and Howard University (1867–1940). Finally, the architect of the Capitol, responsible for construction and maintenance of the United States Capitol, related buildings, and grounds, reported to the secretary of the interior from 1851–1853, 1862–1902, and 1921–1922. Utley and Mackintosh, "Nationwide Concerns."

12.   March 1, 1873 (17 Stat. 484). Utley and Mackintosh, "Territorial Affairs." The territories for which the Interior Department originally had responsibility soon became states: Colorado in 1876; Montana, Washington, North Dakota, and South Dakota in 1889; Wyoming and Idaho in 1890; Utah in 1896; Oklahoma in 1907; Arizona and New Mexico in 1912; and Alaska in 1959. Utley and Mackintosh, "Territorial Affairs."

13.   *Annual Report of the Commissioner of Indian Affairs for 1885*, 314–34, 354.

14.   Utley and Mackintosh, "Western Emphasis."

15.   The Pacific Railroad Act of 1862 (12 Stat. 489) was followed by the Pacific Railroad Act of 1863 (12 Stat. 807), the Pacific Railroad Act of 1864 (13 Stat. 356), the Pacific Railroad Act of 1865 (13 Stat. 504), and the Pacific Railroad Act of 1866 (14 Stat. 66). Ultimately railroads received more than 94 million acres. U.S. Department of the Interior, Bureau of Land Management, *Public Land Statistics*, 1970 (Washington, 1970), 6.

16.   The Morrill Acts included the Morrill Act of 1862 (the Land-Grant College Act), 7 U.S.C. § 301 et seq. and the Morrill Act of 1890 (the Agricultural College Act of 1890, 26 Stat. 417, 7 U.S.C. § 321 et seq.

17.   The *Homestead Act* of 1862 (12 Stat. 392). Homesteaders ultimately claimed 290 million acres. U.S. Department of the Interior, Bureau of Land Management, *Public Land Statistics*, 1970 (Washington, 1970), 6.

18.   Utley and Mackintosh, "Western Emphasis."

19.   Ibid., Organic Act of the U.S. Geological Survey (20 Stat. 394) (March 3, 1879). The USGS was charged with: "classification of the public lands, and examination of the geological structure, mineral resources, and products of the national domain."

20.   The Yellowstone National Park Act (17 Stat. 32) (March 1, 1872).

21.   The National Park Service Organic Act, 16 U.S.C. § 1 et seq. (August 25, 1916). Until creation of the National Park Service (NPS), the secretary of the interior arranged for military units to protect

some of the parks. Utley and Mackintosh, "Western Emphasis." The NPS was given responsibility for fourteen national parks and twenty-one national monuments; the latter included "prehistoric Indian ruins, geologic features, and other sites of natural and cultural significance reserved by presidential proclamations under the Antiquities Act of 1906." Utley and Mackintosh, "Parks and the Park Service."

22.   It was not just the men who had served for whom provisions were made. President Lincoln vowed, "to care for him who shall have borne the battle and for his widow, and his orphan," Abraham Lincoln, Second Inaugural Address; endorsed by Lincoln, April 10, 1865, March 4, 1865; Series 3, General Correspondence, 1837–1897; The Abraham Lincoln Papers at the Library of Congress, Manuscript Division (Washington, D.C.: American Memory Project, 2000–2).

23.   Utley and Mackintosh, "Nationwide Concerns."

24.   "About VA," U.S. Department of Veterans Affairs, http://www.va.gov/about_va/vahistory.asp.

25.   Quoted in Leonard D. White, *The Republican Era*, 1869–1901: *A Study in Administrative History* (New York, 1963), 222. The Patent Office displayed patent models to which Congress added, in 1854, natural specimens and artifacts from Charles Wilkes's South Seas expedition, which was supplemented over the decades with artifacts from government-backed explorations and national treasures such as the Declaration of Independence. The Smithsonian Institution, which was established in 1846, received all of these items by 1879. Utley and Mackintosh, "Nationwide Concerns."

26.   Ibid.; President Cleveland signed the law creating a cabinet-level Department of Agriculture, 25 Stat. 659 (February 9, 1889).

27.   Utley and Mackintosh, "Nationwide Concerns."

28.   Ibid.; The Office of Education is "primarily an establishment for educational research and promotion [with] no administrative functions except those connected with the expenditure of the funds appropriated by the Federal Government for the assistance of colleges of agriculture and the mechanic arts in the several States and Territories, and those connected with the education, support, and medical relief of the natives of Alaska." *Annual Report of the Secretary of the Interior for the Fiscal Year Ended June 30*, 1929 (Washington, 1929), 42.

29.   Utley and Mackintosh, "Nationwide Concerns."

30.   Utley and Mackintosh, "The Conservation Movement." In 1935, the Bureau of Reclamation completed Hoover Dam, which created Lake Mead and the first National Recreation Area, which was managed by the NPS. Utley & Mackintosh, "Parks and the Park Service." Today, eighty-four of the 289 recreation areas created by Bureau of Reclamation projects are managed by federal agencies such as the NPS, the U.S. Forest Service (USFS), the Bureau of Land Management, and the U.S. Fish and Wildlife Service (FWS). Another 159 of the 289 developed recreation areas are managed by non-federal entities, mostly state, county, and city governments. "Reclamation Fast Facts," http://www.usbr.gov/recreation/facts.html.

31.   Utley and Mackintosh, "Managing the Public Domain."

32.   Ibid.; In 1977, Congress passed the "BLM Organic Act," often called the Federal Land Policy and Management Act of 1976, Public Law 94–579, http://www.blm.gov/flpma/organic.htm. The BLM Organic Act established a process for the "final disposal" (a provision from the Taylor Grazing Act) of land "whose potential would best be achieved in nonfederal ownership." Utley and Mackintosh, "Managing the Public Domain."

33.   Ibid.; The Surface Mining Control and Reclamation Act of 1977, P.L. 95–87 (August 3, 1977).

34.   Utley and Mackintosh, "Nationwide Concerns," http://energy.gov/management/history. For example, the Bureau of Mines' research and fact-finding activities regarding fossil fuels technology were transferred to the Department of Energy. Utley and Mackintosh, "Managing the Public Domain."

35.   Utley and Mackintosh, "Fish and Wildlife." "A 1940 reorganization plan (54 Stat. 1232) in the Department of the Interior consolidated the Bureau of Fisheries and the Bureau of Biological Survey into one agency to be known as the Fish and Wildlife Service," http://www.fws.gov/help/about_us.html.

36.   Migratory Bird Conservation Act (16 U.S.C. 715–715d, 715e, 715f–715r) of February 18, 1929, (45 Stat. 1222).

37.   Utley and Mackintosh, "Fish and Wildlife."

38.   These are former Japanese wartime possessions that the United Nations assigned to United States trusteeship in 1947; Utley and Mackintosh, "Territorial Affairs."

39.   Utley and Mackintosh, "Territorial Affairs." Notwithstanding the congressional grant of authority, the Interior Department was not always assigned responsibility for territories. The State Department was responsible for Puerto Rico (1898 from Spain), the War Department for the Philippines and

Cuba (1898 from Spain), and the Navy Department for Guam (1898 from Spain) and American Samoa (1899 from Germany). The Navy Department was also responsible for the Virgin Islands after its purchase from Denmark in 1917.

40. Ibid.; "Welcome to Puerto Rico!," Magaly Rivera, 2013, http://www.topuertorico.org/government. shtml.

41. Utley and Mackintosh, "Territorial Affairs."

INTRODUCTION

1. Kiron K. Skinner, ed., *Turning Points in Ending the Cold War* (Hoover Institution Press, 2007), 110.

2. Ibid.

3. Richard V. Allen, "The Man Who Won the Cold War," *Hoover Digest* no. 1 (January 30, 2000).

4. Robert Cameron Mitchell, "Public Opinion and Environmental Politics in the 1970s and 1980s," in Norman J. Vig and Michael E. Kraft, eds., *Environmental Policy in the 1980s: Reagan's New Agenda* (Congressional Quarterly, 1984) 57–58.

5. Ibid.

6. Ibid.

7. Philip Shabecoff, "Major Environmental Leaders Back Carter Re-election Bid," *New York Times*, September 28, 1980, Section A, 36.

8. "Environmentalists Oppose Land Transfer," *High Country News* (November 2, 1979), 13.

9. Michael E. Kraft, "A New Environmental Policy Agenda: The 1980 Presidential Campaign and Its Aftermath," in Vig, *Reagan's New Agenda*, 38.

10. Ibid.

11. Ibid., 38–40. Reagan, who read *Mandate* cover to cover, had a hardcover version placed before each cabinet officer at an early gathering. "Read the chapter that pertains to your department and make sure you implement it," he instructed them.

12. Ibid., 39.

13. Charles L. Heatherly, ed., *Mandate for Leadership*: *Policy Management in a Conservative Administration* (The Heritage Foundation, 1981), 333–401.

14. "Reagan, environmentalists squawk over policies," *The Milwaukee Sentinel*, March 12, 1983, 3. Earlier President Reagan wrote in his diary, "Anne Burford resigned on her own so the agency could get back to work. This whole business has been a lynching by headline hunting Congressmen. I can't wait to get a question from the Press so I can say that." Ronald Reagan, *The Reagan Diaries* (HarperCollins, 2007), 136.

15. Frank Newport, "Americans: Economy Takes Precedent Over Environment—First time majority has supported economy in 25 years of asking question," *Gallup Economy*, March 19, 2009.

16. "[T]he leak of the internal emails and documents of the Climate Research Unit at the University of East Anglia in November [2009] has done for the climate change debate what the Pentagon Papers did for the Vietnam war debate 40 years ago—changed the narrative decisively." Steven F. Hayward, "In Denial: The meltdown of the climate campaign," *Weekly Standard* vol. 15, no. 25 (March 15, 2010). Even *The Economist*, "decidedly alarmist on global warming through the years," has become a "climate denier." Rich Lowry, "The New Climate Deniers: The world hasn't warmed since 1998, and those obsessed with 'climate change' are ignoring it," National Review Online, April 2, 2013.

17. Bill Vlasic, "Breaking Down on the Road to Electric Cars," *New York Times*, April 24, 2013, B1. Todd Woody, "California's dream to be the Saudi Arabia of solar dries up in the desert," *Quartz*, April 24, 2013, http://qz.com/77898/californias-big-solar-dreams-fizzle-in-the-desert/; Kevin D. Williamson, "Devalued Wind Power: Green-energy delusions inflict a heavy cost on a Massachusetts town," National Review Online, December 3, 2012; Tom Hals and Roberta Rampton, "Beacon Power bankrupt; had U.S. backing like Solyndra," Reuters, October 31, 2011; Matthew L. Wald, "Solar Firm Aided by U.S. Shuts Doors," *New York Times*, September 1, 2011, B1.

18. Review and Outlook, "Cuomo's De-Fracking: New York's Governor favors rich greens over upstate poor," *Wall Street Journal*, October 3, 2012; Glenn Blain, "'Fracking kills': Yoko Ono joins star-studded cast fighting against hydraulic natural gas drilling in upstate New York," *New York Daily News*, January 11, 2013; Jon Entine, "Killing drilling with farcical 'science'," *New York Post*, January 23, 2012.

CHAPTER ONE

1. Kiron K. Skinner, Annelise Anderson, and Martin Anderson, eds., *Reagan, In His Own Hand: The Writings of Ronald Reagan That Reveal His Revolutionary Vision for America* (The Free Press,

2001), 338.; "We're so used to calling this [one third] of our nation, Federal land, isn't it time we remembered that the very term means it belongs, to us—to the people of America?"

2. Ibid.

3. The National Environmental Policy Act (NEPA), 42 U.S.C. 4321 et seq., was signed into law on January 1, 1970, by President Richard Nixon.

4. The late Senator Clifford P. Hansen's great legacy to his beloved Wyoming was the increase, from 37.5% to 50%, of the percentage of mineral royalties paid to the federal government but returned to states in which the oil and gas development takes place. *See* Federal Land Policy and Management Act (FLPMA), Pub. L. No. 94-579, § 317(a), 90 Stat. 2743, 2770 (1976) (amending § 35 of the Mineral Leasing Act of 1920 (30 U.S.C. § 191).

5. In *Miller Bros v. Dep't of Natural Resources*, 203 Mich App 674; 513 NW2d 217 (1994), the court rejected Michigan's nuisance defense for denying a lessee the permit to conduct oil and gas activity in the Nordhouse Dunes area, found a regulatory taking of the lessee's mineral rights, and awarded $71.5 million as just compensation for the value of the property taken, plus interest, costs, and attorney fees. In 1995, Michigan announced a $59.5 million settlement with the Miller Brothers to avoid paying $83 million and perhaps as much as $120 million; http://www.state.mi.us/migov/gov/PressReleases/199509/Nordhous.html. In a case involving federal leases on the OCS issued in 1981 by the Reagan administration in which "[t]wo oil companies.... claim that the [federal] Government repudiated the contracts when [in 1990] it denied them certain elements of the permission-seeking opportunities that the contracts had promised," the Supreme Court ruled 8-1: "We agree that the Government broke its promise; it repudiated the contracts; and it must give the companies their money back." *Mobil Oil Exploration* & *Producing Southeast, Inc. v. United States*, 530 U.S. 604, 607, (2000).

6. One of the environmental groups that objected was the National Audubon Society, which allows energy development on its Rainey Reserve, a privately owned wildlife refuge in Louisiana. C. Brant Short, *Ronald Reagan and the Public Lands: America's Conservation Debate, 1979–1984* (Texas A&M University Press, 1989), 90–91; Steven H. Hanke, "Wise Use of Federal Land," *New York Times*, May 6, 1983, Sec. A, 31; and Steven H. Hanke, letter to the editor, *Wall Street Journal*, August 29, 1983, 13.

7. President Reagan might have been thinking about his conversation with Watt when he said, in his Second Inaugural Address on January 21, 1985, "We've come to a turning point, a moment for hard decisions. I have asked the Cabinet and my staff a question and now I put the same question to all of you. If not us, who? And if not now, when?" Second Inaugural Address, January 21, 1985. http://www.presidency.ucsb.edu/ws/index.php?pid=38688. Reagan commemorates his discussion with Watt thusly: "Friday, September 4[, 1981] Met with Jim Watt. He's taking a lot of abuse from environmental extremists but he's absolutely right. People are ecology too and they can't forage for food and live in caves." Ronald Reagan, *The Reagan Diaries* (Harper, 2007), 36. Reagan wrote something similar in his February 27, 1975, radio commentary titled "Land Planning." "People are ecology too and most of us are looking for answers that will preserve nature to the greatest extent possible consistent with the need to have places where we can work & live." Skinner, *Reagan, In His Own Hand*, 339. As to Reagan's diaries, "I decided to keep a daily journal while I was in the White House.... Each night, I'd write a few lines about the day's events...." Ronald Reagan, *An American Life: The Autobiography* (Simon & Schuster, 1990), 250.

8. The Cache Creek APD was withdrawn subsequently; however, a nearby APD went forward. The leases had been issued years before and were to expire during the Carter administration. Therefore, they were "suspended," that is, they were extended beyond their primary ten-year term. As the controversy brewed, the Interior Board of Land Appeals (IBLA) held that, as to one of the leases, the lease agreement was flawed due to the failure to include a "no-action alternative," that is, the right to bar the lessee from taking any action as to its lease. The IBLA ruling was upheld by a Wyoming federal district court and subsequently, in a brief opinion, by the U.S. Court of Appeals for the Tenth Circuit in Denver. *Getty Oil Company v. Clark*, 614 F.Supp. 904 (D. Wyo. 1985); *Texaco Producing, Inc. v. Hodel*, 840 F.2d 776 (10th Cir. 1988).

9. The first, multi-issue nonprofit, public-interest legal foundation (PILF) that emphasized constitutional liberties and the rule of law was Pacific Legal Foundation, which was founded in 1973 to support Governor Reagan's various initiatives in the courtroom. Ron Arnold, *At the Eye of the Storm: James Watt and the Environmentalists* (Regnery Gateway, 1982), 22. Lee Edwards, *Bringing Justice to the People: The Story of the Freedom-Based Public Interest Law Movement* (Heritage Books, 2004).

Founded in 1968, the National Right to Work Legal Defense Foundation was the first single issue PILF, http://www.nrtw.org/en/about.

10.   Watt's biography is discussed by Arnold, *At the Eye of the Storm*, 1–26; and Short, *Ronald Reagan and the Public Lands*, 51–53, 55–56. Watt's love for and enjoyment of the out-of-doors with friends and family appear at Arnold, *At the Eye of the Storm*, 166–67.

11.   See Ross W. Gorte, et al, "Federal Land Ownership: Overview and Data," Congressional Research Service, February 8, 2012, 4-5.

12.   Kiron K. Skinner, Annelise Anderson, Martin Anderson, Eds., *Reagan's Path to Victory*, *The Shaping of Ronald Reagan's Vision: Selected Writings* (The Free Press, 2004), xiv. "During his radio broadcasting career from 1975 to 1979, it is estimated that he spoke to between 20 and 30 million Americans a week." Ibid.

13.   Ibid., xiv–xv. Of the remaining 354 commentaries, some were written by Reagan but the handwritten drafts were not found and the rest were written by Reagan's staff, primarily Peter Hannaford, and then edited by Reagan. Ibid., xv.

14.   Ibid., xvi. "Over the five-year period, Governor Reagan gave eighty-eight broadcasts on the energy problems and the environment...." Skinner, *Reagan, In His Own Hand*, 318. Of course, Reagan addressed energy issues because he saw them linked both to economic issues and to foreign affairs. In doing so he was also addressing the public's primary concern. "In 1977—as throughout the late 1970s—respondents told the Gallup Poll that the most important problem facing the country was the economic situation—inflation, taxes, and unemployment—by a wide margin. Energy—shortages, fuel prices, and energy policy in general—held second place. Together they almost always accounted for well over 50 percent, outweighing foreign policy and national defense by a 5-to-1 margin." Skinner, *Reagan's Path to Victory*, 105.

15.   Arnold, *At the Eye of the Storm*, 25.

16.   Ibid., 25–26, 51–52. On November 5, 1980, I telephoned my former boss, Senator Hansen, to discuss the election results. He shared my delight but also my astonishment at the Reagan landslide, which put Republicans in charge of the Senate for the first time since 1954. "If I thought that was a possibility I never would have retired," he said. After all, he would have become chairman of the Senate Energy and Natural Resources Committee. (Senator McClure, an Idaho Republican, became chairman instead.) "Senator," I offered, "you should return as Secretary of the Interior." Hansen, known for his self-effacing manner, rebutted, "They have forgotten all about me." I countered that the people who matter had not "forgotten" him and his singular dedication to addressing and resolving Western issues. Then I added, "If Governor Reagan asked you to be Secretary, would you say 'yes'?" "No one can say 'no' to the President," he replied. I could not wait to get off the telephone. I called my friend Sam Ballenger, an aide to Laxalt, and told him of the conversation. Sam told me later that he told Laxalt and that Laxalt told Reagan. Years later, Matt Mead, Hansen's grandson, told me of a time in 1980 when he and his brother were with their grandfather in his front yard. Mrs. Hansen opened the door and told her husband he had a telephone call. "I'll call back," he demurred. "Cliff," she called, "it's Ronald Reagan." Hansen took the call but soon returned silently to the yard and his grandchildren. "Grandpa," said Mead, "Was that really President Reagan?" "Yes," said Hansen. "What did he want?" asked Mead. "He offered me a job," said Hansen. "What did you tell him?" queried Mead. "I told him no," concluded Hansen. (In 2010, Mead was elected Governor of Wyoming.) Some say that Hansen was concerned about whether he could keep federal grazing leases that were essential to the survival of his working ranch. ("Hansen recalls, 'It appeared to me that I just couldn't take the job without going out of the cow business." Arnold, *At the Eye of the Storm*, 26.) In October 1983, after Watt resigned, I again called Hansen and urged him to make himself available. "Perry," he confided, "my doctor told me that being in Washington would take ten years off my life." Hansen, one of the best loved public men in Washington and in Wyoming, died in 2009 at the age of 97, "not far from the log house where he was born." *Remembering Cliff Hansen*, Pete Williams.

17.   Oddly, Laxalt had not heard of Watt despite that Nevada was ground zero of the sagebrush rebellion, that Laxalt had identified himself as a sagebrush rebel, and that MSLF often engaged in litigation in support of sagebrush rebels. Short, *Ronald Reagan and the Public Lands*, 13, 18, 25. For example, one of MSLF's first lawsuits was a challenge to the failure of the BLM to comply with the Wild Free-Roaming Horses and Burros Act of 1971, 16 U.S.C. §1331, as amended by the Public Rangelands Improvement Act of 1978, Pub. L. No. 95-514 (Oct. 25, 1978), by removing excess wild horses from federal lands and from privately owned grazing allotments. *Mountain States Legal Foundation and Rock Springs Grazing Association v. Andrus*, C79-275K, March 13, 1981, as amended by the

February 19, 1982, order. The case was in Wyoming but Laxalt's Nevada had significant wild horse problems as well. McClure knew Watt, however, and arranged a lunch for the two of them with Laxalt; the interview went swimmingly as Watt answered each question with "political red meat," so they would "know where I stood," said Watt. Laxalt brought up coyotes, the bane of Western stockmen. Watt knew the issue was intractable, "I don't know what to do about coyotes." Sensing Laxalt's disappointment, McClure countered. "You do know they are a problem, don't you Jim?" "Are you asking me if I'm a killer?" Watt replied. "If you are, I'm a killer." Laxalt reached for the telephone to call Edwin Meese III, Reagan's close advisor who, in January 1981, became counselor to the president. "We have our secretary of the interior," Laxalt told Meese. Years later, Watt told of this luncheon in a speech and got a call from Laxalt. "Don't ever tell that story again," pleaded Laxalt. Coyotes are not a partisan issue. Colorado Governor Dick Lamm, a Democrat, wrote, "Where there is range, there are coyotes. And where there are coyotes, there is death." Richard D. Lamm and Michael McCarthy, *The Angry West: A Vulnerable Land and Its Future* (Houghton Mifflin, 1982), 252.

18. According to Alan Simpson, the senators in the meeting to identify an interior secretary for President Reagan included Laxalt, Wallop, Simpson, McClure and Senator Pete Domenici, a Republican from New Mexico. Arnold, *At the Eye of the Storm*, 51–52. For a discussion of the process from Watt's selection to his confirmation see ibid., 51–73.

19. Joe Coors, grandson of Adolph Coors who founded the family's Colorado brewery in 1873, was a member of Reagan's "Kitchen Cabinet," helped found The Heritage Foundation in Washington, D.C., and served as founding chairman of MSLF. He hired Watt in 1977 to serve as MSLF's first president. Coors was a frequent visitor to the Oval Office. ("Tuesday, April 5[, 1983] Joe Coors came by for a drink & some talk. He's a fine man." *The Reagan Diaries*, 142.)

20. "The Mountain States Legal Foundation has filed a suit with the Fed. Govt. claiming that constitutional rights of several states are being violated. When Congress voted to extend the time for states to ratify the Equal Rights Amendment it refused to allow several states to change their position and rescind the approval they had given several years ago *earlier*." (Emphasis in original.) Skinner, *Reagan, In His Own Hand*, 416. "Miscellaneous and Goodbye," October 25, 1979. (A photocopy of the handwritten version of this talk is set forth there.)

21. As an IRC 501(c)(3) entity, MSLF is not only "a nonprofit, public-interest legal foundation" (PILF), it is also nonpartisan. Watt's background is most similar to that of another Coloradoan who served as secretary of the interior, Oscar L. Chapman (1949–1953).

22. Ibid.; *An American Life*, 233. "Tip didn't try to hide the fact that he thought I had come to Washington to dismantle everything he believed in—things he and other liberals had spent decades fighting for, starting with the New Deal. As far as he was concerned, I was the enemy." Ibid.

23. Would Reagan have remembered what he wrote about MSLF a little over a year earlier? William P. Clark and Edwin Meese were astonished at his memory. "Reagan had a 'tremendous memory, better than any of ours,' Clark continues. Ed Meese agrees, saying that Reagan probably had a photographic memory." Paul Kengor & Patricia Clark Doerner, *The Judge: William P. Clark, Ronald Reagan's Top Hand* (Ignatius, 2007) 71. George P. Schultz noted, "I could tell dozens of stories about specific times when Ronald Reagan displayed detailed knowledge about policy issues, and when he took decisive action based on that knowledge—without the benefit of someone whispering in his ear or sliding a note into his hand." Skinner, "Foreword," *Reagan, In His Own Hand*, xi.

24. Arnold, *At the Eye of the Storm*, 55. See also, "America – Our Treasure and Our Trust: The Legacy of President Ronald Reagan 1981 – 1988," (U.S. Department of the Interior, December 1988), ii; Joanne Omang, "Watt—A Promise to Support Environmental Laws," *Washington Post*, January 8, 1981, Sec. A, 2. "Significantly, the goals suggested that the secretary intended to implement Reagan's campaign pledges as policy." Short, *Ronald Reagan and the Public Lands*, 53–54. "No other Secretary of the Interior, in recent times, at least, has had a President who understands my department like Ronald Reagan does. He's a Westerner. Fifty percent of his state is owned and managed by the federal government. When I said, 'I want to do this, I want to do that,' he replied, 'Sic 'em.'" Elizabeth Drew, "A Reporter at Large, Secretary Watt," *New Yorker*, May 4, 1981, 112.

25. Kengor, *The Judge*, 257. President Reagan appears to have taken delight in catching the White House staff and outside observers off guard: "made surprise announcement of Bill Clark as new secretary of Interior … ," noted his Thursday, October 13, 1983 diary entry. *The Reagan Diaries*, 187.

26. President Reagan received notice of Clark's confirmation by the Senate on November 18, 1983. *The Reagan Diaries*, 199.

27. Radio Address to the Nation on the Resignation of Secretary of the Interior James G. Watt, November 26, 1983, University of Wyoming, American Heritage Center, James G. Watt Papers, ah07667_00027- 28. On November 28, 1983, Clark said of the radio address, "The President did not have to do it. Jim was gone. But that is the kind of man [Reagan] is."

28. *The Reagan Diaries*, 188. "You'll have to back me and back me until you have to fire me," Watt told President Reagan in their first meeting. Short, *Ronald Reagan and the Public Lands*, 55, quoting James Conway, "James Watt, In the Right with the Lord," *Washington Post*, April 27, 1983, Sec. B, 13. Also, Arnold, *At the Eye of the Storm*, 55.

29. Kengor, *The Judge*, 274–75, 293.

30. Ibid., 107, 143–44. Clark also served as Deputy Secretary of State and Assistant to the President for National Security Affairs or National Security Advisor.

31. See Chapter 14, "Double Duty: Clark's Non-Interior Work at Interior." Ibid., 280–96. President Reagan, the one-time Democrat and admirer of President Roosevelt, no doubt would have known of the unique role Ickes played for FDR when he sent Clark to Interior. Ibid.

32. *The Reagan Diaries*, 292. Hodel earned the respect of President Reagan's most trusted aides. When Attorney General Meese resigned, Reagan noted, "An interesting successor [Meese] suggested was Sec. of Interior Don Hodel." *The Reagan Diaries*, 627.

33. It is impossible to overstate the closeness of the relationship between Reagan and Clark. Clark was "the only person in the entire two terms who had any kind of spiritual intimacy with the President." Edmund Morris, "The Pope and the President," *Catholic World Report* (November 1999): 54. Clark was "one of my most trusted and valued advisers." Ronald Reagan, "Remarks Announcing the Appointment of Robert C. McFarlane as Assistant to the President for National Security Affairs," *Public Papers of the Presidents of the United States*: Ronald Reagan, October 17, 1983, 1471. "When Reagan had a tough task, he called upon Clark, his troubleshooter, his right-hand man."; Kengor, *The Judge*, 16. "Starting in Sacramento … Clark got closer to Reagan than anyone who knew the man, with the exception of Mrs. Reagan. The two were so close that Reagan biographers such as Lou Cannon, Richard Reeves, and others who worked with both men, say that Reagan regarded Clark as a brother."; Ibid.

34. Davis W. Houck and Amos Kiewe, Eds., *Actor, Ideologue, Politician: The Public Speeches of Ronald Reagan* (Greenwood, 1993), 160.

35. Ibid.

36. Ibid., 177–78.

37. Skinner, *Reagan, In His Own Hand*, 319; "Oil I," June 15, 1977 "[I]sn't [Carter's] plea for conservation to reduce consumption by 10% rather futile? If all the oil is going to be gone in 30 years does it really make much difference if we make it last 33?" Ibid. Note: At times in the use of Reagan's radio commentaries, the author has added punctuation, modified the use of upper and lower case, and spelled out abbreviations or symbols for ease of reading.

38. Ibid. Reagan's optimism on the future of oil and gas was in stark contrast to President Carter's pessimism on the subject.

> The oil and natural gas that we rely on for 75 percent of our energy are simply running out. In spite of increased effort, domestic production has been dropping steadily at about 6 percent a year. Imports have doubled in the last 5 years. Our Nation's economic and political independence is becoming increasingly vulnerable. Unless profound changes are made to lower oil consumption, we now believe that early in the 1980's the world will be demanding more oil than it can produce.

President Carter Address to the Nation on Energy, April 18, 1977, http://www.presidency.ucsb.edu/ws/index.php?pid=7369#axzz1R3qJn3vT.

39. Skinner, *Reagan, In His Own Hand*, 319.

40. Houck and Kiewe, *Actor, Ideologue, Politician*, 178.

41. Skinner, *Reagan, In His Own Hand*, 338; "Federal Lands," October 10, 1978.

42. Ibid.

43. Ibid.

44. Ibid. In his December 12, 1978 radio address "Keep Off the Grass," Reagan further detailed the efforts of the federal government under the second so-called Roadless Area Review & Evaluation program, in bureaucratise, "RARE II," to close millions of acres to multiple use, including oil and gas exploration and development, but also motorized recreation. Reported Reagan, "In other words

only those robust enough to go backpacking would have access to those millions of acres of scenic land." Skinner, *Reagan's Path to Victory*, 383.

45. Skinner, *Reagan, In His Own Hand*, 320.

46. Ibid., 321; "OPEC," January 19, 1979.

47. Ibid.

48. Ibid.

49. Ibid., 318–22; Skinner, *Reagan's Path to Victory*, 166–68.

50. Ibid., 167; 257–58.

51. Charles L. Heatherly, ed., *Mandate for Leadership: Policy Management in a Conservative Administration* (The Heritage Foundation, 1981).

52. Ibid., 333–401. Cited by Terrell as deserving "particular mention" were Sam Ballenger, Frank Cushing, Gary Ellsworth, Harry McKittrick, Ray Peck, Perry Pendley, Craig Potter, and Dave Russell.

53. *Webster's Third New International Dictionary* (G. & C. Merriam, 1966) defines conservation as "the wise utilization of a natural product." On one of the granite tablets (the one labeled "Nature") at the Theodore Roosevelt Memorial on Theodore Roosevelt Island in Washington, D.C. is inscribed, "Conservation means development as much as it does protection. (*The New Nationalism*, 1910)," http://www.theodoreroosevelt.org/modern/trisland.htm.

54. Heatherly, *Mandate*, 335–36.

55. Ibid., 333–34.

56. Ibid., 355. "The Solicitor is the chief attorney for the United States Department of the Interior [and] principal legal adviser to the Secretary of the Interior...." http://www.doi.gov/solicitor/index.html.

57. Heatherly, *Mandate*, 354–55. The Carter administration solicitor's opinions' interpretation of such statutory terms as "valid existing rights," "grandfathered rights," "manner and degree," and "nonimpairment," "clearly thwarted the intent of Congress." Ibid., 355.

58. Executive Order 12287–Decontrol of Crude Oil and Refined Petroleum Products, January 28, 1981. The Natural Gas Act of 1938, 15 U.S.C. 717 et seq., gave the Federal Power Commission (later the Federal Energy Regulatory Commission) power to set "just and reasonable rates" for the interstate transmission or sale of natural gas. Price control had "disastrous effects on the natural gas market in the United States." First, with natural gas prices below the market value of the gas, demand surged. Second, there was no incentive for producers to explore for new natural gas deposits. Third, consumers in producing states had an abundance of natural gas, while consumers in other states suffered natural gas shortages, http://www.naturalgas.org/regulation/history.asp. As a result, the Natural Gas Policy Act of 1978, 15 U.S.C. §3301 et seq., initiated price decontrol and elimination of the dual market for natural gas due to competing state and federal regulatory programs. "At the time the [Natural Gas Wellhead Decontrol Act] of 1989 was enacted, more than 60 percent of the domestically produced gas was already price decontrolled, and another 33 percent had never been subject to NGPA price controls," http://www.eia.gov/oil_gas/natural_gas/analysis_publications/ngmajorleg/ngact1989.html.

59. The Mineral Leasing Act of 1920, 30 U.S.C. §181 et seq. provides for leasing of federal land to develop coal, petroleum, natural gas and other hydrocarbons, as well as phosphates, sodium, sulfur, and potassium. Before its enactment, these resources, as well as other minerals were subject to self-initiated exploration by American citizens; that is they were "locatable" under the General Mining Act of 1872. The Mineral Leasing Act gives the secretary total discretion as to when and where and even if to issue leases.

60. http://www.blm.gov/wo/st/en/info/About_BLM.html.

61. http://www.fs.fed.us/.

62. http://www.fws.gov/refuges/. Environmental groups oppose oil and gas drilling especially in wildlife refuges, but one group that owns a refuge developed the natural gas on its property to the tune of $25 million and in doing so maintained that energy development was consistent with the wildlife purposes of the refuge. http://www.perc.org/articles/article167.php. Arnold, *At the Eye of the Storm*, 161.

63. Ross W. Gorte et al., "Federal Land Ownership: Overview and Data," Congressional Research Service, February 8, 2012, 4–5.

64. http://www.npca.org/exploring-our-parks/about-the-national-parks.html.

65. 43 C.F.R. § 3109.2 Units of the National Park System.

66. The Wilderness Act, P.L. 88-577, 78 Stat. 890, "Definition of Wilderness" (1964) at 1014. See generally, William Perry Pendley, *War on the West: Government Tyranny on America's Great Frontier* (Regnery, 1995), Chapter 7, "Where Man Is A Visitor," 114–26. See generally, Arnold, *At*

the Eye of the Storm, 29–31. Are wilderness areas "ecological museums" or "an all-purpose tool for stopping economic activity?" William Tucker, "Is Nature Too Good for Us? It's not much of an environment if you can't get in," *Harper's* (March 1982).

67. Wilderness Fact Sheet, Recreation Management Staff, Forest Service, U.S. Dept of Agriculture (March 8, 1982) (as of 12/31/81). The National Wilderness Preservation System (NWPS) established by the Wilderness Act of 1964 contained 9.1 million acres. C. Coggins and C. Wilkinson, *Federal Public Land and Natural Resources Law* 774 (1981). The largest additions to the wilderness preservation system took place with enactment of the Alaska National Interest Lands Conservation Act of Dec. 1980, P.L. 96-487, §§ 701-05, 94 Stat. 2371, 2417-20, 16 U.S.C. § 1132 (Supp. IV 1980).

68. Stephen S. Edelson, *The Management of Oil and Gas Leasing on Federal Wilderness Lands*, 10 B.C. *Envtl. Aff. L. Rev.* 905 (1983). For a discussion of the seemingly never ending study of potential wilderness lands and the refusal of wilderness proponents to support "hard release" language that would permit multiple use of federal lands, including oil and gas leasing, see Pendley, *War on the West*, 114–26.

69. "1983 – A Year Of Enrichment: Improving The Quality Of Life For All Americans," (U.S. Department of the Interior, October 1983), 13.

70. *Interior Report 1983*, 16, 18. See also, Kornbrath et al., *Petroleum Potential of the Eastern National Petroleum Reserve-Alaska* (State of Alaska Department of Natural Resources Division of Oil and Gas, April 1997). Alaska residents believe the Obama administration is moving in the wrong direction on the NPR-A. "Only in Obama's backwards worldview of anti-energy policies does it make sense to prohibit energy production in a place specifically set aside for energy production at a time when gasoline prices are skyrocketing and federal oil and natural gas production is declining," said U.S. House of Representatives Natural Resources Committee Chairman Doc Hastings (R-WA). Nick Snow, "Salazar, Alaska producers view final NPR-A plan differently," *Oil and Gas Journal* (February 22, 2013). The NPR-A also possesses rich coal and nonfuel mineral resources. Rose Ragsdale, "Bonanza may await explorers in NPR-A South; miners want BLM to include coal, hard rock leasing," *Petroleum News*, August 25, 2006.

71. *Interior Report 1988*, 27.

72. Ibid., 18. The ANWR consists of 1.8 million acres, which is equal in size to South Carolina, but oil and gas exploration would be limited to an area the size of Dulles International Airport outside of Washington, D.C. The amount of recoverable crude oil is estimated at between 5.7 billion to 16 billion barrels. Jonah Goldberg, "Livin' in a Frosty Paradise?," National Review Online, June 13, 2008.

73. William R. Ritz, "Oil Thefts put in Millions," *The Denver Post*, March 16, 1981.

74. Federal Oil and Gas Royalty Management Act of 1982 (30 U.S.C. § 1701 et seq.). See also, "Fiscal Accountability of the Nation's Energy Resources" (FANER), Government Printing Office, January 1982 and Federal Oil and Gas Royalty Simplification and Fairness Act (RSFA), Pub. Law 104-185, 30 U.S.C. §1701.

75. *Interior Report 1983*, 18; Heatherly, *Mandate*, 349; and Secretarial Order No. 3071.

76. See, Abraham E. Haspel, "Drilling for Dollars: The Federal Oil-Lease Lottery Program," *Regulation*, July/August 1985, for a discussion of the problem, the Reagan administration's response, and the potential for legislative relief. The legislative solution successfully urged upon Congress in 1987 is discussed in *Sagebrush Rebel*, chapter 9.

77. Haspel, "Drilling for Dollars," 26. After all, oil companies tended to "control" all the land that might overlay an oil deposit before drilling. Since competition only occurred on lands on a "producing known geological structure" most production occurred on leases that were issued noncompetitively.

78. Ibid., 25. By 2012, however, the big news was on state and private lands where hydraulic fracturing yielded an abundance of oil and natural gas across the country. Jad Mouawad, "Fuel to Burn: Now What?" *New York Times*, April 10, 2012.

79. David Brown, "Crash of '86 Left Permanent Scars," *Explorer*, January 2006.

80. The impressive results are demonstrated graphically in a U.S. Energy Information Administration chart at www.eia.gov/dnav/ng/hist/e_ertw0_xwc0_nus_cm.htm.

81. No one outside Washington may have expected Saudi Arabia to flood the oil market, but President Reagan and a handful of others not only expected it, they also ensured it. Director of the CIA Casey told the Saudis, "Every time the price [of oil] goes up one dollar a barrel, it means $1 billion a year hard currency for Moscow. We can't afford to have that happen again." Casey did not just want to stop oil prices from going up; he wanted to drive them down. "A drop in the price of oil by perhaps $10 a barrel would cost Moscow dearly—$10 billion [a year]." Reagan intended to destroy the Soviet

Union's economy and Casey intended to make it happen. Peter Schweizer, *Victory: The Reagan Administration's Secret Strategy That Hastened the Collapse of the Soviet Union* (Atlantic Monthly Press, 1996), 31, 105.

82.   David Brown, "Crash of '86 Left Permanent Scars," *Explorer*, January 2006. In Denver, Colorado, in those days, it was not unusual to see this bumper sticker: "Please God, One More Oil Boom. I Promise Not To Screw It Up This Time."

83.   Skinner, *Reagan's Path to Victory*, 167. "About 80% of the finding of new oil has been done—not by the giant oil companies but by independents...." Ibid.

84.   Ann Chambers Noble, "The Jonah Field and Pinedale Anticline: A natural-gas success story," http://www.wyohistory.org/essays/jonah-field-and-pinedale-anticline-natural-gas-success-story.

85.   John W. Robinson, "Discovery of Jonah Field, Sublette County, Wyoming," *The Mountain Geologist* 37, no. 3 (July 2000): 135–43.

86.   Skinner, *Reagan, In His Own Hand*, 318–22.

87.   Noble, "The Jonah Field and Pinedale Anticline."

88.   In 2013, the Congressional Research Service reported that, although the United States is the largest natural gas producing country in the world, and in 2012, produced oil at the fastest rate since the first oil well was drilled before the Civil War, production on federal lands is moribund. Marc Humphries, "U.S. Crude Oil and Natural Gas Production in Federal and Non-Federal Areas," Congressional Research Service, February 28, 2013. The latest entry into the long list of exciting new oil and gas plays on state and private land is the Niobrara in the Denver-Julesburg Basin in northeastern Colorado. Cathy Proctor, "Colorado's Niobrara oil play not a flash in the pan," *Denver Business Journal*, April 15, 2013. In addition, south Texas's Eagle Ford shale play continues to impress. Christopher Sherman, "Eagle Ford booms bigger, faster than first thought," *Fort Worth Business Press*, March 29, 2013. North Dakota's Bakken, which like Eagle Ford, produces predominantly oil not natural gas, is well known and getting bigger, but some think California's Monterey/Santos shale play near Bakersfield is even larger. Nathan Slaughter, "The Company With A Hold On The Biggest Shale Play In America," NASDAQ, April 16, 2013. Whether it will be developed is another question. Patrick M. Klemz, "Federal judge stops Monterey Shale fracking leases," [San Luis Obispo County, California] *New Times*, April 11, 2013. At issue is whether the Bureau of Land Management complied with NEPA.

89.   Billions of dollars is a rough estimate; however, it is as likely tens of billions of dollars. Reports abound of green energy companies—despite federal tax credits, refundable tax credits, or commitments to underwrite exorbitant production costs—going out of business and leaving taxpayers to pick up the tab. In January 2010, the White House bragged that $90 billion was being spent on green energy initiatives. "The Economic Impact of the American Recovery and Reinvestment Act of 2009, Second Quarterly Report, Executive Office of the President, Council of Economic Advisors, January 13, 2010, 31–40. In a 2013 report, the General Accountability Office disclosed that 23 federal agencies run hundreds of renewable energy programs at a cost of several billion dollars a year. "Actions Needed to Reduce Fragmentation, Overlap, and Duplication and Achieve Other Financial Benefits," U.S. Government Accountability Office, April 9, 2013, 51. See, for example, "End the DoD's green energy fuelishness," Kenneth P. Green, American Enterprise Institute, July 2, 2012. Even during times of purported tightening budgets, the lavish spending on green energy continues. "DOE awarding more than $1.2 billion in energy subsidies despite sequester," Michal Conger, *Washington Examiner*, April 3, 2013. Meanwhile, in the technological battle to develop more energy resources, fossil fuels are winning! Associated Press, "Oil and gas drillers make technological leaps, while renewable energy industry struggles," *Washington Post*, May 2, 2013. As a result, the abundance of natural gas is causing states to begin to abandon, in the words of Reagan biographer Steven F. Hayward, "their renewable portfolio standards that mandate the purchase of uncompetitive and grid-destabilizing wind and solar power. The rout of the environmentalists continues." Powerlineblog.com, May 8, 2013, referencing Christopher Martin, "Cheap natural gas prompts states to sour on renewable," Bloomberg, May 5, 2013.

90.   Reagan's likely views on Obama's plan to increase taxes on the oil and gas industry to pay for "green energy" boondoggles, including funding alternative energy sources, mandating renewable energy goals, and researching energy efficient transportation are easy to determine. David J. Unger, "Obama budget boosts 'green energy,' but no olive branch to GOP," *Christian Science Monitor*, April 10, 2013. Carter tried it first and drew a withering attack by Reagan. In his 1979 radio address entitled "The Magic Money Machine," Governor Reagan derided Carter's plan to enact a windfall profits tax to bring in huge sums to spend on his synthetic fuels projects. Governor Reagan thought the

better solution was to "encourage the discovery of more oil so as to reduce our dependence on the imported stuff. I have a feeling that if our government was as good at getting oil out of the ground as it is at getting money out of us we'd all be driving gas guzzlers with nothing to worry about except how to pay for them." Skinner, *Reagan's Path to Victory*, 467–68.

91. Reagan complained for years that "experts" in the federal government underestimated the potential for energy development in the United States; thus, it would come as no surprise to Reagan that a 2011 study concluded the U.S. has over 1.4 trillion barrels of technically recoverable oil, which is more than four times Saudi Arabian proven reserves and over 200 years' worth of the nation's oil consumption at its current rate. Total oil resources in the ground are estimated at a whopping 3.75 trillion barrels! "North American Energy Inventory," Institute for Energy Research, December 2011, 1–4. See George Will, "The Specter of Abundance," *Washington Post*, January 2, 2012. Similarly, potential natural gas supplies continue to grow by leaps and bounds. At the end of 2012, "the United States possesses a total technically recoverable resource base of 2,384 trillion cubic feet" of natural gas, the highest resource evaluation ever. "Potential Gas Committee Reports Significant Increase in Magnitude of U.S. Natural Gas Resource Base," Press Release, April 9, 2013, Dr. John B. Curtis, Potential Gas Agency, Colorado School of Mines, Golden, Colorado, http://potentialgas.org/press-release. Meanwhile, Obama, like Carter before him, asserts that it is futile to attempt to drill ourselves out of the nation's oil dependency because, according to Obama, the United States has only "2% of the world's oil reserves." The *Washington Post* awarded this oft-repeated canard "Two Pinocchios" and declared, "We hope he finally drops this specious logic from his talking points." Glenn Kessler, "Pinocchios: Obama gets a downgrade," The Fact Checker: The Truth Behind the Rhetoric, *Washington Post*, March 22, 2012.

92. Stephen Moore, "How North Dakota Became Saudi Arabia, *The Wall Street Journal*, October 1, 2011.

93. In 2012, the Congressional Budget Office estimated the increased federal revenues that would result from leasing and developing federal lands now off-limits to oil and gas development. "Potential Budgetary Effects of Immediately Opening Most Federal Lands to Oil and Gas Leasing," Congressional Budget Office, August 2012. A 2013 report went further, estimating the economic benefits to be enjoyed by the American people from such development to include half a million new jobs annually for the next seven years; almost two million jobs annually over the next 30 years; a $32 billion annual increase in wages over the next seven years; and a $115 billion annual increase in wages over the next seven to 30 years. Joseph R. Mason et al., "Beyond the Congressional Budget Office: The Additional Economic Effects of Immediately Opening Federal Lands to Oil and Gas Leasing," Institute for Energy Research, February 2013, 2.

CHAPTER TWO

1. "America must get to work producing more energy. The Republican program for solving economic problems is based on growth and productivity. Large amounts of oil and natural gas lay beneath our land and off our shores, untouched because the present administration seems to believe the American people would rather see more regulation, taxes and controls than more energy," declared Reagan in his address accepting the presidential nomination of the Republican Party in July 1980. Davis W. Houck and Amos Kiewe, eds., *Actor, Ideologue, Politician: The Public Speeches of Ronald Reagan* (Greenwood, 1993), 160.

2. Kiron K. Skinner, Annelise Anderson, and Martin Anderson, eds., *Reagan's Path to Victory, The Shaping of Ronald Reagan's Vision: Selected Writings* (The Free Press, 2004) 314–15. Reagan was responding to a Massachusetts federal district court that "issued an injunction prohibiting the sale of oil exploration leases for the Georges Bank off Cape Cod on the grounds that 'irreparable' ecological harm would follow such exploration." Reagan noted, "In the 25 years from 1950 to 1975, the total annual catch of fish in Massachusetts dropped from almost 600 million pounds to less than 300 million without any oil or gas drilling activity."

3. Skinner, *Reagan's Path to Victory*, 206–8.

4. Ibid., 207. The U.S. Geological Survey was created on March 3, 1879, by an Act of Congress, 43 U.S.C. § 31. http://www.usgs.gov/aboutusgs/who_we_are/history.asp.

5. Ibid.

6. Ibid.

7. Houck and Kiewe, *Actor, Ideologue, Politician*, 160.

8. Charles L. Heatherly, ed., *Mandate for Leadership: Policy Management in a Conservative Administration* (The Heritage Foundation, 1981), 355–56.

9.   Ibid., 356–57.

10.   Ibid., 357–58.

11.   Ibid., 358.

12.   "[T]he Government of the United States regards the natural resources of the subsoil and sea bed of the continental shelf beneath the high seas but contiguous to the coasts of the United States as appertaining to the United States, subject to its jurisdiction and control." Proclamation 2667 – Policy of the United States With Respect to the Natural Resources of the Subsoil and Sea Bed of the Continental Shelf. September 28, 1945. 10 *Fed. Reg.* 12, 305 (1945), Executive Order 9633 of September 28, 1945. President Truman's first "Whereas," addressed "the long range world-wide need for new sources of petroleum and other minerals." The proclamation originated in the Interior Department with Secretary Ickes. H. L. Ickes to H. S. Truman, July 17, 1945, and Presidential Proclamation 2667, October 2, 1945, White House Official File, Box 273, File 56F "Tidelands Oil," Harry Truman Presidential Library, Independence, Missouri. "Ickes' initiative sparked a major political battle, with coastal states, the oil industry and advocates of states' rights on one side, and the Truman administration, northern oil-consuming states, and spokesmen for consumers and taxpayers on the other." Richard H. K. Vietor, *Energy Policy in America Since 1945: A Study of Business-Government Relations* (Cambridge University Press, 1984), 18.

13.   William K. Wyant, *Westward in Eden: The Public Lands and the Conservation Movement* (University of California Press, 1987), 218–34.

14.   The Submerged Lands Act of 1953, 43 U.S.C. §1301 et seq., which granted coastal states title to the submerged navigable lands within their boundaries (generally three nautical or geographical miles from the coastline) and thereby overturned earlier decisions by the Supreme Court of the United States, *United States v. California*, 332 U.S. 19 (1947), *United States v. Louisiana*, 339 U.S. 699 (1950), and *United States v. Texas*, 339 U.S. 707 (1950), which held that these "submerged lands" belonged to the United States. The exact extent of the title of states adjoining the Gulf of Mexico was not resolved until two subsequent rulings by the Supreme Court holding that the distance for both Texas and the west coast of Florida was nine nautical miles. *United States v. Louisiana*, 363 U.S. 1 (1960), and *United States v. Florida*, 363 U.S. 121 (1960).

15.   The Outer Continental Shelf Lands Act (OCSLA), 43 U.S.C. §1331. Section 1301 further defines "lands beneath navigable waters" to mean: "(1) all lands within the boundaries of each of the respective States which are covered by non-tidal waters that were navigable under the laws of the United States at the time such State became a member of the Union, or acquired sovereignty over such lands and waters thereafter, up to the ordinary high water mark as heretofore or hereafter modified by accretion, erosion, and reliction; (2) all lands permanently or periodically covered by tidal waters up to but not above the line of mean high tide and seaward to a line three geographical miles distant from the coast line of each such State and to the boundary line of each such State where in any case such boundary as it existed at the time such State became a member of the Union, or as heretofore approved by Congress, extends seaward (or into the Gulf of Mexico) beyond three geographical miles, and (3) all filled in, made, or reclaimed lands which formerly were lands beneath navigable waters, as hereinabove defined...." Congress also codified President Truman's 1945 proclamation.

16.   "The Act authorized the Secretary of the Interior to administer OCS properties, set conservation rules and determine leasing schedules, and grant leases of oil and gas properties by sealed, competitive bids on the basis of a cash bonus and a fixed royalty." Vietor, *Energy Policy*, 19, citing, Stephen L. McDonald, *The Leasing of Federal Lands for Fossil Fuels Production* (RFF Press, 1979), 16–20.

17.   "Leasing Oil and Natural Gas Resources – Outer Continental Shelf," U.S. Department of the Interior, Mineral Management Service ("Green Book-Leasing Document"), Appendix C, 49, www.boemre.gov/ID/PDFs/GreenBook-LeasingDocument.pdf. The first offshore oil production in the United States took place in 1896 in state waters from a "wooden pier off Summerland, CA."

18.   Vietor, *Energy Policy*, 18.

19.   Robert Olney Easton, *Black Tide: The Santa Barbara Oil Spill and Its Consequences* (Delacorte Press, 1972), 63–64. Easton recounts high school student Kathy Morales' response when the spill came ashore: "You want to talk about The Establishment?" she asked. "This is my life—out here. I come out here all the time to watch the sea and the birds and animals. I can't think of coming down here for a stroll again. I can't think of some day bringing my children here to watch and to play. I don't know now," she said, with the tears streaming down her cheeks, "if it will ever be the same again, and no one can tell me." An academic study of the impact of the spill concluded, "[D]amage

to the biota [combined flora and fauna of a region] was not widespread, but was limited to several species[;] the area is recovering. In retrospect, it is not surprising that the studies after the Santa Barbara oil spill revealed such a small amount of damage." Dale Straughan, *Biological and oceanographical survey of the Santa Barbara Channel oil spill*, 1969–1970, Allan Hancock Foundation, (University of Southern California, 1971), 217.

20.   42 U.S.C. 4321 et seq. NEPA is referred to as the "National Environmental Policy Act of 1969," but it did not become law until January 1, 1970. 42 U.S.C. §7401 et seq. Nixon was president from January 1969 until August 1974 and supported these environmental laws. Ford was president from August 1974 until January 1977. Carter became president in January 1977 and actively supported these laws.

21.   16 U.S.C. § 1451 et seq. 16 U.S.C. 1362 et seq.

22.   16 U.S.C. §1531 et seq.

23.   33 U.S.C. §1251 et seq.

24.   Outer Continental Shelf Lands Act Amendments of 1978, (P.L. 95–372).

25.   "The Secretary [] shall prepare and periodically revise, and maintain an oil and gas leasing program [that] shall consist of a schedule of proposed lease sales indicating, as precisely as possible, the size, timing, and location of leasing activity which he determines will best meet national energy needs for the five-year period following its approval or reapproval." 43 U.S.C. § 1344(a).

26.   Coastal Zone Management Act Amendments of 1980, (P.L. 96–464). Like much federal legislation, the OCSLA, including its 1978 Amendments, and the CZMA, especially after its 1980 Amendments, are in conflict; in fact, their goals are schizophrenic and even mutually exclusive.

27.   American Petroleum Institute, Two Energy Futures: A National Choice For The 80's (1980), 44. ("API Report"). "In January, 1974, President Nixon ordered the Secretary of the Interior to lease 10 million OCS acres in 1975, more than triple the acreage scheduled for leasing in that year." Karen L. Linsley, *Federal Consistency and Outer Continental Shelf Oil and Gas Leasing: The Application of the "Directly Affecting" Test to Pre-Lease Sale Activities*, 9 B.C. Envtl. Aff. L. Rev. 431 (1980), 432, citing, 10 Weekly Comp. Of Pres. Doc. 72, 83–84 (January 28, 1974).

28.   H.R. Rep. No. 590, 95th Cong., 1st. Sess. 74 (1977), reprinted in [1978] U.S. Code Cong. & Ad. News, 1450, 1481.

29.   "1983 – A Year Of Enrichment: Improving The Quality Of Life For All Americans," (U.S. Department of the Interior, October 1983), 18.

30.   *OCS Oversight-Part 2: Hearings 011 OCS Oversight and Related Issues, the National OCS Program and the Five-Year OCS Leasing Program Before the Subcomm. on the Panama Canal/Outer Continental Shelf of the House Comm. on Merchant Marine and Fisheries*, 97th Cong., 1st Sess. 51 (1981) [hereinafter *OCS Oversight Hearings-Part 2*] (statement of James G. Watt, Secretary of the Interior).

31.   Minerals Management Serv., U.S. Dep't of the Interior, *News Release* I (July 21, 1982) [*News Release* (July 21, 1982)]. The federal OCS, out to a depth of 2500 meters, is estimated at about one billion acres (965.8 million acres). Comptroller General, U.S. General Accounting Office, Pub. No. EMD 81-59, Report To The Congress, "Issues In Leasing Offshore Lands For Oil And Gas Development" 3-4 (1981) [Issues In Leasing Offshore Lands]. Today, Interior estimates the federal OCS as constituting 1.7 billion acres. See, "New Energy Frontier," http://www.doi.gov/whatwedo/energy/index.cfm.

32.   "One or more times during the five-year period, all the tracts in each of the 18 Outer Continental Shelf planning areas ... [are] offered for lease, excepting tracts eliminated for environmental reasons and to accommodate other uses." *News Release* (July 15, 1981). "While the Interior Department offered almost one billion OCS acres for oil and gas leasing, Secretary Watt actually hoped to annually lease between five and twelve million acres." G. Kevin Jones, "Outer Continental Shelf Oil and Gas Development During the Reagan Administration—Part I," *Western New England Law Review* 12, issue 1 (1990): 11. The most federal OCS acreage leased previously in one year was 1.8 million in 1979. Offshore Information & Publications, Minerals Management Serv., U.S. Dep't Of The Interior, OCS Report Mms 89-0058, Federal Offshore Statistics: 1987, Leasing, Exploration, Production & Revenues 12 (1989).

33.   "Offshore Oil-leasing Plans Get Watt's Final Approval," *New York Times*, August 4, 1982, Sec. A, 9.

34.   *Hearings to Review the Secretary of the Interior's Proposed Five-Year Plan for Oil and Gas Development in the Outer Continental Shelf Pursuant to the Outer Continental Shelf Lands Act Amendments of 1978 Before the Subcomm. on Energy Conservation and Supply of the Senate Comm. on Energy and Natural Resources*, 97th Cong., 2d Sess. I (1982), 1 [hereinafter *Senate Hearings on the Five-Year OCS Leasing Plan*] (statement of Senator Lowell Weicker of Connecticut). Staff of The Subcomm.

On Oversight and Investigations of The House Comm. on Interior And Insular Affairs, 98th Cong., 1st Sess., A Report On The Secretary of The Interior James G. Watt's Five Year Oil And Gas Leasing Plan For The Outer Continental Shelf I (Comm. Print 1983), 6 [hereinafter House Rep. On Secretary Watt's Five-year OCS Leasing Plan].

35. *News Release* (July 21, 1982).

36. "A Quiet Point Man for Oil Leasing," *Business Week* 75 (August 30, 1982).

37. *OCS Oversight Hearings-Part* 2, note 1, at 55 (statement of James G. Watt, Secretary of the Interior).

38. Ibid., 370 (statement of Arthur Spaulding, Vice President and General Manager, Western Oil and Gas Ass'n and the Alaska Oil & Gas Ass'n).

39. G. Kevin Jones, 11–13. OCS acres offered went from 1.8 million acres (1977), 3.1 million acres (1978), 3.4 million acres (1979), 2.6 million acres (1980), 7.7 million acres (1981), and 7.6 million acres (1982) to 120 million acres (1983) and 154 million acres (1984). Offshore Information & Publications, Minerals Management Serv., U.S. Dep't Of The Interior, OCS Report MMS 89-0058, Federal Offshore Statistics: 1987, Leasing, Exploration, Production & Revenues 12 (1989) [hereinafter 1987 Federal Offshore Statistics].

40. Issues In Leasing Offshore Lands, 7. Minerals Management Serv., U.S. Department Of The Interior, Fact Sheet: Outer Continental Shelf Five-Year Leasing Program 1 (1982).

41. *OCS Oversight Hearings-Part* 2 (statement of James G. Watt, Secretary of the Interior). Vass, *A Comparison of American and British Offshore Oil Development During the Reagan and Thatcher Administrations. Part* 1, 21 Tulsa L.J. 23, 63 (1985). Bureau Of Land Management, U.S. Dep't Of The Interior, 1 Final Supplement To The Final Environmental Impact Statement: Proposed Five-Year OCS Oil And Gas Lease Sale Schedule, January 1982-December 1986 (1981), 22–29. The time required for the environmental studies was shortened by "telescoping," which is the concurrent, rather than consecutive, performance of required steps, such as issuing a proposed notice of sale at the same time as a Final Environmental Impact Statement (FEIS), and "tiering," which allows the agency to forego redundant discussions and focus instead on the actual matters ripe for decision-making. See, G. Kevin Jones, 18–19. 40 C.F.R. §§ 1502.20, 1508.28 (1988).

42. In January 1982, Watt transferred the Conservation Division's responsibility for onshore oil and gas leasing to the Bureau of Land Management (BLM), both for the minerals estate beneath BLM-managed lands as well as that beneath lands managed by the U.S. Forest Service; he also transferred the Conservation Division's responsibility for outer continental shelf (OCS) oil and gas leasing to the newly created Minerals Management Service (MMS). Secretarial Order No. 3071.

43. Unfortunately, the Deepwater Horizon blowout in 2010 gave the Obama administration an excuse to split these functions anew with resultant inefficiency. In May 2010, all of MMS responsibilities were reassigned to the Bureau of Ocean Energy Management, Regulation and Enforcement (BOEMRE). Secretarial Order No. 3299. In June 2010, the MMS was renamed the BOEMRE. Secretarial Order No. 3302. In September 2010, BOEMRE's federal revenue collection office was reassigned. Secretarial Order No. 3306. In October 2011, the BOEMRE was separated into the Bureau of Ocean Energy Management (BOEM) and the Bureau of Safety and Environmental Enforcement (BSEE). Final Rule, 76 *Fed. Reg.* 64431-64780 (October 18, 2011).

44. There were Republicans who opposed Reagan's OCS program, among them Connecticut Senator Lowell Weicker who led "[a] group of senators from coastal states [who] will try to block plans to accelerate leasing of offshore lands for oil and gas drilling by amending the debt ceiling bill now before the Senate." *Anchorage Daily News*, September 9, 1982, B7. President Reagan viewed Senator Weicker unfavorably: "Lowell Weicker was the head ringmaster against us as he is on everything we want. He's a pompous, no good, fathead." (March 20, 1984.) Ronald Reagan, *The Reagan Diaries* (Harper, 2007), 227.

    Watt recalls a meeting with the California congressional delegation. Democrat Congressmen Phil and John Burton, brothers, "were the trouble makers but the one who taught me the most about our opposition was a GOP member from San Diego." Republican Congressman Ron Packard from San Diego announced that he supported the OCS program if there were no drilling near San Diego. "Those oil companies can find oil anywhere they drill. Have them drill some place other than the Outer Continental Shelf off of San Diego," he demanded.

45. In California, a 1983 statewide survey of voters found that 56 percent of those polled favored new OCS development off the coast of California. *Outer Continental Shelf: Hearings on Outer Continental Shelf Before the Subcomm. on Energy and the Environment of the House Comm. on Interior and Insular Affairs*, 99th Cong., 1st Sess. 450 (1986).

46.   *Interior Report 1983*, 16. Meanwhile, Watt needed to reassure other agencies with offshore interest, including the Department of Defense. Told of an objection by the U.S. Navy to OCS leasing in southern California, Watt scheduled a meeting with Defense Secretary Casper Weinberger. While awaiting Weinberger, Watt chatted with the Chief of Naval Operations. "How fast can those submarines go under water?" Watt asked. "That's classified, but very fast," said the Admiral. "It must take a long distance for them to turn around," Watt queried. "No, not at all, they can turn on a dime," answered the Admiral with pride. "If that is so, why are you worried that your submarines will not see a drilling rig and hit it?" asked Watt. Just then Weinberger entered and Watt began to state the purpose of the meeting but the Admiral interrupted, "Mr. Secretary, the Navy withdraws its objections to Interior's leasing proposal."

47.   *Interior Report 1983*, 16.

48.   Ibid.

49.   Ibid. David C. Russell, the deputy assistant secretary most responsible for the OCS program, reports that he was unable to reach agreement with California's representative "after a full day of working with him on his long list of issues" and that there were "half a dozen or more major items" that remained unresolved. Then the two met with Watt who, according to Russell, "caved on every issue—air quality, onshore impacts, taking out some tracts, marine life protections." Concluded Russell, "Watt wanted the lease sale to go forward, he needed California's support, and he got it."

50.   Although the USGS concluded that Sale No. 53 had the potential for nearly a billion barrels of oil, environmentalists opposed the sale; nonetheless, it drew $2.278 billion in high bids, one of which set a record for the biggest bonus for a single tract and for the highest per-acre bonus. Rintoui, *California's Staggering Sale*, OFFSHORE, (July 1981): 57. Phillips Petroleum Company and Chevron U.S.A. paid a record $333.6 million to drill on a single 5700-acre tract in the Santa Maria Basin off Point Arguello. In 1982, drilling confirmed "a major oilfield," which could make the Santa Maria Basin the largest single American oil discovery since Alaska's Prudhoe Bay in 1968, that is, between 300 million and one billion barrels of oil. "A Billion-Barrel Find?" *Newsweek*, Nov. 29, 1982, at 84; "Black-Gold Rush," *Time*, November 29, 1982, 63.

51.   The program went final only after months of consultation between Interior and twenty-three affected states that resulted in an administrative record of over 5,000 pages that reveals involvement by local governments, environmental groups, industry, and the public. Watt called it "the most comprehensive, exhaustive project in the [Interior] Department's history." *Final Five-Year Plan for Oil and Gas Development in the Outer Continental Shelf: Hearings to Review the Secretary of the Interior's Proposed Five-Year Plan for Oil and Gas Development in the Outer Continental Shelf Pursuant to the Outer Continental Shelf Lands Act Amendments of 1978 Before the Subcomm. on Energy Conservation and Supply of the Senate Comm. on Energy and Natural Resources*, 97th Cong., 2d Sess. I (1982), 9 (statement of James G. Watt, Secretary of the Interior); Minerals Management Serv., U.S. Dep't of the Interior, *News Release I* (July 21, 1982). The release of the OCS plan, which was the work product of hundreds of career civil servants and mere handfuls of political appointees in scores of federal agencies and bureaus demonstrates the remarkable manner in which President Reagan and his officials not only took control of the federal bureaucracy but also inspired the passion, loyalty, and dedicated hard work of its employees. See also, *Sagebrush Rebel*, chapter 9, "Inside the Beltway: Taming the Bureaucracy—Teaming with Congress."

52.   *California v. Watt*, 712 F.2d 584 (1983). In 1981, a different panel of the appeals court held, in a challenge brought against Secretary Cecil Andrus's five-year program for the sale of OCS oil and gas leases in California, that designation of "California" as the area for proposed lease sales 73 and 80 violated the specificity requirement of section 18(a) of the OCSLAA. *California v. Watt*, 668 F.2d 1290, 1303 (D.C. Cir. 1981).

53.   *California v. Watt*, 712 F.2d, 588, 595.

54.   U.S. Representative Gerry Studds, a Democrat from Massachusetts, quoted in Robert Kilborn, Jr., "States face off with Interior in new bout over oil leases," *Christian Science Monitor*, March 16, 1983.

55.   *California v. Watt*, 668 F.2d, 606. Much was made at the time and much continues to be made of the fact that, by refusing to withhold tracts in the manner of a monopolist, the Reagan program made the entire OCS available for bidding and leasing. The complaint by the program's opponents was that the availability of so many tracts drives down the "bonus bid" made by companies on individual tracts. The bonus bid, however, is only a fraction of federal revenues. In fact, in areas where significant production occurs, the bonus bid is but one-third of total federal revenues with royalties and taxes providing one-third each. If no discovery is made, the bonus bid is the only revenue received

by the United States, other than taxes paid in exploring for energy on the leased tracts. Once discovery is made and production begins, the company pays either 12.5 or 16 2/3 percent royalties on the hydrocarbons produced, which has generated billions of dollars. The Outer Continental Shelf Lands Act (OCSLA) of 1953, 43 U.S.C. 1331 et seq. Unlike any other "landowner" the federal government benefits beyond the bonuses and royalties paid because profitable operations with huge payrolls generate major tax revenues. The battle over this issue did not begin when the plan was proposed in 1982. It was the Office of Management and Budget (OMB), which first objected to forgoing the monopolistic profits that the federal government would enjoy by releasing only a handful of tracts during each OCS lease sale. When it came to a choice between government acting as a monopolist to get more money from Americans or the government making energy available, President Reagan sided with Watt. "I have a feeling that if our government was as good at getting oil out of the ground as it is at getting money out of us we'd all be driving gas guzzlers with nothing to worry about except how to pay for them." Skinner, *Reagan's Path to Victory*, 468.

56. James Souby, Director of Policy Development and Planning for Governor Hammond, testified before Congress that: "Sixteen oil and gas lease sales in 10 Alaskan planning areas totaling more than 550 million acres in the next 5 years are simply *too much too soon*." (Emphasis added.) *GAO Disputes OCS Revenue Estimate*, Oil & Gas J., June 28, 1982, 42.

57. *California v. Watt*, 712 F.2d, 589. (Internal citations omitted.)

58. Watt consistently and correctly asserted that the greatest petroleum related risk to the coastal environment is that caused by spills from giant tankers carrying foreign oil to the United States. *U.S. News & World Report* (May 25, 1981): 49. The Congressional Research Service concluded, "offshore OCS production will be less damaging to the environment than importing a like amount of petroleum." Congressional Research Serv., Library Of Cong., 94th Cong., 2d Sess., *A Study On The Effects Of Offshore Oil And Natural Gas Development On The Coastal Zone 1* (1976).

59. *California v. Watt*, 712 F.2d, 594. Meanwhile, of course, Democrat Governor Brown of California continued to issue oil and gas leases in state waters, which unlike federal leases, are directly adjacent to the coast. Ron Arnold, *At the Eye of the Storm: James Watt and the Environmentalists* (Regnery Gateway, 1982), 160–61.

60. *Secretary of the Interior v. California*, 464 U.S., (1984), 312, 315, 317–18.

61. Curry L. Hagerty, "Outer Continental Shelf Moratoria on Oil and Gas Development," Congressional Research Service, March 23, 2011, 2, 5–6. Congress's first OCS moratorium came in December 1981 (P.L. 97–100) long before Watt announced the Reagan five-year plan.

62. Ibid. Unfortunately, President George H.W. Bush adopted moratoria on leasing in the OCS (Statement on Outer Continental Shelf Oil and Gas Development, 26 Weekly Comp. Pres. Doc. 1006 (June 26, 1990)), which President Clinton continued. Memorandum on Withdrawal of Certain Areas of the United States Outer Continental Shelf from Leasing Disposition, 34 Weekly Comp. Pres. Doc. 1111 (June 12, 1998). On July 14, 2008, President George W. Bush issued an executive memorandum rescinding earlier executive moratorium on offshore drilling. Memorandum on Modification of the Withdrawal of Certain Areas of the United States Outer Continental Shelf from Leasing Disposition, 44 Weekly Comp. Pres. Doc. 986 (July 14, 2008).

63. In October 2012, Todd Onderdonk, Senior Energy Advisor in ExxonMobil's Corporate Strategic Planning Department, delivered a talk to the Arkansas Independent Producers and Royalty Owners Annual Meeting entitled "Outlook for Energy: A View to 2040." In response to a question from the audience on the oil and gas potential of the OCS outside the Gulf of Mexico, he stated, "We simply have no idea but we are eager to find out." One area ExxonMobil is "eager" to explore is the North Atlantic. "Consider ExxonMobil's $14 billion plan to develop one of the largest oil fields in the North Atlantic. That drilling will be off Canada's Newfoundland. But the Hebron oil field is believed to extend southward into U.S. waters with its billion-barrel potential. Unfortunately, the United States won't see a drop of it—unless Secretary Jewell and others in the Obama hierarchy open our coasts. Simple permission, not taxpayer funds or new regulations, is all that is required." Robert Bradley Jr., "Peak Oil Will Be Fully Discredited When Peak Government Is Realized," *Forbes*, February 19, 2013.

64. G. Kevin Jones, 59. "I do not think [the moratorium] is in the national interest." "Clark Would End Restrictions on Offshore Leasing," *Washington Post*, June 8, 1984, A21. "Ultimately, [Clark's] biggest disappointment at Interior was not being able to secure offshore drilling," Paul Kengor and Patricia Clark Doerner, *The Judge: William P. Clark, Ronald Reagan's Top Hand* (Ignatius Press, 2007), 272. Clark was echoing comments by President Reagan in 1982 when called upon to respond to a flap created by Capitol Hill Democrats who objected to a letter Watt sent to Israeli Ambassador

Moshe Arens urging greater support for Reagan's OSC program. On two separate occasions, Reagan voiced his support for Watt. In a press conference, Reagan said:

> What [Watt] was suggesting, with regard to the danger to Israel, was our vulnerability as long as we are dependent on … energy from insecure sources[.] [I]f there should be, as we once had, an embargo and if we should find ourselves without the energy needed to turn the wheels in this country and the wheels of industry, we wouldn't be much of an ally to our friends. And that would certainly include Israel. And he was making it very plain that we are morally obligated to the support of Israel.

> I think he was only trying to make the example that some of those who had been the most outspoken up there [on Capitol Hill regarding Watt's letter] have also … had the most objections to us trying to improve our energy situation. And what he was pointing out is, where would the Western world be if someday our source of supply was purely there in the Persian Gulf and it was denied to us?

The President's News Conference, July 28, 1982, http://www.presidency.ucsb.edu/ws/index.php?pid=42796; Dale Russakoff, "Watt Gets Vote Of Confidence from President, *Washington Post*, July 27, 1982, A2; Dale Russakoff, "Jews Now Seek to Quiet Calls for Watt Dismissal," *Washington Post*, July 28, 1982, A2 ("The [Jewish] leaders said they do not view the [Watt] letter as grounds for dismissal and have privately urged Democratic politicians to put the matter to rest."); Dale Russakoff, "Watt Tells Jewish Group He Regrets Energy Warning Letter," *Washington Post*, July 29, 1982, A3; see also, Arnold, *At the Eye of the Storm*, 214–18.

65.   Minerals Management Serv., U.S. Dep't Of The Interior, Proposed Final Five-Year Outer Continental Shelf Oil And Gas Leasing Program Mid-1987 To Mid-1992 (1987). Hodel undertook a major effort to reach a compromise with the California congressional delegation regarding OCS leasing in federal waters offshore California, but "the only OCS program they would accept was no program," he reports.

66.   "Accelerated OCS Leasing A Key to Vital Assessment of U.S. Resources," *Oil & Gas Journal*, Aug. 2, 1982, 45; Hagar, "Gulf of Mexico Area-Wide Sales Draw Kudos from Operators," *Oil & Gas. Journal*, Oct. 28, 1985, 39. Arnold reports that the industry was split with some major oil companies uncertain but the service industry enthusiastic about the new OCS program. ("[The OCS program] is well within our capability.… We're ready to go.") In response to the claim by environmental groups that Watt had not consulted with them about the OCS plan, Watt said he consulted with neither industry nor environmental groups, but with the states, as required by law and President Reagan's Good Neighbor policy. Arnold, *At the Eye of the Storm*, 161–62. "Studies analyzing the contribution of OCS activities to the United States economy found that in 1981 OCS activities generated more than 700,000 jobs, $25 billion in expenditures and nearly 1% of this nation's total economic output. A total ban on OCS leasing off California would negatively affect a wide variety of United States industries and would be felt in virtually all fifty states." G. Kevin Jones, 62.

67.   National Commission on the BP Deepwater Horizon Oil Spill and Offshore Drilling, *The History of Offshore Oil and Gas in the United States*, Staff Working Paper No. 22, 22–23. [hereinafter *SWP22*]

68.   *SWP22*, 24. By 1990, Americans consumed less gasoline on a per capita basis (437 gallons per year) than they did in 1979. U.S. Energy Information Administration (EIA), Annual Energy Review, Petroleum, Table 5.13.c, http://www.eia.gov/emeu/aer/petro.html.

69.   *SWP22*, 24. "A Show of Faith in the Oil Industry," *Newsweek* (June 6, 1983): 77.

70.   *SWP22*; http://www.boem.gov/Oil-and-Gas-Energy-Program/Leasing/Regional-Leasing/Outer-Continental-Shelf-Lease-Sale-Statistics.aspx.

71.   *SWP22*, 22, 25.

72.   Ibid. Shell expended over $40 million on Sonat Offshore Drilling's drillship, *Discoverer Seven Seas*, to improve its depth capability (already rated for 6,000-foot depths) "with a larger marine riser, enhanced dynamic positioning, and a new remote-operated vehicle (ROV) to enable sophisticated work where humans could not venture."

73.   Tyler Priest, *The Offshore Imperative: Shell Oil's Search for Petroleum in Postwar America* (Texas A&M Press, 2007), 221–22.

74.   *SWP22*, 25.

75. Robert Gramling, *Oil on the Edge: Offshore Development, Conflict, Gridlock* (SUNY Press, 1996), 118. See *Sagebrush Rebel*, chapter 1's discussion of Reagan administration's efforts to cause the collapse of the Soviet Union by flooding the world oil market.
76. *SWP22*, 29.
77. Ibid., 26. "During 1985-1986, oil prices collapsed down to $10 per barrel, as both OPEC and non-OPEC producers—principally Mexico and the North Sea—saturated the market with crude. Combined with the rising price of lease bonuses (before area-wide leasing) and disappointing finds, the recession sucked the wind out of drilling in the Gulf of Mexico."
78. Gary Steffens and Neil Braunsdorf, Shell Exploration and Production Technology Company, "The Gulf of Mexico Deepwater Play: 50 Years from Concept to Commercial Reality," AAPG Distinguished Lecture, 1997–1998.
79. *SWP22*, 29.
80. Ibid., 30.
81. Ibid.
82. Ibid.; http://www.boem.gov/Oil-and-Gas-Energy-Program/Leasing/Regional-Leasing/Outer-Continental-Shelf-Lease-Sale-Statistics.aspx.
83. *SWP22*, 34.
84. Ibid., 31.
85. Memorandum on Modification of the Withdrawal of Certain Areas of the United States Outer Continental Shelf from Leasing Disposition, 44 Weekly Comp. Pres. Doc. 986 (July 14, 2008). "Kempthorne starts preparation of next OCS 5-year plan," *Oil and Gas Journal*, August 11, 2008.
86. The Continuing Appropriations Resolution, 2009 (P.L. 110–329) did not extend the annual congressional moratoria on oil and gas leasing activities. On March 11, 2009, the Omnibus Appropriations Act, 2009 (P.L. 111-8) was enacted without moratorium provisions, thus lifting in FY2009 the oil and gas development moratoria that had been in place since 1982 in the OCS along the Atlantic and Pacific coasts, in parts of Alaska, and in the Gulf of Mexico. Hagerty, "Outer Continental Shelf Moratoria on Oil and Gas Development," 1.
87. On January 21, 2009, a notice for Request for Comments on the Draft Proposed 5-Year OCS Oil and Gas Leasing Program for 2010-2015 and the Notice of Intent to Prepare an Environmental Impact Statement (EIS) for the Proposed 5-Year Program were published in the *Federal Register* 74, no. 12 (January 21, 2009): 3631–3635. This new five year program was to replace the last approved program, which ran from 2007-2012.
88. "Ken Salazar's Offshore Charade Continues," Institute for Energy Research, June 22, 2012. In November 2009 and March 2010, the Obama administration indicated that there would be no new OCS 5-year plan until 2012. Under the Bush 5-year OCS plan, 21 lease sales were scheduled; all but 6 of which were to take place in the next administration. The Obama administration, however, cancelled 9 of those 15 lease sales. There were no lease sales during 2011.
89. Nick Snow, "Latest Proposed 5-Year OCS Plan Falls Short, API Official Says," *Oil & Gas Journal*, November 21, 2011; "Obama Administration Imposes Five-Year Drilling Ban on Majority of Offshore Areas," U.S. House of Representatives, November 8, 2011, http://naturalresources.house.gov/news/documentsingle.aspx?DocumentID=267985.
90. "Deepwater-Gate: Administration Modifies 'Peer-Reviewed' Report After It was Reviewed by Scientists," June 11, 2010, Institute for Energy Research; "Protests from experts show drilling moratorium based on politics, not science: An Editorial," *Times-Picayune*, June 11, 2010.
91. Sean Higgins, "Gulf Drilling Ban Casts Doubt on Obama Energy Policy," *Investor's Business Daily*, May 2, 2012.
92. Anna Driver, "Exxon has 3 deepwater Gulf of Mexico discoveries," Reuters, June 8, 2011. One of the blocks, Keathley Canyon Block 919, was acquired by ExxonMobil Corporation at the Gulf of Mexico Lease Sale No. 174 held August 25, 1999 and issued with an effective date of December 1, 1999; http://www.eenews.net/assets/2010/06/02/document_gw_02.pdf. On September 6, 2006, a trio of companies led by Chevron announced that "a test well indicates [a recent Gulf of Mexico oil find] could be the biggest new domestic oil discovery since Alaska's Prudhoe Bay a generation ago." Associated Press, "Oil companies see big Gulf of Mexico discovery," NBC, September 6, 2006.
93. *Wall Street Journal*, Review & Outlook, June 10, 2011.
94. Ibid.
95. A Louisiana federal district court held the Obama administration in contempt of court for continuing its moratorium on the issuance of offshore permits to the detriment of the offshore service industry. *Hornbeck Offshore Services LLC v. Salazar*, 2:10-cv-01663-MLCF-JCW Document 226

Filed 02/02/11, "Order and Reasons;" Laurel Brubaker Calkins, "U.S. in Contempt Over Gulf Drill Ban, Judge Rules," Bloomberg, February 3, 2011.

96.   Jennifer A. Dlouhy, "First rig sails away over deep-water drilling ban: lawmakers and experts fear loss is only the start of offshore exodus," *Houston Chronicle*, July 9, 2010; Kevin Mooney, "Up to 20 Rigs Could Leave Gulf Because of Lack of Permits," *American Spectator*, The Spectacle Blog, September 13, 2011.

CHAPTER THREE

1.   Kiron K. Skinner, Annelise Anderson, and Martin Anderson, eds., *Reagan's Path to Victory, The Shaping of Ronald Reagan's Vision: Selected Writings* (The Free Press, 2004), 484.

2.   "I met alone with Reagan in the Oval Office, and we had a friendly and unrestrained discussion. He listened primarily and made a few remarks, apparently excerpted from his basic campaign speech." Jimmy Carter, *White House Diary* (Farrar, Straus and Giroux, 2010), 486. Carter chose to "omit about three-fourths of the diary [but] decided to make the entire diary (including my detailed hand-written notes) available ... in the near future." Ibid., xiv. Who knows what that redacted portion will hold. William Chedsey, "Carter Insulted Reagan Repeatedly in 'Diary,'" *Newsmax*, September 24, 2010.

3.   "Sagebrush rebels" was a term "coined by the media as a somewhat derogatory characterization of the movement." C. Brant Short, *Ronald Reagan and the Public Lands: America's Conservation Debate, 1979–1984* (Texas A&M University Press, 1989), 14.

4.   For a discussion of the Sagebrush Rebellion generally, see Short, *Ronald Reagan and the Public Lands*, 10–25.

5.   Telegram from Ronald Reagan to Dean Rhodes, Nov. 20, 1980, in U.S. Congress, Subcommittee on Mines and Mining Oversight Hearing, *Sagebrush Rebellion: Impacts on Energy and Minerals*, 96th Cong., 2nd sess. (Government Printing Office, 1980) 287. Governor Reagan campaigned on the Sagebrush Rebellion issue throughout the West. In Idaho Falls, Idaho, he proclaimed, "The next administration won't treat the West as if it were not worthy of attention. The next administration will reflect the values and goals of the Sagebrush Rebellion. Indeed, we can turn the Sagebrush Rebellion into the Sagebrush Solution." "The Sagebrush Rebellion," *U.S. News & World Report*, December 1, 1980. In the summer of 1980, "in a statement little noted by the national press, Mr. Reagan told Utah Republicans in Salt Lake City, 'I happen to be one who cheers and supports the Sagebrush Rebellion. Count me in as a rebel.'" David F. Salisbury, "Sagebrush rebels see open range in Reagan's victory," *Christian Science Monitor*, November 18, 1980.

6.   Richard D. Lamm and Michael McCarthy, *The Angry West* (Houghton Mifflin, 1982), 239–40. Lamm continues, "Time and again [Carter] preached cooperation and partnership. Time and again he pledged to renew federalism. And time and again he was the first to ignore his own call." Other Western Democrat governors agreed. Wyoming Governor Ed Herschler said, "The federal system is badly out of kilter. Federal encroachments on state and local governments are at an all-time high." Arizona Governor Bruce Babbitt said, "[W]hat galls westerners is not so much the fact of ownership, but rather the federal insistence that it is entitled to act not only as landowner, but also as *sovereign*." (Emphasis in original.) After Reagan's election, Governor Lamm declared, "What the federal government fails to do is differentiate between its role as landlord and its role as sovereign. [Government bureaucrats] can't figure out whether they're landlord or king." "The Sagebrush Rebellion," *U.S. News & World Report*, December 1, 1980. See also R. McGreggor Cawley, *Federal Land—Western Anger: The Sagebrush Rebellion & Environmental Politics* (University Press of Kansas, 1993).

7.   For a discussion of the unique nature of the American West given federal land ownership, see generally Lamm, *The Angry West*, and William Perry Pendley, *War on the West: Government Tyranny on America's Great Frontier* (Regnery, 1995).

8.   Ross W. Gorte et al., "Federal Land Ownership: Overview and Data," Congressional Research Service, February 8, 2012, 4–5.

9.   Ibid. Arkansas and Virginia are next at nine percent each.

10. "Garfield County is a large, rural county located in south central Utah. It is about 3.4 million acres in size with a population of about 4700. [It] is larger in area than the state of Connecticut[,] two and a half times larger than Delaware[,] and five times larger than Rhode Island.... We have most of the federal land management agencies represented [in Garfield County], including the Park Service, Forest Service, Bureau of Land Management and the Bureau of Reclamation...." Statement of Garfield County Commission Chairman Maloy Dodds Presented on Behalf of the Western Counties Alliance at the House Resources Committee's Forest and Forest Health Subcommittee Hearing on

"The Impacts of Federal Land Ownership on Communities and Local Governments," June 15, 2005. Garfield County's federal land ownership numbers may be found in the "2011 Utah Counties Factbook" published by the Utah Association of Counties. Inyo County's numbers are here: http:// www.inyocounty.us/.

11.   According to the Department of the Interior, "52.7 million acres of land belong to Indian tribes and individuals" and "66 million acres [are] managed by the Bureau of Indian Affairs," http://www.doi. gov/facts.html.

12.   Gorte, "Federal Land Ownership: Overview and Data," 9–10.

13.   Multiple-Use Sustained-Yield Act of 1960, as amended through December 31, 1996, P.L. 104–333, for example. The Federal Land Policy and Management Act of 1976 (FLPMA) provides, "The Congress declares that it is the policy of the United States that—goals and objectives be established by law as guidelines for public land use planning, and that management be on the basis of multiple use and sustained yield unless otherwise specified by law...." 43 U.S.C. § 1701(a)(7).

14.   Reeves Brown of Colorado once described the difference between being "interested" and being "affected." "A chicken is interested in what you have for breakfast; a pig is affected."

15.   Professor Short argues, "Most observers agree [that passage of FLPMA] represented the last straw for many western ranchers, miners, and loggers." Short, *Ronald Reagan and the Public Lands*, 12.

16.   See generally Ron Arnold, *At the Eye of the Storm: James Watt and the Environmentalists* (Regnery Gateway, 1982), 40–45, 120–124, including an early mention of ACORN, the Association of Community Organizations for Reform, whose "radical politics and controversial tactics" would become notorious decades later. Stanley Kurtz, *Radical-In-Chief: Barack Obama and the Untold Story of American Socialism* (Threshold Editions, 2010), 178.

17.   The Heritage Foundation's *Mandate for Leadership*, described the Carter administration's "initial foray into western water policy" as "an assault against an area long considered the prerogative of western governors and Members of Congress." "Unfamiliar with the nature of western water and hearing only the strident opposition of environmentalists, the Administration sought to kill all such programs." Although more than half of the projects were later pushed through by Congress, Carter destroyed the "quid pro quo" that had government approval in the past and exposed them to attack from "categorical opponents [who] could subject the proposals to delay and death." Charles L. Heatherly, ed., *Mandate for Leadership: Policy Management in a Conservative Administration* (The Heritage Foundation, 1981), 376. See generally Lamm, *The Angry West*, 186–97.

18.   Bryce Nelsen of the *Los Angeles Times*, "Interior Secretary Cecil Andrus of Idaho: Tough stand on Western states," *Anchorage Daily News*, September 25, 1979, B5. Shortly thereafter, Carter's Interior "reversed 50 years of Interior Department policy and pronouncements regarding [the Reclamation Act of 1902] by establishing new acreage, leasing and residency rules ... to administratively repeal the Reclamation Act and fundamentally change the face of western agriculture...." Heatherly, *Mandate*, 376–77.

19.   Bryce Nelsen of *Los Angeles Times*, "Interior Secretary Cecil Andrus of Idaho," *Anchorage Daily News*, September 25, 1979, B5.

20.   "Andrus is the strongest preservationist to ever be secretary, but he hasn't shown a balancing concern for the needs of production. He gives the clear impression of not wanting the public lands to be touched," said Karl Mote, Executive Director, Northwest Mining Association of Spokane, Washington. "I don't think you can have a Sagebrush Rebellion without having a national government that rubs public land users the wrong way. The Department of the Interior has to bear much of the responsibility for that," echoed Senator Pete V. Domenici (R-NM). In his first address to Interior employees in January 1977, Andrus said, "I am a part of the environmental movement and I intend to make Interior responsive to the movement's needs." Arnold, *At the Eye of the Storm*, 94. One early Andrus use of the "rape, ruin and run" phrase was in March 1977, "We intend to exercise our stewardship of public lands and natural resource in a manner that will make the 'three R's'—rape, ruin and run—a thing of the past. We intend and have begun to break up the little fiefdoms which have divided Interior for years. For too long each of the interests—grazing, mining, timber and so forth—has had its own domain. The place was like a centipede with each little pair of feet scuttling off in its own direction. That is going to change. Policy making will be centralized and it will be responsive to my philosophy and the philosophy of President Carter." *News Release*, "Remarks of Secretary of the Interior Cecil D. Andrus Before the National Wildlife Federation," Washington, D.C., March 26, 1977, 5, http://www.fws.gov/news/historic/1977/19770326a.pdf.

21.   Heatherly, *Mandate*, 377.

22.   Ibid.

23.   Ibid.
24.   Ibid. One use proposed was mandated "minimum in-stream flows," that is a federal requirement that a minimum amount of water be retained in the stream to the detriment of those with superior water rights who wish to use the water for economic activity. In most states, such a use does not meet the historic "beneficial use" requirement of the "prior appropriations doctrine," which recognized "first in time, first in right" but only for economic use.
25.   There was more to come. From a philosophical standpoint, Carter's Malthusian energy address in April 1977 not only assailed a key aspect of the Western economy but also allied Carter with a principle theme of the radical environmental movement: "We simply must balance our demand for energy with our rapidly shrinking resources.... Many of [my energy] proposals will be unpopular. Some will cause you to put up with inconveniences and to make sacrifices.... The oil and natural gas that we rely on for 75 percent of our energy are simply running out." Jimmy Carter, *Address to the Nation on Energy*, April 18, 1977, http://www.presidency.ucsb.edu/ws/index.php?pid=7369. For more specifics, *see generally*, Lamm, *The Angry West*, 235–80. According to Lamm, Carter's War on the West included, *inter alia*: his proposal, which "almost defied comprehension[,]" to deploy MX missiles "in horizontal garages scattered through the canyons and valleys of the Nevada-Utah Great Basin." (Ibid., 136; on MX, see generally 134–59); his Energy Mobilization Board, which would "steamroll state agencies, ride roughshod over regional water rights, and destroy environmental laws[,] the arrogant nullification of two hundred years of constitutional history." (Ibid., 28; on synthetic fuels, see generally, 19–50); his Office of Surface Mining, "one of the West's smallest agencies," which "consistently has written ignorant, unreasonable, and unworkable [coal mining reclamation] regulations." (Ibid., 247); his Environmental Protection Agency's "federal blackmail [of Colorado, which was] unprecedented in the West's history." (Ibid., 249); and his wilderness recommendations, which "set off new protests all across the West." (Ibid., 233.) Lamm discusses grazing but failed to mention Andrus' plan "to increase by about 50 percent the fees that the nation's 25,000 cattle and sheep raisers pay to graze their stock on public lands." Carl Hilliard, "[Untitled]," Associated Press, October 21, 1977.
26.   Organized Western outrage over concerns regarding the economic impact of federal regulation of grazing occurred twice earlier in the twentieth century, from 1907 to 1911 and from 1940 to 1943. Short, *Ronald Reagan and the Public Lands*, 10–11.
27.   "What we must do is diffuse the Sagebrush Rebellion. The Sagebrush Rebellion has been caused by an arrogant attitude by the Department land-managers, who have refused to consult and include in their decision-making process State and local governments and land users." *James G. Watt Nomination: Hearings Before the Committee On Energy and Natural Resources, United States Senate, Ninety-seventh Congress, First Session, On the Proposed Nomination of James G. Watt to Be Secretary of the Interior, January 7 and 8, 1981* (Washington: U.S. G.P.O., 1981), 78.
28.   Ibid., 461. Watt declared, "I believe in a 'good neighbor' policy under which the Department seeks to cooperate with local governments and citizens affected by Department actions."
29.   Arnold, *At the Eye of the Storm*, 92.
30.   Ibid. Watt also offered the availability of senior Interior officials during the February 1981 meeting of the National Governor's Association in Washington, D.C. Watt did meet, in February 1981, with eleven Western state governors. Governor List (R-NV), at a press conference afterward, said, "In all candor, I can't recall a single instance in which the governors raised issues ... that the Secretary did not agree." Elizabeth Drew, "A Reporter at Large, Secretary Watt," *New Yorker*, May 4, 1981, 124.
31.   Arnold, *At the Eye of the Storm*, 92.
32.   Ibid.
33.   The gathering was the Western Governors' Policy Office (WESTPO), which became the Western Governors' Association in 1985; http://www.westgov.org/home; Philip Shabecoff, "Watt Says U.S. Defers to States on Water Rights," *New York Times* sec. 1 (September 12, 1981), 1.
34.   Arnold, *At the Eye of the Storm*, 195.
35.   Ibid., quoting J. J. Casserly of the *Arizona Republic*.
36.   Bill Prochnau, "Sagebrush Rebellion Is Over, Interior Secretary Says," *Washington Post*, September 12, 1981, A9. "It was a triumphant beginning to Watt's first major visit to his native West since becoming secretary."
37.   Arnold, *At the Eye of the Storm*, 195.
38.   For example, Watt pledged to delay OCS oil and gas lease sales in Alaska's Bristol Bay, promised to act on nearly 400 requests for transfers of 700,000 acres of federal land to local governments, committed to fight any effort to condemn Western land for coal slurry pipelines, and vowed to propose

that President Reagan support wilderness designation for Arizona's Aravaipa Canyon. Ibid., 95–96. See also Prochnau, "Sagebrush Rebellion Is Over."

39. Michael Reese, Gerald C. Lubenow, and William J. Cook, "Watt Defuses a Rebellion," *Newsweek*, September 21, 1981. Watt continued to meet with Western governors. In November 1982, at their request, Watt met in Denver to discuss coal leasing. At the conclusion of the meeting, Watt summarized, "My position is that we have done all you governors have asked, but that now you just want some redundancy. That's all right with me. I have nothing against redundancy."; "When the meeting broke up, the governors were clearly pleased." David F. Salisbury, "Western politicians close ranks over regional problems," *Christian Science Monitor*, November 24, 1982; Ron Madsen, a staffer for Senator Hatch (R-UT), declared, "Everywhere I go people are now saying that the federal government is a good landlord." Mark Lewis, "What Became of the Sagebrush Rebellion," *Great Falls [Montana] Tribune* sec. B1 (September 26, 1983): 1.

40. Lamm wrote, "Since the Civil War the United States has generally avoided regional conflicts ... But that now is changing. Sectional conflict suddenly has become a Western way of life. Some have called the escalating tension between West and non-West the beginning of the 'Second War Between the States.'" Lamm, *The Angry West*, 123.

41. Lamm was not so restrained in his book *The Angry West* where he praised Watt and Mountain States Legal Foundation and their defense, among other examples, of "134 ranchers, most of them Hispanic, and most of them poor...." Lamm, *The Angry West*, 292. Nor was he earlier in the Reagan administration. "[Watt has] treated us fairly and I don't want to get into a fight with him. I've got a lot riding on the guy." Bill Prochnau, "Out in the Sagebrush, Watt Still Rides High," *Washington Post*, July 26, 1981, A1.

42. Watt's recollection of his meeting with Matheson echoes Matheson's enthusiastic comments in Jackson, where he "told Watt he was 'close to driving the last nail in the coffin of the Sagebrush Rebellion' [and] credited Watt with establishing 'a good neighbor' policy that rapidly dissipated much of the Western political unrest." Prochnau, "Sagebrush Rebellion Is Over." Earlier Matheson declared, "It would be foolish to try running against Watt in Utah." Arnold, *At the Eye of the Storm*, 166.

43. Opinion of William H. Coldiron, September 11, 1981, Non-reserved Water Rights-United States Compliance with State Law, 88 I.D. 1055. In addition, according to former Deputy Assistant Secretary DuBois, the BLM revised its water manual to provide that if a rancher paid for the total cost of the well on a grazing allotment, the rancher who put the water to beneficial use, not the BLM, owned the water right. Previously, the BLM owned the water right and ranchers had no incentive to develop water to improve the rangeland, which also benefitted wildlife.

44. "1983 – A Year Of Enrichment: Improving The Quality Of Life For All Americans," (U.S. Department of the Interior, October 1983), 26. In 1983, the following transfers occurred: Arizona, 55,557 acres; California, 8,002 acres; Colorado, 1,234 acres; Idaho, 2,960 acres; Montana, 25,494 acres; South Dakota, 2,130 acres (this completes South Dakota's entitlement); and, Utah, 93,803 acres. In 1983, a total of 203,806 acres remained to be transferred once states identified the lands; however, by the end of 1987, all but 90,000 acres had been identified and conveyed. "America – Our Treasure and Our Trust: The Legacy of President Ronald Reagan 1981 – 1988," (U.S. Department of the Interior December 1988), 67–68.

45. *Interior Report 1983*, 26. The Carter administration decreased the acreage available for such recreation and public purpose local leases from 50,600 to 41,400 acres but, Reagan's Interior Department increased the available acreage to 113,000 by 1987. Reagan's Interior Department reports that between 10,000 and 20,000 acres a year were transferred to state and local governments through "patents and leases for use as parks or other public purposes." *Interior Report 1988*, 20.

46. *Interior Report 1983*, 26. The Bureau of Land Management finalized five such "cooperative management agreements" in 1983. Sixty plans were completed in 1984. Of course, pursuant to federal law, states receive a share of the mineral leasing bonus, rent, and royalty revenues collected for energy development on federal lands within their boundaries. In 1982, for example, states received $610 million. *Interior Report 1983*, 25. Reagan's Interior Department reported that, over the years, it "collected over $46 billion in royalties, rentals, and bonuses from oil, gas, and solid minerals production on federal and Indian lands. These revenues were disbursed to states, Indians, other surface management agencies, and federal accounts." *Interior Report 1988*, 107–8. States allocate these funds based on state law: "California and Wyoming use these revenues for education, while Colorado uses mineral lease revenues for parks, recreation and road construction." *Interior Report 1983*, 25. In addition, local units of government receive payment-in-lieu of taxes (PILT) funds from the federal

government. In 1983, for example, Interior distributed $95.9 million to 1,693 local units of government. Regrettably, the PILT program has never been funded fully by Congress, nor does the payment justly compensate local government, especially in the instance of national parks, which attract millions of visitors who burden public facilities in adjacent areas with no commensurate tax revenue from the park to cover local costs. See, for example, Statement of Garfield County Commission Chairman Maloy Dodds, June 15, 2005. A federal website on PILT payments is here: http://www.doi.gov/pilt/index.cfm.

47.   *Surface Coal Mining Reclamation: 15 Years of Progress, 1977-1992*, U.S. Office of Surface Mining Reclamation and Enforcement, U.S. Department of the Interior, (Washington, D.C. ,1992), 50–51.; *Interior Report 1983*, 18–19.

48.   *Interior Report 1983*, 25. The states that participated include California, Colorado, Montana, Nevada, New Mexico, North Dakota, Utah, and Wyoming. Ibid.

49.   Ibid., 26.

50.   Robert F. Durant, *The Administrative Presidency Revisited: Public Lands, the BLM, and the Reagan Revolution* (State University of New York Press, 1992), 107–8. Reagan's Interior Department sought to privatize the cost of rangeland maintenance, reduce the discretion of state BLM directors, distribute rangeland improvement funds on the basis of grazing fees paid, and limit the funds spent by the BLM on administrative improvements as opposed to on-the-ground rangeland improvements. Ibid. See also, Tom Arrandale, *The Battle for Natural Resources* (Congressional Quarterly, 1983), 167–68. "In the long run [these] BLM efforts to improve range conditions may offer the Western livestock industry its best chance for economic survival. DuBois reports that grazing allotments were categorized based on their condition: a) excellent, as to which the BLM provided maximum administrative flexibility and innovation; b) good, which the BLM simply monitored; and c) poor or needing improvement, which the BLM assisted and regulated. Thus BLM rewarded good range managers while devoting its resources to problem areas. In addition, ranchers were given greater say in the District Grazing Advisory Boards both as to the expenditure of range improvement funds and the entire rangeland management program. The amount of grazing fees that the BLM could spend on administrative costs was capped and the amount that could be spent on-the-ground range improvements was correspondingly increased."

51.   This applied "particularly in Florida and California." *Interior Report 1988*, 68–69. In addition, following President Reagan's Exclusive Economic Zone (EEZ) proclamation, Reagan's Interior Department created "State-federal cooperative task forces ... to review data, voice concerns, and make recommendations regarding potential development of marine minerals" in the EEZ. *Interior Report 1988*, 69.

52.   *Interior Report 1983*, 26. Interior's U.S. Geological Survey (USGS) provided early warnings to public land users and those nearby regarding active volcanoes at Mt. St. Helens (Washington) and Kilauea (Hawaii), including accurate predictions of eruptions of Mt. St. Helens and Kilauea Volcano. Ibid., 28. In addition, the USGS "completed a nationwide analysis of long-term trends in acid precipitation (acid rain) indicators in streams, which showed a decline in acidity of precipitation in the northeast, and an increase in acidity in some other regions[, based on d]ata ... collected over 10 to 15 years from the [USGS's] water quality records." In doing so, the USGS "worked with 15 states to further define relations between sulfur dioxide emissions and acid deposits, and their effects on streams and lakes." Ibid.

53.   Ibid., 28. In fiscal year 1983, an additional $13 million in grazing fee receipts was earmarked for range improvements. Ibid.

54.   Ibid., 70-71.

55.   Ibid., 10. Reagan's Interior Department also instituted forty "Cooperative Fish and Wildlife Research Units," in cooperation with states and others, to train biologists and scientists; 35 states are now involved. *Interior Report 1988*, 69. In addition, Reagan's Interior Department entered into cooperative agreements with 51 states and territories to implement recovery plans for species listed pursuant to the Endangered Species Act. Ibid., 70.

56.   James D. Linxwiler, *The Alaska Native Claims Settlement Act At 35: Delivering on the Promise*, Rocky Mtn. Min. L. Inst. Vol. 53 Chap. 12, 2007, at 12.03(1)(a)(iv).

57.   Ibid., at 12.03(1)(a)(vii). See generally Richard S. Jones, Alaska Native Claims Settlement Act of 1971 (Public Law 92-203): History And Analysis Together With Subsequent Amendments, Report No. 81–127 GOV, June 1, 1981.

58.   ANCSA also created twelve Native-owned regional corporations and authorized $962 million in "seed money." Linxwiler, *The Alaska Native Claims Settlement Act At 35*, at 12.03(2)(e).

59. ANCSA provided that the withdrawal of the lands would expire in 1978 if Congress had not designated the lands as federal enclaves. John K. Norman Cole and Steven W. Silver, *Alaska's D-2 Lands*, Rocky Mtn. Min. L. Inst., vol. 6B, chap. 5, September, 1978; Raymond A. Peck, Jr., *And Then There Were None: Evolving Federal Restraints on the Availability of Public Lands for Mineral Development*, 25 Rocky Mtn. Min. L. Inst., vol. 25, chap. 3, 1979.

60. Andrus used purported authority under the FLPMA to withdraw 40 million acres and Carter used purported authority under the Antiquities Act of 1906 to withdraw 56 million acres. James D. Linxwiler, *The Alaska Native Claims Settlement Act: The First 20 Years*, Rocky Mtn. Min. L. Inst., vol. 38 chap. 2, 1992 at 2.04(8)(c).

61. Alaska's request for an injunction was denied. *State of Alaska v. Carter*, 462 F. Supp. 1155, 1156 (D. Alaska 1978) (NEPA does not apply to presidential proclamation under the Antiquities Act). Alaska's lawsuit was similar to one filed by Wyoming challenging use of the Antiquities Act to designate the Grand Teton National Monument, *Wyoming v. Franke*, 58 F. Supp. 890 (D. Wyo. 1945). See generally Carol Hardy Vincent and Kristina Alexander, "National Monuments and the Antiquities Act," Congressional Research Service, July 20, 2010. In December 1980, President Carter signed the ANILCA; subsequently, during the Reagan administration, Alaska dropped its lawsuit.

62. Alaska National Interest Lands Conservation Act ("ANILCA"), Pub. L. No. 96–487, 94 Stat. 2371 (1980) (codified as amended in scattered sections of 16 U.S.C., 43 U.S.C., 48 U.S.C.). Joseph J. Perkins, Jr., *The Great Land Divided But Not Conquered: The Effects of Statehood, ANCSA, and ANILCA on Alaska*, Rocky Mtn. Min. L. Inst., vol. 34, chap. 6, 1988 at 6.02.

63. News Release, "Watt Outlines 'Good Neighbor' Policy for Land Management in Alaska," March 12, 1981. Watt assigned Deputy Under Secretary of the Interior William P. Horn lead responsibility for coordinating with Alaska in Reagan's Interior Department's implementation of ANILCA.

64. Master Memorandum of Understanding Between the Alaska Department of Fish and Game, Juneau, Alaska and the U.S. National Park Service, Department of the Interior, Anchorage, Alaska, October 14, 1982; Master Memorandum of Understanding Between the Alaska Department of Fish and Game, Juneau, Alaska and the U.S. Fish and Wildlife Survey, Department of the Interior, Anchorage, Alaska, March 13, 1982; and Master Memorandum of Understanding Between the Alaska Department of Fish and Game, Juneau, Alaska and the Bureau of Land Management, Department of the Interior, Anchorage, Alaska, August 3, 1983.

65. *Interior Report 1983*, 25.

66. Ibid. The conveyances by the Reagan administration to Alaska and Native Alaskans greatly exceeded the amount of land transferred to each during the Carter administration. *Interior Report 1988*, 86–87.

67. Sadly, for Alaskans, the bad old days have returned. "Despite its claims, it is clear the [Obama] Interior Department yet again has made a decision about Alaska land use that ignores what Alaskans want," Senator Mark Begich, a Democrat declared. Chris Klint, "Alaska Delegation Questions NPR-A Management Plan," Associated Press, February 21, 2013; Tim Bradner, "Alaska's delegation scolds Salazar over NPR-A withdrawals," *Alaska Journal of Commerce*, August 31, 2012. The Interior Department's decision "represents the largest wholesale land withdrawal and blocking of access to an energy resource in decades."; NPR-A possesses rich coal and nonfuel mineral resources. Rose Ragsdale, "Bonanza may await explorers in NPR-A South; miners want BLM to include coal, hard rock leasing," *Petroleum News*, August 25, 2006.

68. The Santini-Burton Act, Public Law 96-586, provided for the sale of Bureau of Land Management Lands near Las Vegas and the acquisition of environmentally sensitive lands as national forest lands around Lake Tahoe.

69. These sales are permitted by the Federal Land Policy and Management Act if the land, "because of its location or other characteristics is difficult and uneconomic to manage as part of the public lands, and is not suitable for management by another Federal department or agency," or if it was "acquired for a specific purpose" but "is no longer required for that or any other Federal purpose," or if the land's sale "will serve important public objectives … [,]" "which outweigh other public objectives and values" served by being retained as federal land. 43 U.S.C. § 1713(a)-(g).

70. *Interior Report 1988*, 68.

71. The Nevada-Florida Land Exchange Authorization Act, Public Law 100-275 (102 Stat. 52), approved March 3, 1988, provided for the transfer of 28,000 acres of BLM land in Nevada to a private corporation in exchange for 4,650 acres of Florida wetlands owned by the corporation; the Florida lands were to be sold to the South Florida Water Management District and the revenue used by the U.S. Fish and Wildlife Service to purchase inholdings at Florida refuges. *Interior Report 1988*,

17–18. The Arizona Idaho Conservation Act, Public Law 100-696 (102 Stat. 4577), approved November 18, 1988, also known as the Big Cypress Exchange, provided for the exchange of 68.4 acres at the Phoenix Indian School in Arizona for 107,800 acres of land in Collier County, Florida, and $34.9 million, from corporations owned by the Collier family. Under the law, 80,070 acres of the Florida land were added to the Big Cypress National Preserve, 5,109 acres added to the Florida Panther National Wildlife Refuge, and 19,620 acres used to establish a new Ten Thousand Islands National Wildlife Refuge in Collier County on the southwest coast of Florida. The Santa Rita Exchange, Public Law 100-696 (102 Stat. 4593), approved November 18, 1988, provided for an exchange of lands between the United States and the State of Arizona: 51,000 acres from the BLM and the Bureau of Reclamation and 2,500 acres from the Fish and Wildlife Service lands at Havasu and Imperial National Wildlife Refuges were exchanged for 91,600 acres of state lands at the Buenos Aires National Wildlife Refuge. In addition, extensive state acreage elsewhere was transferred to the BLM, Forest Service, and Bureau of Reclamation.

72. Bernard J. Lewis, "The Reagan Administration's Federal Land Sales Program: Economic, Legal and Jurisdiction Issues," Staff Paper Series Number 37, College of Forestry, Department of Forest Resources, and the Agricultural Experiment Station, St. Paul, MN, November 1983 (Published as Paper No. 1914 of the Miscellaneous Journal Series of the Minnesota Agricultural Experiment Station), 14; *Public Land News*, 7(4), February 18, 1982.

73. Lewis, *Federal Land Sales*, 14.

74. Ibid.

75. Ibid.

76. Ibid., 15. The Property Review Board included the Counselor to the President, Director of the Office of Management and Budget, President's Assistant on National Security, and other presidential appointees.

77. Ibid., 16.

78. Ibid., 17. *Public Lands News*, 7(4), February 18, 1982.

79. *Land Use Planning Report* 10 (22): May 31, 1982.

80. Lewis, *Federal Land Sales*, 18.

81. Environmental groups were not the only ones demanding that their narrow interests be served. For example, when the Forest Service attempted to dispose of 13,000 isolated, formerly distressed farm-land acres in upstate New York, the public outcry was fierce; apparently locals like their "cost-free" park. *USA Today*, March 7, 1983. Most surprising of all was opposition to the disposal by the General Services Administration of small parcels in urban areas; city dwellers also like "cost-free" parkland. Lewis, *Federal Land Sales*, 23.

82. In August 1982, *Time* magazine's cover featured a sneering Watt before the slogan, "GOING, GOING … !" Peter Stoler, "Land Sale of the Century," *Time* (August 23, 1982): 16. Stoler wrote that the scope of the sale, involving a mere 5% of federal lands, was "enormous." One writer later argued that the connection between Watt's land sales program, which he described as "minuscule," and the Council of Economic Advisor's privatization program was "weak." Short, *Ronald Reagan and Public Lands*, 82. Some newspapers, especially out West, got it right: "The idea of raising a few dollars via the sales, controlling maintenance costs and putting some of these lands back on the tax rolls may well make sense when the entire process has been completed." *Springfield (Oregon) News*, Editorial, February 13, 1983.

83. "Democratic Governors Spar with Watt," *Great Falls Tribune*, June 30, 1983, Sec. A, 1.

84. "Watt Pulls Agency Out of Reagan Land-Sale Program," *Missoulian*, July 28, 1983, Sec. A, 2; "Land Removed from Sale Plan," *Great Falls Tribune*, July 28, 1983, Sec. A, 1. For a discussion of the ideological battle in the Reagan administration over public land sales, see Chapter 6: "Selling the Public Lands—Lock, Stock, and Barrel," in Short, *Ronald Reagan and the Public Lands*, 81–99. "Unlike Watt's asset management program which stressed the sale of unwanted and unused lands, the privatizationists wanted *all* land targeted for eventual sale." (Emphasis in original.) Ibid., 85–86.

85. Chairing a meeting of the Cabinet Council on Natural Resources and Environment, Watt sought to resolve the ongoing turf battle between the Interior Department and the Property Review Board regarding the disposal of federal land. Meese, both on behalf of President Reagan and as a member of the Property Review Board, sided with Watt.

86. http://www.usbr.gov/mp/ccao/newmelones/history.html; The New Melones Dam replaced the original 211-foot high Melones Dam built in 1926 by two irrigation districts to provide water for agriculture.

87. Ibid. Part of the Central Valley Project, the reservoir provides water to arid areas in central California, minimizes downstream flooding, and creates recreational opportunities on its 12,500 surface acres and 100 miles of shoreline.

88. Hodel, standing at his ubiquitous flip chart making notes as Watt and various assistant secretary level officials planned for the days and months ahead, quipped, "Tell the protesters we will have to deal with their estates."

89. Janet Krietemeyer, "New Melones Reservoir to be filled up," *Lodi [California] News-Sentinel*, July 2, 1981, 1. Not all projects got a green light from Watt. He stopped a plan to add two generating turbines to the Glen Canyon Dam on the Colorado River above the Grand Canyon. Although the turbines would have added 250 megawatts of power to the dam's power capacity, they would have increased the river flow during peak generating periods with unpredictable impacts on beach erosion, wildlife, and river rafters. Arnold, *At the Eye of the Storm*, 218–19.

90. *Interior Report 1983*, 23.

91. Ibid.

92. Ibid.

93. Ibid., 24.

94. Ibid.

95. Ibid.

96. Ibid., 23. The U.S. Geological Survey, the "federal government's largest science research agency … and the employer of the nation's largest number of professional earth scientists" not only completed the annual *National Water Summary*, but also worked with the Environmental Protection Agency and other bureaus and agencies to assess water quality, including groundwater. *Interior Report 1988*, 52–53, 58–60. Reagan's Interior Department developed cooperative water use programs with all 50 states, Puerto Rico, and the Virgin Islands to create a "more uniform and consistent set of water use estimates [to permit] trends in water demand and use to be determined throughout the country." Ibid., 72.

97. *Interior Report 1983*, 24. The Bureau of Reclamation's 290 recreational areas, including those managed by other agencies, provided 45 million visitor-days of outdoor recreation in 1983.

98. Ibid.

99. Ibid., 23. See also *Interior Report 1988*, 52–53. Reagan's Interior Department "[re]established states' rights as the guiding principle within the federal government, particularly in dealing with the acquisition of water rights[,] was responsible for refuting the 'non-reserved' water rights claim, by which the prior Administration had preempted the long-established state control of water resources[, and] was responsible for reestablishing the government-wide policy that directs agencies seeking water rights for wilderness areas to act within the confines of state water law." Ibid., 53, 67.

100. Executive Order 12612 – Federalism, October 26, 1987, http://www.presidency.ucsb.edu/ws/index.php?pid=33607. See also, *Interior Report 1988*, 66.

101. See *Sagebrush Rebel*, chapter 9. In addition, Reagan's Interior Department sought and won amendments to the Safety of Dams Act, Public Law 95-578, November 2, 1978, as amended by Public Law 98-404 (August 28, 1984), which increased financial authorization ($650 million) along with cost sharing (15%), for the rehabilitation and repair of potentially unsafe Western dams. Subsequently, Reagan's Interior Department reviewed dam safety needs and ranked them in order of priority. *Interior Report 1988*, 55.

102. Reagan's Interior Department adopted "principles and guidelines" to provide for a more realistic economic assessment of planned water projects by providing for "computation of benefit/cost ratios that reflect the actual situation of each project," rather than a one-size fits all bureaucratic standard. Ibid.

103. Ibid., 53.

104. Ibid.

105. Ibid., 56.

106. Ibid., 54.

107. Resolution of the Westland Water District (California) litigation allowed the department to address a naturally occurring phenomenon that threatened the environmental quality of the Kesterson Reservoir. Ibid., 56–57. Negotiations resolved water rights issues involving the Ak Chin and Salt River Pima-Maricopa in Arizona and affecting American Indians on Colorado's Animas-LaPlata project. Ibid., 54.

108. Davis W. Houck and Amos Kiewe, eds., *Actor, Ideologue, Politician: The Public Speeches of Ronald Reagan* (Greenwood, 1993), 178.

109. *Interior Report 1988*, 67. The Quiet Title Act provides in relevant part:

> The United States may be named as a party defendant in a civil action under this section to adjudicate a disputed title to real property in which the United States claims an interest, other than a security interest or water rights.
>
> Any civil action under this section, except for an action brought by a State, shall be barred unless it is commenced within twelve years of the date upon which it accrued. Such action shall be deemed to have accrued on the date the plaintiff or his predecessor in interest knew or should have known of the claim of the United States.

    28 U.S.C. § 2409a(a) and (g).

110. Statement on Signing the Bill Amending the Quiet Title Act, November 4, 1986, http://www.presidency.ucsb.edu/ws/index.php?pid=36693.

111. http://www.archives.gov/federal-register/codification/executive-order/12612.html. On November 17, 1986, President Reagan wrote in his diary, "A Domestic Policy Council meeting to receive the first results of the studies I'd asked for. This one was on Federalism and how the National government has violated the Constitution in making our states administrative districts of the Federal Government rather than sovereign states. I want this reversed." Ronald Reagan, *The Reagan Diaries* (Harper, 2007), 451. Earlier, in Executive Order 12372, President Reagan sought "to foster an intergovernmental partnership and a strengthened federalism by relying on State and local processes for the State and local government coordination and reviews" during the federal grant making process. Intergovernmental Review of Federal Programs, July 14, 1982, http://www.presidency.ucsb.edu/ws/index.php?pid=42735.

112. Executive Order 12612.

113. Ibid. A few weeks before signing the Executive Order, President Reagan met with Republican Senators Steve Symms of Idaho and Chic Hecht of Nevada and Secretary of Transportation Elizabeth Dole:

> The two Cong. Men want to return speed laws to the states & so do I. Liz is worried that lifting the Fed 55 mile limit may lead to an increase in traffic fatalities. I held out on the side of turning power back to the states—it was none of Wash's business in the 1st place. I think Liz left a little upset—but the 2 Reps [senators] were happy and so am I.

    The Reagan Diaries, 432 (August 11, 1986).

114. "The Sagebrush Rebellion," *U.S. News & World Report*, December 1, 1980.

115. Clinton revoked President Reagan's executive order on federalism with an executive order of his own (Executive Order 13083, 1998) while in England; however, it created such an outcry that he suspended and then replaced it (Executive Order 13132, 1999).

116. Proclamation No. 6920, 61 *Fed. Reg.* 50,223 (1996).

117. Robert Redford, *Perspective On The West: This Land is Your Children's Land; Setting aside 1.7 million acres of virgin land in Utah may become a defining legacy of the Clinton presidency*, Los Angeles Times, Sept. 19, 1996, B9.

118. See generally Pendley, *War on the West*.

119. Thomas Pyle, "Obama's War on Coal Will Only Get Worse If He Is Re-Elected," *U.S. News & World Report*, November 5, 2012; Geoff Liesik, "Mining company blames Obama for its 102 Utah lay offs," *Deseret News*, November 8, 2012.

120. Ben Wolfgang, "EPA offers details of its controversial fracking study," *Washington Times*, December 21, 2012; Edward McAllister, "U.S. EPA to test water near Penn. Fracking site," Reuters, January 19, 2012; Christopher Helman, "EPA Official Not Only Touted 'Crucifying' Oil Companies, He Tried It," *Forbes*, April 26, 2012.

121. Paul Foy, "U.S. limits oil-shale development in Rockies," *The Durango Herald*, November 10, 2012. The Obama plan is "a third of the range lands that President George W. Bush planned to offer...." "'The Obama Administration should cancel this plan and work with Congress and governors on solutions that will create jobs and strengthen our energy security,' said Sen. John Barrasso, R-Wyo."

122. John Fund, "Jobs Are Also an Endangered Species: The Obama administration backs down on the dunes sagebrush lizard," National Review Online, June 15, 2012; Felicity Barringer, "U.S. Reaches a Settlement on Decisions About Endangered Species," *New York Times*, May 10, 2011; Milan Simonich, "Lesser prairie chicken considered for endangered protection status," *Las Cruces Sun-*

News, November 30, 2012. "Unfortunately, our jobs and our way of life in southern New Mexico continue to come under assault," said U.S. Representative Steve Pearce, a Republican from New Mexico.

123.   Journal Staff, "Senators Seek To Protect 2 N.M. Sites," *Albuquerque Journal*, October 27, 2012, C1. Representative Pearce, in whose district the Organ Mountains lie, urges congressional action to protect a small area to permit "broader [public] access."

124.   Gov. Matthew H. Mead, "Hydro-fracking regulations should be left to states: Federal government bogs down process," *Washington Times*, September 17, 2012.

125.   Valerie Richardson, "Is Utah primed for another Sagebrush Rebellion? State wants millions of acres of public lands transferred to its control," *Washington Times*, March 7, 2012; Kirk Johnson, "Utah Asks U.S. to Return 20 Million Acres of Land," *New York Times*, March 23, 2012.

126.   Robert Gehrke, "Utah alone in Sagebrush Rebellion after Arizona governor's veto," *The Salt Lake City Tribune*, May 15, 2012.

127.   Katherine Wutz, "Lawmakers: Feds should give up land—Senate passes federal land transfer resolution," *Idaho Mountain Express*, April 3, 2013. "In the past year, legislatures in seven western states—Utah, Arizona, Wyoming, New Mexico, Colorado, Nevada, and Idaho—have passed, introduced, or explored legislation demanding that the federal government turn over millions of acres of federal public lands to the states." Jessica Goad and Tom Kenworth, "State Efforts to 'Reclaim' Our Public Lands," Center for American Progress, March 11, 2013, 2; Brian Maffly, "Bills aiming to curb federal clout in Utah are gaining momentum," *Salt Lake City Tribune*, March 4, 2013; Jim Kalvelage, "Takeover of fed lands could be costly, profitable," *Carlsbad* [NM] *Current-Argus*, February 26, 2013; Laura Hancock, "Wyoming may look at ways to manage federal land," *Star-Tribune*, February 26, 2013; Dianne Stallings, "Village backs federal land transfer legislation," *Ruidoso* [NM] *News*, January 31, 2013; Rocky Barker, "Can Idaho turn a profit with federal lands?" *Idaho Statesman*, February 20, 2013.

CHAPTER FOUR

1.   Benjamin C. Bradlee, former executive editor (1968–1991) of the *Washington Post* maintained, "We are unable to admit any of this publicly, as I once found out, for as soon as we admit that we don't always print the truth, someone will immediately pounce on the admission.... We don't print the truth. We print what we know, what people tell us. So we print lies." Ben Bradlee, *A Good Life: Newspapering and Other Adventures* (Simon & Schuster, 1996), 432.

2.   Kiron K. Skinner, Annelise Anderson, and Martin Anderson, eds., *Reagan, In His Own Hand: The Writings of Ronald Reagan That Reveal His Revolutionary Vision for America* (The Free Press, 2001), 250. Ronald Reagan had written out, but then scratched through—that is, deleted—the following line: "I used to say they probably thought I ate my young but Nancy made me quit that." The handwritten version of this address is reproduced on pages 248–49.

3.   Art. II, Sec. 2, cl. 2.

4.   Ilie, Cornelia. 2006. Parliamentary Discourses. In Keith Brown, ed., *Encyclopedia of Language and Linguistics*, 2nd Edition, vol. 9, (Oxford: Elsevier), 189.

5.   The House Committee on Public Lands was created on December 17, 1805. With passage of the Legislative Reorganization Act of 1946, five committees were combined into the House Committee on Public Lands, including Territories (1825), Mines and Mining (1865), Indian Affairs (1821), Irrigation and Reclamation (1893), and Insular Affairs (1899). On February 2, 1951, the House Committee on Public Lands was renamed the House Interior and Insular Affairs Committee; it became the House Committee on Natural Resources in 1993. In 1995, the jurisdiction of the House Merchant Marines and Fisheries Committee (1887) was transferred to the House Committee on Natural Resources. http://naturalresources.house.gov/about/history.htm. See, "Historical Information on the Committee on Resources and Its Predecessor Committees 1807 – 2002," 107th Congress 2d Session, Committee Print 107-G, NOV02. Enabling legislation is a federal law passed by Congress and signed by the president that permits a federal agency or department to perform a function; however, the agency may only perform that function if Congress passes an appropriation bill, which must originate in the House of Representatives, that is signed by the president and provides the funds necessary to do so. "[A]n agency literally has no power to act.... unless and until Congress confers power upon it.... An agency may not confer power upon itself. To permit an agency to expand its power in the face of a congressional limitation on its jurisdiction would be to grant to the agency power to override Congress. This we are both unwilling and unable to do." *Louisiana Pub. Serv. Comm'n v. F.C.C.*, 476 U.S. 355, 374-375 (1986). Congress often withholds funds for agency action

that it opposes, as Congress did for decades regarding oil and gas leasing on the Outer Continental Shelf. See *Sagebrush Rebel*, chapter 2.

6.   http://www.loc.gov/pictures/collection/hlb/background.html.

7.   Ibid. "During a 55-year career at *The Post*, [Block] counted Richard M. Nixon and Ronald Reagan as his least favorite chief executives, and, boy, does it show. [H]is dead-eyed, prune-faced Reagan visually lives up to the artist's characterization of him as an 'amiable dunce.'" "Political Lines, Sharply Drawn," Michael O'Sullivan, *Washington Post*, June 6, 2008.

8.   "Only Interior Secretary James Watt's phiz ("physiognomy") made him a more suitable subject for [cartoonists'] satire [than David Stockman]." Laurence I. Barrett, *Gambling with History, Ronald Reagan in The White House* (Doubleday, 1983), 188. "It's easy enough to laugh at Interior Secretary James Watt. With his bald head and glasses ... he's a cartoonist's delight—an eggheaded exploiter out to nail Bambi's hide to his office wall." Jack Anderson, "Watt's poor attempt at secrecy carries scent of Watergate," *Lakeland [Florida] Ledger*, May 10, 1982, 9A.

9.   It appears that Block drew his "inspiration," not from the hearing, which he did not attend, or its transcript, which he did not read, but instead from an execrable commentary by one of his *Post* colleagues. Colman McCarthy, "James Watt and the Puritan Ethic," *Washington Post*, May 24, 1981, L5. Other commentators, no better informed than McCarthy or Block, soon piled on to "the-hate-Watt-and-his-purported-religious-beliefs" bandwagon.

10.   Leilani Watt, *Caught in the Conflict: My Life With James Watt* (Harvest House, 1984), 91–94.

11.   Why did "the Secretary [bring] up the Lord?" "[A]s a fundamentalist Christian, his commitment calls for witness. Otherwise, he could see himself as hypocritical." John J. "Jack" Casserly, "Mr. Watt of the West," *Petroleum Independent*, December 1981, quoted in Ron Arnold, *At the Eye of the Storm: James Watt and the Environmentalists* (Regnery Gateway, 1982), 10.

12.   Briefing by the Secretary of the Interior, Oversight Hearing before the Committee on Interior and Insular Affairs, House of Representatives, Ninety-Seventh Congress, 1st Sess., held in Washington, D.C., February 5, 1981 (Government Printing Office, 1981), 37–38. The verbatim account of the hearing was available to anyone who sought the truth as early as 1982. See Arnold, *At the Eye of the Storm*, 74–76.

13.   Some reporters outside the Washington, D.C., Beltway took the time to understand what all the fuss was about and if it were true. John D. Lofton, after listing the comment of those who attacked Watt for his alleged comments, set the record straight and then declared: "So there you have it: The allegations regarding James Watt's religious views and his actual religious views. Any fair-minded observer would have to admit they are not one and the same. Not by a long shot." John D. Lofton, "What Watt says and what others say he says," *Beaver County [Pennsylvania] Times*, August 18, 1981, A7. Little wonder that President Reagan described Washington, D.C. as "an island, surrounded on all sides by reality." Dinesh D'Souza, *Ronald Reagan: How an Ordinary Man Became an Extraordinary Leader* (The Free Press, 1997), 219.

14.   Over the decades, environmentalists, leftists, and anti-Christians used Watt's mythical statement to attack Reagan, Watt, and other Christians, and those who espouse environmental views inconsistent with what the attackers regard as required by environmental or liberal orthodoxy. In 2004, Bill Moyers's use of the lie about Watt came to Watt's attention, as did a February 6, 2005, *Washington Post* article by Blaine Harden entitled, "The Greening of Evangelicals: Christian Right Turns, Sometimes Warily, to Environmentalism," at page A01, which contained this statement: "James G. Watt, President Ronald Reagan's first interior secretary, famously made this argument before Congress in 1981, saying: 'God gave us these things to use. After the last tree is felled, Christ will come back.'" Watt contacted the *Washington Post*, which published the following: "Correction to This Article – A Feb. 6 story incorrectly quoted James G. Watt, interior secretary under President Ronald Reagan, as telling Congress in 1981: 'After the last tree is felled, Christ will come back.' Although that statement has been widely attributed to Watt, there is no historical record that he made it." Moyers called Watt to apologize for his inadvertent use of a nonexistent statement. Moyers used a subsequent written apology to Watt to attack Watt for his actions as Reagan's Interior secretary, his views on environmental issues, and his ignorance of Christian doctrine. The *Washington Post* published Watt's views on the subject on May 21, 2005. On February 4, 2005, *Grist* website published the following: "In fact, Watt did not make such a statement to Congress. The quotation is attributed to Watt in the book *Setting the Captives Free* by Austin Miles, but Miles does not write that it was made before Congress. *Grist* regrets this reporting error and is aggressively looking into the accuracy of this quotation. The *Star Tribune* also regrets the error, and will report any further developments in the *Grist* inquiry." On February 11, 2005, *Grist* provided this update: "*Grist* has been unable to sub-

stantiate that Watt made this statement. We would like to extend our sincere apologies to Watt and to our readers for this error."

15. "This quotation ricocheted about Washington...." Elizabeth Drew, "A Reporter at Large, Secretary Watt," *New Yorker*, May 4, 1981, 111. Some members of the media, like Muckraker Jack Anderson, could not resist. "When he's not thinking of ways to use up the nation's natural resources in time for the Second Coming, [Watt's] scheming...." Jack Anderson, "Watt's poor attempt at secrecy carries scent of Watergate," *Lakeland [Florida] Ledger*, May 10, 1982, 9A. Congressman Weaver would not let it go. At a subsequent hearing Weaver, in a disagreement with Watt over policy, accused Watt of being motivated by the imminent arrival of the Lord. Republican members demanded that Chairman Udall rebuke Weaver, but Udall demurred. Weaver later apologized to Watt. Arnold, *At the Eye of the Storm*, 170–71; David S. Broder, "Watt Says He's Reined In Udall on Hostile Hearings," *Washington Post*, August 19, 1981, A1; C. Brant Short, *Ronald Reagan and the Public Lands: America's Conservation Debate, 1979–1984* (Texas A&M University Press, 1989), 58–59.

16. Unfortunately, even members of the Reagan administration could be taken in by a *Post* "hit piece" *if* it concerned an issue, official, or agency regarding which the reader was uninformed. If the *Post* story hit closer to home, the assumption was the reporter got it wrong and the record could be corrected with a call to the reporter, the editor, or a friendly columnist or by means of an official letter to the editor. Most of the time, however, nearly everyone who read of a department's misdeeds in the *Post*, even Reagan officials, wondered aloud, "What is wrong with them over there?"

17. "With a city full of whispers concerning James G. Watt's ability to keep his job, the interior secretary is engaged in an aggressive anti-media campaign designed, he says, 'to get out the truth.'" Martin Crutsinger and Ann Blackman, "Watt blames problems on media," Associated Press, *Lakeland [Florida] Ledger*, April 11, 1983.

18. President Reagan was used to such personal attacks. Nicholas von Hoffman wrote that it was "humiliating to think of this unlettered, self-assured bumpkin being our president." Nicholas Von Hoffman, "Contra Reaganum," *Harper's* (May 1982): 35; Robert Wright declared Reagan "virtually brain dead." Robert Wright, "Legacy: What Legacy?" *New Republic*, (January 9, 1989), 6. Michael Kinsley asserted that Reagan was "not terribly bright." Michael Kinsley, *Curse of the Giant Muffins: And Other Washington Maladies* (Summit Books, 1987), 89. Thanks to Paul Kengor's remarkable research, President Reagan's deep Christian faith is today well known; however, during his presidency that was not the case, in part, because, in the words of Judge Clark, the "media and biographies have for the most part bypassed the President's total faith and trust in God." Reagan biographer Steven F. Hayward maintains that "Reagan kept [his deep religious faith] hidden in plain sight...." Paul Kengor, *God and Ronald Reagan: A Spiritual Life* (Harper, 2004), flyleaf. Kengor relates that Secretary Heckler suggested that cabinet meetings should open with a prayer. President Reagan replied, "I do." "That is, he was already in the habit of praying alone and to himself, before each meeting." Hodel relates, "He both responded to the suggestion and closed the subject. There was no debate. No controversy. That was it. He prayed himself." Ibid, 173–74.

19. Philip Shabecoff, "Major Environmental Leaders Back Carter Reelection Bid," *New York Times*, September 28, 1980, Sec. A, 36.

20. "And God blessed them, and God said unto them, 'Be fruitful, and multiply, and replenish the earth, and subdue it: and have dominion over the fish of the sea, and over the fowl of the air, and over every living thing that moveth upon the earth.'" Genesis 1:28, King James Version (Cambridge).

21. "Environmentalism is a proselytizing religion. Skeptics are not merely people unconvinced by the evidence: They are treated as evil sinners. I probably would not write this article if I did not have tenure." "Environmentalism as Religion," Paul H. Rubin, *Wall Street Journal*, April 22, 2010.

22. Arnold, *At the Eye of the Storm*, 76–87.

23. The Herblock cartoon became ubiquitous; it took on a life of its own. Even thoughtful analyses of the policies of Reagan's Interior Department and Watt's views included the scurrilous cartoon, albeit with a disclaimer ("That quote has been unfairly interpreted as a justification for using up our resources willy-nilly; Watt says it means nothing of the sort.") and a quote from Watt's former minister. Jerry Adler, William J. Cook, Mary Hager, and Tony Fuller, "James Watt's Land Rush," *Newsweek*, June 29, 1981, 29, 32.

24. The anti-Christian bias of the *Washington Post* was revealed late in 1981 when, in printing the transcript of President Reagan's December 23, 1981, "Address to the Nation About Christmas and the Situation in Poland," the *Post* deleted the first five paragraphs, including the phrase, "Others of us believe in the divinity of the child born in Bethlehem, that he was and is the promised Prince of Peace."; "Reagan: 'Their Crimes Will Cost Them Dearly,'" *Washington Post*, December 24, 1981,

A8. The negative response of readers, who had seen the address on television, was so overwhelming that the *Post* had to explain itself nearly two months later. It "lamely argued," writes Professor Paul Kengor, that it just did not have space for the 100 words that included mention of Jesus. Robert J. McCloskey, "The 'Tyranny of Space,'" *Washington Post*, February 22, 1982, A10. See Paul Kengor, "Candles in Solidarity," *The American Spectator*, December 23, 2012. A more direct assault on President Reagan's Christianity occur in February 1984 when the *New York Times* blasted him for his acknowledgement that Jesus is Lord to a meeting of the National Religious Broadcasters. Editorial, "Sermon on the Stump," *New York Times*, February 3, 1984. Eleven years later, the *Post* again revealed its bias, perhaps inadvertently—the article was quickly scrubbed as an oversight—in a front page story describing Christians as "largely poor, uneducated and easy to command." Michael Weisskopf, "Energized by Pulpit or Passion, the Public Is Calling," *Washington Post*, February 1, 1993, A1; Mona Charen, "Evangelical prey," February 10, 1993. More recently the *New York Times* demonstrated its ignorance of Christianity with a correction to a March 31, 2013, article entitled "Pope Calls for 'Peace in All the World' in first Easter Message," by Elisabetta Povoledo: "Correction: April 1, 2013: An earlier version of this article mischaracterized the Christian holiday of Easter. It is the celebration of Jesus's resurrection from the dead, not his resurrection into heaven."

25. President Reagan keenly followed what was said, written, and drawn about members of his family, personal and political. "I phoned Berke Breathed—cartoonist who does *Bloom County*. He obviously thought I was calling to bitch about something. I called to thank him for the Sunday strip where he had Nancy in the strip looking lovely. He's sending me the original." Ronald Reagan, *The Reagan Diaries* (Harper, 2007), 297, January 28, 1985.

26. "One of Reagan's most remarkable leadership qualities [was] his ability to maintain his course and not to be deterred even in the face of intense opposition." D'Souza, *Ronald Reagan*, 235.

27. Arnold, *At the Eye of the Storm*, 58; Paul Slansky, *The Clothes Have No Emperor, A Chronicle of the American 80s* (Fireside, 1989), 48.

28. Jeremiah O'Leary, "Reagan Says He Supports Watt Fully," *Washington Star*, August 5, 1981. At the National Press Club, Chief of Staff James Baker said regarding Watt's efforts: "We are aware that there is a great deal of tension with respect to some of these policies. The President has absolute faith and confidence in Jim Watt. This has been discussed. The President thinks Jim is doing a fine job." Arnold, *At the Eye of the Storm*, 175.

29. January 20, 1982; http://www.reagan.utexas.edu/archives/speeches/1982/12082e.htm.

30. Arnold, *At the Eye of the Storm*, 159–60, sets forth a series of attacks made by environmental groups on what Reagan's Interior Department "is planning" to do. Another example was based on a leaked document that never went to the level of department policy. Jack Anderson, "This Land is Your Land, Or is It?," *Washington Post*, July 18, 1982, Sec. B, 7.

31. Sometimes the media took the time to get the story right. *Newsweek* reported, regarding claims by environmental groups that Reagan's Interior Department planned to mine the parks, "Parks are inviolate, by decree of Congress, and [Watt] has no quarrel with that." *Newsweek*, June 29, 1981, 24.

32. During the lunch break at Watt's Confirmation Hearing, veteran newsman and Watt's future press secretary (assistant to the secretary for public affairs) Doug Baldwin, and I sat at a small table with Watt preparing for the afternoon session. Baldwin had learned of a hostile question that Colorado Senator Hart, a Democrat, planned to ask. Watt rehearsed an answer neither Baldwin nor I liked, and I said we should develop a better response. Watt refused; "I'm ready," he said. But when Hart asked the question, Watt was not ready. I regretted that I had not pressed the matter; however, the issue raised by Hart died. During Watt's tenure, others approached him with similar advice, but Watt kept his own counsel on what he would say and when and how he would say it. Those in Watt's office when he learned of and was struck by the diversity of the blue ribbon coal panel kicked themselves later for not warning Watt off of the phrase that became, "A Black, a woman...." But it would not have made any difference. At some point down the road, there would have been another fatal, self-inflicted wounding witticism. One remarkable aspect of this matter is that the words that ended his tenure came from Watt's lips and not via a leak in the department. It was not because Hodel quickly highlighted many a controversial Watt statement with, "You did NOT hear the Secretary say that," which was as much a not-so-subtle suggestion to his friend Watt as it was a caution to everyone in the room; it was out of a sense of loyalty felt by political appointee and careerist alike.

33. Once, Baldwin saw a large crowd of reporters at an early Watt event. "What are you here for? He's just going to give the same speech." "We think one of these days he'll say something that will get him fired and we want to be there for it," replied one. On one trip to Glacier National Park, reporters

from *Newsweek*, the Associated Press, and newspapers from Spokane, Kalispell, as well as almost every television and radio station in Montana followed Watt. Mark Brunson, "Watt's Antagonism Toward Press Part of Road Show," *Daily Interlude*, July 15, 1983, Sec. A, 1.

34.   Arnold, *At the Eye of the Storm*, 200–1, 238.

35.   In a private meeting with Subcommittee Chairman John Dingell, a Democrat from Michigan, whom Watt knew from previous appearances as Commissioner of the Federal Power Commission, Watt related that he did not see what the fuss was all about, but he stood fast on President Reagan's right to assert the privilege.

36.   *United States v. Nixon*, 418 U.S. 683, at 705-06, 708, 711 (1974).

37.   *Nixon v. Administrator of General Services*, 433 U.S. 425, 446, 449 (internal citations omitted), and 453 (1977).

38.   *Watkins v. United States*, 354 U.S. 173, 187 (1957).

39.   Letter from Attorney General William French Smith to President Reagan, October 31, 1981, reprinted in 5 Op. O.L.C. 27, 30 (1981). In his opinion, Smith maintained that "the interest of Congress in obtaining information for oversight purposes is, I believe, considerably weaker than its interests when specific legislative proposals are in question." Moreover, he argued, Congressional oversight "is justifiable only as a means of facilitating the legislative task of enacting, amending, or repealing laws." 43 Op. Att'y Gen. 327, 331 (1981). Subsequent presidents, including George H.W. Bush, Clinton, and George W. Bush have made the same distinction. Todd Garvey, Alissa M. Dolan, "Presidential Claims of Executive Privilege: History, Law, Practice, and Recent Developments," Congressional Research Service, August 21, 2012, 3, note 20.

40.   Martha M. Hamilton, "Executive Privilege Invoked to Back Watt, *Washington Post*, October 15, 1981, D12.

41.   "House Subcommittee Moving to Cite Interior Secretary Watt for Contempt," *Washington Post*, November 27, 1981, A9.

42.   William Chapman, "House Subcommittee Votes to Cite Watt for Contempt," *Washington Post*, February 10, 1982, A1.

43.   "Watt Says Congress Likely to Hold Him in Contempt," *Washington Post*, February 11, 1982, A9.

44.   Eleanor Randolph, "Watt Says He'd Rather Go to Jail Than Give Papers to Subcommittee," *Los Angeles Times*, (February 11, 1982), 10. During this period, Watt and his wife were at the White House for a function. As they passed through the reception line, President Reagan pulled Leilani aside, wrapped his arm around her shoulders, and whispered, "Lani, don't you worry. If Jim ends up in jail, I'll visit him every Thursday."

45.   Philip Shabecoff, "House Panel Finds Watt in Contempt," *New York Times*, February 26, 1982, D16; William Chapman, "Hill Panel Votes to Cite Watt for Contempt," *Washington Post*, February 26, 1982, A5; William Kronholm, "Full panel cites Watt," *Lakeland (Florida) Ledger*, February 26, A1. One Republican who voted to cite Watt opined that "the White House was setting Watt up for the contempt vote as a way of ridding itself of a controversial Cabinet member." Ibid., A12.

46.   Carew Papritz, ed., *100 Watts: The James Watt Memorial Cartoon Collection* (Khyber Press, 1983), 39, 84. That the media focused on Watt and not on Reagan was not surprising. "[Reagan's] aura of serenity … forced subordinates like David Stockman and James Watt to absorb animosity created by Reagan's policies. Barrett, *Gambling with History*, 40–41.

47.   On December 16, 1982, the House of Representatives voted 259 to 105 to support a similar contempt citation against EPA Administrator Anne Burford; 55 Republicans joined 204 Democrats. 128 *Cong. Rec.* 31746-76 (1982). Less than three months later, on March 9, 1983, Ms. Burford resigned; http://www.reagan.utexas.edu/archives/speeches/1983/30983e.htm.

48.   Anderson, "Watt's poor attempt at secrecy carries scent of Watergate." A few months later, Congress again sought documents, this time from Reagan's Interior Department regarding the Powder River Basin coal lease sale. A team of lawyers from the Justice Department advised Watt that he should assert executive privilege and that he would prevail. After the lawyers left, Watt had the boxes of documents loaded on a truck and hauled down the street to the Justice Department. When Watt learned the boxes were on the loading dock, he called Smith and told him he had the documents and was free to assert executive privilege. The documents were returned to Reagan's Interior Department where Watt had copies made and sent them to Capitol Hill.

49.   Edwin Meese III, *With Reagan: The Inside Story* (Regnery, 1992), 63.

50.   Clark's biographer writes, "The purpose of the leaks was to control the President. By feeding information to the public via the media, men inside the White House could bring external pressure upon Reagan to abandon or stay clear of policies they did not support." Paul Kengor and Patricia Clark

Doerner, *The Judge: William P. Clark, Ronald Reagan's Top Hand* (Ignatius, 2007), 153. In that context, Jim Baker and Mike Deaver treated President Reagan "like a grandfather whom one humors but does not take very seriously." Richard Pipes, *Vixi: Memoirs of a Non-Belonger* (Yale University Press, 2003), 176. Quoted in Kengor, *The Judge*, 152.

51.   *The Reagan Diaries*, e.g., 61 ("Laid down the law to Cabinet on leaks."); 113 ("I know what my decision is but if I reveal it there will be a leak [d—n it] so I've taken it under study."); and 634 ("We started by talking leaks to the press—suddenly there is a new wave.").

52.   *The Reagan Diaries*, 278 ("We're all in an uproar over the continued leaks. Yesterday's Cabinet meeting was on the front P. of the Wash. Post.... From now on we dispense with the back benchers—only Cabinet members will attend meetings.").

53.   Ibid., 144, 147, 151. Regarding Secretary of State Al Haig, President Reagan wrote, "One or more people in the White House were trying to do him in with malicious leaks to the press. [T]he jealousies and turf battles had gone too far." Ronald Reagan, *An American Life: The Autobiography* (Simon & Schuster, 1990), 361.

54.   *The Reagan Diaries*, 144. In January 1983, President Reagan was quoted as saying, "I've had it up to my keister with these leaks." Associated Press, *Lakeland* [Florida] *Ledger*, January 11, 1983, 8A.

55.   Watt, *Caught in the Conflict*, 11. The U.S. Park Police was created in 1791; http://www.nps.gov/uspp/.

56.   Ibid.

57.   Phil McCombs, "Watt Outlaws Rock Music on Mall for July 4," *Washington Post*, April 6, 1983, A1.

58.   Ibid.

59.   Watt's Assistant Secretary for Fish, Wildlife, and Parks, Ray Arnett, a friend and appointee of Governor Reagan in his days in California, kidded Watt, "Jim, you don't know the Beach Boys from beach balls, do you?" Watt admitted that he did not.

60.   Phil McCombs and Richard Harrington, "Watt Sets Off Uproar With Music Ban," *Washington Post*, April 7, 1983, A1.

61.   Ibid.

62.   Ibid.

63.   The question remains, what did Nancy Reagan know about the Beach Boys and when did she know it? Her personal knowledge of the Beach Boys, their music, or her children's interest in or appreciation of them and their music appears unlikely. Patti Davis, the President and Mrs. Reagan's daughter, reports on "introducing a rock musician [not Dennis Wilson of the Beach Boys who she once dated apparently without her mother's knowledge] to the governor's wife [Mrs. Reagan] who still played Frank Sinatra on 78's." Patti Davis, *The Way I See It* (G. P. Putnam's Sons, 1992), 186–91, 200–1. Given the family dynamics revealed by Ms. Davis, it is unlikely that Nancy Reagan interceded in defense of the Beach Boys out of concern for her daughter, her friendship with a "Beach Boy," or her love of his music.

64.   Phil McCombs and Richard Harrington, "Watt Beached on July 4 Music Ban," *Washington Post*, April 8, 1983, A1. See Watt, *Caught in the Conflict*, 9–22.

65.   Watt never criticized the First Lady. When Watt's wife asked him why he had not told the First Lady of the facts of the controversy, he replied, "Mrs. Reagan was defending her husband, and I like that." Watt, *Caught in the Conflict*, 22.

66.   Watt, *Caught in the Conflict*, 19.
        Fuller provides this recollection:

> Jim Watt was a bit of a target of some within the administration, certainly outside, and yet he was so loyal. He had a marvelous—his commitment I guess to doing what the President wanted was great. Yet he got himself in trouble with the Beach Boys. [S]omehow the Beach Boys play big in this administration. [*laughs*] [Watt] had a criticism about their appearing on the Mall and we were sitting around going, "Oh my God, what are we going to do now?" I said, "You know, David Gergen showed me this foot that he had. It was a foot, a cast mold of a foot with a hole through the middle. I said, "Jim Watt's coming over here, why don't we give him the award for shooting himself in the foot?" We all thought it was funny. We said, "If we can't laugh our way through this, we're going to have a problem." So he comes over. I said, "Jim, let me tell you what we're going to do. We're going to give you an award." "Really?" he said, "I thought I was in trouble." I said, "Well, you are, but we're going to try and get you out of it. Trust us, we think this will work." He was good-

natured enough to accept the Shot Myself in the Foot award. We got a nice little picture with him doing that, and we got through the crisis of the Beach Boys on the Mall.

George H. W. Bush Oral History, Interview with Craig Fuller, http://millercenter.org/president/bush/oralhistory/craig-fuller.

67.   Watt, *Caught in the Conflict*, 15, 18. President Reagan wrote, "Lunch with V.P. A strain has developed between George S. and Bill C. I've invited the Schultz's to Camp D. for the weekend. I don't think the problem is serious." *The Reagan Diaries*, 142. Little wonder that Reagan did not mention the forty-five second presentation to Watt before which he whispered, "I'm sorry you had to go through this."

68.   Watt, *Caught in the Conflict*, 19.

69.   George H. W. Bush Oral History, Interview with Craig Fuller, http://millercenter.org/president/bush/oralhistory/craig-fuller. One wonders, when Fuller declared, "Jim Watt was a bit of a target of some within the administration," if he meant himself, or Deaver, or Gergen?

70.   "When James Watt, Reagan's secretary of the interior, barred the Beach Boys from playing a Fourth of July concert on the National Mall in 1983 because he thought they attracted 'the wrong element,' Reagan invited them to the White House." George Will, "They Get Around," *St. Louis Post Dispatch*, June 22, 2012.

71.   This is particularly the case in rural counties in the eleven Western states, where the Interior Department together with the U.S. Forest Service (under the U.S. Department of Agriculture) own the overwhelming majority of the land.

72.   The American people are largely unfamiliar with the public policy issues that affect the West; for example, they do not know the difference between a federally designated "wilderness" and wide open spaces, that a national park is not a national forest, or that the coyote is not on the Endangered Species Act list. Arnold, *At the Eye of the Storm*, xiv–xvi.

73.   Of course, decisions regarding natural resources, especially energy, affect jobs, families, and communities throughout the country and not just in the West; however, people are so figuratively far from the farm that they forget milk comes from cows. Arnold writes of an "urban v. rural" divide as well as a split between the "services v. goods" economy. Arnold, *At the Eye of the Storm*, xvii–xix. Abraham Maslow has a fancy name for the distance and even disdain many urban dwellers harbor for those who provide the food, fiber, fuel, and minerals that make our lives so comfortable. He calls it, "postgratification forgetting and devaluation." Abraham H. Maslow, *Motivation and Personality* (Harper & Row, 1954), 61.

74.   In June 1981, a poll conducted by *Newsweek* asked how people viewed "Increasing oil exploration and other commercial uses of Federal lands (not including national parks)." Seventy-eight percent favored such a policy; 19% opposed. *Newsweek*, June 29, 1981, 29.

75.   This unfortunate turn of phrase was first used by Al Gore in *Earth in the Balance, Ecology and the Human Spirit* (Houghton Mifflin Harcourt, 1992), 245.

76.   *Newsweek*, June 29, 1981, 23.

77.   For example, Arnold discusses favorable newspaper coverage of actions by Reagan's Interior Department backing an "Open Lands Project" in Chicago, preventing use of federal funds for private development on coastal barrier islands in Louisiana, and killing a plan to add turbines to the Glen Canyon Dam that would have increased water flows in Grand Canyon in Arizona. Arnold, *At the Eye of the Storm*, 218–19, referring to coverage in the *Chicago Sun-Times* (see also Eve Endicott, ed., *Land Conservation Through Public/Private Partnerships* [Island Press, 1993], 209–11), the *New Orleans Times-Picayune*, and the *Arizona Daily Sun*.

78.   "When the environmentalists [go] to the media prior to my arrival … and drill all these press people on how I'm supposedly destroying the world … the journalists then know the right questions to ask." Arnold, *At the Eye of the Storm*, ix.

79.   Watt ensured headlines, even if the stories beneath them were hardly newsworthy; for example, the headline for President Reagan's first claim of executive privilege contained "Watt" not "Reagan." Thus the media gave prominent and continuing coverage to charges that: the wrong account had been charged for a Watt gathering; Reagan's Interior Department stopped paying membership dues to environmental organizations saving $85,000 a year; and appointees to advisory committees were reviewed by the Republican Party. Arnold, *At the Eye of the Storm*, 214, 238–39, 240–41.

80.   Watt became "the Republican Party's fund-raising star, cranking out bucks from the faithful at prodigious rates, second only to President Reagan himself." Arnold, *At the Eye of the Storm*, 203;

see also 203–7 and 241–42. Lyn Nofziger proclaimed, "If [any Republican] takes on Jim Watt, their funding dries up." Ibid., 207. Short, *Ronald Reagan and the Public Lands*, 57, 59.

81. "Watt's Off-the-Cuff Remark Sparks Storm of Criticism," Dale Russakoff, *Washington Post*, September 22, 1983, A1. One member of the commission said, "I am disturbed that he decided to describe our race, religion and other characteristics. The point should be that we are intelligent, experienced, well-informed people undertaking a serious and conscientious study." Ibid. In 1977, Congress mandated the awarding of government contracts on the basis of race and ethnicity; these programs not only remain in place today but have been expanded, notwithstanding a ruling of the Supreme Court of the United States that leaves their constitutionality in question. *Adarand Constructors, Inc. v. Peña*, 515 U.S. 200 (1995). Without intent or apparent irony, in the same paragraph in which he discusses Watt's selection as Secretary of the Interior, Professor Pfiffner writes of the need for a president to appoint "a woman or black, a Jew or Catholic, to demonstrate his commitment to a broadly based administration." James P. Pfiffner, *The Strategic Presidency: Hitting the Ground Running* (University Press of Kansas, 1996), 35. On August 22, 2012, James Taranto quipped in the *Wall Street Journal*: "Barack Obama, Heir to Reagan: '[On my staff] I have a black, a woman, two Jews and a cripple. And we have talent.'—Interior Secretary James Watt, Sept. 21, 1983; 'Holder Justice Department Recruits Dwarfs, Schizophrenics, and the ["]Intellectually Disabled["]'—headline, PJ Media.com, August 21, 2012." Reagan biographer Steven Hayward best describes why Watt's relatively innocuous remark was his undoing:

> Crude and obsolete language, to be sure, but Watt's real sin was transgressing the chief dialectical convention of modern liberalism, which is that while we are to be always conscious of race and ethnicity, we are never to be explicit or direct about it. Watt was explicit. For that he had to go. Even Gerald Ford and Bob Dole said so.

Steven F. Hayward, *The Age of Reagan: The Conservative Counterrevolution, 1980–1989* (Crown Forum, 2009), 307.

82. "Senate Is Ready to Ask for Watt's Resignation, *Gainesville (Florida) Sun*, September 29, 1983.
83. Watt, *Caught in the Conflict*, 166, 170.
84. Ibid.
85. Dale Russakoff, "Watt's Support on the Hill Erodes," *Washington Post*, September 24, 1983, Sec. A, 1; Marin Crutsinger, "Watt Losing Western Base?" *Great Falls [Montana] Tribune*, October 1, 1983, Sec. A, 2.
86. "Secretary of the Interior James Watt resigns," *Bangor* (Maine) *Daily News*, October 10, 1983, 1. See Watt, *Caught in the Conflict*, 161–83. What did he say? In a bill of particulars of sorts, the Associated Press published, in a separate article accompanying news of Watt's resignation, a list of his offensive pronouncements (*Bangor* [Maine] *Daily News* [November 1981], 3):
    - "I never use the words Democrats and Republicans. It's liberals and Americans." (A partisan remark from a political appointee is hardly surprising.);
    - January 19, 1983: Indian reservations are examples of "the failures of socialism." (Who should Watt have blamed, American Indians or the federal government? See, John Koppisch, "Why Are Indian Reservations So Poor? A Look At The Bottom 1%," *Forbes*, December 13, 2011.);
    - January 20, 1983: Watt compared environmentalists to communists in their pursuit of "centralized planning and control of the society." ("Environmentalism," says Czech President Vaclav Klaus, "is the new communism, a system of elite command-and-control that kills prosperity and should similarly be condemned to the ash heap of history." *Washington Times*, May 30, 2008.);
    - April 5, 1983: [The Beach Boys fiasco];
    - April 13, 1983: Watt said he and his wife as "persecuted evangelical Christians" had "experienced the hatred that has been poured out...." (What else would one call the Herblock cartoon?);
    - August 20, 1983: Watt compared Germans who did not speak out against Nazism to those who do not speak out against abortion. (According to figures from the Centers for Disease Control and the Guttmacher Institute, between the ruling of *Roe v. Wade* in 1973 and mid-1983 when Watt spoke, between 11.2 and 13.6 million abortions had been performed in the United States.);
    - June 17, 1982, Watt wrote a letter to Israel's ambassador to the U.N. contrasting U.S. support for Israel with what Watt perceived of as the lack of support by liberal Jews for

the Reagan administration's energy program. (Watt, a *goyim* from Lusk, Wyoming, unfamiliar with the diversity of Jewish opinion, might be forgiven for his ham-handed attempt at diplomacy. Sandee Brawarsky and D. Mark, *Two Jews, Three Opinions: A Collection of 20th Century American Jewish Quotations* [Perigee Trade, 1998].)

87. "Reagan accepts resignation, wishes Watt and wife well," *Bangor* [Maine] *Daily News*, October 10, 1983, 3.

88. *The Reagan Diaries*, 185.

89. Ibid., 188.

90. Radio Address to the Nation on the Resignation of Secretary of the Interior James G. Watt, November 26, 1983; http://www.presidency.ucsb.edu/ws/index.php?pid=40809. Peter M. Robinson, White House speechwriter wrote the author on August 21, 2012, regarding the talk: "I recall that radio address well. Why? Because the speechwriting shop had already composed an address—I don't recall the subject, although it may have been the economy. The President sent back our address with a couple of pages from a legal pad on which he had composed his own, the tribute to Sec. Watt. The President included a warm note, explaining that he hoped we speechwriters wouldn't mind if he set aside our draft for his own. We all marveled at his draft. He had composed it, single-spaced, with scarcely more than a word or two crossed out and re-written. He had simply sat down with a pen in his hand and written what he had wanted to say. Beautiful."

91. Could Watt have survived? In retrospect, the phrase that was his undoing hardly seems the stuff of head-toppling scandal. Of course, Reagan and Watt's opponents seized upon it and attacked once again, as they had done in the past. The difference this time was Watt. He was spent, withdrawn, depressed. The years of fighting back had taken their toll. His aide Steve Shipley related to an encouraging caller, "Jim has got no gas left in his tank." Republicans in Washington, D.C., got the word: they need not expend political capital defending Watt. Only Reagan continued to defend him. Watt, *Caught in the Conflict*, 161–181.

92. Kengor, *The Judge*, 252. President Reagan told Clark: "I want you to consider going to Interior to place some oil on Jim Watt's water—to calm the waves." To "pour oil on troubled waters" is "to resolve a quarrel by the exercise of tact and diplomacy." Daphne M. Gulland and David G. Hinds-Howell, *Dictionary of English Idioms* (Penguin Books, 1986), 25. See Benjamin Franklin, Of the Stilling of Waves by means of Oil. *Philosophical Transactions of the Royal Society of London* (1774) 64, 445–60.

93. Kengor, *The Judge*, 258.

94. Their loyalty was born of respect. "Clark agreed with Reagan on all of the important issues, respected him, and trusted his political instincts," as a result, his was a "'let Reagan be Reagan' approach to White House policy making." Ibid., 247. Likewise, it was Watt who, during a gathering of all Reagan administration political appointees at the Department of Commerce's vast auditorium in January 1982, brought the audience to its feet with a closing cry of "Let Reagan be Reagan."

95. Ibid., 259, quoting, in part, Lyn Nofziger, "Clark as Troubleshooter (again)," *Washington Times*, October 19, 1983, C1.

96. Kengor, *The Judge*, 260–63. One Friends of the Earth spokesman said, "Clark doesn't know any more about national parks or endangered species than he did about Angola or Zimbabwe," referencing Clark's confirmation hearing in February 1981 for Deputy Secretary of State when he was hammered mercilessly by Delaware Senator Joseph Biden, a Democrat. "What They're Saying about Clark," *The Denver Post*, October 14, 1983, 10A. A Sierra Club leader declared, "Secretary Watt was bored by the Grand Canyon. I worry that Judge Clark may not know where it is." Dale Russakoff, "Environmental Groups Prepared to Oppose Clark at Hearing," *Washington Post*, November 1, 1983, A2.

97. Kengor, *The Judge*, 68–69, 265. The vote to confirm Watt was 83 to 12, with five not voting; http://www.govtrack.us/congress/votes/97-1981/s13. "Interior post nominee, seven others confirmed on late-night Senate votes," *Lawrence* [Kansas] *Journal-World*, January 23, 1981, 2.

98. Kengor, *The Judge*, 266–67.

99. Ibid., 267. Watt believed he had a good working relationship with Udall, but Udall, in a *Washington Post* article, "viciously attacked" Watt. Watt stormed to Capitol Hill, barged into the Chairman's office, and red-faced but silent confronted Udall as Udall's staff scurried from the room. After several uneasy minutes, Udall replied softly, "I lied." Watt took it as apology, spun on his heels, and left. Thereafter, the two never spoke privately but were cordial ("Mr. Chairman" and "Mr. Secretary") in public. President Reagan had a similar encounter with Washington's unusual approach to friendship, but his response differed from Watt's reaction. A month or so after the 1981 inauguration,

Speaker Tip O'Neill and his wife and a few others were guests of the President and First Lady in the family quarters. "It was a warm, pleasant evening, and a good time was had by all. By the time it was over, I was certain Tip and I had worn out Nancy and the other guests by trying to top each other with Irish stories passed on by our fathers. I also thought I'd made a friend." A day or so later, however, in a story in a newspaper, "Tip really lit into me personally because he didn't like the economic recovery program and some of the cuts I proposed in spending. Some of his remarks were pretty nasty. I was not only surprised but disappointed and also a little hurt." President Reagan called O'Neill who said "Ol' buddy, that's politics. After six o'clock we can be friends; but before six, it's politics." So, whenever President Reagan saw the Speaker he said, "Look, Tip, I'm resetting my watch; it's six o'clock." Reagan, *An American Life*, 250–51. Some close to Watt believed he had a "chip on his shoulder." Watt himself tells of an early confrontation, on behalf of his boss, Senator Milward Simpson, with the Harvard Law educated aide of another Senator. "My nerves just turned steel tough. I wasn't going to yield to that guy on anything just because he was from Harvard." Said a close friend from Wyoming, "His idea is not to roll with the punches. One sure way of not changing him is to fight him." Arnold, *At the Eye of the Storm*, 9–10.

100. Kengor, *The Judge*, 267.
101. Philip Shabecoff, "Watt Successor Offers Olive Branch to Critics," *New York Times*, December 8, 1983, A24.
102. Dale Russakoff and Ward Sinclair, "Cost Allocations to Change; Reagan Revises Water-Project Policy," *Washington Post*, January 24, 1984, A1.
103. Kengor, *The Judge*, 269–70.
104. Ibid., 270.
105. Ibid.; Ronald A. Taylor, "Environment: A New Leaf for Reagan," *U.S. News & World Report*, February 27, 1984, 59. Clark consistently assured the political appointees from Watt's tenure that he did not want to deviate substantively from Watt's policies.
106. Kengor, *The Judge*, 291. Although three out of every four voters who listed environmental protection as one of the issues most important to them voted for Mondale, according to a *Los Angeles Times* poll, only four percent of voters labeled environmental protection as one of the issues of most importance to them. Lou Cannon, *President Reagan: The Role of a Lifetime* (Simon & Schuster, 1991), 463. The *New York Times* asserted that, "for the first time, the environment as an issue emerged, if only temporarily, as a dominant feature on the nation's political landscape. It was an issue that captured and then held the public's attention for weeks and preoccupied the Government at its highest levels." Philip Shabecoff, "Politics and the E.P.A. Crisis: Environment Emerges as a Mainstream Issue," *New York Times*, April 29, 1983. This is an odd assertion given that the headlines regarding Watt, the media's biggest boogieman, rarely addressed his policies. Moreover, six months later, the *New York Times* concluded that it was Watt's "indiscretions, not his—or Mr. Reagan's—policies, that did him in." "What James Watt Said—and Did," *New York Times*, October 11, 1983.
107. Kengor, *The Judge*, 271–72.
108. Ibid., 277–79; Phil Gailey and Warrant Weaver, Jr., "Comes a Horseman," *New York Times*, February 5, 1985, 20; and Dale Russakoff, "Mornings on Horseback: Interior Secretary Clark's Final Canter in the Park," *Washington Post*, February 11, 1985, B1.
109. Margaret Shapiro, "Senate Confirms Education, Interior, Energy Secretaries," *Washington Post*, February 7, 1985, A4. United Press International reported that Proxmire "attack[ed] Hodel, warning that his 'tenure will be a disaster' and calling him a 'hatchet man' for James Watt, former interior secretary under whom Hodel worked for 21 months. 'If you liked Watt, you'll love Hodel,' Proxmire said. 'I did not like Watt, so I cannot go for the son of Watt.'" February 7, 1985.
110. "Interior Secretary James Watt has developed an unofficial seal for his office—one with the Interior Department's buffalo facing right. The department's official seal depicts a buffalo, facing left." *Dallas Times-Herald*, April 2, 1982.
111. Cass Peterson, "Interior Secretary Fires Iacocca From Statue of Liberty Panel," *Washington Post*, February 13, 1986, A1. See Statue of Liberty and Ellis Island discussion in *Sagebrush Rebel*, chapter 11. Hodel had become convinced that Iacocca, because of his management style and personality, controlled each of the boards on which he served. The buffer that a blue-ribbon panel normally provides a cabinet officer did not exist. Iacocca would be the only one making decisions and that presented a conflict of interest, in Hodel's opinion.
112. Cass Peterson, "Iacocca Assails Hodel's Action As Almost 'Un-American,'" *Washington Post*, February 14, 1986, A1. Iacocca's press conference included a rant where he posed a series of rhetorical questions. That evening, Hodel appeared on McNeil-Lehrer, a must watch program for Washington

insiders. Robert McNeil was in New York and Jim Lehrer was in Washington, D.C. Hodel appeared with Jim Lehrer who had each of Iacocca's questions played and then asked Hodel to respond to them in order. The next day the story all but disappeared from the news.

113.   Cass Peterson, "Hodel Avoided Asking Permission To Fire Iacocca From Statue Panel: Interior Secretary Says He Feared White House Would Veto Idea," *Washington Post*, February 15, 1986, A5. In Hodel's conversations with "the White House," he advised the caller that he could be ordered to put Iacocca back on the panel but the story would not be that Iacocca had rolled Hodel or even Donald Regan, White House Chief of Staff; instead, the story would be that Iacocca had rolled President Reagan!

114.   Cass Peterson, "Administration Ozone Policy May Favor Sunglasses, Hats," *Washington Post*, May 29, 1987, A1; from News Services, "Alternative to Ozone Pact Hit: Sunglasses, Hats Idea Is Not Serious Option, EPA Says," *Washington Post*, May 30, 1987, A2. Not surprisingly, Hodel asserts wryly that the phrase, though it never passed his lips, "will be my epitaph."

115.   Ibid.

116.   See Montreal Protocol discussion in *Sagebrush Rebel*, chapter 9.

117.   "Was it only two years ago that the Fourth of July in Washington was a birthday party and not a Beach Boys promotion? Could that be the real reason James Watt tried to ban the Boys from the Mall?" Richard Harrington, "Beach Boys: The Surf's Down: Succumbing to The Sands of Time," *Washington Post*, July 4, 1985, D1.

118.   Jacqueline Trescott, "Beach Boys, Better Late … The Long Wait Backstage," *Washington Post*, July 5 1985, B1. Hodel reports that the Park Police were preparing to call in reserves when they heard talk of "rushing the stage."

119.   http://www.brown.edu/Research/Understanding_the_Iran_Contra_Affair/about.php.

120.   Hodel purposefully deflected conflict and defused controversy. In addition, he encouraged Interior Department assistant secretaries and bureau chiefs to issue news releases in their names rather than in the name of the secretary thereby assuring less media interest.

121.   See generally Arnold, *At the Eye of the Storm*, 209–25.

122.   Bernard Goldberg, *A Slobbering Love Affair: The True (and Pathetic) Story of the Torrid Romance Between Barack Obama and the Mainstream Media* (Regnery, 2009), inside flap. See also Bernard Goldberg, *Bias: A CBS Insider Exposes How the Media Distort the News* (Regnery, 2001).

123.   Richard Viguerie, *America's Right Turn: How Conservatives Used New and Alternative Media to Take Over America* (Taylor Trade Publishing, 2004); Glenn H. Reynolds, *An Army of Davids: How Markets and Technology Empower Ordinary People to Beat Big Media, Big Government, and Other Goliaths* (Thomas Nelson, 2006).

124.   John Hinderaker, "Bill Moyers Smears A Better Man Than Himself," *Powerline*, February 6, 2005, http://www.powerlineblog.com/archives/2005/02/009377.php; see also John Hinderaker, "Lies and the Lying Liberals Who Tell Them," *Powerline*, May 21, 2005, http://www.powerlineblog.com/archives/2005/05/010372.php.

CHAPTER FIVE

1.   "Several weeks ago our modern day Luddites were out in full force. For those who don't know, the Luddites were people who wanted to stop the industrial revolution back in the last century. They took to the streets and tried to smash factory machinery then." Kiron K. Skinner, Annelise Anderson, and Martin Anderson, eds., *Reagan's Path to Victory, The Shaping of Ronald Reagan's Vision: Selected Writings* (The Free Press, 2004), 454. "Eco-terrorists are not preservers of the status quo, or even 'New Luddites' anxious about technology stealing their jobs, but rather deeply primitivist activists opposed to industrial civilization itself." Ron Arnold, *At the Eye of the Storm: James Watt and the Environmentalists* (Regnery Gateway, 1982), 40. Steward Brand, survivalist and creator of *The Whole Earth Catalog* declared, "We have wished, we eco-freaks, for a disaster or for a social change to come and bomb us into the Stone Age, where we might live like Indians in our valley, with our localism, our Appropriate Technology, our gardens, and our homemade religion, guilt-free at last." Ibid., 36. In late 1977, Reagan quoted with approval a report calling "the environmental crusade … one of the greatest hoaxes ever perpetrated on the people of this country." Skinner, *Reagan's Path to Victory*, 229–31, (November 8, 1977).

2.   Kiron K. Skinner, Annelise Anderson, and Martin Anderson, eds., *Reagan, In His Own Hand: The Writings of Ronald Reagan That Reveal His Revolutionary Vision for America* (The Free Press, 2001), 339. "A majority of us are somewhere in an environmental middle between those who'd pave over everything in the name of progress and those who wouldn't let us build a house unless it

looked like a bird nest.... Those of us who are neither anti-ecology [n]or environmental extremists seek an answer. How do we protect our constitutional right to own a piece of this earth at the same time we insure open space and natural beauty for generations not yet born? Is it oversimplification to suggest we don't need restrictive laws or government land planning but simply the law of supply and demand operating in the free market?" Ibid.

3. Built by Henry Cordes Brown, an Ohio carpenter turned real estate developer, designed by Denver architect Frank E. Edbrooke in the Italian Renaissance style with Colorado red granite and Arizona sandstone on its exterior, and constructed at a cost of $1.6 million (not including furniture), the Brown opened on August 12, 1892; http://www.brownpalace.com/About-the-Brown/From-the-Archive.

4. Spencer Rich, "Hickel to Hire U.S. Chamber Ex-Lobbyist," *Washington Post*, January 28, 1969, A5.

5. "President Nixon chose a businessman with exactly the wrong kind of background." Editorial, "The Hickel Nomination," *New York Times*, January 22, 1969. "I believe he is not qualified by understanding, experience and outlook to become the nation's chief conservationist and the major advocate of the American Indian," said South Dakota Senator George McGovern, a Democrat. Ibid. Drew Peterson and Jack Anderson, "Hickel Believes in More Oil and Fewer Reindeer," *Washington Post*, January 6, 1969, A19. Drew Pearson and Jack Anderson, "Hickel's Acts as Governor Questioned," *Washington Post*, January 15, 1969, 67.

6. Carroll Kilpatrick, "Hickel Fired: Morton Is Named," *Washington Post*, November 26, 1970, A1.

7. Arnold, *At the Eye of the Storm*, 12–13. C. Brant Short, *Ronald Reagan and the Public Lands: America's Conservation Debate, 1979–1984* (Texas A&M University Press, 1989), 56. The dramatic difference between Nixon's Interior and Ford's Interior and that of President Reagan was made clear six months after the 1981 Inauguration when former top Department of the Interior official under both Nixon and Ford, Nathanial Reed, decried the policies of Reagan's Interior Department as a "disaster," "bankrupt and infantile." Bill Prochnau, "'Crusade' at Interior Apparently Is Causing Political Problems for President in the West: The Watt Controversy," *Washington Post*, June 30, 1981, A1.

8. Jules Witcover, "Ford Names Hathaway to Interior," *Washington Post*, April 5, 1975, A2.

9. After World War II, Hathaway earned his college and law degrees in Nebraska, then practiced law in Torrington, Wyoming, served as Goshen County Attorney, and led the Wyoming Republican Party. Sally Vanderpoel, *Stan Hathaway: A Biography* (Wodehouse Enterprise, 2003). In April 2012, the balance in the Permanent Wyoming Mineral Trust Fund (PWMTF), Governor Hathaway's proudest achievement, was $5.758 billion; http://www.wyotax.org/PMTF.aspx.

10. United States Congress, Senate Committee on Interior and Insular Affairs, "Interior Nomination: Hearings before the Committee on Interior and Insular Affairs, United States Senate, Ninety-Fourth Congress, 1st Sess, on the Nomination of Stanley K. Hathaway to be Secretary of the Interior" (Government Printing Office 1975); John Gingles, "The Hathaway Hearings,"" *Washington Post*, June 2, 1975. Various Senators made great sport of Hathaway. It was the type of derisive treatment often accorded conservatives by those from the left. Six years later, Senator Biden would harangue William P. Clark relentlessly during his confirmation hearings for Deputy Secretary of State. "Hey, Judge, no hard feelings," Biden laughed afterwards, "[A]nd don't worry; I didn't know the answers to those questions either." *The Judge*, 113. So horrific was the treatment that Hathaway—who had survived the worst that Nazi anti-aircraft fire and the *Luftwaffe* had to offer—refused to return to Washington, D.C. If he had business with clients in the nation's Capital, he met them at the Marriott on the Virginia side of Key Bridge. It was Watt who prevailed upon Hathaway to return to Reagan's Interior Department for the unveiling of his official portrait as secretary.

11. Hathaway was victimized by the back channel that exists between bureaucrats in Interior's various offices and agencies and Capitol Hill, its senators, members, and personal and committee staffers. He wondered in each meeting of every day: what comment that he made would find its way to Capitol Hill or to the front pages of the *Washington Post*.

12. Lusk, Watt's hometown, and Wheatland, where he graduated from high school, are both less than sixty miles from Torrington, where Hathaway practiced law.

13. James Conway, "James Watt, In the Right with the Lord," *Washington Post*, April 27, 1983, B13.

14. Arnold, *At the Eye of the Storm*, 61–62.

15. For a discussion of Watt's efforts at MSLF see Short, *Ronald Reagan and the Public Lands*, 52–53. For the view of liberals and environmental groups as to what constitutes the public interest for the purposes of public interest litigation, see Arnold, *At the Eye of the Storm*, 176–189. Watt testified that 20 percent of MSLF's cases involved the Department of the Interior. *James G. Watt Nomination*:

Hearings Before the Committee On Energy and Natural Resources, United States Senate, Ninety-seventh Congress, First Session, On the Proposed Nomination of James G. Watt to Be Secretary of the Interior, January 7 and 8, 1981 (Washington: U.S. G.P.O., 1981), 51.

16.   Watt reflected on the meeting with the Colorado leaders during his hearing. Ibid., 75–76.

17.   Watt's "damage[] my hearing" by "shrill" talk came up at the confirmation hearing. Ibid., 61; Arnold, *At the Eye of the Storm*, 69.

18.   Ibid., 62.

19.   In December 2000, for example, seventeen years after Watt left the scene, the Sierra Club attacked President George W. Bush's Interior Secretary nominee, Gale Norton, as "James Watt in a skirt." Douglas Jehl, "The 43rd President; Interior Choice Sends a Signal on Land Policy," *New York Times*, December 30, 2000. Seventeen years is nothing, however; thirty years after Watt did NOT bar the Beach Boys, George Will wrote that he famously had done just that. George F. Will, "Good vibrations: The Beach Boys & Their World," *New York Post*, June 20, 2012.

20.   Kathy Fletcher, "Where Does Carter Stand with Environmentalists?" *High Country News*, May 30, 1980, 2.

21.   Jeffrey K. Stine, "Natural Resources and Environmental Policy" in W. Elliot Brownlee and Hugh Davis Graham, eds., *The Reagan Presidency: Pragmatic Conservatism & Its Legacies* (University Press of Kansas, 2003), 235.

22.   William Perry Pendley and J. Michael Morgan, *The Clean Air Act Amendments of 1977: A Selective Legislative Analysis.* 13 Land & Water L. Rev. 747 (1978).

23.   "Environmentalists Agree to Endorse President Carter," UPI, *The Hour* (Norwalk, CT), September 12, 1980, 26. "President Carter has picked up the endorsement of leaders of almost every major environmental group—a potent constituency that backed him in 1976 but showed some signs of disenchantment since. 'On balance, we believe President Carter has been sensitive to environmental concerns and committed to conservation principles,' said Tom Kimball of the National Wildlife Federation, speaking for the 22 leading environmentalists and conservationists who met with Carter for an hour this week.... Group members also took turns delivering blistering attacks on Ronald Reagan." See also Arnold, *At the Eye of the Storm*, 171–72.

24.   Philip Shabecoff, "Major Environmental Leaders Back Carter Re-election Bid," *New York Times*, September 28, 1980, Sec. A, 36.

25.   Ibid.

26.   Ibid.

27.   Ibid.

28.   Short, *Ronald Reagan and the Public Lands*, 27; "Environmentalists Oppose Land Transfer," *High Country News*, November 2, 1979, 13.

29.   Short, *Ronald Reagan and the Public Lands*, 13, 18, 25–29. In chapter 3, Short addresses, "'Save Our Public Lands' – The Environmental Response to the Sagebrush Rebellion."

30.   See *Sagebrush Rebel*, Chapter 3.

31.   See generally Richard D. Lamm and Michael McCarthy, *The Angry West: A Vulnerable Land and Its Future* (Houghton Mifflin, 1982).

32.   See generally, Short, *Ronald Reagan and the Public Lands*, 38–39.

33.   "More than two-thirds of the commentaries were explicitly on domestic issues, most often the economy.... [e]nergy and the environment were also frequent topics." Skinner, *Reagan's Path to Victory*, xvi. See also, Skinner, *Reagan, In His Own Hand*.

34.   Laurence I. Barrett, *Gambling with History* (Doubleday, 1983), 126.

35.   Elizabeth Drew, *Portrait of an Election* (Simon & Schuster, 1981), 268.

36.   "Text of President Debate Between Carter and Reagan," *Congressional Quarterly* (November 1, 1980): 3289.

37.   Davis W. Houck and Amos Kiewe, eds., *Actor, Ideologue, Politician: The Public Speeches of Ronald Reagan* (Greenwood, 1993), 160.

38.   Ibid. Governor Reagan was opposed to conservation "so that we will run out of oil, gasoline, and natural gas a little more slowly," which in the process would make Americans suffer. Ibid. President Reagan may have eschewed conservation as a national mandate or policy, but he embraced it personally.

> At this point in the diary, five lines were crossed out [inconsequentially] by President Reagan: it seems that pages were stuck together, and the president started writing on those pages, then realized he was wasting paper, so he crossed out the lines and went back and rewrote them two pages earlier.

Ronald Reagan, *The Reagan Diaries* (Harper, 2007), 17; editor's note.

39.   "Carter-Reagan Debate Text," 3286. Governor Reagan's remarks on the economy, natural resources, and the environment, both in speeches and in interviews, came as no surprise to anyone who had heard his radio addresses. Getting government off the people's back, opening up the public lands to energy and mineral development, and getting the government out of the energy business were common themes.

40.   Short, *Ronald Reagan and the Public Lands*, 40. Nevertheless, environmentalists continue to argue that Governor Reagan's true beliefs on natural resources and the environment were hidden in plain sight. "[T]he environment never really emerged as a major campaign issue for any of the principal candidates … both relegated environmental and natural resources questions to a minor role." In fact they argue, more than two decades later, that it was only after the election that the environmental movement was "sobered" by the "new political landscape apparently hostile toward their core values." Stine, "Natural Resources and Environmental Policy," 235 and note 21. How can this be explained? "The media helped Reagan deemphasize his right-wing views by reporting extensively on [his] overtures ['to build a unified Republican party']." Michael E. Kraft, "A New Environmental Policy Agenda: The 1980 Presidential Campaign and Its Aftermath," in Norman J. Vig and Michael E. Kraft, eds., *Environmental Policy in the 1980s: Reagan's New Agenda* (CQ Press, 1984), 33.

41.   Arnold, *At the Eye of the Storm*, xix. "What price do we wish to pay [to meet the demands of environmentalists]? But it is forbidden to raise this question and the environmentalists will not even discuss it. Indeed, anyone who does raise it will quickly find himself being excoriated and slandered as an unprincipled enemy of the true, the good, the beautiful." Irving Kristol, *Two Cheers for Capitalism* (Basic Books, 1978), 45.

42.   Lou Cannon, *Reagan* (G. P. Putnam's Sons, 1982), 349. Reagan valued open space:

> It bothers me not to be in church on Sunday but don't see how I can with the security problem. I'm a hazard to others. I hope God realizes how much I feel that I am in a temple when I'm out in his beautiful forest & countryside as we were this morning.

The Reagan Diaries, 41 (October 4, 1981).

43.   Cannon, *Reagan*, 49, citing Lou Cannon, *Ronnie & Jessie, A Political Odyssey* (Doubleday, 1969), 226.

44.   Cannon, *Reagan*, 353.

45.   Ibid.; Remarks to the Association of California Water Agencies, Sacramento, CA 1973-04-27.

46.   Cannon, *Reagan*, 352.

47.   Ibid, 351.

48.   This discussion is drawn largely from Arnold's *At the Eye of the Storm*, 27–50, 74–87. Arnold prefaces his lengthy and scholarly discussion with this:

> I spent many years at the grass-roots level of the [environmental] movement.… As my involvement grew deeper, it became apparent to me that the movement was concerned with more than simply protecting environmental quality. I began to see deliberate alarmism, calculated political moves and a difficult attitude toward basic American values such as individual liberties and private property. I left the movement quietly but finally in 1972. The conflict between economics and ecology concerned me deeply and became a major study; I have consulted many experts in relevant disciplines and over time have assembled a number of findings that I think will be of interest to all Americans.

See also, Short, *Ronald Reagan and the Public Lands*, 3–9.

49.   Webster's Third New International Dictionary (G. & C. Merriam Company, 1969), 483, defines "conservation" as "the wise utilization of a natural product.… "

50.   *Organic Administration Act.* • Act 01 June 4, 1897 (Ch, 2, 30 Stat. 11, as amended; 16 V.S.C.. 473-475, 477-482,551). "No national forest shall be established, except to improve and protect the forest within the boundaries, or for the purpose of securing favorable conditions of water flows, and to furnish a continuous supply of timber for the use and necessities of citizens of the United States.… "

51.   Yellowstone National Park is "dedicated and set apart as a public park or pleasuring ground for the benefit and enjoyment of the people.…" 16 U.S.C. §21. Environmentalists love this statute; however, they loathe another federal law enacted by the same far-sighted Congress, the General Mining Law of 1872. Act of May 10, 1872 (17 Stat. 91) 30 U.S.C. § 21 et seq.

52. Arnold, *At the Eye of the Storm*, 28; Rachel Carson, *Silent Spring* (Houghton Mifflin, 1962). Carson's book is dedicated to Albert Schweitzer, "Man has lost the capacity to foresee and to forestall. He will end by destroying the earth." Arnold, *At the Eye of the Storm*, 28–29. See George Clause and Karen Bolander, *Ecological Sanity* (David McKay, 1977) for an early criticism of Carson's work. That Carson misused, mis-cited and misinterpreted the information in her book is irrelevant to many environmentalists:

> Is it morally defensible to use shock tactics, to exaggerate, to distort the facts or color them with emotive words, or to slant the television camera in order to excite the public conscience? My experience leads me reluctantly to believe that *in the present social climate* some dramatization is necessary.

> Eric Ashby, *Reconciling Man With His Environment* (Stanford University Press, 1979), 22. (Emphasis in original.)

53. Stewart L. Udall, *The Quiet Crisis* (Avon Books, 1964).
54. Paul R. Ehrlich, *The Population Bomb* (Buccaneer Books, 1968). "Giving Society cheap, abundant energy at this point would be the equivalent of giving an idiot child a machine gun." Paul Ehrlich, "An Ecologist's Perspective on Nuclear Power," May/June 1978 issue of *Federation of American Scientists Public Issue Report*. Ehrlich famously lost a bet about the future with Julian L. Simon. Simon believed "the human propensity to take advantage of new opportunities and innovate meant that commodities are likely to become less scarce." http://www.perc.org/articles/article588.php. See Julian L. Simon, *The Ultimate Resource* (Princeton University Press, 1981). As part of Watt's "Resource Learning Sessions" for political appointees and their spouses at Reagan's Interior Department, Dr. Simon addressed these issues. Another speaker was Dr. Robert Ballard of the Woods Hole Oceanographic Institute—who today expresses grave concerns regarding human survival in the face of global warming—and Dr. Sylvia Earle, a world-renowned oceanographer whose discussion of singing whales fascinated Watt. Arnold, *At the Eye of the Storm*, 174, 194, 254.
55. Donella H. Meadows, *The Limits to Growth: A Report for the Club of Rome's Project on the Predicament of Mankind* (Signet, 1972).
56. Wilderness Act of 1964 (16 U.S.C. 1131-1136, 78 Stat. 890); Public Law 88-577, approved September 3, 1964. Despite the designation of millions of acres of federal land as "wilderness," studies of non-wilderness lands for possible designation by Congress and pressure for such designation continue to date. Arnold, *At the Eye of the Storm*, 29–31.
57. Arnold, *At the Eye of the Storm*, 35–40.
58. Robert Cameron Mitchell, "Public Opinion and Environmental Politics" in Vig, *Reagan's New Agenda*, 58, quoting Riley E. Dunlap, "Paradigmatic Change in Social Science: From Human Exemptionalism to an Ecological Paradigm," *American Behavioral Scientist* 24 (1980): 5–14.
59. Ibid. One history of the environmental movement and its federal statutory victories is set forth in Arnold, *At the Eye of the Storm*, 27–50.
60. Ibid., 77. Arnold quotes Donald McKinley, M.D., from his article *Why Wilderness?* in the February 1963 issue of *Forest Industries* magazine: "The emotional aspects of a wilderness experience might be compared to a religious experience."
61. Arnold, *At the Eye of the Storm*, 80. See generally, 76–87. Professor Short explains it this way:

> Both the preservationists and utilitarians traditionally held a human-centered worldview; for them, as Nash put it, "either man's stomach or man's spirit is the paramount concern." In contrast, the emerging new ecological view radically transformed this perspective by defining humans as part of the biotic community.... In the 1960s, concluded Nash, there "occurred a convergence of the utilitarian and aesthetic streams toward the ecological. The intellectual collision toward the end of the decade helps to explain the gospel of ecology."

> Short, *Ronald Reagan and the Public Lands*, 5, citing Roderick Nash, "American Environmental History," *Pacific Historical Review* 41 (1972): 368. Bestor Robinson, a Sierra Club president and director in the 1930s and 1940s declared, "Never let your love of nature overshadow your concern for human needs. I want wilderness to contribute to the American way of life." Arnold, *At the Eye of the Storm*, 82.

62. Susan R. Schrepfer, "Conflict in Preservation: The Sierra Club, Save-the-Redwoods League, and Redwood National Park," *Journal of Forest History* (April 1980), 76.
63. Ibid., 70, 76.

64. Skinner, *Reagan's Path to Victory*, 140–41, 266–68 ("Again I say, 'the Calif. Save the Redwoods league'—[bless them]—with cooperation not opposition from the lumber companies has *already* saved basically all the Superlative Redwoods without a Nat. park." [emphasis in original]), 268.

65. "I was really no longer a Democrat by 1960.... After that, the more I learned how some liberal Democrats wanted to rein in the energy of free enterprise and capitalism, create a welfare state, and impose a subtle kind of socialism, the more my view changed. Upon reflection, I'm not so sure I changed as the parties changed." Ronald Reagan, *An American Life: The Autobiography* (Simon & Schuster, 1990), 134.

66. Llewellyn King, publisher of *Energy Daily*, quoted in H. Peter Metzger, "Environmental Activists Capture Washington, *Reason*, May 1979, 1. Secretary of the Interior Cecil D. Andrus self-identified with this "gaggle." "I am a part of the environmental movement and I intend to make Interior responsive to the movement's needs." Arnold, *At the Eye of the Storm*, 94.

67. Kristol, *Two Cheers for Capitalism*, 14. "But there is now considerable evidence that the environmentalist movement has lost its self-control, or, to put it bluntly, has become an exercise in ideological fanaticism."

68. O'Sullivan's Law provides that any organization or enterprise that is not expressly conservative will become liberal over time. The law is named after British journalist John O'Sullivan. Thus it is that the major special interest groups of the day are arms of the Democratic Party, which include the NAACP, the AARP, and all environmental groups.

69. Arnold, *At the Eye of the Storm*, 72, quoting David Brower of the Friends of the Earth. See generally ibid., 71–73. National environmental groups had not waited for the confirmation hearings. Once Watt's nomination appeared likely, they came out swinging; in fact, 12 major environmental groups sent a telegram to Reagan demanding a different nominee. One environmentalist was quoted as saying. "[Watt] represents the blind faith in technology of the large corporations who believe that we can develop our way out of resource scarcity." Ibid., 58. At Watt's confirmation hearings, environmental groups knew they could not prevent his confirmation but savaged him anyway. Ibid., 71–72. Watt and Anne Gorsuch at the EPA "quickly became the environmentalists' bogeypersons." Laurence I. Barrett, *Gambling with History, Ronald Reagan in The White House* (Doubleday, 1983), 63. With 17 television cameras in the Senate hearing room, Watt's confirmation "was the most heavily reported and attended confirmation event of the Reagan Cabinet selection process, and perhaps of all U.S. history." Arnold, *At the Eye of the Storm*, 66. Senator Simpson opened the morning session by quoting poetry, "If," by Rudyard Kipling; http://www.kipling.org.uk/poems_if.htm; Senator Bumpers opened the afternoon session by reading from Chief Seattle's famous letter. William Safire, ed., *Lend Me Your Ears: Great Speeches in History* (W. W. Norton, 1992), 574–77. Arnold, *At the Eye of the Storm*, 68–69. *Watt Nomination Hearings*, 14-15, 57–58.

70. See *Sagebrush Rebel*, Chapter 4.

71. Arnold, *At the Eye of the Storm*, 76. See generally, "The Religious War." Ibid., 74-87. "The religious fervor of environmentalists is a fact America must face up to [and that, for example,] is revealed in uncompromising demands that preservation always come[s] before economics." Ibid., 86.

72. Ibid. Ron Wolf, "God, James Watt, and the Public Land," *Audubon* 83(3) (May 1981): 65. Arnold concludes:

> Watt's fundamentalist Christianity had to be attacked, because the idea of a sacred nature has certain political advantages: if nature is sacred, any environmental issue becomes a moral issue, and since most of us want to be moral, the issue is easier to win from the moral high ground. Thus, the truth of the matter is that behind the doctrinal wrangling of The Religious War [over Watt's remarks] raged an intense political war.

Arnold, *At the Eye of the Storm*, 80. Andrus, despite his alleged self-imposed silence regarding the activities of his successor and his personal knowledge that a secretary's views might get distorted, attacked Watt immediately. "I do not believe the Lord expects his place to be a barren desert used up by man...." In an appearance on National Public Radio's "Morning Edition," and NBC's "Today" shows, he also asserted that Watt violated both the law and the Constitution. UPI, "Andrus: Watt is 'rape, ruin boy,'" *Spokane Daily Chronicle*, July 17, 1981, 6.

73. Arnold, *At the Eye of the Storm*, 172. Jay Hair's assertion, in a May 1981 interview, that when the National Wildlife Federation "come[s] off the fence it'll be with more and greater credibility than if we had attacked from the first," was laughable. His organization came off the fence regarding Reagan when it met at the White House in September 1980 with Carter. "[S]ince Watt's first days in

office[, t]he Special-Interest Breakfasts were a weekly feature giving special-interest group representatives an hour of the Secretary's undivided attention. The first groups invited had been the large
environmentalist organizations, whose leaders had used the breakfast as a springboard for a media
event to denounce Watt and his policy." Ibid., 193–94.

74.   Otto Von Bismarck, August 11, 1867.
75.   As occurred with President Reagan, environmentalists repeatedly demanded that Watt explain his
       views, especially, for example, his position that no mining, oil and gas drilling, or logging could take
       place in the parks; it is illegal. They never took his word for it. Make it "more clear, if that is [your]
       position." "Watt gives environmentalists veto power over dam," *Modesto (California) Bee*, Novem-
       ber 3, 1081, 1. *Newsweek* reported, "It is simply false to suggest, as some of his critics have, that
       Watt would favor mining or timbering in the National Parks. "Parks are inviolate, by decree of
       Congress, and [Watt] has no quarrel with that." *Newsweek*, June 29, 1981.
76.   Arnold, *At the Eye of the Storm*, 207. In June and August 1981, environmental groups reached
       agreements with Watt's Interior Department on two high visibility Alaska issues.
77.   See "Besieged," Arnold, *At the Eye of the Storm*, 157–75.
78.   Scott Thompson, "Interior's Watt draws environmentalist fire from all sides," *The Christian Science
       Monitor*, July 16, 1981. James Naughtie, "Wildlife Group Urges President to Dismiss Watt," *Wash-
       ington Post*, July 15, 1981, A1.
79.   Leilani Watt, *Caught in the Conflict: My Life With James Watt* (Harvest House, 1984), 74–77. It is
       easy for environmental groups and the media to confuse the public on Interior related issues. The
       public and much of the media are simply uninformed on the difference between a wide-open piece
       of federal land in the middle of nowhere and a "wilderness area" as designated by Congress under
       the Wilderness Act of 1964. In fact, many do not know the difference between a National Forest
       and a National Park and that the former is managed by the U.S. Department of Agriculture and the
       latter by Interior. Arnold, *At the Eye of the Storm*, xiv–xvi, citing a 1978 public opinion survey by
       Opinion Research, Inc.
80.   Ibid., 201. A CONFIDENTIAL memorandum from the Sierra Club disclosed that the document
       was developed based on "'inside' advice from Capitol Hill. Arnold reveals that the "inside" advice
       came from Senator Alan Cranston, and Representatives Phillip Burton, John Sieberling, James
       Weaver, and Toby Moffet. Ibid. *The Dallas Morning News*' take on the story was that the Sierra
       Club petition left "a mere 225,404,825 Americans who didn't sign…. Now that the vote's in, maybe
       he can get down to work." Ibid., 203.
81.   James K. Kilpatrick, "Why Don't They Like James Watt?" *Washington Post*, August 10, 1981, A17.
       "Not to drop names or anything, but one day last week I lunched with James Watt and found him
       an eminently rational fellow. Then I came back to the office and found a great red-bound notebook
       awaiting me from the Wilderness Society. The society thinks he's a bum." Reagan's Interior Depart-
       ment responded with a "Fact and Fiction" packet in late 1981 with citations to the U.S. Code
       demonstrating that its actions were in accordance with federal law. Arnold, *At the Eye of the Storm*,
       213.
82.   Outside the Washington, D.C., Beltway, local newspapers and reporters saw through the carefully
       orchestrated media event, which was coordinated with Capitol Hill Democrats, for what it was,
       "the 1981 version of a lynch mob." *Kansas City Star* editorial quoted in Arnold, *At the Eye of the
       Storm*, 201. See generally, ibid., 200–3.
83.   Watt's "four cornerstones of the Reagan conservation policy" gave great offense to environmental
       groups because each one "emphatically rejected Aldo Leopold's ecological conscience and land ethic
       as the guiding standards for public land management…." "'America must have a sound economy'
       to be a good steward of the land; America must have 'orderly development' of resources to prevent
       the ravages of 'crisis development'; America's resources are for the 'enjoyment' of all people, not
       only the 'elitist groups'; and much of the nation's expertise in land management exists in the private
       and local sector, not the federal bureaucracy." Short, *Ronald Reagan and the Public Lands*, 59–60.
       Watt's speeches are analyzed ibid., at 58–62.
84.   Arnold, *At the Eye of the Storm*, 58. Paul Slansky, *The Clothes Have No Emperor, A Chronicle of
       the American 80s* (Fireside, 1989), 48.
85.   *The Reagan Diaries*, 36.
86.   The attacks on the Reagan administration were vicious. See generally, Short, *Ronald Reagan and
       the Public Lands*, 100–15. Russell Peterson, in a speech in Wisconsin, claimed that "the plume
       hunters are back in business." Ibid., 104. William Turnage, in a speech at Yale, said the Reagan
       administration will "return us to a barbarous age—a time of Robber Barons and Economic Royal-

ists." Ibid., 105. Gaylord Nelson, in a speech in Montana, said Reagan officials "intend to squeeze the world inside ['their little prefabricated cubicles'] whether it fits or not." Ibid., 106. Over-the-top remarks were issued frequently by writers Wallace Stegner and Edward Abbey. Ibid., 108–12. Cecil Andrus claimed that Reagan and Watt believed "if you can't dig it up or cut it down, it has no value at all." Ibid., 113. Finally, Steward Udall faulted Reagan and Watt for "breaking the national bipartisan consensus that developed over environment and ecology," a consensus that Udall himself initiated when he served as interior secretary under President Kennedy. Ibid., 115. Even the "analysis" by scholars was over the top. "Policy making that violates constitutional norms, democratic accountability, and empirical evidence is doomed to frustration and failure. From that perspective, Reagan's performance as president loses much of its alleged luster." Norman J. Vig and Michael E. Kraft, "Preface," in Vig, *Reagan's New Agenda*, x. One can disagree with the decision to make all of the OCS available for oil and gas leasing or to return regulatory authority for coal mining reclamation to the states, but one cannot truthfully say that such policies are contrary to the Constitution, democratic principles, or factual evidence.

87. Dale Russakoff, "The Critique: Ansel Adams Takes Environmental Challenge to Reagan," *Washington Post*, July 3, 1983, A1.
88. Ibid.
89. Ibid., the *Post* reported that the Adams quote appeared in the May 1983 issue of *Playboy*.
90. Ibid.
91. White House staff leaked that President Reagan would give a speech to "comprehensively define his environmental policies." Lou Cannon, "Reagan to Define Policy on Environment," *Washington Post*, March 23, 1983, Sec. A, 5.
92. The new administrator at the EPA was William Ruckelshaus. President Reagan so trusted Watt's advice that he told Meese to bring Watt into the Oval Office to discuss the possible nominee. Watt had met Ruckelshaus at a business leaders' event in Seattle where Ruckelshaus worked for Weyerhaeuser. During the question and answer session, Ruckelshaus stood to praise the policies of the Reagan administration. Watt advised President Reagan that he vouched for him wholeheartedly.
93. President Reagan's Radio Address to the Nation on Environmental and Natural Resources Management delivered on June 11, 1983, at 12:06 p.m. from Camp David, Maryland, http://www.presidency.ucsb.edu/ws/index.php?pid=41463.
94. *The Reagan Diaries*, 163–64.
95. "Ansel Adams Takes Environmental Challenge to Reagan," A6. UPI, "Ansel Adams Meets Reagan, Disapproves," *New York Times*, July 4, 1983. Years later, Watt and his wife had a chance encounter with Adam's daughter Anne. She related that she had become a Christian, apologized for her father's harsh words, and told Watt that she believed in what he and Reagan sought to accomplish.
96. *The Reagan Diaries*, 185.
97. Ibid.
98. Ibid.,188.
99. Reagan biographer Lou Cannon, no hagiographer he, adds to the evidence of Reagan's phenomenal, even photographic memory. He recounts that an article he wrote against the Dos Rios Dam was handed "to the governor to read on July 4, 1968, during a time when he was waiting to deliver a patriotic speech. He read the piece and, several weeks later, surprised some state water officials who were advocates of the dam by quoting portions of it verbatim—including a section about Indian burial sites in the valley that were important both to archeologists and Indians." Cannon, *Reagan*, 353, fn.
100. Nonetheless, environmental groups attacked Clark as they had attacked Watt, if not personally, then for his policies. "The fact that somebody owns a ranch is only a reflection that he has the money to own a ranch," said National Audubon Society president Russell Peterson. Paul Kengor & Patricia Clark Doerner, *The Judge: William P. Clark, Ronald Reagan's Top Hand* (Ignatius, 2007), 261. In fact, with Clark barely in his chair at Reagan's Interior Department, "[a]t the end of 1983[,] environmental groups already were at work planning for the 1984 election. While they had not yet settled on a candidate for president, the League of Conservation Voters made an unusual announcement[:] any Democratic candidate would be preferable to Ronald Reagan in 1984." Kraft, "A New Environmental Policy Agenda," in Vig, *Reagan's New Agenda*, 47.
101. Clark kept President Reagan informed on his progress. "Sec. Bill Clark checked in with a report on progress we're making in calming the normal hysteria of our more extreme environmentalists." *The Reagan Diaries*, 227 (March 22, 1984). Clark had a direct line on his desk at Interior to the Oval Office.

102. Ibid., 242.

103. Cass Peterson, "The President Meets With Conservationist," *Washington Post*; May 25, 1984, A47.

104. Ibid.; Jonathan Lash, Katherine Gillman and David Sheridan, *A Season of Spoils* (Pantheon Books, 1984).

105. Skinner, *Reagan's Path to Victory*, xvi–xvii. This is part of a letter (dictated) that Reagan wrote to Tommy Thorson. See Kiron K. Skinner, Annelise Anderson, and Martin Anderson, eds., *Reagan: A Life in Letters*, (The Free Press, 2003), 335.

106. *The Reagan Diaries*, 252–53.

107. Ibid. In a front page story the next day, the environmentalists at the meeting called the Burford appointment "outrageous" and "arrogant." Dale Russakoff and Cass Peterson, "Burford's Return Attacked: Conservationists Angry," *Washington Post*, July 4, 1984, A1. Hair, who attended the meeting only after receiving two telephone calls from Clark, two from EPA Administrator Ruckelshaus, three from Craig Fuller, and one from Mike Deaver, blasted the appointment as did the leaders of every other environmental group. Ibid., p. A11. The last paragraph of the article noted that President Reagan, in a Rose Garden ceremony, honored the federal migratory bird stamp program: "'Too many still consider our resources inexhaustible,' [Reagan] told an audience of conservationists, hunters, and business executives." Ibid.

   Two days later, on a back page, came Anne Burford's response. Dale Russakoff, "Burford Decries 'Demagogue' Critics," *Washington Post*, July 6, 1984, p. A17. Russakoff reported, "Administration officials who have tried to moderate Reagan's image on environmental matters expressed dismay this week at Burford's appointment [by their boss President Reagan]." Ibid.

108. Kent Jenkins Jr. and Michael D. Shear, "Reagan Issues Letter Denouncing North: Former President Cites 'False Statements,'" *Washington Post*, March 18, 1994, A1. "I do have to admit that I am getting pretty steamed about the statements coming from Oliver North."

109. *The Reagan Diaries*, 253.

110. "Conservationists Rap Reagan Stance," *Louisville Courier-Journal*, June 26, 1984, Sec. A, 3.

111. Remarks to the National Campers and Hikers Association in Bowling Green, Kentucky, July 12, 1984, http://www.reagan.utexas.edu/archives/speeches/1984/71284a.htm.

112. Ibid.

113. The local media did report on President Reagan's appearances. "Quality of life means more than protection and preservation … [it means] a good job, accommodation for a growing population, and the continued economic and technological development essential to our standard of living." "Reagan Sells Environmental Record, But Some Aren't Buying," *Louisville Courier-Journal*, July 12, 1984, Sec. A, 4. Speaking at a wildlife refuge in Maryland, Reagan said that his concern for the environment was "one of the best kept secrets" of his presidency. See Michael Putzel, "Environmental Issues of 'Great Interest' to Him, Reagan Says," *Louisville Courier-Journal*, July 11, 1984, Sec. A, 5.

114. *The Reagan Diaries*, 255.

115. Ibid., 659.

116. "By the time of Reagan's first inauguration, the lines were being drawn for the most important public land debate since conservationists prevented the Eisenhower administration from developing Echo Park in Utah." Short, *Ronald Reagan and the Public Lands*, 54.

117. Ibid., 78.

118. Ibid., 60. At Reagan's Interior Department, "Watt began the challenge of Big Environmentalism's power and self-righteousness." Arnold, *At the Eye of the Storm*, 262.

119. Short, *Ronald Reagan and the Public Lands*, ix. Arnold sees the conflict this way:

   > [Reagan's Interior Department] is optimistic about the future and environmentalists tend to be pessimistic. [Reagan's Interior Department] sees a future of human action, risk and danger, of the will to overcome and solve problems, of liberty and plenty derived from proper management of our natural and human resources. Environmentalists … see a future of dwindling resources and growing scarcity, of withdrawal from resource management in favor of resource preservation, and of authoritarian government deciding how the scarcity will be shared.

   Arnold, *At the Eye of the Storm*, 245.

120. Short, *Ronald Reagan and the Public Lands*, ix. Short argues that, "as Gifford Pinchot had rejected John Muir's quasi-religious perception of the wilderness, so too did Watt reject the ecological views of Muir's modern descendants.…" Ibid., 62. The late Bil Gilbert, an environmentalist, writing from

his 35 years of experience with public lands issues, declared that the three individuals who have made the greatest impact on how Americans view nature are Aldo Leopold, Rachel Carson, and James Watt. "The last name is listed with absolutely no ironic or sarcastic intent." Bil Gilbert, "Alone in the Wilderness," *Sports Illustrated* (October 3, 1983): 111.

121.   "What you & I must realize is that just possibly [environmentalists'] cause is much broader than whether electricity should be generated by nuclear power or some other sources.... In other words is there a larger purpose behind their anti-nuclear stand or their environmentalism? Is their goal in reality to block any increase in energy supply & even to reduce it with the idea that by stopping progress the world will remain as it is. The deer 'will loll in his rilly place' as the poet puts it and we'll give up many of the latest electric powered gadgets that have made life a little easier and yes more simple by any definition but theirs." Skinner, *Reagan's Path to Victory*, 214.

122.   See generally, Ron Arnold and Alan Gottlieb, *Trashing the Economy: How Runaway Environmentalism is Wrecking America* (Merril Press, 2010), and Ron Arnold, *Undue Influence: Wealthy Foundations, Grant Driven Environmental Groups, and Zealous Bureaucrats That Control Your Future* (Merril Press, 1999).

123.   Of course, as Al Gore and his ilk have demonstrated, the misery that results from mandated scarcity and coercive governmental policies will not affect them! Environmentalists are schizophrenic on the matter. On the one hand, they believe that President Reagan's confidence in the ability of technology to solve our problems of resource scarcity is foolishness. Arnold, *At the Eye of the Storm*, 58, quoting Wilderness Society member Bill Cunningham. On the other hand, they believe that we may have the ability to discover and develop heretofore unknown resources, but we will use them all up before our grandchildren benefit from them. Ken Olson, "Stewart Udall: Watt's Interior Contrary to the Tide of History," *High Country News*, (November 13, 1981): 10. "I'd like my grandchildren to have a little bit of oil 30 years from now...." No worries, thirty-one years later this article or one with a similar headline and news appeared across the country: Mike W. Thomas, "U.S. sets record for domestic oil production in 2012," *San Antonio Business Journal*, December 19, 2012.

CHAPTER SIX

1.   Kiron K. Skinner, Annelise Anderson, and Martin Anderson, eds., *Reagan, In His Own Hand: The Writings of Ronald Reagan That Reveal His Revolutionary Vision for America* (The Free Press, 2001), 329.

2.   Ibid.

3.   Ibid., 330.

4.   Ibid.

5.   Ibid., 330–31. (Emphasis in original.)

6.   *Tennessee Valley Authority v. Hill*, 437 U.S. 153 (1978).

7.   Ibid., 437 U.S. at 184.

8.   Ibid., 437 U.S. at 188. "As it was finally passed, the Endangered Species Act of 1973 represented the most comprehensive legislation for the preservation of endangered species ever enacted by any nation.... Lest there be any ambiguity as to the meaning of this statutory directive, the Act specifically defined 'conserve' as meaning 'to use and the use of *all methods and procedures which are necessary* to bring *any endangered species* or threatened species to the point at which the measures provided pursuant to this chapter are no longer necessary.'" (Citation omitted.) (Emphasis added.) Ibid., 437 U.S. at 180.

9.   None of the justices approved of the statute. Justice Marshall commented, "Congress can be a jackass." Justice White, who had urged overturning the injunction issued below, switched sides and agreed to affirm. Chief Justice Burger then voted with the other five and assigned himself the opinion to "serve notice on Congress that it should take care of its own 'chestnuts'." Holly Doremus, *The Story of TVA v. Hill: A Narrow Escape for a Broad New Law* in Oliver A. Houck & Richard J. Lazarus, eds., *Environmental Law Stories: An In-Depth Look at Ten Leading Cases on Environmental Law*, 130–31 (Foundation Press, 2005). Although the article does not cite a source for the comments in conference, Professor Doremus explains, "All the information in that piece about what was said at conferences (including Marshall's "jackass" comment) and what passed between the [justices] before and after oral argument (including the White note) came from Justice Blackmun's files at the Library of Congress."

10.   Here the Chief Justice tells Congress, to paraphrase Justice Marshall, why its law is asinine:

> In Tennessee alone there are 85 to 90 species of darters, [] of which upward to 45 live in the Tennessee River system. [] New species of darters are being constantly

> discovered and classified—at the rate of about one per year. [] This is a difficult task
> for even trained ichthyologists since species of darters are often hard to differentiate
> from one another.

(Citations omitted.) *T.V.A. v. Hill*, 437 U.S. at 159, n. 7.

11.   Ibid., 210.

12.   Ibid., 204, n. 13, quoting Keith Shreiner, Associate Director and Endangered Species Program Manager of the U. S. Fish and Wildlife Service, quoted in a letter from A. J. Wagner, Chairman, TVA, to Chairman, House Committee on Merchant Marine and Fisheries, dated Apr. 25, 1977, quoted in Wood, On Protecting an Endangered Statute: The Endangered Species Act of 1973, 37 Federal B. J. 25, 27 (1978).

13.   Endangered Species Act Amendments of 1978, Pub. L. No. 95-632, 92 Stat. 3752. Congress did make a significant alteration in the ESA with its 1978 Amendments, a change that permitted the FWS to be more cautious. Congress required designation of critical habitat for a species at the same time as its listing but, to address public fears that critical habitat designation would result in land use restrictions on federal and fee land, Congress allowed the Secretary to consider the economic impact of critical habitat designation. Moreover, if critical habitat could not be determined, the Secretary could delay or even withdraw the proposed listing. 16 U.S.C. § 1533(b)(1)(B)(2). Congress's decision to link these two decisions almost completely halted new listings; listing proposals for 2000 species were withdrawn by the FWS in 1978. *The Endangered Species Act (Stanford Environmental Law Society Handbook)* (Stanford University Press, 2002), 23.

14.   The Endangered Species Committee (ESC) was empowered to grant exemptions to federal projects barred by the ESA if it found the economic benefits outweighed the benefits of conserving the species. The ESC consisted of the Secretary of the Interior, the Secretary of Agriculture, the Secretary of the Army, the Chairman of the Council of Economic Advisors, the Administrator of the EPA, the Administrator of the National Oceanic and Atmospheric Administration, and an individual nominated by the governor of the state where the project is located and appointed by the President. Endangered Species Act Amendments of 1978, Pub. L. No. 95-632, 92 Stat. 3752.

15.   Section 7 of the ESA, which requires federal agencies undertaking projects that may result in jeopardy for a listed species to consult with the Fish and Wildlife Service, played a crucial role in *TVA v. Hill*, especially before the Supreme Court. At the time Section 7 was a short two sentences long, but the Court held its meaning was clear. *T.V.A. v. Hill*, 437 U.S. at 181–88. Congress took steps in 1978, 1979, and 1982 to make the statutory mandate for consultation even more explicit.

16.   "Tellico Dam Gets Go-Ahead," *Endangered Species Tech. Bull.*, Oct. 1979, 1, 3. There is a happy ending all around: the snail darter did not go extinct; there were more of them elsewhere. In 1984, the FWS down-listed the species to threatened with no need for further monitoring. U.S. Fish and Wildlife Service, Final Rule Reclassifying the Snail Darter (*Percina tanasi*) From an Endangered Species to a Threatened Species and Rescinding Critical Habitat Designation, 49 *Fed. Reg.* 27510 (July 5, 1984).

17.   Much earlier statutes included the Migratory Bird Treaty Act of 1918, ch. 128, 40 Stat. 755 (1918) (codified as amended at 16 U.S.C. §§ 703-711), which prohibited hunting migratory birds without a federal permit; the Bald Eagle Protection Act, Pub. L. No. 567, 54 Stat. 278 (codified at 16 U.S.C. § 668), which sought to save the species from extinction; and the Lacey Act of 1920, ch. 553 §, 16 U.S.C. § 3372, which, among other things, barred interstate commerce in animals or birds killed contrary to state law. Congressman Lacey's oft-cited floor statement was persuasive. He told of the damage to agriculture done by the decline in bird populations, listed various wildlife problems such as extinction of the carrier pigeon, depletion of grouse, prairie chicken, and buffalo, and addressed problems created by importation of foreign species such as the French pink flower and the English sparrow (Lacey called it "that rat of the air, that vermin of the atmosphere"). Lacey considered the chief threats to America's bird populations to be: (1) excessive hunting of game birds by market hunters, (2) introduction of harmful exotic species that threaten native birds, and (3) the use of bird feathers in ladies' hats. 33 *Cong. Rec.* 4871 and H.R. Rep. 474, 56th Cong., 1st Sess. (1900) (statement of Rep. John Lacey). Although the Lacey Act applied to animals, it was primarily a bird preservation and restoration measure enacted to protect and improve agriculture given Congressman Lacey's passion for preserving birds that benefitted agriculture and eliminating exotic species that were harmful to agriculture. Mr. Lacey, a Republican, was from Iowa.

18.   Pub. L. No. 89-669, 80 Stat. 926 (1966). Experts believe that Congress was becoming more aware that states were not up to the task of protecting species. See generally, William Perry Pendley, *War on the West: Government Tyranny on America's Great Frontier* (Regnery, 1995), 85–98 (chapter

5, "The Pit Bull of Environmental Laws"). The Endangered Species Act defines "take" to include "harass, harm, pursue, hunt, shoot, wound, kill, trap, capture, or collect, or to attempt to engage in any such conduct." 16 U.S.C. § 1532(19) (1988). The statute does not define these terms, but Fish and Wildlife Service regulations provide some guidance. For example, "harm" includes "significant habitat modification or degradation where it actually kills or injures wildlife by significantly impairing essential behavioral patterns, including breeding, feeding or sheltering." 50 C.F.R. § 17.3 (1993). As a result of the ambiguity surrounding the concept of "take," the term has been litigated extensively over the years.

19. Pub. L. No. 91-135, 83 Stat. 275 (1969). That effort led to the Convention on International Trade in Endangered Species of Wild Fauna and Flora (CITES), http://www.cites.org/eng/disc/what.php. Changes in the 1969 Act regarding domestic wildlife were minor; however, the definition of "fish and wildlife" was expanded beyond vertebrates and the Lacey Act was amended to prohibit interstate commerce in illegally taken reptiles, amphibians, mollusks, and crustaceans.

20. H. R. Rep. No. 93-412, 93rd Cong., 1st Sess. (1973).

21. Legislative History, P.L. 93-205, Senate Report No. 93-307, 2990.

22. H. R. Rep. No. 93-412, 93rd Cong., 1st Sess. (1973).

23. Ibid.

24. *Congressional Record*, S25674, July 24, 1973.

25. *Congressional Record*, S25694, July 24, 1973; *Congressional Quarterly*, 1973 Almanac, 673.

26. U.S. Senator James A. McClure, a Republican from Idaho, reflected on what he and his colleagues envisioned: "I think we just never contemplated, in 1973, that the [ESA] would reach as far and wide as it has. I can say with some confidence that many of my colleagues would have been surprised to learn that a legal and administrative structure originally designed to protect 109 species might one day be asked to accommodate not only ten times that number of threatened species, but also potentially 4,000 or more candidate species." National Endangered Species Act Reform Coalition Newsletter (Summer 1994): 4.

27. *Congressional Record*, S25691, July 24, 1973.

28. Ibid.

29. *Congressional Record*, S25676, July 24, 1973.

30. Mr. Gordon founded the National Wilderness Institute in 1989. He is Senior Advisor for Strategic Outreach of The Heritage Foundation in Washington, D.C. He refers to this as "bait and switch."

31. "The authorization for funding of the ESA expired on October 1, 1992, though Congress has appropriated funds in each succeeding fiscal year to ensure continued implementation of the law."; http://nesarc.org/faq/.

32. Interestingly enough, an environmental group did not file an ESA lawsuit to stop Tellico Dam; instead, one filed a lawsuit under the National Environmental Policy Act (NEPA) alleging a paperwork violation. It was a University of Tennessee ichthyologist who discovered the snail darter while snorkeling. Allegedly he emerged from the stream and cried out to a bystander that he had discovered "the fish that will stop the Tellico Dam." William Bruce Wheeler and Michael J. McDonald, *TVA and the Tellico Dam 1936–1979: A Bureaucratic Crisis in Post-Industrial America* (University of Tennessee Press, 1986), 157. A law student and his law professor filed the ESA litigation that reached the Supreme Court. *The Story of TVA v. Hill*, 118–23.

33. Chastened by their experience with Tellico Dam, environmental groups were reluctant to sue. That reluctance would last nearly a decade. Ironically, and akin to what happened with the Tellico Dam ESA litigation, it was not one of the major groups that first sued over the northern spotted owl in the late 1980s. A tiny outfit in Massachusetts filed the first petition to list the owl; 30 other environmental groups soon did the same. *Stanford Environmental Law Society Handbook*, 26–27, note 13.

34. "1983 – A Year Of Enrichment: Improving The Quality Of Life For All Americans," (U.S. Department of the Interior, October 1983), 7–8. The FWS published final regulations providing guidelines for setting species listing and recovery priorities and to achieve early resolution of conflicts regarding projects through informal consultation with other federal agencies. Ibid., 9. In 1988, Reagan's Interior Department reported that it had "completed more than 205 recovery plans," compared with 39 recovery plans completed prior to 1981. "America – Our Treasure and Our Trust: The Legacy of President Ronald Reagan 1981 – 1988," (U.S. Department of the Interior, December 1988), 16. The plans included those for the American alligator, the East Coast population of the brown pelican, and the California sea otter. Ibid., 16–17.

35.   *Interior Report 1983*, 4. The FWS undertook cooperative studies with the state of Wyoming and Idaho State University to ascertain numbers and distribution in northwestern Wyoming of the endangered black-footed ferret. Ibid., 9.
36.   Ibid., 9.
37.   Ibid., 10.
38.   Ibid., 9. Three years of technical discussions culminated in an agreement between the United States and Canada to conserve the porcupine caribou herd, as it migrates between Yukon Territory and the Arctic National Wildlife Refuge. *Interior Report 1988*, 18.
39.   *Interior Report 1983*, 10.
40.   Ibid., 7. Once, as many as 25,000 bald eagles inhabited the lower 48 states; by 1963, only 417 active bald eagle nests could be found. In 1983, active eagle nests totaled 1,450. Ibid. The bald eagle breeding program at the Patuxent Wildlife Research Center, Maryland, as a result of a $150,000 grant from the DuPont Company, was able to double eaglets produced in captivity for later release to suitable nests in the wild. Ibid., 9. Thanks to the corporate sponsorship of DuPont, Eagle Rare Bourbon, and American Airlines and with the assistance of the Tennessee Wildlife Resources Agency and Tennessee Conservation League, three bald eagle chicks from Patuxent were transferred to reestablish eagles in the "Land Between the Lakes," administered by the TVA. Ibid. As a result of these early efforts, in August 2007, bald eagles were removed from the ESA list; http://www.fws.gov/migratorybirds/baldeagle.htm.
41.   *Interior Report 1988*, 19. The FWS transferred 13 fish hatcheries to state ownership or management to permit states to assume a greater role in managing fisheries within their boundaries. *Interior Report 1983*, 10. In 1983, the FWS distributed $139.8 million to state and territorial fish and wildlife agencies, through the Pittman-Robertson and Dingell-Johnson Acts, to restore fish and wildlife and to improve hunter safety education programs. Some $261 million was provided to states in 1981 and 1982. In addition, the FWS supported a modified expansion of the Dingell-Johnson Act to yield up to $90 million annually by way of a federal excise tax program to fund state fishery efforts, which could mean a three-fold increase for some state fishery programs. Ibid., 9.
42.   *Interior Report 1988*, 19.
43.   Ibid., 7. In August 1999, the peregrine falcon was removed from the ESA list; http://www.fws.gov/endangered/what-we-do/peregrine-falcon.html; http://library.fws.gov/Pubs/brown_pelican1109.pdf.
44.   *Interior Report 1988*, 17. http://www.fws.gov/hoppermountain/index.html. As of May 2012, population counts put the number of known condors at 405, including 226 in the wild and 179 in captivity. Katy Muldoon, "California condors hit a milestone – a population of 405 – after nearly going extinct," *The Oregonian*, May 20, 2012.
45.   Reagan's Interior Department also gave attention to big game animals on public lands: antelope using Bureau of Land Management (BLM) land increased from 190,000 (1974) to 275,000 (1987) and the number of elk using public land went from 96,000 to over 134,000 during the same period. BLM land provides habitat for one of every five big game animals. In October 1988, Reagan's Interior Department dedicated the first wild horse sanctuary, the culmination of efforts by the Institute of the Range and the American Mustang, the South Dakota Community Foundation, and the BLM. *Interior Report 1988*, 18.
46.   *Interior Report 1983*, 9; http://www.fws.gov/idaho/Caribou.html.
47.   *Interior Report 1983*, 9. In August 1999, the Arctic peregrine falcon was removed from the ESA list; http://www.fws.gov/endangered/what-we-do/peregrine-falcon.html. 49 *Fed. Reg.* 22330, http://www.fws.gov/mountain-prairie/species/mammals/UTprairiedog/.
48.   *Interior Report 1988*, 16. Reagan's Interior Department's efforts included "production of over 5 million sea turtles," reintroduction of "four pairs of red wolves to the Alligator River National Wildlife Refuge," new plans for the "Puerto Rican parrot," and actions to reduce the need for listing of the "southeastern big-eared bat, spring pygmy sunfish, Rio Grande cutthroat trout, and Guadalupe bass." Ibid.
49.   *Interior Report 1983*, 9.
50.   Endangered Species Act Amendments of 1982, Pub. L. No. 97-304, 96 Stat. 1417. Reagan's Interior Department and Congress provided a mechanism that allowed the FWS—faced with the absolute prohibitions against the "take" of a species set forth in Section 9 following a Section 7 jeopardy finding—to authorize, under Section 10, an "incidental take" of a species if the action is part of "an otherwise lawful activity." § 6(1)(B) and 16 U.S.C. §1539(a). During this period few permits were applied for or granted. See Robert Meltz, *Where the Wild Things Are: The Endangered Species Act and Private Property*, 24 Envtl. L. 369 (1994). Concerns regarding the impact of species on private

land grew out of a decision by the Ninth Circuit that grazing by feral goats on state lands violated the ESA by degrading the habitat of a protected bird and causing an "illegal take" of an endangered species. *Palila v. Hawaii Dept. of Land & Natural Resources*, 639 F.2d 495 (9th Cir. 1981). Subsequently, the habitat conservation program was developed to allow similar flexibility on private property affected by the ESA.

51.   Exec. Order No. 12,630, 53 *Fed. Reg.* 8859 (1988). That Executive Order required that federal agencies assess the "takings implications" of any major federal action, hence the preparation of "taking implication assessments" (TIAs); however, the Executive Order lacked an enforcement mechanism.

52.   16 U.S.C. § 1533(b)(3)(C)(iii).

53.   *Stanford Environmental Law Society Handbook*, 27, note 13.

54.   "NBC Nightly News," September 17, 1993. "In 1972, biologist Dr. Eric Forsman located his first 59 pairs of spotted owls in Oregon. At that time he predicted, 'Within the next five years, the majority of the population may be gone.' [The latest] spotted owl counts were: 1988 about 1,500 pairs, 2,022 pairs in 1990, and 1992, 3,461." Network News, Oregon Lands Coalition, February 4, 1994. See Pendley, *War on the West*, 247, n. 67.

55.   http://www.fws.gov/oregonfwo/Species/Data/NorthernSpottedOwl/BarredOwl/default.asp.

56.   Robin Silver, co-founder of the Center for Biological Diversity in Nicholas Lemann, "No People Allowed: A radical environmental groups attempts to return the Southwest to the wild," *New Yorker*, November 22, 1999, 106.

57.   There are currently more than 2,052 species listed. U.S. Fish and Wildlife Service, "Summary of Listed Species Listed Populations and Recovery Plans as of Wed, March 21, 2012."

58.   Scott Learn, "Obama administration increases 'critical habitat' for northern spotted owl," *The Oregonian*, November 21, 2012.

59.   Ros Krasny, "US lawmakers cry 'fowl' over move to help lesser prairie chicken," Reuters, November 30, 2012.

60.   Editorial, "Protecting Endangered Farmers: A tale of modern California," *Wall Street Journal*, February 29, 2012.

61.   Christy Goodman, "Cliff residents might lose homes to save endangered beetles," *Washington Post*, January 25, 2012.

62.   "[A] single, dime-sized, translucent, subterranean spider has brought a $15 million traffic reduction project to a dead stop." Robert Gordon, "Little meshweaver brings San Antonio to a screeching stop," *Washington Times*, October 17, 2012. At least one federal judge found not only the FWS's paperwork deficient, but also found its scientists dishonest. Felicity Barringer, "More Interior Scientists Are Taking Heat," *New York Times*, Green: A Blog About Energy and the Environment, September 21, 2011; Colin Sullivan, "Judge Discards "Sloppy Science' by FWS on Delta Smelt," Greenwire, *New York Times*, December 15, 2010.

63.   When a Montana federal district court overturned a decision by Interior to delist the northern rocky mountain wolf in Idaho and Montana, Congress barred the agency from returning the wolf to the ESA listing. Environmental groups sued contending that Congress's action violated the Constitution; the U.S. Court of Appeals for the Ninth Circuit ruled that Congress had merely amended the ESA, which it had every right to do even during ongoing litigation. *Alliance for the Wild Rockies v. Salazar*, 672 F.3d 1170 (9th Cir. 2012).

64.   Dr. J. Gordon Edwards, "The Endangered Species Act," San Jose State University, undated and unpublished manuscript, 5.

65.   Quoted by Associated Press reporter Robert Greene. See, Pendley, *War on the West*, 246, n. 67.

66.   Some environmental group petitions appear to rely on NatureServe (http://www.natureserve.org/). NatureServe, however, provides this disclaimer: "The purpose of the conservation status ranks developed by NatureServe is to assess the relative risk facing a species and does not imply that any specific action or legal status is needed to assure its survival.... However, NatureServe status assessment procedures have different criteria, evidence requirements, purposes and taxonomic coverage than government lists of endangered and threatened species, and therefore these two types of lists should not be expected to coincide."

67.   William Perry Pendley, "Killing jobs to save the sage grouse: Junk science, weird science, and plain nonsense," *Washington Times*, May 31, 2012.

68.   Joshua Rhett Miller, "Environmental groups collecting millions from federal agencies they sue, studies show," Fox News, May 8, 2012; William Perry Pendley, "Green groups exploit law for financial gain: Citizens suffer while environmentalists make bank," *Washington Times*, August 15, 2012.

69. See generally J. B. Ruhl, "The battle over Endangered Species Act methodology," *Environmental Law*, March 22, 2004. The ESA requires the use of "best scientific and commercial data available" when deciding whether to list a species (16 U.S.C. § 1533(b)(1)(A) (2000)) and the use of "the best scientific data available" when designating critical habitat (16 U.S.C. § 1533(b)(2) (2000)) as well as when issuing "no jeopardy" and "no adverse modification" decisions to federal agencies during the mandated consultation process (16 U.S.C. § 1536(a)(2), (b)-(c) (2000) and 16 U.S.C. § 1536(c); 50 C.F.R. 402.14(g)(8) (2004)). Sometimes the FWS merely "assumes" facts that the ESA mandates it use "scientific data" to determine. For example, in the case of the delta smelt, listed and protected with devastating impact on the San Joaquin Valley in California, the agency declared:

> [T]he [FWS is] … assuming that delta smelt abundance trends have been driven by multiple factors, some of which are affected or controlled by CVP/SWP operations and others that are not.

> [The FWS] assumes that the proposed CVP/SWP operations affect delta smelt throughout the year either directly through entrainment or indirectly through influences on its food supply and habitat suitability.

> [The FWS] also assumes that any of these three major categories of effects described above will adversely affect delta smelt, either alone or in combinations.

    Biological Opinion on the Coordinated Operations of the Central Valley Project (CVP) and the State Water Project (SWP) in California, U.S. Fish and Wildlife Service, December 15, 2008, 203; http://www.fws.gov/sfbaydelta/documents/SWP-CVP_OPs_BO_12-15_final_signed.pdf.

70. In the course of Section 7 consultations in which the FWS determines whether to issue a jeopardy opinion regarding a land management agency's proposed activities by requiring adoption of restrictions ostensibly to protect a species, the FWS, out of sloth or chicanery:

    - sets forth a "boilerplate" list of activities or conditions that adversely affect the species generally that may or may not exist on the land in question; or
    - fails to provide data to support its demands; or
    - ignores the agency's land management plans and the species protections set forth there; or
    - asserts that it lacks proof that the agency is enforcing those restrictions.

    Megan Maxwell, "BLM's NTT Report: Is It the Best Available Science or a Tool to Support a Predetermined Outcome?" (Unpublished report prepared for the Northwest Mining Association), May 20, 2013.

71. CFR 50 § 424.10 General. The Secretary may add *a species* to the lists or designate critical habitat, delete *a species* or critical habitat, change the listed status of *a species*, revise the boundary of an area designated as critical habitat, or adopt or modify special rules (see 50 CFR 17.40–17.48 and parts 222 and 227) applied to *a threatened species* only in accordance with the procedures of this part. (Emphasis added.)

    CFR 50 § 424.14 Petitions [excerpt] (ii) Contains detailed narrative justification for the recommended measure, describing, based on available information, past and present numbers and distribution of the species involved and any threats faced by the species; (iii) Provides information regarding the status of the species over all or a significant portion of its range; http://www.fws.gov/endangered/esa-library/pdf/petition_guidance_for_internet_final_for_posting_12-7-10.pdf.

72. Skinner, *Reagan, In His Own Hand*, 330–31.

73. In addition to the deficiencies enumerated by Dr. Ramey, another ESA legal practitioner suggests addressing the following: 1) definition of species including distinct population segments, (2) the petition process, (3) reestablishing differential treatment for endangered v. threatened species, (4) limiting citizen suits and payment of attorney fees and (5) reversing the *T.V.A. v Hill* holding that species be protected "whatever the cost." 437 U.S. at 184.

CHAPTER SEVEN

1. Kiron K. Skinner, Annelise Anderson, and Martin Anderson, eds., *Reagan, In His Own Hand*: *The Writings of Ronald Reagan That Reveal His Revolutionary Vision for America* (The Free Press,

2001), 480. See also, "Cuba and Africa," May 4, 1977: "It is unrealistic for us to fail to recognize the Soviet Union has opened a new stage in its campaign to achieve strategic dominance over Africa with all its mineral riches." Ibid., 184. "Cuba," July 1978: "There are now 50,000 Cubans in Africa ... threatening to cut off minerals to the industrialized Western world." Kiron K. Skinner, Annelise Anderson, and Martin Anderson, eds., *Reagan's Path to Victory, The Shaping of Ronald Reagan's Vision: Selected Writings* (The Free Press, 2004), 339.

2.   Congressman Raymond P. Kogovsek, a Democrat from Colorado, was the only other member who joined Santini's small group, which flew commercial rather than via U.S. Department of Defense aircraft due to its size and the need for DOD aircraft to fly congressional delegations to Europe.

3.   Despite the delegation's small size, it did draw local media attention. Gary Thatcher, "Will Rhodesia play politics with scarce metals?" *The Christian Science Monitor*, January 25, 1980.

4.   Five minerals—cobalt, chromium, manganese, platinum, and titanium—were of most significance based on these factors: "(1) the critical need for the mineral in defense or industry, (2) the lack of adequate domestic resources, (3) the limited potential for developing substitutes, and (4) the lack of alternative or more secure sources of supply." G. Kevin Jones, "Onshore and Offshore Solutions to the Nonfuel Minerals Shortage," *Brigham Young University Law Review*, 618, 623–24 (1982), quoting Subcomm. on Econ. Stabilization, House Comm. on Banking, Finance & Urban Affairs, 97th Cong., 1st Sess., A Congressional Handbook On U.S. Materials Import Dependency/Vulnerability 129 (Comm. Print 1981). In fact, one expert labeled the five the "metallurgical Achilles' heel of our civilization." Herbert E. Meyer, "Russia's Sudden Reach for Raw Materials," *Fortune*, July 28, 1980, 68.

5.   "And oh yes! We've ordered a halt to buying Chrome from Rhodesia. It looks like we're going to lose more than a basketball game [with Cuba] before the foolishness ends." Skinner, *Reagan, In His Own Hand*, 184–85. "Cuba and Africa," May 4, 1977.

6.   Cobalt has an array of military and industrial uses. See generally Murphy, *A Report on the Potential for Supply Dislocation of Selected Nonenergy Materials*, in 2 Special Study on Economic Change, Energy and Materials: A Shortage of Resources or Commitment?, 96th Cong., 2d Sess. 185, 199–200, 223–25 (Joint Comm. Print 1980). Specifically:

> The aircraft industry is critically dependent on cobalt, which is used in jet engines to withstand high temperatures. Because of its unique hardening qualities and resistance to corrosion and abrasion, cobalt is required in the manufacture of machine tools and drill bits; it also functions as a desulfurizing catalyst in petroleum refining.

Jones, "Onshore and Offshore Solutions to the Nonfuel Minerals Shortage," 624, note 4.

7.   "Strategic Mineral Supplies Shaky," UPI, *Florence [Tennessee] Times*, February 14, 1980, 3.

8.   Charles L. Heatherly, ed., *Mandate for Leadership: Policy Management in a Conservative Administration* (The Heritage Foundation, 1981), 333. "When [the United States] jostle[s] with Western Europe and Japan for strategic minerals, that's competition," declared Frank Shakespeare, former director of the United States Information Agency. "When the Russians get into the act, that's war." Meyer, "Russia's Sudden Reach for Raw Materials," 43–44, note 4.

9.   Heatherly, *Mandate*, 334.

10.   30 U.S.C. § 21 et seq.

11.   Heatherly, *Mandate*, 338.

12.   Ibid., 339.

13.   Ibid., 339–40.

14.   Ibid., 343–44.

15.   *Staff of House Subcomm. on Mines and Mining of the Comm. on Interior And Insular Affairs, 96th Cong., 2d Sess., Report On U.S. Minerals Vulnerability: National Policy Implications* 1 (Comm. Print 1980) (*U.S. Minerals Vulnerability Report* or the Santini report). The report was transmitted to the members of the Committee on Interior and Insular Affairs by Committee Chairman Morris K. Udall, the former chairman, before Congressman Santini, of the Mines and Mining Subcommittee. In his transmittal letter, Chairman Udall warned of "an emerging awareness in this nation that oil is not the only mineral in short supply...." cautioned that "[a]ccess to nonfuel minerals cannot be left to chance in view of the critical role these resources play in our defense, economy, and everyday lives...." and cited the Santini report's conclusion that "the Federal government ... has exerted an adverse influence on domestic mineral development." Ibid., III. See generally *Nonfuel Minerals Policy Review: Oversight Hearings on Nonfuel Minerals Policy Review Before the Subcomm. on*

Mines and Mining of the House Comm. on Interior and Insular Affairs, Parts I, II and III, 96th Cong., 1st Sess. 44 (1979). The Santini report was written almost single-handedly, under the direct supervision of Chairman Santini, by Wilbert L. Dare, consultant to the Mines and Mining Subcommittee. Mr. Dare, a decorated Marine Corps veteran who fought in the Pacific and served as a career employee of the U.S. Bureau of Mines, died in May 2012.

16. *U.S. Minerals Vulnerability Report*, 1. An irony of minerals' essential nature is that, in terms of output value and numbers employed, they represent but one percent each of the nation's economy and work force, that is, the U.S. economy might be visualized as "an inverted pyramid where the bulk of the economy overshadows the raw materials that is its base." Ibid., 1–2.

17. D. A. Viljoen, *Minerals From the Dawn of Mankind to the Twenty-First Century*, 79 J.S. African *Inst. Mining & Metallurgy*, 410-420 (1979).

18. *One Third of the Nation's Land, A Report to the President and to the Congress by the Public Land Law Review Commission*, Washington, D.C., June 1979, 121. On September 19, 1964, President Johnson signed Public Law 88-606 to create the Public Land Law Review Committee (PLLRC), which completed a review of public land laws and rules and regulations, policies and practices of Federal, state, and local governments and agencies; recommended needed modifications; and, prepared a final report. Six PLLRC members were appointed by the president, six by the U.S. Senate, and six by the U.S. House of Representatives. Thirty-four people were selected by the PLLRC and federal agencies as an Advisory Council and the PLLRC was permitted to hire fifty-four staff members. Jerome C. Muys, The Public Land Law Review Commission Study—Issues and Interests, *Natural Resources Lawyer* 3, no. 2 (May 1970): 315–26.

19. *U.S. Minerals Vulnerability Report*, 5. "Few realize that their colored television set contains about 35 mineral commodities and that a telephone contains about 40." Ibid., citing, A. G. Chynoweth, "Electronic Materials, Functional Substitutes," *Science* 191 (February 20, 1976), 725–32. The National Mining Association reports: "Every American uses an average of nearly 40,000 pounds of newly mined materials each year; Telephones are made from as many as 42 different minerals, including aluminum, beryllium, coal, copper, gold, iron, limestone, silica, silver, talc and wollastonite[, and w]ithout boron, copper, gold and quartz, your digital alarm clock would not work; a television requires 35 different minerals, and more than 30 minerals are needed to make a computer."; http://www.nma.org/statistics/fast_facts.asp.

20. *U.S. Minerals Vulnerability Report*, 5. In 1980, the United States imported 21 percent of its basic raw material requirements resulting in a $1 billion trade deficit in mineral materials; however, Western Europe and Japan had much greater trade imbalances with Western Europe importing 80 percent of its needs and Japan importing 95 percent. Calingaert, *U.S. Strategic Minerals Dependency*, Dep't State Bull., April 1981, 23. See also Crowson, *British Foreign Policy to* 1985: *Dependence on Non-Fuel Minerals*, 54 Intl. Aff. 48 (1978).

21. *U.S. Minerals Vulnerability Report*, 8.

22. Ibid. A little over a year after the end of World War II, Secretary of the Interior J.A. Krug advised the mining industry:

> [A minerals] policy must have universal understanding and endorsement. No one person or group can satisfactorily devise it. The problems involved are too numerous, too diverse in technical nature, and too interrelated in political aspect. The legislative and executive branches of the Federal government must work together in creating mineral policy.

Secretary of the Interior J. A. Krug address to American Mining Congress, Denver, Colorado (September 11, 1946). Ibid. "We have moved in this century from a time of abundance to a time of scarcity for many of the essential minerals." Secretary of the Interior James G. Watt address to the American Mining Congress, Denver, Colorado (September 28, 1981). "Until the late 1920s, America had a surplus balance of trade in both fuel and nonfuel minerals. Less than 50 years later, a trade deficit in raw and processed nonfuel minerals reached $8 billion, growing fourfold since 1973." *U.S. Minerals Vulnerability Report*, 5.

23. Ibid., 12.
24. Ibid.
25. Ibid., 13.
26. Ibid.
27. Ibid.

28. Ibid., 16. "Interior has a long history of benign neglect regarding the mining and minerals industry. However, its confession of powerlessness to deal with the woes confronting that industry is of recent [Carter administration] vintage." Ibid. Secretary Andrus did more than confess institutional impotence and concede his individual indifference; "Andrus termed the mining industry 'the rape, ruin and run boys' when he became secretary, and that rhetoric permeates his department." Bryce Nelson of *The Los Angeles Times*, "Interior Secretary Cecil Andrus of Idaho: Tough stand on Western states," *Anchorage Daily News*, September 25, 1979, B-5. Indifference regarding minerals policy was indeed bipartisan; for example, the Ford administration did not send Congress an annual report in 1974 as a result of an internal policy disagreement over whether the federal government "should be concerned with the health of the private mineral sector and the increase in mineral imports." *U.S. Minerals Vulnerability Report*, 18–19. In 1975, the Ford administration disclosed no sense of "urgency regarding [mineral] imports." Ibid., 19.

29. Ibid., 13.

30. Ibid. The Santini report maintained that "[g]ood mineral policy should not be a policy of reaction, but rather the product of a steady commitment that recognizes the indispensability of minerals to the Nation's industrial base and its national security." Ibid., xii.

31. Ibid., 58–59. The Santini report, as do other studies, recognizes the impact on the production of domestically available minerals of a host of environmental laws. *U.S. Minerals Vulnerability Report*, 50–58. *Nonfuel Minerals Policy Review Hearings, Part II*, 444–49, note 15. The equitable and predictable (as opposed to arbitrary and capricious) application of most federal environmental laws does not pose the barrier to domestic mineral production that results from the closure of vast amounts of federal land to mineral exploration and development. The only two exceptions are the National Environmental Policy Act (NEPA), which often yields an endless cycle of studies and litigation, that is, total paralysis by analysis, and the Endangered Species Act, which, often accompanied by perpetual litigation, may result in a total ban on any use of the land encumbered by a given species. America's environmental laws mean, however, that only truly "world-class mineral deposits" can be developed, such as the New World Mine in southern Montana. One commentator argues, "Perhaps the government action that has most significantly impeded domestic mineral production has been the restriction of access to Federal lands for mineral exploration and development." Jones, "Onshore and Offshore Solutions to the Nonfuel Minerals Shortage," 630, note 4.

32. *One Third of the Nation's Land*, 122. (Emphasis added.) The rarity of "economic concentrations of nonfuel minerals" is demonstrated by "the fact that between 1,150 and 1,200 mines supply about 90 percent of the free world's mineral requirements." Furthermore, "the geologic uniqueness of mineral deposits" yields the "rule-of-thumb that the average mining company can stay in business if it makes one significant discovery every 20 to 30 years." Of course, to make that discovery, it "must continue searching for new deposits." *U.S. Minerals Vulnerability Report*, 58.

33. Ibid., 59. See Raymond A. Peck, Jr., "And Then There Were None," Evolving Federal Restraints on the Availability of Public Lands for Mineral Development, 25 *Rocky Mtn. Min. L. Inst.* 3-1, 3-13 (1979).

34. *U.S. Minerals Vulnerability Report*, 60. See, "Final Report of the Task Force on the Availability of Federally Owned Mineral Lands," U.S. Department of the Interior, 1977, 48. (A disclaimer added by Secretary Andrus states that the report's "findings and recommendations do not represent the official views or policy of the Department of the Interior.") Ronald Reagan was well aware of this report and its suppression by the Carter administration. "That study ... revealed that no one in Washington knows how much of the Federally owned mineral lands have been removed from use. And it doesn't look as if we're going to find out because Secretary of the Interior in this administration, Cecil Andrus has suppressed this report." "Federal Land," October 10, 1978, Skinner, *Reagan, In His Own Hand*, 338.

35. "Much of the restricted access results from the designation of increasing amounts of public lands as wilderness areas, which ... single-use designations rule out access, add costs, and increase the uncertainties of efforts to find and produce minerals.... The potential Federal acreage designated for wilderness preservation and withdrawn from mineral development is approximately twenty-six percent of all Federal lands, or nearly nine percent of total U.S. acreage." Jones, "Onshore and Offshore Solutions to the Nonfuel Minerals Shortage," 631–32, note 4, citing "Minerals Management at the Department of The Interior Needs Coordination and Organization," General Accounting Office, EMD-81-53, June 5, 1981), 50. See also, Ferguson, *Forest Service and BLM Wilderness*

Review Programs And Their Effect On Mining Law Activities, 24 Rocky Mtn. Min. L. Inst. 717 (1978); Hall, *Mineral Exploration And Development In Bureau Of Land Management Wilderness Study Areas*, 21 Ariz. L. Rev. 351 (1979); Hubbard, *Ah, Wilderness! (But What About Access and Prospecting?)*, 15 Rocky Mtn. Min. L. Inst. 585 (1969); Short, *Wilderness Policies and Mineral Potential On The Public Lands*, 26 Rocky Mtn. Min. L. Inst. 39 (1980).

36. The Santini report took particular umbrage at the ubiquitous land classification, "areas of critical environmental concern." "The rarity of a mineral occurrence necessitates the adoption of a concept of 'areas of strategic mineral potential' whereby mineral areas would be so designated and hence protected from restrictive classification." *U.S. Minerals Vulnerability Report*, 82.

37. *U.S. Minerals Vulnerability Report*, 60.

38. "Mining Law Reform and Balanced Resource Management," General Accounting Office, EMD-78-93, Feb 27, 1979, 16, cited by *U.S Minerals Vulnerability Report*, 61, note 90.

39. "In effect, the owner of one-third of the Nation's lands has not yet even considered a title search of its property to learn the extent of the non-development liens it has placed against it." Ibid., 61. The General Accounting Office declared there to be "no single source of cumulative withdrawal statistics." Mining Law Reform and Balanced Resource Management, General Accounting Office, 1979, 16. As it had regarding the National Park Service's land acquisition policy during the Carter administration, the General Accounting Office issued three reports during this period regarding the absence of, and the need for, a national nonfuel mineral policy. "Need to Develop a National Non-Fuel Mineral Policy," General Accounting Office, RED 76-86, July 2, 1976; "Learning to Look Ahead: The Need for a National Minerals Policy and Planning Process," General Accounting Office, EMD 79-30, April 19, 1979; "The U.S. Mining and Minerals Processing Industry: An Analysis of Trends and Implications," General Accounting Office, ID-80-04, October 31, 1979. The 1979 report concluded: "Even though materials are central to America's industrial health and economic welfare, the Federal Government has never given materials availability the serious, sustained attention it deserves." EMD 79-30, 49.

40. *U.S. Minerals Vulnerability Report*, 58–59. The Carter administration's head-in-the-sand approach regarding the oil and gas potential of federal lands drew this from Ronald Reagan, "Why is the government so anxious to lock up this land.... Is it a fear that more [natural gas] strikes will be made? Hard as it may be to believe that—is there any other explanation?" Skinner, *Reagan, In His Own Hand*, 338.

41. *U.S. Minerals Vulnerability Report*, 59, note 84, and also page 62.

42. Ibid., 62–63; see generally 60–65. "The most precious asset and the most fundamental requirement, access to land—primarily the mineral-rich public land—in which to search for minerals could well become the scarcest component in America's mineral supply future." Ibid., xv.

43. Ibid., 46. Small miners have discovered "most of the existing important mineral deposits that have been mined in the U.S." Ibid., note 69. According to a survey of 41 major mining companies, from 1970 to 1975, "12-18 mines were being planned or brought into production annually from mineral properties submitted to major companies by small miners." Ibid., citing David W. Delcour, "The Role of the Small Miner," paper presented at the American Mining Congress Convention, September 13, 1977.

44. *U.S. Minerals Vulnerability Report*, 64.

45. Ibid., 61–62, note 92. When the Blackbird cobalt deposit in Idaho was proposed for inclusion in wilderness, Carter's Interior Department remained silent notwithstanding that supplies from southern Africa could be disrupted and that the alternative source of supply was the U.S.S.R. When the Bureau of Mines director urged removal from wilderness consideration of the Stillwater Complex in Montana due to its chromite and platinum deposits—minerals that, like cobalt, were at risk of serious social or political disruption—the assistant secretary ordered the director to remove his recommendation. Ibid.

46. Ibid., 22. Little wonder it was doomed given that it was placed in the hands of the secretary who, after all, referred to miners as practitioners of "rape, ruin, and run." Associated Press, "Andrus To Crack Down On Mining Firms," *Sarasota Herald-Tribune*, March 27, 1977, 9-A. Andrus said he intends to "end what I see as the domination of the department by mining, oil and other special interests ... [to] make the three r's—rape, ruin and run—a thing of the past." Ibid.

47. *U.S. Minerals Vulnerability Report*, 23–24.

48. In this regard, the Santini report faulted "the development within government of a belief that government, not the marketplace, should mandate the fundamental decision as to whether an ore deposit should be mined or its minerals processed.... Over the past decade the development of ore deposits

in the United States has become increasingly dependent upon decisions of government—a government increasingly opposed to such development. In fact, in some cases, the Federal government's opposition to mineral development has been accomplished by the open solicitation of public opinion against such development." Ibid., 27.

49.   Ibid., 25–26.

50.   Ibid., 26. See generally, "The Nonfuel Minerals Policy Review," 22–27. Chairman Santini, in an interview conducted in Salisbury, Rhodesia, called the report, "a whitewash." Gary Thatcher, "Will Rhodesia play politics with scarce metals?" *Christian Science Monitor*, January 25, 1980.

51.   *U.S. Minerals Vulnerability Report*, 26.

52.   See *Sagebrush Rebel*, chapter 1. See generally "Minerals and Energy Policy," Arnold, *At the Eye of the Storm*, 117–20.

53.   Ibid., 28.

54.   National Materials and Mineral Program Plan and Report to Congress, submitted by President Reagan, April 5, 1982.

55.   Ibid., 3. President Reagan also emphasized the need to renew and improve stockpiling. In fact, President Reagan ordered the first major stockpile acquisition in two decades, including purchases of cobalt and the acquisition of Jamaican bauxite "by purchase, barter of agricultural products, and swap of excess stockpile materials." *Strategic Materials: Technologies to Reduce U.S. Import Vulnerability* (Washington, D.C.: U.S. Congress, Office of Technology Assessment, OTA-ITE-248, May 1985), 117. In 1984, President Reagan signed into law the National Critical Mineral Act, 30 U.S.C. § 1801 et seq., which established a national Critical Materials Council in the Executive Office of the President; the secretary of the interior chaired that Council for President Reagan. (Pub. L. 98-373, title II, Sec. 202, July 31, 1984, 98 Stat. 1249.

56.   President Ronald Reagan, "Message to the Congress Submitting the National Materials and Minerals Program Plan and Report," April 5, 1982. http://www.presidency.ucsb.edu/ws/index.php?pid=42363.

57.   President Reagan's objections went beyond the seabed mining provisions: "Decided in [National Security Council] meeting—will not sign 'Law of the Sea' treaty even without seabed mining provision." Ronald Reagan, *The Reagan Diaries* (Harper, 2007), 91. *Business Week*, May 24, 1982, 196. In April 1982, the United Nations voted 130 to four, with seventeen abstentions, to approve the Law of the Sea Treaty; the United States voted no. *New York Times*, May 1, 1982, 9, col. 1. For a lengthy discussion of the complex international organization that would oversee deep seabed mining, see Jones, "Onshore and Offshore Solutions to the Nonfuel Minerals Shortage," 666–75, note 4. The objections of the United States to the Law of the Sea Treaty are set forth at 675–88.

58.   Proclamation 5030–Exclusive Economic Zone of the United States of America, March 10, 1983; http://www.presidency.ucsb.edu/ws/index.php?pid=41037; "It has been estimated that by 1985 the United States could produce four to five million tons of seabed ore annually; in terms of current consumption, this could provide 92% of America's cobalt, 33% of its ferromanganese, 18% of its nickel, and 1.5% of its copper." Jones, "Onshore and Offshore Solutions to the Nonfuel Minerals Shortage," 638, note 4, citing, Alfred E. Eckes, *The United States and The Global Struggle for Minerals* (University of Texas Press, 1979), 252. Of course, the costs of developing the deep seabed nodules would be substantial; the mining industry estimated "cumulative expenditures of at least $140 million to develop deep ocean mining technology, and cumulative investments of $2.1 billion to $3.1 billion to achieve commercial operations." "Deep Ocean Mining: Actions Needed to Make It Happen," General Accounting Office, PSAD-77-127, June 28, 1978, 15.

59.   Act of May 10, 1872 (17 Stat. 91) 30 U.S.C. § 21 et seq. Opponents attack the General Mining Law because it was enacted during the Grant administration; ironically President Grant also signed the federal law that created Yellowstone National Park.

60.   From 1981 through 1987, for example, the Bureau of Land Management (BLM) "patented 497 mining claims, where only 143 claims had been patented from 1976 through 1981." *Interior Report 1988*, 37. During the Reagan administration, the BLM received notices or plans for 16,000 mining operations. Ibid. The Reagan administration also conducted the first combined offshore mineral sale for sulfur and salt in the Gulf of Mexico Region. Ibid., 38.

61.   The location of a mining claim is only the first step in the lengthy, difficult, and costly process that leads to obtaining a "patent" (title) to the mining claim, including the ore body and the overlying land, and mining the mineral deposit. For a lengthy discussion of the General Mining Law, its value to the American West, and the challenges to the development of even extremely valuable ore bodies,

see generally William Perry Pendley, *War on the West: Government Tyranny on America's Great Frontier* (Regnery, 1995), 141–56.

62.   Ibid., 145.
63.   In 1981, Andrus defended his opposition to energy and mineral exploration in wilderness areas: "Now the law *permitted* it but it did not *mandate* it, and it has been the view of all administrations—from 1964 on through 1980, Republican and Democrat alike, elephants and donkeys, that you just don't do it." "Cecil Andrus on Windmills and Balance," *High Country News* (Nov. 13, 1981), 16. (Emphasis added.)
64.   The Santini report specifically criticized a Solicitor's Opinion from Carter's Interior Department that barred all mineral activity on lands being considered for wilderness designation. *U.S. Minerals Vulnerability Report*, 59, note 95.
65.   The Wilderness Act of 1964, Act of September 3, 1964 (Public Law 88-577, 78 Stat. 890 as amended; 16 U.S.C. § 1133(d)(2). "[S]uch areas shall be surveyed on a planned, recurring basis consistent with the concept of wilderness preservation by the Geological Survey and the Bureau of Mines to determine the mineral values, if any, that may be present; and the results of such surveys shall be made available to the public and submitted to the President and Congress." Ibid.
66.   Pendley, *War on the West*, 146. Marc Humphries, "New World Gold Mine and Yellowstone National Park," Congressional Research Service Report for Congress, 96-669, August 27, 1996, 1.
67.   P.L. 96-312, specifically, Section 5(d)(1), which provides:

> Notwithstanding the provisions of the Wilderness Act of 1964 (78 Stat. 890; 16 U.S.C. 1131), including section 4(d)(3), closing wilderness areas after December 31, 1983, to the United States mining laws, and the designation of the River of No Return Wilderness by this Act, within that portion of the wilderness depicted on a map entitled "Special Mining Management Zone—Clear Creek", (hereinafter referred to in this section as the "Special Management Zone"), dated June 1980, all prospecting and exploration for, and development or mining of cobalt and associated minerals shall be considered a dominant use of such land and shall be subject to such laws and regulations as are generally applicable to National Forest System lands not designated as wilderness or other special management areas, including such laws and regulations which relate to the right of access to valid mining claims and private property[.]

Notwithstanding staff chicanery, this provision was included due to the hard work and persistent efforts of Chairman Santini, Congressman Steven D. Symms, Republican of Idaho and Senator James A. McClure, Republican of Idaho.

68.   The Santini report recommended that Interior allow "more access for mineral exploration and development" as a "general policy" and acquire a better understanding of the various restrictive land classifications and the extent to which they bar or limit mineral exploration and development. *U.S. Minerals Vulnerability Report*, 81. The Santini report also recommended that Interior "permit full exploration and development of nonfuel minerals" within wilderness areas as intended by Congress and recommended that Congress enact federal legislation permitting mineral exploration on wilderness lands until 2000 and on lands designated as wilderness after 1980, for a period of 20 years. Ibid., 82.
69.   "1983 – A Year Of Enrichment: Improving The Quality Of Life For All Americans," (U.S. Department of the Interior, October 1983), 20–21. Other Interior mineral studies included an extensive analysis of strategic and critical minerals from South Africa—addressing mineral supply contingencies and embargo implications— in support of Bureau of Mines and other Reagan administration witnesses regarding anti-apartheid legislation, a study on the impact of research and development in improving the nation's competitive posture regarding minerals on the world market and mechanisms for government and industry to improve America's competitive position, and research to advise international leading institutions with regard to the underwriting of foreign mineral projects that may compete with domestic producers. "America – Our Treasure and Our Trust: The Legacy of President Ronald Reagan 1981 – 1988," (U.S. Department of the Interior, December 1988), 38–39.
70.   Ibid., 38.
71.   Ibid., 40–47. The research projects include: soldering of aluminum (after electroplating with a nickel-copper alloy), regenerating spent chromic acid solutions, recycling stainless steel, recycling waste chromic solutions, recovering cobalt from Missouri lead ores and copper leaching solutions,

recycling minute amounts of gold and platinum in military applications, recycling lead from scrap automobile batteries, and developing titanium alloy molds. Ibid.

72.   Associated Press, "Reagan Vetoes Wilderness Bill," *New York Times*, January 15, 1983, Sec. 1, 10, Col. 1.

73.   Philip Shabecoff, "Reagan Vetoes Bill to Protect 1.4 Million Acres in Montana," *New York Times*, November 4, 1988.

74.   Todd S. Purdum, "Clinton Unveils Plan to Halt Gold Mine Near Yellowstone," *New York Times*, August 13, 1996.

75.   Alison Mitchell, "President Designates A Monument Across Utah," *New York Times*, September 1996.

76.   Marc Humphries, "Rare Earth Elements: The Global Supply Chain," Congressional Research Service, R41347, September 30, 2010; Kalee Thompson, "There Is No Substitute, Rare Earths' Story," *Popular Mechanics* 190, no. 1 (January 2013).

77.   Jack Perkowski, "Behind China's Rare Earth Controversy," *Forbes*, June 21, 2012.

78.   Developing rare earths in states with significant resources could yield $40 billion in increased gross state product, add almost 3,600 well-paying jobs, and increase state revenues by $724 million. Tom Tanton, "Rare Earths Mining Potential in the United States," National Center for Policy Analysis, Policy Report no. 348 (April 2013): 10.

79.   Daniel McGroarty, "America's Growing Mineral Deficit," *Wall Street Journal*, January 30, 2013. "[T]here are now 19 strategic metals and minerals for which the U.S. is currently 100% import-dependent—and for 11 of them a single country, China, is among the top three providers." Ibid. The Obama White House's "Material Genome Initiative … is a double-edge sword: Will the U.S. policies be guided by sound science? Or will they be unduly influenced by environmental politics.…" Ibid.

80.   Phil Taylor, "Cobalt Deposit Solidifies Idaho's Place on Mineral Map," *New York Times* (Greenwire), August 26, 2010.

CHAPTER EIGHT

1.   "I wonder how many Americans are aware of their govt's. insatiable hunger for land. Probably not as many as should be." Skinner, *Reagan's Path to Victory*, 357, September 19, 1978. In attacking the federal government's land acquisition activities, Reagan wrote of the National Park Service, which during the 1970s became notorious for its questionable practices and the cost to the American people of its voracious appetite. Of course, given his experiences in Sacramento, Reagan knew of the other federal agencies that acquire private property. It was not just the agencies, however; Congress often took the initiative and even exerted tremendous pressure, over the protestations of the agencies, to acquire more private land. For example, Congress appropriated and mandated the expenditure of funds to purchase an Arizona ranch, which uniquely in the country—according to congressional proponents and FWS scientists—could serve as the only habitat that would ensure the recovery of a particular endangered species. After buying the ranch for nearly $9 million, spending millions of dollars on upkeep and modifications, and sacrificing thousands of the masked bobwhite quail recovery population, the venture is a costly failure. Nathan F. Sayre, *Ranching, Endangered Species, and Urbanization in the Southwest: Species of Capital* (University of Arizona Press, 2002), 21–233; *Interior Report* 1998, 17. One local cowboy opined, "I remember when the Buenos Aires Ranch was sold to USFWS – it was a beautiful ranch [but] its last owner needed money and only the govt. would pay that amount.… The FWS moved in, and with the help of the Sierra Club and God knows how much Federal money, tore all the fences and corrals out – which were worth millions in place and will never be replaced. I understand they have mostly neglected the waters, and it is now a freeway for cartels moving drugs from Mexico north. Every neighboring ranch gets cattle that stray onto the place and because the waters are in such poor condition it is a death trap for cattle (because it takes a cowboy to maintain the waters, not some government employee – they're too lazy and have to hire a contractor, which means letting a contract, which means getting an appropriation, which means an EA, you get the picture). I'm told that the bobwhite quail on the place (and they're not endangered or if they are it is not man's doing – they were all over our ranches in S. Arizona when I was a kid) haven't done well. The bird lovers rhapsodize about the place, but I don't think many of them know what they've really done there because they don't know anything about managing large blocks of rural land (or in the Buenos Aires' case, mis-managing). Anyway, [it's] just a silly idea for spending public money on a place that is managed by idiots that has worked out predictably. No wonder we have a national debt problem."

2.   Kiron K. Skinner, Annelise Anderson, and Martin Anderson, eds., *Reagan's Path to Victory, The Shaping of Ronald Reagan's Vision: Selected Writings* (The Free Press, 2004), 140. President Reagan continued to follow this issue:

> ABC news had a story about a woman with a country restaurant in Texas along a hi-way in a National Park. The Park service wants to bulldoze her café to improve the view. I called Jim Watt (in California). He's going to look into it.

Ronald Reagan, *The Reagan Diaries* (Harper, 2007), 110 (November 4, 1982).

3.   Skinner, *Reagan's Path to Victory*, 278.

4.   Ibid.

5.   Ibid., 279.

6.   Ibid., 278. The "special interest group" was the Sierra Club, which, beginning in 1948 in the years before it became radicalized, supported the Mineral King ski resort. "The Sierra Club—which had still approved a Mineral King recreational development as recently as 1965—attempted to use the courts to stop the project." http://www.yesterland.com/mineralking.html.

7.   Skinner, *Reagan's Path to Victory*, 279.

8.   Kiron K. Skinner, Annelise Anderson, and Martin Anderson, eds., *Reagan, In His Own Hand: The Writings of Ronald Reagan That Reveal His Revolutionary Vision for America* (The Free Press, 2001), 337.

9.   Constitutional Amendment V.

10.   Skinner, *Reagan, In His Own Hand*, 341.

11.   The GAO undertakes investigations at the request of Senators and Members of Congress. These reports were prepared at the request of Republican Senator Ted Stevens of Alaska and his staffer and later Reagan Interior Department official, Ric Davidge.

12.   "Federal Protection and Preservation of Wild and Scenic Rivers is Slow and Costly" (CED-78-96) (May 22, 1978); "Review of the National Park Service's Urban National Recreation Area Program" (CED-79-98) (June 19, 1979); "The Federal Drive to Acquire Private Lands Should be Reassessed" (CED-80-14) (December 19, 1979); "Federal Land Acquisitions by Condemnation—Opportunities to Reduce Delays and Costs" (CED-80-54)(May 14, 1980); "Lands in the Lake Chelan National Recreation Area Should be Returned to Private Ownership" (CED-81-10) (January 22, 1981); "The National Park Service Should Improve its Land Acquisition and Management at the Fire Island National Seashore" (CED-81-78) (May 8, 1981).

13.   According to the GAO:

> [O]n April 26, 1979, the National Park Service issued its "Revised Land Acquisition Policy." The purpose of the policy was to provide guidance on how to critically evaluate the need to purchase land. The Service's policy states that each park area's land acquisition plan must identify the reasons for fee simple acquisition versus alternative land protection and management strategies such as acquiring easements, relying on zoning, making cooperative management agreements with State and local governments and communities, and acquiring right-of-way through private property. The Park Service's policy before this was to acquire all lands in fee simple within park area boundaries.
>
> Even though the Park Service revised its land acquisition policy to stress less than fee simple acquisition, little improvement has been made. For example, during the period September 30, 1979, to December 31, 1980, the Service acquired an interest in 160,530 acres of land of which only 3 percent was acquired in other than fee simple. Before the policy change, the Park Service had acquired less than 1 percent in other than fee simple.

Statement of Roy J. Kirk, Senior Group Director Community and Economic Development Division [U.S. General Accounting Office], Before The Subcommittee On Public Lands And Reserved Water Committee On Energy And Natural Resources United States Senate During Its Workshop On Public Land Acquisition And Alternatives Regarding Adjacent Lands And Intermingled Ownership Problems, July 9, 1981, 2.

14.   At a congressional hearing in 2001, Chuck Cushman testified, "Only 29 homes were to be taken for the [Cuyahoga NRA] ... [y]et the number of homes purchased was well over 300." House Resources Committee, U.S. House of Representatives, June 20, 2001, Conservation and Reinvestment Act (H.R. 701), http://www.landrights.org/CARA_CushmanTestimony010620.pdf. The

sponsor of the act creating the Cuyahoga Valley National Recreation Area, Ohio Congressman John F. Seiberling, a Democrat, had a home in the NRA, but he was allowed to keep it after donating a scenic easement to the NPS. Given that the NPS allowed "some landowners to keep their homes while ['well over 300'] others were required to sell," the GAO investigated Mr. Seiberling's circumstance but concluded that he had received no "preferential treatment." "Allegations That Congressman Seiberling Received Preferential Treatment Regarding Land Transactions in the Cuyahoga Valley National Recreation Area," CED-80-135, Aug 27, 1980.

15. "For the Greater Good," PBS Frontline, produced and directed independently by Mark and Dan Jury and produced for Frontline by Stephanie Tepper, aired June 6, 1983. Jessica Savitch concluded the recitation of what happened to the people of the Cuyahoga Valley, "But perhaps it is in pursuit of the greatest good that we should take the greatest care."; http://www.youtube.com/watch?v=rWhruoZq7qQ. Savitch introduced the program with, "It is rarely if ever that we get to see a story about the implementation of a government program charting its affects on the lives of people over time and outlining the details of how it works."

16. "The National Inholders Association estimated that there are between 50,000 and 60,000 private land owners in national areas." Statement of Roy J. Kirk, 1. The GAO also reported that number had "undoubtedly increased over the years as the Congress has authorized new or expansions to existing national parks, forests, wildlife refuges, wild and scenic rivers, and the like. For example, the National Park Service's purchases of land and the addition of 46 new areas with many private landowners, in the last decade doubled the acreage of the Park Service system to nearly 72 million and increased the number of areas managed by the Service to 323." Ibid.

17. "The Encyclopedia of Cleveland History," A joint effort by Case Western Reserve University and the Western Reserve Historical Society, Cuyahoga Valley National Park, last modified September 26, 2003, http://ech.case.edu/ech-cgi/article.pl?id=CVNP.

18. "Lands in The Lake Chelan National Recreation Area Should Be Returned to Private Ownership," (CED-81-10) (January 22, 1981).

19. "In 1978 Interior Secretary Cecil Andrus told Congress that expansion of Redwood National Park would cost $359 million. The actual cost when all landowners were paid has exceeded $1.4 billion. Consequently, Secretary Andrus' estimate was off by 417 percent." Statement of Congressman James V. Hansen (R – 1st UT), *Congressional Record* 140, no.133 (Wednesday, September 21, 1994) (House).

20. See Ron Arnold, *At the Eye of the Storm: James Watt and the Environmentalists* (Regnery Gateway, 1982), 184; see generally 181–87. This practice was documented and criticized by Interior's Inspector General in a 1992 report regarding a NPS practice in place since 1983 and no doubt prior to that date. U.S. Department of the Interior, Office of the Inspector General, "Audit Report: Department of the Interior Land Acquisitions Conducted With the Assistance of Nonprofit Organizations," Report No. 92-I-833, May 1992, 4–5.

21. Ibid., 9, 16–19. Even when the government did make an appraisal to determine the fair market value, it was done months and even years before the sale, rendering its worth highly questionable. In all, the inspector general concluded that, on sixty-four federal purchases with a fair market value of $44 million, the American people lost $5.2 million. Ibid., 5.

22. Apparently this activity is quite profitable. According to documents accompanying a press release issued by the Trust for Public Lands (TPL), "Sixty percent of TPL's operating income comes primarily from its land sales to government." Trust for Public Land, "Land Protection Group Calls DOI Report 'Biased,'" June 5, 1992, 5.

23. See William Perry Pendley, *War on the West: Government Tyranny on America's Great Frontier* (Regnery, 1995), 112–13.

24. Arnold, *At the Eye of the Storm*, 185. One example was Sweeney Ridge in San Francisco. Ibid.,186–87.

25. See generally Arnold, *At the Eye of the Storm*, 102–17, from which this discussion draws heavily.

26. Elizabeth Drew, "A Reporter at Large, Secretary Watt," *New Yorker*, May 4, 1981, 126.

27. See generally "The National Parks" in Arnold, *At the Eye of the Storm*, 103–17. In April 1832, Congress first set aside an area that would become a national park when President Jackson signed legislation to protect natural thermal springs and adjacent mountainsides for future use by the federal government in an area now known as Hot Springs, Arkansas; http://www.nps.gov/hosp/index.htm; In June 1864, President Lincoln signed legislation ceding Yosemite Valley and the Mariposa Grove of Giant Sequoias to California for "public use, resort, and recreation," http://www.nps.gov/yose/index.htm; When the wonders of what became Yellowstone National Park were discovered the area

was federal territory; there was no state to which to cede the property. The Northern Pacific Railroad played a crucial role in the designation and early development of Yellowstone National Park. Phyllis Smith and William Hoy, *The Northern Pacific Railroad & Yellowstone National Park* (Keystone Press, 2009).

28. Golden Gate National Recreation Area (CA), http://www.nps.gov/goga/index.htm; Gateway National Recreation Area (NY), http://www.nps.gov/gate/index.htm; Chattahoochee River National Recreation Area (GA), http://www.nps.gov/chat/index.htm.

29. Arnold, *At the Eye of the Storm*, 107.

30. 16 U.S.C. §§ 460*l*-4 through 460*l*-11, September 3, 1964, as amended 1965, 1968, 1970, 1972–1974, 1976–1981, 1983, 1986, 1987, 1990, 1991, 1993–1996. Ironically, "the [Land and Water Conservation F]und accumulates revenues from oil and gas leases on the Outer Continental Shelf (OCS). For many years, the OCS revenues have accounted for almost all of the deposits." Carol Hardy Vincent, "Land and Water Conservation Fund: Overview, Funding History, and Issues," Congressional Research Service, August 13, 2010, 1.

31. See "Anatomy of a Condemnation Case" at http://www.justice.gov/enrd/4610.htm. See, in particular the discussion of a Declaration of Taking pursuant to the Declaration of Taking Act, 40 U.S.C. §3114. The NPS has been known to use "low valuations," engages in "appraisal shopping," including the use of appraisers who work exclusively for the federal government, and often is accused of acting in "bad faith." One appellate judge seemed to agree as to the NPS's bad faith. *United States of America v. Bradac*, 910 F.2d 439 (7th Cir. 1990). J. Pell, "I dissent because the Bradacs simply have not had their day in court on the issue of bad faith [by the NPS regarding the Lower St. Croix National Scenic Riverway]." 910 F.2d at 443. In 1972, Public Law 92-560 added fifty-two miles of the Lower St. Croix River to the National Wild and Scenic Rivers System.

32. Act creating Yellowstone National Park, March 1, 1872:

> *Be it enacted by the Senate and House of Representatives of the United States of America in Congress assembled,* That the tract of land [described herein] is hereby reserved and withdrawn from settlement, occupancy, or sale under the laws of the United States, and dedicated and set apart as a public park or *pleasuring-ground for the benefit and enjoyment of the people....*
>
> SEC 2. That said public park shall be under the exclusive control of the Secretary of the Interior, whose duty it shall be, as soon as practicable, to make and publish such rules and regulations as he may deem necessary or proper for the care and management of the same. Such regulations shall provide for the *preservation, from injury or spoliation, of all timber, mineral deposits, natural curiosities, or wonders within said park, and their retention in their natural condition.* (Emphasis added.)

33. http://www.pbs.org/nationalparks/history/ep6/3/.

34. Harry Anderson et al., "The U.S. Economy in Crisis," *Newsweek*, January 19, 1981, 30–34.

35. Leon Lindsay, "'Battle of Sweeney Ridge': Californians clash with Watt," *Christian Science Monitor*, February 3, 1982.

36. "Facilities in Many National Parks and Forests Do Not Meet Health and Safety Standards" (CED-80-115) (October 10, 1980); "National Parks' Health and Safety Problems Given Priority; Cost Estimates and Safety Management Could Be Improved" (RCED-83-59) (April 25, 1983).

37. October 1980 GAO Report, i–ii. Little wonder the Carter administration's NPS took little or no action to address parkland health and safety issues. Beginning with a restoration and improvement budget of $176.2 million in FY1978, by FY1981 that budget was a mere $77.9 million. "1983 – A Year Of Enrichment: Improving The Quality Of Life For All Americans," (U.S. Department of the Interior, October 1983), 2.

38. "Reagan Proposals Detail Further Trims in Budget," *New York Times*, March 11, 1981.

39. Statement of Roy J. Kirk, 3, note 13.

40. Russell Dickenson, the careerist Watt kept as Director of the National Park Service, supported the plan by Reagan's Interior Department to repair the parks. Arnold, *At the Eye of the Storm*, 96–97.

41. *Interior Report 1983*, 2–3.

42. President Eisenhower's "Mission 66" program was larger, but much of it was for new construction.

> As President Dwight D. Eisenhower pushed plans through Congress to spend $25 billion over 10 years to build an interstate highway system, the new Park Service director, Colin Wirth, proposed a similar 10-year plan for the parks. He named the

ambitious project "Mission 66," timing its completion to coincide with the agency's 50th anniversary in 1966. Wirth called for spending $787 million, more than half for new construction and the rest for repairs, better maintenance and more staff. Once the president agreed, work began almost immediately. Roads were fixed, sewer systems upgraded, campgrounds improved, and visitor centers added.

http://www.pbs.org/nationalparks/history/ep6/3/.

43. *Interior Report 1983*, 2.
44. Ibid. Much of the work was performed by local loggers and American Indians hard-hit by the slump in the timber industry via 70 contracts with local small businesses. In addition, the Youth Conservation Corps and Comprehensive Employment Training Act participants were used throughout the project.
45. Ibid, 3.
46. Ibid.
47. Ibid.
48. Ibid. "America – Our Treasure and Our Trust: The Legacy of President Ronald Reagan 1981 – 1988," (U.S. Department of the Interior, December 1988), 12. In addition, $300 million was raised, with the support of the NPS, by the private sector for the Statue of Liberty/Ellis Island rehabilitation project. Ibid. See, *Sagebrush Rebel*, chapter 11.
49. *Interior Report 1983*, 5.
50. *Interior Report 1983*, 3. The national parks and their projects included: Glacier National Park (water quality monitoring and protection); Olympic National Park (reestablishing salmon and steelhead fisheries); Death Valley National Park (fencing to eliminate trespassing animals); Yellowstone National Park (geothermal monitoring); Isle Royale National Park (wolf-moose endangered species studies); Everglades National Park (fishery ecosystem studies); Glacier Bay National Park (humpback whale studies); Great Smoky Mountains National Park (wildlife management); Mammoth Cave National Park (protecting cave resources); Hawaii Volcanoes National Park (feral pig and goat control). Ibid.
51. Ibid., 4.
52. *Interior Report 1988*, 11.
53. Ibid., 20.
54. *Interior Report 1983*, 5; *Interior Report 1988*, 11. From 1981 to 1983, the NPS collected $65.6 million (compared to $26.9 million collected from 1977 to 1980) in recreation user fees in the National Park System thanks to increased efficiency, including establishment of fee comparability and extended collection hours. *Interior Report 1983*, 5. In 1987, Interior sought and received authority to raise park fees for the first time since 1972 and to collect entrance fees; over the next ten years, $.5 billion would be collected, most of which went directly for resources management in the National Parks. *Interior Report 1988*, 11 and 102. The ability of the NPS to "keep" a substantial portion of the fees it collected provided a powerful incentive for the agency to do something that it had not done before it was allowed to keep that portion of the fees: collect the fees diligently, daily, and throughout each day.
55. See ibid., notes 12 and 13.
56. http://www.nps.gov/policy/DOrders/DO25_Refs/LWCFpolicy.pdf, at 19785. Under this policy, notes Davidge, if a federal area were set aside to preserve an historical site, proposed land acquisitions must serve that purpose and must be ranked in the degree to which they serve that purpose. No longer could lands be bought by federal agencies because of "purchase opportunities" or political objectives.
57. The U.S. Forest Service under the U.S. Department of Agriculture adopted the policy through the Federal Land Policy Group, as part of the Cabinet Council on Natural Resources and Environment.
58. *The Reagan Diaries*, 255.
59. *Interior Report 1983*, 1. Davidge maintains that the federal land acquisition policy of the Carter administration was to "follow the cement truck," that is, to buy land before it was developed whether it had any specific resource value consistent with the purpose for which a conservation unit was established.
60. Ibid., 3–4.
61. The Great Basin National Park was established in October 1986 by incorporating Lehman Caves National Monument, created by presidential proclamation in January 1922 by President Harding, into a new park.
62. By acts of Congress and with President Reagan's signature the National Trails System was expanded with the addition of the Florida National Scenic Trail, the Natchez Trace National Scenic Trail, and

the Potomac Heritage Scenic Trail. In addition, Reagan's Interior Department administratively designated four National Recreational Trails bringing the total to 729 trails, which extend over 7,300 miles. *Interior Report 1983*, 5. "The National Recreation Trail program is administered jointly by the National Park Service and the U.S. Forest Service in conjunction with a number of other federal and nonprofit partners...." http://www.americantrails.org/nationalrecreationtrails/.

63.   *Interior Report 1983*, 4. These designations brought to 548 the areas listed on the National Registry of Natural Landmarks. Ibid. See also http://nature.nps.gov/nnl/. Because private property may be designated, the National Natural Landmark program is not without considerable controversy. Pendley, *War on the West*, 113–14, 125. Reagan's Interior Department took unprecedented action to protect some 46,200 cultural resources on public lands: from 1981 through 1983, protective management, including periodic patrols, interpretive signing, fencing, and site stabilization was implemented at 114,639 cultural resource sites, as compared to such management practices at 10,365 sites from 1970 through 1980. *Interior Report 1983*, 7. In addition, at Reagan's Interior Department, the Bureau of Land Management (BLM) designated 5.0 million acres of federal land, out of the 5.1 million acres designated, as Areas of Critical Environmental Concern (ACEC) because of their "wildlife habitat, geological features and archeological sites." *Interior Report 1988*, 20. See also http://www.blm.gov/co/st/en/fo/ufo/areas_of_critical.html.

64.   *Interior Report 1983*, 4. The sites are Mammoth Cave National Park, Olympic National Park, and Cahokia Mounds [Illinois] State Historic Site. World Heritage Site designation can become controversial as when a U.N. panel asserted that Yellowstone National Park, a World Heritage Site, was "in danger" as a result of a proposed gold mine on private property far outside the park. Valarie Richardson, "U.N. 'Intrusion' Stirs Anger at Yellowstone," *Washington Times*, February 1, 1996, A1. See also, Pendley, *War on the West*, 145–47.

65.   *Interior Report 1983*, 6. In 1983 alone, the NPS designated 23 properties as National Historic Landmarks. Ibid. http://www.nps.gov/nhl/. Reagan's Interior Department reported in 1988 that it had "doubl[ed] the number of places now listed on the National Registry of Historic Places [and] designat[ed] more than 300 new National Historic Landmarks. *Interior Report 1988*, 15.

66.   The areas include Valley Forge National Historical Park (Pennsylvania), Women's Rights National Historical Park (New York), and Harry S Truman National Historic Site, which became the National Park System's 334th area. The Truman site was his residence for over fifty years; during the Truman Presidency, it served as the "summer White House." *Interior Report 1983*, 6.

67.   (ERTA) Pub. L. No. 97-34, 95 Stat. 172. ERTA dramatically increased the size and scope of the tax credits available, which provided substantial economic incentives to investors, constituted one of the most generous credits in the tax code, and caused remarkable growth in rehabilitation of older buildings. Information on Historic Preservation Tax Incentives (GAO/GGii-84-47) (Mar. 29, 1984), 8–9.

68.   *Interior Report 1988*, 15.

69.   *Interior Report 1983*, 5.

70.   Ibid., 4.

71.   Ibid., 6.

72.   Ibid.

73.   http://www.fws.gov/refuges/. The overarching effort of Reagan's Interior Department regarding the FWS was two-fold. First, reestablish a partnership with state fish and game agencies, recognizing that states have primacy regarding their fish and wildlife resources, akin to what Reagan's Interior Department did regarding Alaska. This effort continues to be largely successful today. Second, prevent the FWS from becoming the "U.S. Endangered Species Service" and allow it to focus its resources on its traditional programs, including, migratory birds, management of wildlife refuges, and fisheries restoration. This effort languished beginning in 1989 with the "environmental president" and subsequently with actions by federal courts mandating FWS actions regarding the Endangered Species Act. See *Sagebrush Rebel*, chapter 6.

74.   President Reagan visited one wildlife refuge:

> Marine 1 & off to Chesapeake Bay. First stop the Wildlife Refuge (14,000 acres).
> A briefing, then a town. Saw 2 bald eagles among other things. Then on to an island
> where the oyster & crab boats headquarter. They are fearful of the growing pollu-
> tion of the bay. We're working with 3 states, Va., Maryland & Pa. on a clean-up
> program.

The Reagan Diaries, 254 (July 10, 1984). Reagan "declared 'the time for action is now' to clean up Chesapeake Bay" and "touted the $10 million-a-year cleanup program he announced in his State of the Union address...." Norman D. Sandler, "Reagan, on Environmental Stump, Calls for Chesapeake Bay Cleanup," *Schenectady (New York) Gazette*, July 11, 1984, 1.

75.   *Interior Report 1983*, 1.

76.   Ibid.

77.   Ibid. An additional $20 million received under the Emergency Jobs Act was used for maintenance and rehabilitation activities at refuges, fish hatcheries, and research laboratories. Ibid. The FWS also began a volunteer program for public participation at refuges and other FWS facilities. For example, in 1983, more than 7,100 volunteers donated 193,000 hours at FWS facilities. Ibid., 9.

78.   Ibid., 5. See also *Interior Report 1988*, 14–15. Coastal Barrier Resources Act (CBRA), Public Law 97-348 (96 Stat. 1653; 16 U.S.C. § 3501 et seq.), enacted October 18, 1982. The FWS prepared an inventory to identify undeveloped barrier beaches along the Atlantic and Gulf coasts that were not included in the Coastal Barrier Resource System. *Interior Report 1983*, 5. The FWS also completed detailed wetland maps for 390,000 square miles of the Continental United States and 30,000 square miles of Alaska to aid in wetlands conservation. Ibid., 9.

79.   *Interior Report 1988*, 12. In addition, Reagan's Interior Department added acreage to existing units of the National Wildlife Refuge System, including 100,000 acres of environmentally sensitive land in south Florida. Ibid., 13. Reagan's Interior Department also sought to prevent the loss of wetlands. It established a task force, developed federal legislation, and worked with Congress to enact a law to address the issue. See *Sagebrush Rebel*, chapter 9.

80.   By federal law, wilderness areas are not just wide open spaces in the vast federal estate, but are set aside by acts of Congress as separate and "where man is a stranger who departs," where motorized vehicles are barred, and where other stringent management conditions apply. The areas to be studied, in accordance with federal law, for future designation, by Congress, as wilderness areas, that is, wilderness study areas (WSAs) were selected, not by Congress, but by bureaucrats. Once identified, those areas were managed as *de facto* wilderness areas until Congress, in adopting wilderness legislation for a particular state, enacted "release language" that permitted those WSAs to return to multiple-use management. A mere handful of bills had such release language. Although Reagan's Interior Department issued policy directives more in keeping with the intent of Congress on what could be a WSA, millions of acres of land remained in WSAs.

81.   Great controversy surrounded the purported plans of Reagan's Interior Department to drill in wilderness areas; however, the forty-five oil, gas, and geothermal leases had been issued by Carter's Interior Department without apparent notice. Arnold, *At the Eye of the Storm*, 207. Of course, federal law allowed for such energy activity; plus, many if not all of the leases were encumbered with "no surface occupancy" provisions, which meant that the drilling had to be done off-site by directional drilling. Nonetheless, the existence of these leases on Watt's watch permitted local representatives to become outraged and to receive media coverage. See, for example, ibid., 162–64 and 206–7. See also, C. Brant Short, *Ronald Reagan and the Public Lands: America's Conservation Debate, 1979–1984* (Texas A&M University Press, 1989), 118–24.

82.   Under Sections 202 and 603(a) of the Federal Land Policy and Management Act (FLPMA), the BLM inventoried and categorized lands of 5,000 acres in size or more that were suitable for designation by Congress as wilderness, that is WSAs. Reagan's Interior Department withdrew some WSAs designated by Carter's Interior Department that were 1) less than 5,000 acres in size; 2) contained privately owned oil, gas, or mineral rights (split estates); or 3) used the presence of adjacent wilderness lands with wilderness characteristics to support a finding that the BLM land has wilderness characteristics. The third category was the result of an Interior Board of Land Appeal ruling. Don Coopes et al., IBLA 81-14, 81-63 (February 3, 1982), 61 IBLA 306.

83.   *Interior Report 1983*, 10.

84.   Ibid.

85.   *Interior Report 1988*, 19, *Interior Report 1983*, 10. "Reagan Signs Wilderness Bills," *New York Times*, UPI, October 1, 1984, B9. Only Carter put more federal land into wilderness and that was simply as a result of the passage of the ANILCA. If Alaska is excluded, Reagan outranks Carter and outranks all presidents to follow in the number of wilderness bills signed, wilderness areas created or added to and land designated as wilderness. Ross W. Gorte, "Wilderness: Overview and Statistics," Congressional Research Service, January 25, 2010, 2. Most of the wilderness designations were on U.S. Forest Service lands. *Interior Report 1988*, 9.

86. President Reagan signed nearly 40 wilderness bills and vetoed only two of them: In January 1983, President Reagan vetoed a Florida wilderness bill because it could have required that taxpayers provide $200 million in compensation for privately owned minerals in the restricted area. President Reagan called it "unnecessarily costly to the federal taxpayer." The Florida Sierra Club was "shocked and outraged." "Florida wilderness bill vetoed by Reagan," *St. Petersburg [Florida] Times*, UPI, January 15, 1983, 8A. Watt, in order to prevent mining, denied lease applications by four companies seeking to mine phosphate within the Osceola National Forest and withdrew the eligibility of these lands for future mining. In November 1988, President Reagan "pocket vetoed" a Montana wilderness bill because, at 1.43 million acres, it did not free up enough land and would put "miners and loggers out of work." "Demos hoping wilderness bill veto backfires," *The [Spokane, WA] Spokesman-Review*, Associated Press, November 5, 1988, A6. In addition, the legislation lacked bi-partisan support. Philip Shabecoff, "Reagan Vetoes Bill to Protect 1.4 Million Acres in Montana," *New York Times*, November 4, 1988. Former Senator Gaylord Nelson, lead sponsor of the Wilderness Act of 1964 and "counselor to the Wilderness Society," cried out, "The president's action is unprecedented.... It is a dark day for wilderness preservation." Ibid.

87. One of President Reagan's biographers points out, "[B]y the time Reagan left office his administration had added 38 million acres to various categories of permanent protection (3.1 million acres of additional national park land, and 11.7 million to the National Wilderness Preservation System, for example), and nearly 5,000 miles to the National Wild and Scenic Rivers program and the National Estuarine Reserves." Steven F. Hayward, "Ronald Reagan and the Environment," *inFocus Quarterly* 3, no. 3 (Fall 2009). Reagan was proud of these accomplishments:

> Then I went downstairs & signed a bill—the Wild Scenic Rivers Act—HR 4350—very important to Colorado. For one thing it marks the 1st Colorado stream to be classed as a wild river & preserved as such.

   The Reagan Diaries, 448 (October 30, 1986).

88. U.S. Department of the Interior, National Park Service, "National Parks for the 21st Century: The Vail Agenda," Report and Recommendations to the Director of the National Park Service, 1992, 20. In 1988, Reagan's Interior Department revised the NPS Management Policies to reflect that the Organic Act of 1916 viewed parks as areas to be conserved with a purpose, that is, for the enjoyment of the public. Clinton's Interior Department, as the Vail Agenda suggests, reversed those policies to write people out of the parks.

89. The NPS also returned to its old rapaciousness in seizing private property. Desperate to declare a park a wilderness area, Secretary Salazar ignored the bad science his agency handed him and relied on legalese to eject a family-owned oyster farm and with it the employees and 40 percent of California's oyster production. Felicity Barringer, "A Park, an Oyster Farm and Science: Epilogue," *New York Times*, Green: A Blog About Energy and the Environment, December 4, 2012.

90. Letter from Michael V. Finley, superintendent of Yosemite National Park, to Jesse Brown, dated April 7, 1994. In an attached cover letter Finley notes: "Secretary of the Interior Babbitt has also reviewed the letter and is supportive of the National Park Service position."

91. *Denver Post*, May 28, 1994, 11B.

92. Todd S. Purdum, "Clinton Unveils Plan to Halt Gold Mine Near Yellowstone," August 13, 1996. The article did not discuss that the owner of the mining claims, an elderly local resident, had not been consulted, nor did it mention the lost jobs. The article closed, instead, by noting that Clinton had lost weight. "The President also looks unusually trim. Aides said he had told them he was down to 207 pounds—10 pounds below past confessed levels—and aiming for 200. One secret of his success may be an unusually low-fat diet: On Sunday, he had a whole wheat vegetarian pizza with no cheese and extra artichoke hearts, a far cry from his fattier favorites."

93. Clinton's use of the Land and Water Conservation Fund (LWCF) was unprecedented:

> Until FY1998, LWCF funding rarely exceeded $400 million; from FY1977-FY1980, funding ranged from $509 million (FY1980) to $805 million (FY1978), and averaged $647 million annually. *LWCF appropriations spiked dramatically in FY1998—to $969 million—from the FY1997 level of $159 million.* FY1998 was the first year that LWCF appropriations exceeded the authorized level of $900 million. They included $270 million in the usual funding titles for land acquisition by the four federal land management agencies; *an additional $627 million in a separate title, funding both the acquisition of the Headwaters Forest in California and New World Mine outside Yellowstone National Park*; and $72 million for other programs.

(Emphasis added.) Carol Hardy Vincent, "Land and Water Conservation Fund: Overview, Funding History, and Issues," Congressional Research Service, August 13, 2010, 5.

94.   Paul Richter and Frank Clifford, "Clinton Designates Monument in Utah," *Los Angeles Times*, September 19, 1996. "In his remarks, Clinton implied that he intended to block the mine, which some have said could produce high quality coal with a value of $1 trillion. Clinton said he was 'concerned' about the prospect of the mine. 'We can't have mines everywhere, and we shouldn't have mines that threaten our national treasures,' he said." Ibid.

95.   Marc Lacey, "President Expands Protection For Groves of Giant Sequoias," *New York Times*, April 16, 2000. Tulare County sued President Clinton over his monument decree and its impact on logging jobs and recreational access; however, its lawsuit was dismissed. *Tulare County v. Bush*, 306 F.3d 1138 (D.C. Cir. 2002).

96.   Skinner, *Reagan's Path to Victory*, 279. Obama's Interior embarked on a similar attempt to circumvent the need to enact federal laws to designate wilderness areas by having the Bureau of Land Management designate "wildlands," that is *de facto* wilderness, under Salazar's infamous Order No. 3310. In response to outrage from across the West, Salazar withdrew the order. Amy Joi O'Donoghue, "Critics celebrate death of Salazar's wildlands policy," *Deseret News*, June 1, 2011.

CHAPTER NINE

1.   Ronald Reagan, *Speaking My Mind* (Simon & Schuster, 1989), 392. Senator Alan K. Simpson (R-WY) told his fellow Western senators, "Jim Watt is the man who can grab that [Interior] monster by the throat and make it behave. He knows where all the bones are buried. He knows where the deadwood accumulates. He knows where all the blockage systems are built in. He knows where all the conduits and shunts and leaks are. He knows the bureaucracy." Ron Arnold, *At the Eye of the Storm: James Watt and the Environmentalists* (Regnery Gateway, 1982), 52.

2.   Seth S. King, "Outgoing Interior Secretary Expects No Major Shift Under His Successor," *New York Times*, November 18, 1980, B9.

3.   Arnold, *At the Eye of the Storm*, 26.

4.   Ibid., 47.

5.   See generally, for example, Kiron K. Skinner, Annelise Anderson, and Martin Anderson, eds., *Reagan, In His Own Hand: The Writings of Ronald Reagan That Reveal His Revolutionary Vision for America* (The Free Press, 2001), 318–341, and Kiron K. Skinner, Annelise Anderson, Martin Anderson, Eds., *Reagan's Path to Victory, The Shaping of Ronald Reagan's Vision: Selected Writings* (The Free Press, 2004).

6.   James P. Pfiffner, *The Strategic Presidency: Hitting the Ground Running* (Dorsey Press, 1988), 47.

7.   On January 20, 1982, in a gathering of about 1,500 of the Reagan administration's 2,200 political appointees in the gargantuan Commerce Department auditorium, Watt delivered a stirring paean to President Reagan that closed, to growing and then thunderous applause, as President Reagan entered, "Let Reagan be Reagan." See generally "Reagan toasts his first anniversary: Time to drain the swamp," *The* [Nashua, NH] *Telegraph*, January 21, 1982. Clark was Reagan's "top hand" from Sacramento and the first man to whom he turned for help. Hodel, unknown to President Reagan when Hodel was selected as Watt's first Under Secretary, demonstrated such personal loyalty that he earned two cabinet appointments: Energy (1982) and Interior (1985). He nearly became Reagan's final Attorney General.

8.   Pfiffner, *The Strategic Presidency*, 35. See generally ibid., 25–33, for a discussion of the "troika" composed of Edwin Meese III, James A. Baker III, and Michael Deaver. "[O]nly Meese among the three [was seen by conservatives] as the protector of the 'real Reagan' of ideological purity." Ibid., 26.

9.   Ibid., 48.

10.   David Stockman, *The Triumph of Politics* (Harper & Row, 1986), 113. "The [newly appointed cabinet officers were] in the position of having to argue against the group line," said Stockman. "And the group line is cut, cut, cut." William Greider, "The Education of David Stockman," *Atlantic*, December 1981, 33.

11.   Pfiffner, *The Strategic Presidency*, 13. One "major problem" with the Reagan administration's transition, "the largest and most elaborate in history," was size: "There were 588 listings in the transition telephone directory, but the total number of those involved might have been twice that number." Ibid., 14, citing *Washington Post*, December 15, 1980.

12.   Pfiffner, *The Strategic Presidency*, 13.

13. Ibid. The transition teams received office space in the departments and agencies and full access to budget and program, but not personnel, files. Ibid.

14. Charles L. Heatherly, ed., *Mandate for Leadership: Policy Management in a Conservative Administration* (The Heritage Foundation, 1981), ix, vii. "Chapter 8 – The Department of the Interior" was 68 pages long. Ibid, 333–401.

15. Arnold, *At the Eye of the Storm*, 25. Weeks later, Watt received a rough draft of the chapter; however, due to a copying error, "he had been sent two copies of even-numbered pages and none at all of odd-numbered pages." Ibid.

16. Ibid. Watt remembers with a laugh, "I didn't know enough about Interior to serve on the Heritage Foundation committee and I couldn't get on President Reagan's transition team to help set Interior policy, so the only thing left for me to be was Secretary of the Interior." Ibid., 25–26.

17. See generally ibid., 88–101.

18. Watt met with a transition personnel team—chaired by Helene A. von Damm—that provided Watt a booklet of presidential appointment recommendations. Watt hired an associate of Ms. von Damm, Katherine Baier, as his personal assistant. Subsequently, she served as Deputy Assistant Secretary, Territorial and International Affairs. After the Inauguration, Pen James, Assistant to the President for Presidential Personnel, became a great supporter of Reagan's Interior Department.

19. Arnold, *At the Eye of the Storm*, 14, 17, 200. Watt's successor, Judge Clark, shared Watt's views on deputies. "Nobody voted for them and they are rarely found in the spotlight, but decisions made every day by top deputies in the Reagan administration will go a long way in shaping the nation's future." While their bosses "glide around in their limousines to cabinet meetings and congressional hearings [it is] their top assistants left back at the office who often run the show." "It's the No. 2 Men Who Really Run Government," *U.S. News & World Report*, March 2, 1981, 36.

20. They included these men and women, their positions in late 1980 and (their future positions at Interior): Stephen P. Shipley of Jackson, Wyoming, current and former colleague, MSLF Vice President (Executive Assistant to the Secretary); Douglas P. Baldwin of Lander, Wyoming, former congressional aide and colleague, Director of Communications, Interstate Commerce Commission (Assistant to the Secretary for Public Affairs); Emily DeRocco of Carlisle, Pennsylvania, former colleague, Assistant Executive Director, Interstate Commerce Commission (Assistant to the Secretary); Moody R. Tidwell III, Esq. of Miami, Oklahoma, former colleague, U.S. Department of Labor (Deputy Solicitor and Counselor to the Secretary); David C. Russell of Arlington, Virginia, new friend, Professional Staff Member, U.S. Senate Energy and Natural Resources Committee (Deputy Assistant Secretary – Land and Water Resources); and William Perry Pendley of Cheyenne, Wyoming, old friend, Minority Counsel, Mines and Mining Subcommittee, U.S. House of Representatives Interior and Insular Affairs Committee (Deputy Assistant Secretary—Energy and Minerals). See Arnold, *At the Eye of the Storm*, 56–57.

21. Hodel, former head of the Bonneville Power Administration (BPA), in the private sector in 1980, was a former Chairman of the Oregon Republican Party. Oregon Senators Mark Hatfield and Bob Packwood, both Republicans, supported his nomination. Watt hired Hodel in 1969 as Deputy Administrator, BPA; over the years, they became close friends.

22. The appointees and their political sponsors included: G. Ray Arnett, former Director, California Department of Fish and Game under Governor Ronald Reagan, selected, from a list of one, as Assistant Secretary, Fish, Wildlife and Parks; Garrey E. Carruthers, Professor, New Mexico State University (Senator Pete V. Domenici (R-NM)), selected as Assistant Secretary, Land and Water Resources; Daniel N. Miller, Jr., Wyoming State Geologist (Senator Malcolm Wallop (R-WY)), selected as Assistant Secretary, Energy and Minerals; Kenneth L. Smith, General Manager of the Warm Springs Tribe in Oregon (Senators Hatfield and Packwood (R-OR)) selected as Assistant Secretary, Indian Affairs; William H. Coldiron, Esq., Director, Montana Power Company (Congressman Ron Marlenee (R-2nd MT)), selected as Solicitor; Richard Mulberry, Executive Partner Fox & Co., Dallas, Texas (Senator John G. Tower (R-TX)), selected as Inspector General; Robert F. Burford, Speaker, Colorado House of Representatives (Senator William L. Armstrong (R-CO)), selected as Director, Bureau of Land Management; James R. Harris, Indiana State Senator (Senator Richard Lugar (R-IN)), selected as Director, Office of Surface Mining Reclamation and Enforcement; Robert C. Horton, Director, Geology Division, Bendix Field Engineering Corp. (Senator Paul Laxalt (R-NV)), selected as Director, Bureau of Mines; Robert A. Jantzen, Director, Arizona Game and Fish Department (Senator Barry Goldwater (R-AZ)), selected as Director, U.S. Fish and Wildlife Service; Robert N. Broadbent, Clark County (Nevada) Commissioner (Senator Paul Laxalt (R-NV)), selected as Commissioner, Bureau of Reclamation; Derrell P. Thompson, selected as Western Representative,

Department of the Interior; and Vernon R. Wiggins, Executive Director and Secretary, Citizens for the Management of Alaska Lands, Inc., (Senator Ted Stevens (R-AK)), selected as Federal Cochairman of the Alaska Land Use Council.

23. J. Robinson West of Bryn Mawr, Pennsylvania, was selected as Assistant Secretary, Policy, Budget and Administration. In addition, Pedro San Juan of Havana, Cuba, who had served on the State Department Transition Team, was selected as Assistant Secretary, Territorial and International Affairs.

24. As to the U.S. Geological Survey, Governor Reagan had blasted Secretary Andrus for firing the director for partisan reasons. After the National Academy of Sciences "highly recommended" the chief geologist, Dallas L. Peck, as director, Watt forwarded the recommendation to the White House. Watt recognized that the director of the National Park Service should be someone who bled "green and grey" and therefore recommended the retention of Russell E. Dickenson, who had been named director in March 1980 by the Carter administration. The White House agreed to both. Senator Henry Jackson (D-WA) brought up the "revolving door directorship" at the NPS. *Watt Nomination Hearings*, 76–77.

25. The deputies included: William P. Horn of Dover, DE, Minority Counsel to the House Interior Committee recommended by Senator Ted Stevens (R-AK) and Congressman Don Young (R-AK), Deputy Under Secretary; Frank DuBois, a New Mexico cowboy and policy analyst with the New Mexico Department of Agriculture recommended by Senator Domenici, Deputy Assistant Secretary for Land and Water Resources; John W. Fritz of St. Paul, MN, counsel to 3M in Minneapolis, Minnesota, Deputy Assistant Secretary, Indian Affairs; Richard R. Hite of Columbus, GA, a career civil servant known to Watt from Watt's prior service at Interior, Deputy Assistant Secretary for Policy, Budget, and Administration; Diane Kay Morales, a Texan with 3D/International in Houston, Deputy Assistant Secretary for Territorial and International Affairs; J. Craig Potter, a Wyomingite with the U.S. Senate Appropriations Committee recommended by Senator James A. McClure (R-ID), Deputy Assistant Secretary for Fish, Wildlife, and Parks; J. Steven Griles, a Virginian and Deputy Director, Virginia Department of Conservation and Economic Development, recommended by Senator John Warner (R-VA), Deputy Director, Office of Surface Mining Reclamation and Enforcement; Mary Lou Grier, a Texan, Deputy Director, National Park Service; James F. McAvoy of Elizabeth, NJ, Deputy Director, Bureau of Mines; Roy Sampsel, from Oregon, Executive Director of the Columbia River Inter-Tribal Fish Commission in Portland, recommended by Senators Hatfield and Packwood, Deputy Assistant Secretary for Indian Affairs; and Gordon S. Jones of Salt Lake City, UT, and David S. Brown of Athens, OH, Congressional and Legislative Affairs responsibility for the Senate and House respectively. The Associate Solicitors included: Maurice O. Ellsworth, born in Globe, AZ, but an Idaho lawyer, Audit and Inspection; Alexander H. Good of Los Angeles, CA, Energy and Resources; Lawrence J. Jenson of Salt Lake City, UT, Indian Affairs; William H. Satterfield, Birmingham, AL, General Law; J. Roy ("JR") Spradley, Jr. of Washington, D.C., Conservation and Wildlife; and Donald R. Tindal of Washington, D.C., Surface Mining.

26. Doyle G. Frederick, a career USGS employee, was named Deputy Director to Peck; F. Eugene Hester, a career Fish and Wildlife Service employee, was named Deputy Director to Jantzen; and James M. Parker, a career Bureau of Land Management employee, was named Deputy Director to Burford.

27. Watt also named Stanley W. Hulett of California, a former Interior colleague, Assistant to the Secretary for Congressional and Legislative Affairs, and Theodore J. Garrish, Esq. of Michigan and a veteran of the Nixon White House, Chief Legislative Counsel. See generally "Taming the Bureaucracy," Arnold, *At the Eye of the Storm*, 125–42.

28. Earlier in the day, Watt issued a directive reaffirming, as to Interior, President Reagan's hiring freeze, a ban on all but the "most essential" travel, a survey of all consulting contracts currently in place, and a review of all proposed foreign travel. Arnold, *At the Eye of the Storm*, 92. "You have to strike fast in this business. Influence is a very perishable commodity. You can lose it practically overnight. You have to use what you've got when you've got it. For me that's right now." Tony Brown, "Watt: Development Right, Time Wrong," *Argus Leader* [Sioux Falls], April 7, 1982, located in *Newsbank*, EVN 34: F13.

29. Arnold, *At the Eye of the Storm*, 93.

30. Ibid. The "Schedule C" positions to which Watt referred, "are excepted from the competitive service by law, by Executive Order, or by the Office of Personnel Management (OPM) based on their responsibility for determining or advocating agency policy or their confidential character" and "the incumbent serves at the pleasure of the agency head." http://www.opm.gov/transition/trans20r-ch1. htm#top. Nonetheless, *Rolling Stone* described Watt's dismissal of Carter's Schedule C appointees

thusly: "It was like a Russian purge ... to take control of the Interior Department." Howard Kohn, "After James Watt, What?" *Rolling Stone*, October 15, 1981, xx.

31.   Arnold, *At the Eye of the Storm*, 93.

32.   Ibid. Four years earlier, Secretary Andrus advised many of these same employees:

> I am a part of the environmental movement and I intend to make Interior responsive to the movement's needs. We intend to break up the little fiefdoms which have divided Interior for years ... The place is like a centipede with each little pair of feet scuttling off in its own direction. That is going to change. Policy-making will be centralized and it will be responsive to my philosophy and the philosophy of President Carter. And, our philosophy does not include allowing developers to crank up the bulldozers and run rough-shod over the Public Domain.

Ibid., 94.

33.   Ibid., 93–94.

34.   Early on, Watt decided to stop reading the *Washington Post* and its unrelenting attacks on President Reagan, the president's policies, and Watt's efforts to implement those policies at Interior. One piece of advice he gave frequently—using his own experience as an example—was not to permit the *New York Times* or the *Washington Post* to set the daily agenda of Reagan's Interior Department. This was especially the case for those appearing on Capitol Hill. Typically the *Washington Post* writers worked with Senate and House aides and radical environmental groups to frame the day's congressional hearings with front page "news" stories. In the 1980s, long before cable news, talk radio, and the internet, there was only one spin on the news, and it spun left.

35.   Watt was generous with advice, which was typically professional but could be personal, whether it came straight on with a "Remember ... " or was the result of a discussion following a question such as, "Why in the world would you say that?" "Remember, your true friends were your friends before you got your fancy title." "Hire people you trust then trust them." "Remember what's important: your wife and your family." "Make the right policy decision as quickly as possible but take the time to implement it in the smartest way possible." "Be honest with those you trust." "Make as many decisions as you can; if you work hard, your successor will not be able to undo everything you've done." "Test people who bring you recommendations that you are supposed to approve to make sure they did their homework and will stand their ground; then sign!" "When someone gives you a document, ask, 'Is this your best work?' Read it only if the answer is 'Yes!'" "Anyone can manage down; it takes talent to manage up."

36.   Tidwell once asked Watt who should attend a particular meeting. Watt told him, "Those who are supposed to be there will come." Tidwell asked the origin of that point of view. Watt said that, in high school, when the football coach told the first string to take the field, the first string took the field. "They knew they were supposed to be there," said Watt.

37.   See generally Arnold, *At the Eye of the Storm*, 137–42. Watt first used an MBO program when he became Director of the Bureau of Outdoor Recreation in 1972. Ibid., 17–20. Not surprisingly, by this time, there was already a nascent MBO program in place covering the initial tasks and crisis level aspects of assuming command. From his first days at the Interior Department, before anyone but Watt had been confirmed, Hodel kept a list of assignments, the person responsible, and accompanying milestones, which became a "mini-MBO" that Hodel ran out of his notebook.

38.   Ibid., 139.

39.   Ibid.

40.   Assistant Secretary for Indian Affairs Kenneth L. Smith recalled that the MBO system required that those in charge "bear down to make it happen." "You have to spend time ... asking about target dates, are we on target, and continuously use it, because if you stop, everybody else will just go back to the easy way." Ibid., 141.

41.   Arnold, *At the Eye of the Storm*, 126. See generally 125–30.

42.   As a result, "Every senior manager in every bureau of the Department, about 800 of them, has personal contact with the Secretary once each month." Ibid., 128.

43.   Ibid., 129–30. Watt's insistence on being visible and available was the result of his experience at Interior. "When I was working here in the Bureau of Outdoor Recreation and in Water and Power Resources, I know that months went by without an Assistant Secretary seeing the Secretary. Bureau heads would go long periods of time without seeing the Secretary. They might see him on television or giving testimony up on the Hill, but not in one-on-one conversations." Ibid., 130. Aware that

thousands of Interior employees spread throughout the West knew him only by what they saw on television or read in magazines and newspapers, Watt met personally with Interior employees, discussed President Reagan's policies and his efforts, with their help, to implement those policies, and then opened up for long question and answer periods. In the summer of 1981, he met with more than 5,000 employees in eight states. Arnold, *At the Eye of the Storm*, 196–97.

44.   Watt's office was a small spartan one off the ornate ceremonial office used by other secretaries. Two framed plaques were posted near his desk: "'Duty, Honor, Country' General Douglas MacArthur" and "'Persistence Forges Results' Calvin Coolidge." The longer Coolidge quote is "Nothing in the world can take the place of persistence. Talent will not; nothing is more common than unsuccessful men with talent. Genius will not; unrewarded genius is almost a proverb. Education will not; the world is full of educated derelicts. Persistence and determination alone are omnipotent. The slogan Press On! has solved and always will solve the problems of the human race." Arnold, *At the Eye of the Storm*, 1.

45.   The MBO program even made its way into field offices, including a Bureau of Land Management office in Battle Mountain, Nevada. Arnold, *At the Eye of the Storm*, 238.

46.   Congressional hearings, for example where attendance is mandatory, exact a considerable cost in time, energy, manpower, and angst. The official testifying does not travel to Capitol Hill alone, and that appearance is preceded by days of preparation during which much paperwork is generated. During its first two years, Reagan's Interior Department participated in 152 congressional hearings for an average of 1.25 hearings each legislative day. Watt testified on the average of once every twelve legislative days. "1983 – A Year Of Enrichment: Improving The Quality Of Life For All Americans," (U.S. Department of the Interior, October 1983), 37.

47.   Davis W. Houck and Amos Kiewe, eds., *Actor, Ideologue, Politician: The Public Speeches of Ronald Reagan* (Greenwood, 1993), 178–79.

48.   "The Reagan Revolution was about shrinking the size of the federal government, not merely slowing its rate of growth nor fine-tuning specific federal programs." Robert F. Durant, *The Administrative Presidency Revisited: Public Lands, the BLM, and the Reagan Revolution* (State University of New York Press, 1992), 52.

49.   Arnold, *At the Eye of the Storm*, 132. On March 10, 1981, the Reagan administration released its detailed budget proposal. Ibid. In January and early February 1981, with the assistance of each of Interior's budget managers, his top advisors and deputy assistant secretaries, and selected career professionals, Watt went line-by-line through "the entire budget of 8 major divisions, 11 major bureaus, 13 major offices, hundreds of programs, and 80,000 employees." Ibid. "How, then, was President Reagan able to make such dramatic changes in President Carter's lame-duck budget? By March 10, only forty-nine days after taking office, he submitted to Congress a complete revision of the FY 1982 budget.... The personal wills and political skills of Ronald Reagan and David Stockman were crucial to the Reagan administration's unprecedented budget victories in 1981." Pfiffner, *The Strategic Presidency*, 104.

50.   Watt's announced criteria for screening budget proposals included these three questions: "(1) Was there a compelling reason why the government should exercise its power to do the activity or could it be done by the private sector? (2) If it were properly a governmental function, should it be done by the federal government or could state and local governments do it? (3) If it were a federal responsibility, was it being done well or was the federal government, in fact, a part of the problem?" Arnold, *In the Eye of the Storm*, 137.

51.   "Facilities in Many National Parks and Forests Do Not Meet Health and Safety Standards" (CED-80-115) (October 10, 1980).

52.   Mission 66 was a National Park Service–wide plan to update the parks in preparation for the 50th anniversary of the NPS in 1966. National Park Service Archives, Harpers Ferry, General Collection Box A8213, Folder entitled, "Cabinet Meeting, Mission 66 Presentation, January 27, 1956." "Channeling use" for "visitor enjoyment" was the principle that revised how the parks functioned as public places. Ethan Carr, Mission 66: *Modernism and the National Park Dilemma* (University of Massachusetts Press, 2007), 266–68.

53.   Over a decade (1971–1982), the fund had financed nearly a threefold expansion of the national park system, from 24.4 to 68.5 million acres. Paul J. Culhane, "Sagebrush Rebels in Office: Jim Watt's Land and Water Politics," in Norman J. Vig and Michael E. Kraft, eds., *Environmental Policy in the 1980s: Reagan's New Agenda* (CQ Press, 1984), 309.

54.   See *Sagebrush Rebel*, Chapter 8. "Federal Protection and Preservation of Wild and Scenic Rivers is Slow and Costly" (CED-78-96) (May 22, 1978); "Review of the National Park Service's Urban

National Recreation Area Program" (CED-79-98) (June 19, 1979); "The Federal Drive to Acquire Private Lands Should be Reassessed" (CED-80-14) (December 19, 1979); "Federal Land Acquisitions by Condemnation—Opportunities to Reduce Delays and Costs" (CED-80-54) (May 14, 1980); "Lands in the Lake Chelan National Recreation Area Should be Returned to Private Ownership" (CED-81-10) (January 22, 1981); "The National Park Service Should Improve its Land Acquisition and Management at the Fire Island National Seashore" (CED-81-78) (May 8, 1981).

55.   "Virtually every park in the National Park Service was touched by a $1 billion Park Restoration and Improvement Program begun in 1982 to rehabilitate deteriorated and unsafe facilities. Significant improvements were made to water and sewer systems, overnight accommodations and the correction of health and safety problems." "America – Our Treasure and Our Trust: The Legacy of President Ronald Reagan 1981 – 1988," (U.S. Department of the Interior, December 1988), 96. "In our first three years we sought a billion dollars to repair and rehabilitate the dilapidated infrastructure within our national parks. In the past eight years, we have put more than $3.5 billion into fixing up our national parks so that visitors and employees alike could safely enjoy the beauty and wonders of our parks." *Interior Report 1988*, 10. Reagan's Interior Department obtained congressional approval to increase entrance fees at many parks and to authorize collection of fees at refuges; these new and increased fees will generate $.5 billion over a ten year period. Ibid., 11.

56.   In a speech to the Conference of National Park Concessioners, Watt declared, "We will use the budget system to be the excuse to make major policy decisions." Elizabeth Drew, "A Reporter At Large," *New Yorker*, May 4, 1981, 128–30.

57.   Durant, *The Administrative Presidency Revisited*, 53, citing Jeanne N. Clark and Daniel McCool, *Staking Out the Terrain: Power Differentials Among Natural Resource Management Agencies* (Albany State University of New York Press, 1985), ch. 4; Paul R. Portney, ed., *Natural Resources and the Environment: The Reagan Approach* (Urban Institute Press, 1984); John D. Leshy, "Natural Resources Policy"; "Watt's Clashes with Congress Stall Program," *Congressional Quarterly Weekly* Reports, July 11, 1981, 1256–1258. Arnold reports that Reagan's Interior Department "slashed $66.6 million from the Office of Surface Mining, leaving a $179.8 [million] budget. Funding for regulatory enforcement was cut $10 million, reflecting Watt's intent to stress state primacy in surface mining enforcement." Arnold, *At the Eye of the Storm*, 134.

58.   For the record, Watt declared, "[The decision] provides a good opportunity to absorb skilled personnel from HCRS into the Park Service where a substantial number of vacancies exist." On a related note, that is, a moratorium on recreation funding, Watt said, "State and local government funding for recreation in 1981 is about $5.7 billion; our total moratorium is less than $300 million. The nation will not be without recreation opportunities while this moratorium is in effect." Arnold, *At the Eye of the Storm*, 133.

59.   *Interior Report 1983*, 37. In addition to the HCRS, functions of both the Office of Minerals Policy and Research Analysis and the Office of Water Research and Technology were absorbed by other bureaus. In addition to cost and personnel savings, the mergers "eliminated overlapping jurisdictions and duplicative functions." Similar streamlining occurred when Reagan's Interior Department consolidated onshore mineral leasing activities in the Bureau of Land Management. Ibid. Reagan's Interior Department continued to initiate and implement major reorganizations to eliminate redundancies, achieve efficiencies, and reduce federal expenditures and full-time employees. For example: a Bureau of Reclamation reorganization removed a layer of bureaucracy at headquarters, reduced overlap in the planning, engineering, and research operations, and realigned the regional offices from seven to five. At the same time, the Bureau of Reclamation expanded its role to include water management while preserving its traditional construction orientation. *Interior Report 1988*, 54, 96. A Bureau of Mines reorganization reduced directorates from six to three, reduced programmatic divisions from twelve to seven, reduced the number of Grade 15 positions from forty-seven to thirty-six and the number of Grade 13 and 14 positions from 208 to 196, while improving the supervisor-to-employee ratio from 1:8 to 1:9. At the same time, a Bureau of Mines research facility (Avondale, Maryland) was closed to achieve an annual savings of $1.2 million. Ibid., 96–97.

60.   Durant, *The Administrative Presidency Revisited*, 53. Arnold reports that Reagan's Interior Department "reduced the Carter administration's Fiscal Year (FY) 1982 budget request by $877 million to a total of $5.76 billion, as well as rescission of $383 million in FY 1981 funds." Arnold, *At the Eye of the Storm*, 132.

61.   *Interior Report 1988*, 93–94. Nonetheless, over the course of the Reagan administration, Interior's budget declined by 15% in real spending power. Ibid., 94. DuBois recalls the rare instance when the OMB thought a Reagan Interior cut in the BLM grazing budget was too large. DuBois fought back

and got the cut he wanted through OMB and the House; however, a conservative Western senator put the funds back into the budget on the advice of a Western ranching association.

62. *Interior Report 1983*, 38. Some members of the media reported correctly that, in March 1981, Watt fired 51 Interior employees hired by Carter's Interior Department, in Watt's words, in "blatant disregard of the budget and hiring laws." "The 'Sagebrush Rebel' Shaking Up Interior," *U.S. News & World Report*, March 30, 1981, 8. In fact, Carter's Assistant Secretary for Policy, Budget, and Administration had faulted the Solicitor's office for the hires because they exceeded budget authority by $1.3 million. Discharged were 14 full-time lawyers, 4 part-time lawyers, and 33 clerks; later Watt authorized the hiring of four full-time lawyers, an action that was authorized by Watt's budget authority. Arnold, *In the Eye of the Storm*, 88, 98.

63. *Interior Report 1988*, 94. In fiscal year 1982, which began on October 1, 1981, the full-time equivalent (FIE) personnel target for Interior was 79,225, but Interior's actual usage was 73,225. By fiscal year 1988, the FTE target had decreased by 8,768 and actual usage had declined by 2,890. Ibid. The Office of Personnel Management (OPM) reported that, during President Reagan's first term, over 39,000 voluntary and involuntary separations occurred at Interior as a result of reductions in force (RIFs), reductions in grade, forced furloughs, and reorganization. Nonetheless, the number of full-time permanent employees increased at Reagan's Interior Department; however, not surprisingly, the increases took place "predominantly in positions related to energy and mineral production." Durant, *The Administrative Presidency Revisited*, 57–58. Attempts to eliminate unnecessary or redundant federal full-time employees (FTEs) continued throughout the Reagan administration. In 1984, the consolidation of "payroll input offices" to two locations resulted in the elimination of 55 FTEs and an annual savings of $1 million. *Interior Report 1988*, 110. In 1988, for example, reorganization of the Bureau of Reclamation resulted in creation of a Technical Service Center to ensure "better use of scarce technical expertise." The projected savings of $7.5 million a year were the result of elimination of 200 FTEs. *Interior Report 1988*, 109. In an anomalous example, when the United States ended its administration of the Trust Territories of the Pacific Islands (including the Republic of the Marshall Islands and the Federated States of Micronesia) in 1986, Reagan's Interior Department had a reduction of 20 full-time employees. *Interior Report 1988*, 105.

64. President Reagan's initiatives included those of the White House, the President's Task Force on Management Reform, the President's Council on Integrity and Efficiency, the Grace Commission, the Inspectors General, the Office of Management and Budget, the General Service Administration, the Office of Personnel Management, the Assistant Secretaries for Management and Administration Group, and departments and agencies. All of these efforts were backed by the Cabinet Council on Management and Administration. Mark A. McBriarty, "Reform 88: A Sense of Déjà Vu," *The American Review of Public Administration* 18, no. 1 (March 1988): 56, (DOI: 10.1177/027507408801800104).

65. President Ronald Reagan, "Radio Address to the Nation on Organ Donorship and on Reform 88," July 30, 1983, http://www.presidency.ucsb.edu/ws/index.php?pid=41663; Reform 88 was launched officially by Meese in a White House Press Release, Washington, D.C., September 22, 1982. OMB Deputy Director Joe Wright called it "[T]he biggest reform ever undertaken in this government." *The Bureaucrat* 12 (Summer 1983), 11.

66. President Reagan's remarks to the Management Reform Group, Press Release, White House, August 2, 1983.

67. Mark A. McBriarty, "Reform 88: A Sense of Déjà Vu," *The American Review of Public Administration* 18, no. 1 (March 1988): 47 (DOI: 10.1177/027507408801800104).

68. Ibid., 54.

69. Ibid., 55.

70. Edwin Meese, *White House Press Release*, Washington, D.C., September 22, 1982, 2. See also, Chester Newland, "The Reagan Presidency," *Public Administration Review* 43 (Jan/Feb 1983), 1–22, and Dick Kirschten, "OMB's Wright Plots 'Quiet Revolution' in the Way U.S. Agencies Do Business," *National Journal* (October 30, 1982), 1846–47.

71. John Cole, "An Interview with Joe Wright," *The Bureaucrat* 12 (Summer 1983), 10. Reform 88 differed from past efforts not only because it was about process and not policy and because it recognized the political organization in Washington, including Congress and the bureaucracy, but also because it had presidential interest, cabinet-level support, and direct agency participation; because OMB worked, not as a commander but as a collaborator; and because OMB did not invade the traditional territory of agency budget examiners but did insist, to the advantage of the agency, on a Management Review of costs savings as a result of Project 88 and their recognition in the budget

statement. Mark A. McBriarty, "Reform 88: A Sense of Déjà Vu," *The American Review of Public Administration* 18, no. 1 (March 1988): 55–56 (DOI: 10.1177/027507408801800104).

72. *Interior Report 1983*, 37 and *Interior Report 1988*, 110. The conversion to one system in one location also "reduced staffing, improved consistency in classifying and reporting data, simplified payroll/personnel training, enhanced consistent interpretation of laws and regulations, improved responsiveness to internal and external requests, improved user satisfaction, and strengthened internal control." Ibid.

73. Ibid., 109. For example, "outstanding travel advance balances were reduced from $11.9 million in 1981 to an expected $3.7 million by the end of calendar 1988." Ibid. Moreover, early institution of "wire transfers for major minerals royalty receipts and abandoned mined land fees [saved] taxpayers an estimated $1.2 million in interest carrying costs." *Interior Report 1983*, 38.

74. *Interior Report 1988*, 96.

75. *Interior Report 1983*, 38. This exceeded the requirement of the Paperwork Reduction Act.

76. Ibid., 37–38. *Interior Report 1988*, 108, reports that the program "increased receipts on federal mineral leases and Indian mineral leases by over $300 million and denied improper requests for refunds for over $90 million."

77. *Interior Report 1983*, 38. These efforts by the Interior Department were also in furtherance of the requirements of the Federal Managers' Financial Integrity Act of 1982, September 8, 1982, P.L. 97-255. Interior chaired an interagency study group on paperwork requirements associated with implementing the Act, which resulted in revisions OMB Circular A-123. *Interior Report 1988*, 111.

78. *Interior Report 1988*, 109–10.

79. Ibid., 103.

80. Ibid., 110.

81. Ibid. Interior was one of only four civilian agencies to achieve that rate of savings and was rated "the most efficient user of energy (measure in BTU/gsf) in [a] federally owned building[]." Ibid.

82. Ibid., 111. Subsequently, more than 8,000 units owned by the U.S. Forest Service, Bureau of Prisons, and other agencies were added to the QMIS system. Ibid.

83. This effort to devolve federal responsibilities to the private sector is in addition to the devolution to state and local entities of various responsibilities pursuant to President Reagan's Good Neighbor policy and in accordance with his Executive Order 12612 on Federalism.

84. Ibid., 104. Issued on November 19, 1987, Executive Order 12615 sought to "[e]nsure that new Federal Government requirements for commercial activities are provided by private industry, except where statute or national security requires government performance or where private industry costs are unreasonable."; http://www.archives.gov/federal-register/codification/executive-order/12615.html.

85. *Interior Report 1988*, 55, 104.

86. Ibid., 103. In FY 1983, 58% of Interior's procurement obligations was with small businesses, compared to 42% in FY 1980; 11.5% was with minority businesses, compared with 10% in 1983; and 20% was set aside for award to businesses located or performing in areas of high unemployment, compared to 8% in 1980. In 1983, Interior created the Office of Historically Black Colleges and University Programs and provided $2.5 million in contracts, procurement and training. *Interior Report 1983*, 38. From 1981 through FY 1988, Interior's contracting with small businesses averaged nearly 59% and peaked at 67% in FY 1984. *Interior Report 1988*, 105.

87. Ibid., 109.

88. Ibid., 110.

89. Ibid., 103. Interior's study of the preexisting systems found them to be "labor intensive, expensive, technologically outdated, and incompatible." Ibid.

90. Congressional amendments to the Volunteers in the Parks Act during FY 1985 through FY 1988 barred the Bureau of Land Management, Fish and Wildlife Service, and National Park Service from any private sector contracts involving fewer than ten full-time federal employees unless specifically approved by Congress. In FY 1988, the House and Senate Appropriations Committee reports required a specific request of Congress for Bureau of Reclamation to conduct a private sector contracting review (OMB Circular A-76) and the Indian Self Determination and Education Assistance Act provides tribes with the right of first refusal of any activity conducted pursuant to A-76. Ibid., VI–12.

91. Ronald Reagan, Executive Order 12291–Federal Regulation, February 17, 1981, http://www.presidency.ucsb.edu/ws/index.php?pid=43424.

92. Remarks Announcing the Establishment of the Presidential Task Force on Regulatory Relief, January 22, 1981, http://www.reagan.utexas.edu/archives/speeches/1981/12281c.htm.
93. See, for example, *Sagebrush Rebel*, chapter 1, chapter 2, chapter 3, and chapter 10.
94. For the history of regulations, see "Regulationism," Arnold, *At the Eye of the Storm*, 143–56.
95. http://www.presidency.ucsb.edu/ws/index.php?pid=43424; The Office of Management and Budget (OMB) reports that President Reagan's regulatory reform effort differed from past efforts "in a number of important respects:"

> First, it required that agencies not only prepare cost-benefit analyses for major rules, but also that they issue only regulations that maximize net benefits (social benefits minus social costs). Second, OMB, and within OMB the Office of Information and Regulatory Affairs (OIRA), replaced CWPS [President Ford's Council on Wage and Price Stability] as the agency responsible for centralized review. Third, agencies were required to send their proposed regulations and cost-benefit analyses in draft form to OMB for review before they were issued. Fourth, it required agencies to review their existing regulations to see which ones could be withdrawn or scaled back. Finally, President Reagan created The Task Force on Regulatory Relief, chaired by then-Vice President Bush, to oversee the process and serve as an appeal mechanism if the agencies disagreed with OMB's recommendations. Together these steps established a more formal and comprehensive centralized regulatory oversight program.

    http://www.whitehouse.gov/omb/inforeg_chap1#trbrp.
96. *Interior Report 1983*, 37. Watt sought to remove "excessive regulations," "unnecessary red tape," and "unnecessary burdens." Regulations should not be "ends unto themselves, [but only] a means to an end … protecting the environment and the basic values of our nation…. " Arnold, *At the Eye of the Storm*, 135.
97. *Interior Report 1988*, 111–13.
98. *Interior Report 1988*, 111. Major regulatory reform efforts continued in the Solicitor's office, which addressed a number of statutes, including the Trans-Alaska Pipeline Authorization Act, the Program Fraud Civil Remedies Act, and the Civil Rights Restoration Act; in addition, the Solicitor's Hazardous Waste Task Force addressed the environmental protection requirements of a number of environmental statutes. Ibid., 112-113. Meanwhile, Interior's technical experts in the Bureau of Mines advised other federal agencies regarding the feasibility of draft regulations regarding asbestos as distinguished from other mineral particles. Ibid.,113.
99. Ibid., 11. In 1985, President Reagan further strengthened regulatory review during his administration by issuing Executive Order 12498, Regulatory Planning Process, January 4, 1985, http://www.presidency.ucsb.edu/ws/index.php?pid=38024. Under that order, federal agencies were required to send OMB annually "detailed plans" of the "significant rules" they had under development as to which OMB could recommend modifications. OMB then published the descriptions of the most important rules, typically about 500, in a large volume entitled, *Regulatory Program of the U.S. Government*, http://www.whitehouse.gov/omb/inforeg_chap1#trbrp.
100. Ronald Reagan, *An American Life: The Autobiography* (Simon & Schuster, 1990), 250–51.
101. President Reagan was "the quintessential practitioner of the administrative presidency, wielding its tools with a comprehensiveness, vigor, and relentlessness unparalleled in his predecessors." Durant, *The Administrative Presidency Revisited*, xi. President Reagan "relentlessly applied an administrative strategy to the pursuit of his policy goals in a fashion and to an extent unprecedented in terms of its strategic significance, scope, and philosophical zeal." He sought to "alter the size, scope, and ends of the federal government" by (1) changing budgets and personnel; (2) revising regulations; (3) appointing "movement" conservatives; (4) reorganizing departments and agencies; (5) monitoring agency performance; and, (6) devolving federal activities to the states. Ibid., 4.
102. Watt recognized this immediately, of course. Arnold, *At the Eye of the Storm*,130–31.
103. "Perhaps at no time has the administrative presidency been more rabidly applied in pursuit of an incumbent's agenda than in the Reagan administration. And perhaps nowhere did this Administration more enthusiastically, contentiously, and with less apology apply the strategy than in the area of natural resource policy [as to which] several of the President's most passionately committed and resourceful devotees labored…." Durant, *The Administrative Presidency Revisited*, 11. "Ronald Reagan pursued an energetic, enterprising, and philosophically based politicizing strategy that far eclipsed all his recent predecessors' efforts, with the probable exception of FDR. Indeed, many

concluded that Reagan's cabinet and subcabinet appointments were the most partisan and ideological of any president of the past twenty years." Ibid., 37.

104. The numerous federal land laws "give the interior secretary broad administrative powers over the use of federal lands." C. Brant Short, *Ronald Reagan and the Public Lands: America's Conservation Debate, 1979–1984* (Texas A&M University Press, 1989), 148–49, citing Kathy Koch, "Reagan Shifts U.S. Land Policies on Public Land Management," *Congressional Quarterly* (October 3, 1981): 1899. Nonetheless, environmentalists attacked Reagan's Interior Department for using the mechanisms at its and every other incoming administration's disposal to effect the change desired by the President: budget, personnel, and regulations. "Rather than using a legislative approach, Reagan relied on 'administrative fiat'—reorganizing federal agencies; significantly reducing or reallocating money and personnel; altering, withdrawing, or weakening the enforcement of federal regulations; and placing like-minded loyalists in key positions within the federal bureaucracy." Jeffrey K. Stine, "Natural Resources and Environmental Policy," 233, in W. Elliot Brownlee and Hugh Davis Graham, eds., *The Reagan Presidency: Pragmatic Conservatism & Its Legacies* (University Press of Kansas, 2003).

105. "Watt is everything Reagan wanted at Interior, a conservative hardliner, a business sympathizer who would reduce government regulation and appease members of the Sagebrush Rebellion, a tough administrator determined to stimulate more energy and minerals production from public lands." Ron Wolf, "New Voice in the Wilderness," *Rocky Mountain Magazine* (March/April 1981): 34. Hodel praised Watt's accomplishments. "If I had been Secretary, we'd still be holding meetings with the Sierra Club trying to figure out if we didn't have some common ground and none of this would have gotten done.... Watt has done more in this single year than most Secretaries achieve in a whole Presidency, and he did it under the most appallingly stressful conditions imaginable." Arnold, *At the Eye of the Storm*, 229.

106. During his confirmation hearings, Watt advised the Senate that he would not seek additional legislative authority. Short, *Ronald Reagan and the Public Lands*, 57. During House hearings regarding the fiscal year 1982 budget, Watt admitted that he was making major policy changes by revising the budget. Arnold, *At the Eye of the Storm*, 136–37.

107. "I'm ready to make a decision and if it's wrong and someone can talk me out of it, I'm ready to make a new one," was a frequent opener for Watt during secretarial decision meetings. In response, the presenter, most usually a career professional, would quickly chide, "Not yet, Mr. Secretary, let us brief you fully on the options." Watt would grin, look around the room, and open his briefing book. One brief account of a decision meeting is set forth in Arnold, *At the Eye of the Storm*, 2.

108. Watt was always laudatory in his praise of career employees:

> Skeptics had warned me that I would get little cooperation and that changing the direction of the Department would be slow, tedious, and frustrating, and, in the end, fruitless. Boy, were they wrong! Instead of opposition and resistance, most of these people agreed with the need for changes in programs and policies. With very few exceptions, the career workers pitched in with the new leadership and revamped programs, made constructive suggestions, trimmed budgets, and implemented mandated changes. They were terrific.

Arnold, *At the Eye of the Storm*, 197.

109. "The lesson from the Reagan years is that, at least under the conditions of the administrative presidency and at the upper echelons of federal agencies, presidents can expect a fairly high degree of responsiveness from the career bureaucrats in the executive branch.... [C]ivil servants cooperated with the administration out of respect for their appointed bosses [and] because the agency's leadership engendered good will through their own attitudes and behavior...." Marissa Martino Golden, *What Motivates Bureaucrats? Politics and Administration During The Reagan Years* (Columbia University Press, 2000), 152, 154.

110. Clark and Hodel operated in the same manner. The absence of "back channels" and the presence of clear lines of authority not only built confidence in the assistant secretaries and their deputies, but also created respect for those officials in the leadership and employees of the bureaus that reported to them.

111. "Watt left office with a substantial record." Short, *Ronald Reagan and the Public Lands*, 78. Reporter Philip Shabecoff credited him with opening up a record amount of federal land for oil, gas, and coal development, changing the use of federal dollars for national parks from land acquisitions to land improvements, and "institutionalized [policy changes] through new guidelines." Philip

Shabecoff, "Watt Played Incandescent Role," *Herald-Review* [Decatur, Ill.], October 14, 1983, Sec. A, 10. "He was a consummate bureaucrat. He knew how to make a big, sprawling agency do what he wanted." "The Legacy of James Watt," *Time* (October 24, 1983): 25.

112.   Dale Russakoff and Ward Sinclair, "Cost Allotments to Change; Reagan Revises Water-Project Policy," *Washington Post*, January 24, 1984, A1.

113.   A 1993 Grazing Fee Task force would conclude: "The government is not collecting the full market value for grazing public lands, but ranchers are paying full value through the current fee, non-fee grazing costs, and the grazing permit." "The Value of Public Land Forage and the Implications for Grazing Fee Policy" (A Summary of the Bureau of Land Management and Forest Service Incentive-Based Grazing Fee Study, Grazing Fee Task Group), New Mexico State University, College of Agriculture and Home Economics, Las Cruces, New Mexico, December 1993, IV. "The current grazing fee, or even a lower fee, would be justified in all cases if even a minimal allowance were made for ranchers' grazing permit investments." Ibid., V.

> Unlike the private landlord, the U.S. government has a plethora of interests and concerns that are, in turn imposed upon the grazing lessee. For example, there are requirements to own base property, to construct and maintain improvements, and to provide for public access, as well as restrictions relating to multiple use, forage use, and watershed and wildlife issues, not to mention time-consuming meetings with federal agencies and officials as well as interest members of the public.

William Perry Pendley, *War on the West: Government Tyranny on America's Great Frontier* (Regnery, 1995), 75, citing Drs. Gerhard N. Rostvold and Thomas J. Dudley, "Report to Congress: New Perspectives on Grazing Fees and Public Land Management in the 1990's," Pepperdine University, June 1992, 9, 12–13, 80–81.

114.   President Ronald Reagan Executive Order 12548 – Grazing, signed February 14, 1986; 51 *FedReg* 5985, February 19, 1986.

115.   "Cabinet Council meeting on Natural Resources & Environment. A lot of decisions to be made on Western Water policies...." Ronald Reagan, *The Reagan Diaries* (Harper, 2007), 213.

116.   Over the objections of the Reagan administration, a Colorado federal district court ruled, in *Sierra Club v. Block*, 622 F.Supp. 842 (1985), that congressional designation of a wilderness area created a federal reserved water right, but ruled against the Sierra Club in its contention that Secretary Block was arbitrary and capricious in not asserting that right regarding wilderness areas in Colorado. In *Sierra Club v. Yeutter*, 911 F.2d 1405 (10th Cir. 1990), a three-judge panel dismissed the Sierra Club's lawsuit holding that the harm it alleged was "speculative and contingent." Ibid., 1421.

117.   See generally Stine, "Natural Resources and Environmental Policy," 233–34, note 104.

118.   *James G. Watt Nomination: Hearings Before the Committee On Energy and Natural Resources, United States Senate, Ninety-seventh Congress, First Session, On the Proposed Nomination of James G. Watt to Be Secretary of the Interior, January 7 and 8, 1981.* (Washington: U.S. G.P.O., 1981), 60–61. Governor Reagan wrote about the issue needing federal legislation in one of his radio addresses. *Reagan's Path to Victory*, 211–12 (October 18, 1977). The Reclamation Act of 1902 (P.L. 57-161), also known as the Lowlands Reclamation Act, the National Reclamation Act, or the Newlands Reclamation Act after Nevada Senator Francis G. Newlands, a Democrat, the author of the bill, provided for the construction and maintenance by the federal government of irrigation projects; the irrigated land would be sold and the funds used to finance additional projects. President Theodore Roosevelt, often credited with ensuring the Act's passage, signed it into law on June 17, 1902.

119.   "The Reclamation Reform Act of 1982," U.S. Department of the Interior, Bureau of Reclamation, Lower Colorado Region. http://www.usbr.gov/lc/phoenix/AZ100/1980/reclamation_reform_act. html.

120.   Hamilton Wright, "Millions of New Acres for American Farmers," *National Magazine*, November 1905, 198. See also William D. Rowley, "The Bureau of Reclamation: Origins and Growth to 1945," vol. 1. U.S. Department of the Interior, Bureau of Reclamation, Denver, CO, 2006.

121.   Ibid. "Under the reclamation act the government will construct the largest irrigation works in history, far excelling those of Egypt and India." Wright described completed and proposed projects in Arizona, California, Colorado, Idaho, Montana, Nevada, New Mexico, Oregon, Nebraska, North Dakota, South Dakota, Utah, Washington, Wyoming. Ibid.

122.   John W. Powell, "A Report on the Arid Regions of the United States, with a More Detailed Account of the Lands of Utah," (1876). Powell, a soldier, geologist, explorer, professor, director of various scientific and cultural entities, and second director of Interior's U.S. Geological Survey, lived to see

the Reclamation Act of 1902 signed into law. James M. Aton, *John Wesley Powell: His Life and Legacy* (Bonneville Books, 2009). Arnold, *At the Eye of the Storm*, 148.

123.   http://www.usbr.gov/main/about/.

124.   http://www.usbr.gov/lc/phoenix/AZ100/1980/reclamation_reform_act.html. In the mid-1970s, a lawsuit alleged violations and abuses of the various provisions of the law, which led to a court injunction, *National Land for People, Inc. v. Bureau of Reclamation of the Dep't of the Interior*, 417 F. Supp. 449, 452-453, (D.D.C. 1976), which resulted in regulations by Carter's Interior Department, 42 *Fed. Reg.* 43,044 (1977), which led finally to a counter lawsuit that barred the regulations pending preparation of an environmental impact statement, *County of Fresno v. Andrus*, Civ. No. F-77-202 (E.D. Cal. Dec. 7, 1977). In early 1981, Watt ordered cessation of water deliveries to the Westlands Water District by the end of 1981 if the district refused to pay the required higher price for its water. Letter from Assistant Secretary of Interior to General Manager of the Westlands Water District (May 21, 1981).

125.   Reclamation Reform Act of 1982, Pub. L. 97-293, title II, Oct. 12, 1982, 96 Stat. 1263 (43 U.S.C. 390aa et seq.) In addition to Watt, other key players in this legislative success story include Hal Furman, Principal Deputy Assistant Secretary for Water and Science, Alexander H. Good, Associate Solicitor for Energy and Resources, and Robbie Aiken, Director of Congressional and Legislative Affairs, Bureau of Reclamation.

126.   http://www.usbr.gov/lc/phoenix/AZ100/1980/reclamation_reform_act.html.

127.   Letter from Chairman David F. Linowes to Secretary James G. Watt dated January 21, 1982, "Fiscal Accountability of the Nation's Energy Resources" (FANER), Government Printing Office, January 1982, unnumbered first page. The report was also delivered to the Chairman of the Council on Integrity and Efficiency, Edwin L. Harper, at the White House, ibid., unnumbered second page.

128.   William R. Ritz, "Oil Thefts put in Millions," *The Denver Post*, March 16, 1981. According to the Commission, "Reports of oil theft came to public notice in June 1980...." Ibid., 26–27.

129.   Ibid., Appendix A, 271273. "Oil and Gas Royalty Collections—Serious Financial Management Problems Need Congressional Attention," FGMSD-79-24, April 13, 1979. Bill Prochnau, "Watt Probes Oil 'Theft' on Indian Lands," *Washington Post*, July 16, 1981, A3.

130.   FANER, 39, note 127.

131.   Arnold, *At the Eye of the Storm*, 231–34.

132.   Secretarial Order No. 3071, January 19, 1982. Amendment No. 1 to this order was issued on May 10, 1982. The Commission concluded, "[R]oyalty management[, which is] a demanding, complicated job ... is especially difficult for an agency such as the USGS which has an overriding scientific and research mission that has nothing to do with royalty management." FANER, 39, note 127.

133.   In late 1983, Reagan's Interior Department reported that it had completed or was in the process of completing audits of "23 of the 25 largest royalty payers and eight of the medium-size royalty payers," which, during 1983 identified potential underpayments of $20 million. Underpayments identified by the audits ordered by Watt totaled $32.8 million; 85 percent of those underpayments involved interpretive issues. *Interior Report 1983*, 38.

134.   Arnold, *At the Eye of the Storm*, 232. See generally ibid., 231–32.

135.   http://thomas.loc.gov/cgi-bin/bdquery/z?d097:SN02305:@@@L&summ2=m&.

136.   Federal Oil and Gas Royalty Management Act of 1982, 30 U.S.C. 1701 et seq. Implementing regulations followed. In 1988, Reagan's Interior Department reported that the Mineral Management Service's Royalty Management Program (RMP) developed and installed an Auditing and Financial System (AFS) to account for royalties; a Bonus and Royalty Accounting System (BRASS) to account for bonuses and rentals from onshore leases; and a Production Accounting and Auditing System (PAAS) to account for production data from offshore and onshore oil and gas leases and solid mineral leases. RMP includes a 200-person audit team that audits cyclically and achieved additional royalties and interest as well as refund denials of more than $450 million. The AFS exception reporting system, which seeks out late payments, late reporting, and failure to report, collected $36 million. PAAS, which compares production data to sales data (from the AFS) collected $26 million since early 1985. *Interior Report 1988*, 108–9.

137.   President Ronald Reagan Statement on Signing the Federal Oil and Gas Royalty Management Act of 1982, January 12, 1983, http://www.presidency.ucsb.edu/ws/index.php?pid=41254.

138.   S. Rep. No. 188, 100th Cong., 1st Sess. 2 (1987). See generally Patricia J. Beneke, "The Federal Onshore Oil and Gas Leasing Reform Act of 1987: A Legislative History and Analysis," 4 *J. Min. L. & Pol'y* 11 (1988–1989), 11–47.

139. "'Known geological structure' '(KGS)' means technically the trap in which an accumulation of oil and gas has been discovered by drilling and determined to be productive, the limits of which include all acreage that is presumptively productive." E. Finley, *The Definition of Known Geological Structures of Producing Oil and Gas Fields*, in U.S. GEOLOGICAL SURVEY, Circular no. 419, 1 (1959); BLM Minerals Management, 43 C.F.R. § 3100.0-5(1) (1987).

140. Most leases issued noncompetitively are issued under the simultaneous oil and gas leasing (SIMO) system. BLM Minerals Management, Simultaneous Filing, First Qualified Applicant, 43 C.F.R. Subpart 3112.4 (1987). The SIMO system has potential for fraud, abuse, and speculation. U.S. General Accounting Office, "Issues Surrounding Continuation Of The Noncompetitive Oil And Gas Lottery System 36," (GAO/RECD-85-88, 1985).

141. S. REP. No. 188, 100th Cong., 1st Sess. 2 (1987). In 1947, Congress allowed oil and gas leasing under the Mineral Leasing Act of 1920 on acquired lands when it enacted the Mineral Leasing Act for Acquired Lands, 30 U.S.C. § 351 (1986), but it excluded acquired lands "set apart for military or naval purposes," 30 U.S.C. § 352 (1986), which included land such as those within Fort Chaffee. Congress eliminated the military and naval exemption when it enacted the Federal Coal Leasing Amendments Act of 1976, Pub. L. No. 94-377, Sec. 12, 90 Stat. 852 (1976).

142. S. REP. No. 188, 100th Cong., 1st Sess. 2 (1987).

143. *Arkla Exploration Co. v. Watt*, 562 F. Supp. 1214, 1222 (W.D. Ark. 1983), *aff'd sub nom. Arkla Exploration Co. v. Texas Oil and Gas Corp.*, 734 F.2d 347 (8th Cir. 1984).

144. *Arkla Exploration Co. v. Texas Oil and Gas Corp.*, 734 F.2d, 361.

145. The area involved was the Amos Draw field in Campbell County a few miles West of Gillette. U.S. General Accounting Office, "Issues Surrounding Continuation Of The Noncompetitive Oil And Gas Lottery System 12," (GAO/RCED-85-85, 1985).

146. Ibid.

147. Ibid.

148. Bureau Of Land Management, U.S. Dep't. Of The Interior, Instruction Memorandum 84-35 (October 14, 1983); Bureau Of Land Management, U.S. Dep't. Of The Interior, Instruction Memorandum 84-36 (October 14, 1983); Bureau Of Land Management, U.S. Dep't. Of The Interior, Instruction Memorandum 84-439 (April 1984).

149. *Bender v. Clark*, 744 F.2d 1424 (10th Cir. 1984).

150. *Oversight Hearing on Federal Onshore Oil and Gas Leasing Program Before the Subcomm. on Mining and Natural Resources of the House Comm. on Interior and Insular Affairs*, 99th Cong., 1st Sess. 19 (1985) (statement of J. Steven Griles, Acting Assistant Secretary, Land and Minerals Management). The oil and gas industry agreed. *Hearing on S. 66 and S. 1388 Before the Subcomm. on Mineral Resources Development and Production of the Comm. On Energy and Natural Resources*, 100th Cong., 1st Sess. 113 (1987) (statement of Kenneth A. Wonstolen, Executive Director and General Counsel, Independent Petroleum Ass'n of Mountain States).

151. See generally Beneke, *"The Federal Onshore Oil and Gas Leasing Reform Act of 1987*, 28–41.

152. Abraham E. Haspel, "Drilling for Dollars: The New and Improved Federal Oil Lease Program," *Regulation*, Fall 1990, 64. Clark had ordered an overall review of the program. Ibid., 63. Reagan's Interior Department sought to address concerns of independent oilmen regarding both the loss of the noncompetitive system, which provided them an opportunity to participate fully by obtaining leases in frontier areas where the hydrocarbon potential is unknown and the likely payoff in the event of a discovery is greatest, and the risk of new environmental restrictions on the availability of federal lands for oil and gas activity. Ibid., 64–65. "Independent producers develop 95 percent of domestic oil and gas wells, produce 54 percent of domestic oil and produce 85 percent of domestic natural gas," www.ipaa.org/about-ipaa/.

153. *Hearing on S. 66 and S. 1388 Before the Subcomm. on Mineral Resources Development and Production of the Senate Comm. on Energy and Natural Resources*, 100th Cong., 1st Sess. 48-49, 51 (1987) (statement of Robert F. Burford, Director, Bureau of Land Management, U.S. Department of the Interior).

154. Congress also withdrew from oil and gas leasing all wilderness study areas. See, Beneke, *"The Federal Onshore Oil and Gas Leasing Reform Act of 1987*, 42–47.

155. For example, Reagan's Interior Department proposed legislation to combat "wildcat" coal miners, which was enacted. *Interior Report 1988*, 35. *See, Sagebrush Rebel*, chapter 10. Reagan's Interior Department created a task force (Protect Our Wetlands and Duck Resources [POWDR]) composed of "corporate, State and conservation officials," to develop recommendations to "address the rapid loss of wetlands in the United States—estimated at 458,000 acres per year." *Interior Report 1983*,

8. Based on the recommendations by POWDR, Reagan's Interior Department transmitted legislation to Congress that led to enactment of the Emergency Resources Act of 1986, which President Reagan signed into law. *Interior Report 1988*, 13. In addition, Reagan's Interior Department urged enactment of the Coastal Barrier Resources Act of 1982 to prevent the loss of coastal wetlands. *Interior Report 1983*, 5, *Interior Report 1988*, 14–15. See *Sagebrush Rebel*, chapter 8. Reagan's Interior Department's Wilderness Protection Act did not receive favorable attention, not because it was unwise or unreasonable, but because Congress could not reach agreement itself on how to address the balancing of national security, economic well-being, and environmental preservation. The Act, introduced on request by New Mexico Representative Manuel Lujan, Jr., a Republican, provided: wilderness areas and wilderness study areas (both RARE II and BLM study areas) are off-limits upon enactment to all oil, gas and mineral development; wilderness studies and congressional action designating wilderness areas would be completed by 1985 or 1988 after which the lands would be released; mineral inventories would be performed on all wilderness lands; "buffer zones" around wilderness areas would be prohibited; however, specific oil, gas, or mineral development of a specific mineral could occur in a specific wilderness area in the event of "urgent national need," by order of the President with consent of Congress. Arnold, *At the Eye of the Storm*, 232–33.

156. Don Oberdorfer, "Sea Law Treaty Being Blocked At White House," *Washington Post*, March 4, 1981, A1. The treaty remains in the news. Iain Murray, "LOST at Sea: Why America Should Reject the Law of the Sea Treaty," National Center for Policy Analysis, Policy Backgrounder No. 167, March 25, 2013.

157. No doubt informed of what happened at the meeting by someone at the State Department, one reporter gave Watt credit. Drew, "A Reporter at Large," 104, 120.

158. President Ronald Reagan, "Statement on United States Oceans Policy," March 10, 1983, http://www.presidency.ucsb.edu/ws/index.php?pid=41036.

159. Ibid. President Ronald Reagan, Proclamation 5030–Exclusive Economic Zone of the United States of America, March 10, 1983. http://www.presidency.ucsb.edu/ws/index.php?pid=41037.

160. In Sacramento, Governor Reagan put in place "an inner cabinet of 'executive directors' intended to serve as a board of directors of his administration." Lou Cannon, *Governor Reagan: His Rise to Power* (Public Affairs, 2003), 178. The idea of such an "inner Cabinet" composed of the Secretaries of State, Defense, Treasury, and Justice, and four senior White House aides, which would act, as had the California group, as a board of directors was rejected as "unworkable" in the federal government. Pfiffner, *The Strategic Presidency*, 49. President Washington first used "his department heads as a 'cabinet.'" Ibid., 34.

161. For example, President Reagan's statement on Indian policy originated with a working group that reported to and through the Cabinet Council on Human Resources, as described in *Sagebrush Rebel*, chapter 11. An issue being addressed by the Cabinet Council on Natural Resources and Environment was at the heart of a controversy involving President Reagan's exercise of executive privilege as described in *Sagebrush Rebel*, chapter 4. See generally Arnold, *At the Eye of the Storm*, 130.

162. Ibid., 49–53. This is evidenced by President Reagan's diary entries regarding Cabinet Council and Domestic Policy Council. There were 16 entries for "Cabinet Council" of one kind or another during the first term and only six during the second term, the last one made on July 11, 1985. There were sixteen entries for "Domestic Policy Council" during the second term beginning on June 4, 1985, and ending on August 1, 1988. *The Reagan Diaries*, 712, 719.

163. Pfiffner, *The Strategic Presidency*, 53.

164. Cass Peterson, "Administration Ozone Policy May Favor Sunglasses, Hats: Support for Chemical Cutbacks Reconsidered," *Washington Post*, May 29, 1987, A1.

165. Associated Press, "EPA Rejects 'Hat, Sunglasses' for Ozone," *Los Angeles Times*, May 31, 1987; Opinion, "Through Rose-Colored Sunglasses," *New York Times*, May 31, 1987; Associated Press, "EPA says Hodel's alleged ozone plan is hot air," *Houston Chronicle*, May 30, 1987, Section 2, 8.

166. *The Reagan Diaries*, June 18, 1987, 508–9. President Reagan expressed such concerns even earlier. On January 17, 1984, he wrote, "Cabinet Council meeting on Natural Resources and Environment. A lot of decisions to be made on … doing something about acid rain. This last calls for more research." Ibid., 213. Again on January 20, 1984, "Back to a meeting with several Gov's. regarding Acid Rain. It's a tough problem. Do we know enough for sure that mid west plant burning sulphur coal is the cause. The solution is terribly expensive—too much so if we're wrong about the cause, we're upping our research efforts." Ibid., 214. Again on February 18, 1986, "[L]ong meeting with Domestic Policy Council regarding 'Report on Acid Rain….'" Ibid., 391. Again on April 6, 1987, "About 10:30 a plenary meeting in Cabinet Rom. It went well & I think we resolved some difficult

problems having to do with Acid rain, Arctic waters sovereignty problems, & defense budget." Ibid., 488. Again on January 14, 1988, "Domestic Council meeting regarding acid rain...." Ibid., 568. Again on August 1, 1988, "Back to Cabinet Room for a Domestic Policy Council meeting. Subject was about international program calling for reduction of pollutants—Nitrates & Oxides etc. We are ahead of most nations in eliminating or reducing emissions now." Ibid., 635.

167.   Ibid., 531, September 18, 1987.
168.   "President Reagan on Montreal Protocol Ratification," EPA press release, December 21, 1987, http:// www.epa.gov/history/topics/montreal/01.html.
169.   Ben Lieberman of The Heritage Foundation reports:

> The thinning of the ozone layer that occurred throughout the 1980s apparently stopped in the early 1990s, too soon to credit the Montreal Protocol. A 1998 World Meteorological Organization (WMO) report said that, "since 1991, the linear [downward] trend observed during the 1980s has not continued, but rather total column ozone has been almost constant"[http://www.esrl.noaa.gov/csd/assessments/ ozone/1998/executive_summary.html] even though the stratospheric concentrations of the offending compounds were still increasing through 1998. This lends credence to the skeptical view, widely derided at the time of the Montreal Protocol, that natural variations better explain the fluctuations in the global ozone layer. WMO concedes that no statistically significant long-term trends [in ground level UVB radiation] have been detected, noting [in 2007] that "outside the polar regions, ozone depletion has been relatively small, hence, in many places, increases in UV due to this depletion are difficult to separate from the increases caused by other factors, such as changes in cloud and aerosol," [http://www.esrl.noaa.gov/csd/assessments/ ozone/2006/executivesummary.html] In short, the impact of ozone depletion on UVB over populated regions is so small that it's hard to detect.

Ben Lieberman, "Ozone: The Hole Truth," September 14, 2007, http://www.heritage.org/ research/commentary/2007/09/ozone-the-hole-truth.

CHAPTER TEN

1.   Kiron K. Skinner, Annelise Anderson, and Martin Anderson, eds., *Reagan's Path to Victory, The Shaping of Ronald Reagan's Vision: Selected Writings* (The Free Press, 2004), 477.
2.   Energy Information Administration, *Quarterly Coal Report*, 2010, Table 2. Pennsylvania, Texas, North Dakota, and Ohio round out the top ten. Ibid. "The U.S. has nearly 261 billion tons of recoverable coal reserves, according to the Energy Information Administration; That's a 235-year supply at current rates of use; Coal accounts for approximately 94 percent of the nation's fossil energy reserve; Coal is found in 38 states, under 458,600 square miles or about 13 percent of the nation's land area." http://www.nma.org/statistics/fast_facts.asp.
3.   "The U.S. is, after all, the Saudi Arabia of coal." Cathy Booth Thomas, "Is Coal Golden" *Time*, October 2, 2006, http://www.time.com/time/magazine/article/0,9171,1541270,00.html.
4.   The "locally available coal" provision pleased both the United Mine Workers and environmental groups. See, "Beyond the New Deal: Coal and the Clean Air Act" by Bruce A. Ackerman and William T. Hassler, in *Yale Law Journal* 89 (July 1980): 1466–1571, reprinted in *Regulation* – AEI Journal on Government and Society (March/April 1981), 52.
5.   Surface Mining Control and Reclamation Act of 1977 (SMCRA), 30 U.S.C. §1201 et seq. President Ford vetoed the predecessor to SMCRA twice. H.R. REP. NO. 95-218, at 57 (1977), reprinted in 1977 U.S.C.C.A.N. 593, 595 (explaining the purposes behind and history of SMCRA). The Supreme Court of the United States upheld the constitutionality of the act in *Hodel v. Virginia Surface Mining and Reclamation Association, Inc.* 452 U.S. 264 (1981) and *Hodel v. Indiana*, 452 U.S. 314 (1981). The Reagan administration defended the constitutionality of the statute; however, Watt was recused given the presence in the litigation of MSLF, which filed *amicus curiae* briefs arguing that the law is unconstitutional. The Court ruled, in a facial challenge, that SMCRA did not violate the Commerce Clause or run afoul of either the Fifth Amendment (Due Process Clause and Takings Clause) or the Tenth Amendment (Reservation Clause). Justice Powell concurred but raised concerns regarding federalism and the impact of SMCRA on the Commonwealth of Virginia: "The Surface Mining Act mandates an extraordinarily intrusive program of federal regulation and control of land use and land reclamation, activities normally left to state and local governments.... The Act could affect seriously the owners and lessees of the land and coal in the seven westernmost counties of Virginia.... Because

of thin soil and rugged terrain, the land in its natural state is not suited for agricultural use or the growing of merchantable timber. Its value lies, in most instances, solely in its coal. Mining the coal is a major industrial activity in an otherwise impoverished area of Virginia.... In sum, if the Act is implemented broadly in accordance with its terms, the consequences to individual lessees and owners, and to the area as a whole, could be far-reaching." 452 U.S. 305-307. Justice Rehnquist added a cautionary note regarding the Commerce Clause: "Congress must show that the activity it seeks to regulate has a substantial effect on interstate commerce. It is my uncertainty as to whether the Court intends to broaden, by some of its language, this test that leads me to concur only in the judgments." 452 U.S. 313.

6.   42 U.S.C. §7401 et seq.
7.   30 U.S.C. §§1253 and 1254.
8.   http://thomas.loc.gov/cgi-bin/bdquery/z?d095:HR00002:@@@L&summ2=m&.
9.   Under the federal Clean Air Act (42 U.S.C. § 7401 et seq.) even after the Environmental Protection Agency (EPA) approves a "state implementation plan," for the purposes of deciding how the National Ambient Air Quality Standards for various criteria pollutants (NAAQS) will be met (42 U.S.C. § 7407(a)), the EPA may still enforce state-issued permits and regulations after providing notice to the state. 42 U.S.C. § 7407(d)(1)(B); 7413(a).
10.   *Bragg v. W.Va. Coal Association*, 248 F.3d 275, 288 (4th Cir. 2001) citing Mark Squillace, Cooperative Federalism Under the Surface Mining Control and Reclamation Act: Is This Any Way to Run a Government? 15 *Envtl. L. Rep.* 10039 (1985) (calling SMCRA's "broad delegation" to states "unparalleled").
11.   SMCRA, 30 U.S.C. §1201(f). "The Congress finds and declares that [because of that diversity] the primary governmental responsibility for developing, authorizing, issuing, and enforcing regulations for surface mining and reclamation operations subject to this chapter should rest with the States...." Ibid.
12.   "1983 – A Year Of Enrichment: Improving The Quality Of Life For All Americans," (U.S. Department of the Interior, October 1983), 19.
13.   Skinner, *Reagan's Path to Victory*, 363.
14.   Watt intervened in the OSM's regulatory reform only as to one matter. He advised Harris that the "Two Acre Exemption" was a loophole that was being abused—especially in Virginia, and he wanted it closed. Ron Arnold, *At the Eye of the Storm: James Watt and the Environmentalists* (Regnery Gateway, 1982), 200. Harris responded to Watt's directive by revising OSM's regulations to set forth specific and exacting criteria required to claim the exemption in order to reflect more accurately Congress's intent to apply the exemption only to "the one-man operation" that "would cause very little environmental damage." 47 *Federal Register* 33424 (August 2, 1982). Additionally, a two-acre exemption task force was established to enforce violations and to collect unreported fees in Virginia and Kentucky from operations previously granted improper exemption from the law. Finally, Watt urged that Congress completely eliminate the Two Acre Exemption. On June 6, 1987, Public Law 100-34 eliminated the two-acre exemptions for newly permitted operations and set November 8, 1987, as the final day for such exemptions. Surface Coal Mining Reclamation: 15 Years of Progress, 1977–1992, U.S. Office of Surface Mining Reclamation and Enforcement, U.S. Department of the Interior, Washington, D.C. 1992, 51. See also "America – Our Treasure and Our Trust: The Legacy of President Ronald Reagan 1981 – 1988," (U.S. Department of the Interior, December 1988), 35–36, on legislative and regulatory actions to combat illegal "wildcat" coal mining operations as opposed to "the great majority [of all surface coal mines] that operate in full compliance with the law." Ibid., 35.
15.   Richard D. Lamm and Michael McCarthy, *The Angry West: A Vulnerable Land and Its Future* (Houghton Mifflin, 1982), 247. "Let's abolish OSM and take them to Lower Slobbovia. They're a pain in the backside," said Herschler, a Democrat. Ibid., 248. *Mandate* also addresses an aspect of the SMCRA that affected Western coal: the unsuitability criteria by which the OSM could designate federal land as "unsuitable" for the surface mining of coal. Of particular concern was the retroactive application of the criteria to federal leases issued prior to SMCRA's enactment. Charles L. Heatherly, ed., *Mandate for Leadership: Policy Management in a Conservative Administration* (The Heritage Foundation, 1981), 358–59.
16.   *15 Years of Progress*, 50.
17.   *Interior Report 1983*, 18–19; *15 Years of Progress*, 50.
18.   *15 Years of Progress*, 50.

19.   One Watt proposal involved moving 50 to 100 OSM employees out of Denver, Colorado, and closer
       to the actual mining operations including, mostly Casper, Wyoming, but also Albuquerque, New
       Mexico, and Olympia, Washington. Colorado Representative Patricia Schroeder, a Democrat,
       objected to the loss of that many constituents out of a population of 500,000; Casper at the time had
       51,016 residents. The media focused on this flap for days. Watt believes focus of the media and the
       House of Representatives on the Denver to Casper OSM move allowed him to implement all other
       aspect of the OSM reorganization. Arnold, *At the Eye of the Storm*, 168–71.

20.   *15 Years of Progress*, 50. Nonetheless, in 1983, nearly 170,000 inspections of surface mines were
       conducted, nearly three times the 58,822 inspections performed during each of the previous three
       years. *Interior Report 1983*, 19. OSM also engaged in research, formerly performed by the Bureau
       of Mines. "Established the fifth generic mineral technology center in the field of respirable dust—the
       single greatest health hazard in underground coal mining—jointly at Pennsylvania State and West
       Virginia Universities, and awarded a research grant of $1.84 million to support the center's research
       program." *Interior Report 1983*, 21.

21.   In April 1984, for example, after detecting deficiencies in Oklahoma and Tennessee programs, OSM
       assumed direct federal enforcement of the inspection portion of those programs and, in October
       1984. OSM instituted a full federal program in Tennessee after the state repealed its program. *15
       Years of Progress*, 51.

22.   In October 1987, OSM's Applicant Violator System (AVS) became operational; the AVS ensures
       compliance with Section 510(c) of SMCRA, which prohibits issuance of a new permit to any appli-
       cant who owns or controls mining operations having unabated or uncorrected violations anywhere
       in the United States until those violations are abated or corrected or are in the process of being abated
       or corrected to the satisfaction of the agency with jurisdiction over the violation. *15 Years of Progress*,
       51. http://www.arcc.osmre.gov/Divisions/AVSO/AVSO.shtm. In June 1987, OSM's first "Annual
       Excellence in Surface Coal Mining and Reclamation Award" was presented to nine operators. *15
       Years of Progress*, 51.

23.   30 U.S.C. §1202(h) and 30 U.S.C. § 1231(a). Three U.S. Bureau of Mines abandoned mine land
       programs were transferred to OSM (P.L. 738, Extinguishment of Outcrop and Underground Fires;
       P.L. 162, Anthracite Mine Drainage Act; and P.L. 89-4, Appalachian Regional Development Act,
       Section 205). *15 Years of Progress*, 50.

24.   The Reagan administration's OSM issued the nation's first Abandoned Mine Land policy statement
       to ensure that AML funds are used to reclaim mined lands. AML funds are collected by the OSM
       from coal producers, deposited in the U.S. Treasury, and disbursed to states and tribes to correct the
       damage associated with past mining. *Interior Report 1983*, 19. *15 Years of Progress*, 50–51.

25.   J. Steven Griles, OSM Deputy Director during the period, reflected, "We rewrote 90% of the regula-
       tions and got sued over 10% of them. Of that 10% that ended up in federal court, the courts held
       in 50% of the cases that we failed to dot the 'i's' and cross the 't's' and sent them back for republica-
       tion; then they went final. On the other 50% of the ten percent, the judges disagreed and substituted
       their judgment for ours." See also Short, *Ronald Reagan and the Public Lands*, 61. There were fewer
       lawsuits against Reagan's Interior Department in its first year (138) than against Carter's Interior
       Department in its last year (197). Arnold, *At the Eye of the Storm*, 137. "This Administration
       modified and simplified more than 90 percent of the [OSM] regulations.... These modifications
       resulted in more than 25 judicial challenges from states, industrial groups, coal companies, and citi-
       zen groups, which were ultimately consolidated into one case. The U.S. Court of Appeals issued a
       final opinion, *National Wildlife Federation v. Hodel*[, 839 F.2d 694] (D.C. Cir. 1988), endorsing the
       regulatory approach taken by this Administration in implementing the Surface Mining Act." *Interior
       Report 1988*, 35, 112–13.

26.   30 U.S.C. §181 et seq. Previously coal was "locatable" under the General Mining Law of 1872.

27.   One expert puts the impact of the NEPA requirements this way:

           By the mid-1970s the writing of environmental impact statements [EISs] had become
           a central concern throughout the Interior Department. Many Department projects
           and programs stopped or started according to the fate of their EISs.... "Telephone-
           book" EISs became commonplace as Interior agencies sought to cover every conceiv-
           able subject that might cause an EIS to be rejected by a court.... Few EISs ever
           discovered any very surprising or unexpected impacts of projects on the environment.
           Rather, the EIS requirement gave environmental organizations and the judiciary a
           powerful new handle to influence Interior decisions. The judiciary often showed
           little restraint; for a couple of years in the late 1970s the Interior coal, rangeland,

and timber management programs—a major part of the Department's overall responsibilities—were operating under court orders imposing significant management directions. Many Department meetings were preoccupied with EIS matters: How could the Department regain its former decision-making role? What concessions would be necessary to placate environmental opposition to prevent a suit or to gain a favorable court verdict on the "adequacy" of an EIS, allowing an Interior project to proceed?

Robert H. Nelson, *The Making of Federal Coal Policy* (Duke University Press, 1983), 99.

28.   *Kleppe v. Sierra Club*, 427 U.S. 390 (1976). The four states included in the Powder River Basin are Montana, North Dakota, South Dakota, and Wyoming.

29.   *NRDC v. Hughes*, 437 F.Supp. 981 (D.D.C. 1977). Professor Nelson says this about the NRDC:

A threat to sue from NRDC was no idle matter. NRDC had just won a suit against the entire BLM livestock-grazing program and the Department was being forced to agree to prepare 212 separate environmental impact statements stretching over thirteen years that might ultimately cost several hundred million dollars. NRDC was by a wide margin the most successful environmental litigant against the federal government in the 1970s, winning numerous major cases. The organization had been founded by Yale law school graduates and was supported by the Ford Foundation. Several NRDC staff attorneys had been law clerks for Supreme Court Justices. Its staff attorneys in an earlier era would have been bright young lawyers in the New Deal or corporate advisors in the best law firms. In short, the legal artillery NRDC could bring to bear was formidable.

Nelson, *The Making of Federal Coal Policy*, 99.

30.   Ibid., 131.

31.   Ibid., 114. Of course, President Carter also issued his National Energy Plan, which envisioned coal production doubling from 1976 to 1985. The National Energy Plan (Apr. 29, 1977) (White House doc.).

32.   Stat. 1083–1092. *Mandate for Leadership* especially faults the Federal Coal Leasing Amendments Act of 1976 as having been "enacted at the height of the so-called environmental movement." It was enacted over the veto of President Ford. "[T]he Act contains numerous burdensome, complex and in many cases experimental concepts which inhibit coal development ... including diligent development, logical mining units, extensive land-use planning and numerous studies and reviews...." Heatherly, *Mandate for Leadership*, 362–63.

33.   43 U.S.C. § 1701 et seq.

34.   30 U.S.C. §1272(e), (2008).

35.   Heatherly, *Mandate*, 363.

36.   Ibid.

37.   *Interior Report 1983*, 13.

38.   Ibid.

39.   Act of July 30, 1983, Pub.L. No. 98-63, 97 Stat. 328. In May 1983, the General Accounting Office (GAO) opined that Interior issued leases in the Powder River Basin for $100 million less than the GAO's estimates of fair market value. See Comptroller General, Report to the Congress: "Analysis of the Powder River Basin Federal Coal Lease Sale: Economic Valuation Improvements and Legislative Changes Needed" (May 11, 1983).

40.   Watt sought to move forward with a long-planned (since the Carter administration) and well-papered (pursuant to NEPA) federal coal lease sale for Eastern Montana and Western North Dakota (the Fort Union sale); however, the House Interior Committee adopted, along party lines, a resolution pursuant to Section 204(e) of FLPMA (30 U.S.C. § 1714(e), which directed Watt to remove the area from coal leasing temporarily as a result of an "emergency situation." Environmental groups sued Watt to prevent the Secretary from accepting the bids received from the sale. Chairman Udall intervened in the lawsuit as did the successful bidders in the Fort Union coal lease sale. Watt argued that Section 204(e), essentially a "one-House veto," is contrary to the Presentment Clause of the Constitution. The federal district court for the District of Columbia declined to reach the constitutional question and issued a preliminary injunction, which it later made final. *National Wildlife Federation v. Watt*, 571 F.Supp. 1145 (D.D.C. 1983), *National Wildlife Federation v. Clark*, 577 F.Supp. 825 (D.D.C. 1984). The constitutional question asked by Watt and Clark remains unresolved today. See *Northwest Mining Association v. Salazar*, No 12-08042-DGG (D. Az.).

41. Federal Coal Management Program, "Final Environmental Impact Statement," U.S. Department of the Interior, Bureau of Land Management, October 1985. This EIS supplements the 1979 Final Environmental Impact Statement for the Federal Coal Management Program.

42. *Mandate* recommended that Interior complete the processing of the preference right lease applications (PRLA) (non-competitive coal leasing) expeditiously but recommended that the determination as to whether commercial quantities were discovered should use the standard when the permit was issued. Heatherly, *Mandate*, 360. With the 1985 Final EIS, Interior committed to completing the processing of the PRLA. *Mandate* also asserted that new requirements set forth in the Federal Coal Leasing Amendments Act, such as advance royalty payments, logical mining units, diligent development, and continuous operations, should not be applied retroactively to pre-existing leases. Ibid., 359–63.

43. *Mandate* recommended specifically:

> Subsequent to the initial lease sale, the new Administration must issue regulations instituting specific changes in the coal management program including: deletion of the requirement that only high and medium potential coal lands be evaluated; retention of all coal lands through the process despite declared applicability of the various screening criteria; elimination of the "threshold development" concept; restriction of the "unsuitability" criteria, as well as numerous others.

     Ibid., 363.

44. http://www.blm.gov/wy/st/en/programs/energy/Coal_Resources/PRB_Coal/history.html. "Since decertification, from 1992 to present, 21 LBA tracts have been offered for sale in the Wyoming portion of the PRB with 20 leased. At present 12 LBA tracts are pending, all of which have been recommended for processing by the PRB RCT and are in various stages of processing." Ibid.

45. Energy Information Administration, *Quarterly Coal Report*, 2010, Table 2.

46. Robert F. Durant, *The Administrative Presidency Revisited: Public Lands, the BLM, and the Reagan Revolution* (State University of New York Press, 1992), 205.

47. Reagan's Interior Department proposed to lease 1.2 to 1.5 billion tons of coal in September 1983 with 2.3 billion tons more coal available after the Bureau of Land Management processed 26 PRLAs. Ibid., 207.

48. Ibid., 208.

49. Watt's decision to withdraw from review so-called Wilderness Study Areas (WSAs) of less than 5,000 acres, which was based on a correct interpretation of the Federal Land Policy and Management Act, and his decision to withdraw from potential wilderness designation lands as to which the United States did not own the mineral rights ("split estates") and would be subjected to taking without just compensation lawsuits, drew heavy fire from environmental groups. "Bisti Dropped as Potential Wild Area," *Albuquerque Journal*, December 28, 1982; "Wilderness Sites May Be Cut," *Albuquerque Journal*, October 26, 1982.

50. "Reagan Signs Four Corners Wilderness Bill" [The San Juan Wilderness Act of 1984], *Albuquerque Journal*, October 31, 1984.

51. Energy Information Administration, *Annual Energy Review*, Table 7.2 "Coal Production, 1949-2011," September 27, 2012.

52. Mark Wilcox, "BLM condemned for coal lease practices after Peabody sale," *Wyoming Business Report*, June, 29, 2012. http://www.wyomingbusinessreport.com/article.asp?id=63516. Peabody Energy leased 721 million tons of ultra-low-sulfur coal reserves adjacent to its North Antelope Rochelle Mine in the Powder River Basin of Wyoming for $1.10 per ton for a total of $793 million. After lease issuance, an annual rental payment of $3 per acre is required, which totals just over $19,000 per year for the 6,364 acre property, along with a royalty payment of 12.5 percent based on the value of surface mine produced coal. Although the 12.5 percent royalty fluctuates with the market value of the coal, at current market value, the 721 million tons of mineable coal will yield an additional $825 million payment to the federal government. Wyoming Governor Matt Mead called the lease "good news" for the state, "Over five years, Wyoming will get a little over $400 million from that sale." Ibid. Days earlier, the General Accountability Office (GAO) announced an investigation in concert with Interior's Inspector General in response to a demand from a Democrat congressman from Massachusetts. Juliet Eilperin, "Powder River Basin coal leasing prompts IG, GAO reviews," *Washington Post*, June 25, 2012, A5.

53. Ibid.

54. The Sierra Club has embarked on a "Beyond Coal" effort. http://www.beyondcoal.org/.

55. January 17, 2008 interview with reporter from *San Francisco Chronicle*. Daniel Halper, "Obama Warned that His Policies Would Bankrupt Coal Power Plant Owners," *Weekly Standard*, May 11, 2012, http://www.weeklystandard.com/blogs/obama-warned-his-policies-would-bankrupt-coal-power-plant-owners_644384.html (audio link).

56. John M. Broder, "'Cap and Trade' Loses Its Standing as Energy Policy of Choice," *New York Times*, March 25, 2010.

57. Proposed Endangerment and Cause or Contribute Findings for Greenhouse Gases Under Section 202(a) of the Clean Air Act, December 7, 2009. http://www.regulations.gov/#!documentDetail;D=EPA-HQ-OAR-2009-0171-0001.

58. *Mingo Logan Mine v. EPA*, Case No. 1:10-cv-00541 (D.D.C.)(March 23, 2012). A three-judge panel of a federal appeals court reversed. *Mingo Logan Coal Co. v. U.S. E.P.A.*, No. 12-5150, 2013 WL 1729603 (D.C. Cir. Apr. 23, 2013).

59. U.S. Environmental Protection Agency. 2012. Proposed Rule. Standards of Performance for Greenhouse Gas Emissions for New Stationary Sources: Electric Utility Generating Units. *Federal Register* 77, n. 72, 22392 (April 13). Not all facilities in all areas of the country can meet the proposed new standards merely by shifting to natural gas. Matthew J. Kotchen and Erin T. Mansur, "How Stringent is the EPA's Proposed Carbon Pollution Standard for New Power Plants?" University of California Center for Energy and Environmental Economics Working Paper Series, April 2012.

60. http://www.epa.gov/airquality/powerplanttoxics/actions.html. http://www.epa.gov/ttn/atw/utility/utilitypg.html. "[T]he so-called "frankenplant" problem in the [EPA's] proposed [Mercury and Air Toxics Standards] rule [is that] EPA required new and existing plants to meet standards based on the best performing units for each individual [hazardous air pollutants]. In reality, few if any plants could meet all of these standards at the same time." "House Passes Bill To Restrict EPA Power Sector Rules," Troutman Sanders, LLP, September 26, 2011, http://www.martindale.com/energy/article_Troutman-Sanders-LLP_1349798.htm.

61. In April 2010, the OSM published notice of intent to prepare an EIS to revise the so-called stream protection rule, 75 *Federal Register* 22723, to replace the 2008 Stream Buffer Zone (SBZ) Rule (73 *Federal Register* 75815). Taylor Kuykendall, "House Committee Makes Final Document Request in Mining Rule Rewrite," [*West Virginia*] *State Journal*, February 26, 2012; Patrick Reis, "Bush's Stream-Buffer Rule for Mining Will Remain Until 2011," *New York Times* (Greenwire), November 2, 2009.

62. Mark Burton, Michael J. Hicks, and Calvin A. Kent, "Coal Production Forecasts and Economic Impact Simulations in Southern West Virginia: A Special Report to the Senate Finance Committee," Center for Business and Economic Research, Marshall University, June 2000, 37.

63. "Economic Analysis of Proposed Stream Protection Rule," ENVIRON International Corporation, Project Number 20-28301A, March 5, 2012, ES-1.

CHAPTER ELEVEN

1. "There were many unrelated functions, for Interior became a Department of miscellany, the most likely place for any new government activity." Eugene P. Trani, *The Secretaries of the Department of the Interior*, 1849–1969 (University of Michigan Library, 1975), 3.

2. Kiron K. Skinner, Annelise Anderson, and Martin Anderson, eds., *Reagan's Path to Victory, The Shaping of Ronald Reagan's Vision: Selected Writings* (The Free Press, 2004), 390, 393. President Reagan wrote: "Norman Podhoretz sent me his book on 'Why We Were In Vietnam' personally inscribed: He wrote 'To Pres. RR—Who always knew and still knows why we were in Vietnam and why it was indeed ["]a noble cause.["]'" Ronald Reagan, *The Reagan Diaries* (Harper, 2007), 74.

3. Barry Moreno, *The Statue of Liberty Encyclopedia* (Simon & Schuster, 2000), 204–5. See also F. Ross Holland, *Idealists, Scoundrels, and the Lady: An Insider's View of the Statue of Liberty-Ellis Island Project* (University of Illinois Press, 1993), 2.

4. Ibid., 216–81; http://www.ellisisland.org/EIinfo/about.asp.

5. Richard Seth Hayden and Thierry W. Despont, *Restoring the Statue of Liberty* (McGraw-Hill Book Company, 1986), 75.

6. http://www.ellisisland.org/EIinfo/about.asp.

7. Ibid.

8. Ibid.

9. Ibid. "Volunteerism has manifested itself in many ways [including] the contributions made by tens of thousands of citizens of their time, talents, and goods to help us manage our parks and refuges."

"America – Our Treasure and Our Trust: The Legacy of President Ronald Reagan 1981 – 1988," (U.S. Department of the Interior, December 1988), 13.

10.	http://www.ellisisland.org/EIinfo/about.asp.

11.	*Interior Report 1988*, i.

12.	Ibid., 4.

13.	Ibid., 3. Litter cleanup in national parks alone cost $15 million annually; 85 percent of the work done by Bureau of Land Management law enforcement officers involves crimes against property; and highway sign vandalism costs between $50 million and $2 billion annually. Ibid.

14.	Ibid., 5.

15.	Ibid. An average of 900 inquiries a month were received in response to the PSAs. Ibid., 6.

16.	Ibid.

17.	Title XI of Public Law 101-628, signed November 28, 1990, established the Take Pride in America Program (TPIA) within the Department of the Interior. (16 USC 4601 note; 104 Stat. 4502), the purposes of which include: (1) Establishing and maintaining a public awareness campaign to instill in the public an appreciation for federal, state, and local lands, facilities, and cultural and natural resources. (2) Conducting a national awards program to honor individuals and entities that distinguish themselves in the appreciation, conservation, and stewardship of these resources. (3) Administering the "Take Pride in America" slogan and logo, http://www.fws.gov/laws/lawsdigest/TAKEPRI. HTML.

18.	"Reagan was unimpressed that the federal government would bear the cost of the dam. ('It's all our money,' he told me.) Livermore had support from Bill Clark, who asked Caspar Weinberger about the cost-effectiveness of Dos Rios. Weinberger, adding another voice to the opposition, told him that the economics were questionable." Lou Cannon, *Governor Reagan: His Rise to Power* (Public Affairs, 2005), 312.

19.	Lou Cannon, *Ronnie and Jesse: A Political Odyssey* (Garden City, 1969), 226.

20.	Kiron K. Skinner, Annelise Anderson, and Martin Anderson, eds., *Reagan, In His Own Hand: The Writings of Ronald Reagan That Reveal His Revolutionary Vision for America* (The Free Press, 2001), 388–89.

21.	Dean J. Kotlowski, "From Backlash to Bingo: Ronald Reagan and Federal Indian Policy," *Pacific Historical Review* 77, no. 4 (November 2008), 624.

22.	Ibid.

23.	Robert J. McCarthy, "The Bureau of Indian Affairs and the Federal Trust Obligation to American Indians," *BYU Journal of Public Law* 19, no. 1 (December, 2004), 6. "1983 – A Year Of Enrichment: Improving The Quality Of Life For All Americans," (U.S. Department of the Interior, October 1983), 31. The present day Department of the Interior's description of the relationship is here: http://www.bia.gov/WhatWeDo/index.htm.

24.	*James G. Watt Nomination: Hearings Before the Committee On Energy and Natural Resources, United States Senate, Ninety-seventh Congress, First Session, On the Proposed Nomination of James G. Watt to Be Secretary of the Interior, January 7 and 8, 1981.* (Washington: U.S. G.P.O., 1981), 52. Ron Arnold, *At the Eye of the Storm: James Watt and the Environmentalists* (Regnery Gateway, 1982), 67. Numerous tribes supported Watt's nomination and Norm Wilson, chairman of the Rosebud Sioux Tribe in South Dakota had a reason for why some tribes opposed Watt: "[S]ome of our chairmen are staunch Democrats, and they're going through a period of crying in their beer, so to speak." Ibid, 60.

25.	News release, "Kenneth L. Smith, Western Tribal Leader, to Be Nominated Assistant Interior Secretary," April 1, 1981. Smith's two deputies were Roy H. Sampsel, a Choctaw Indian from Oregon, and John W. Fritz of the Cherokee Tribe of Oklahoma. Arnold, *At the Eye of the Storm*, 99.

26.	Minutes, Cabinet Council on Human Resources, Sept. 20, 1982, folder: Indian Policy Schedule Proposal, file OA9724, box 3, Neal Files. Morton Blackwell, White House liaison to Native Americans, played a critical role in the issuance of President Reagan's American Indian policy and related issues. Kotlowski, "From Backlash to Bingo."

27.	U.S. Department of the Interior press release on "Indian Issues," June 1, 1983, folder: Indians [3 of 4], file OA10054, box 1, Lee L. Verstandig Files, Reagan Library, as cited by Kotlowski, "From Backlash to Bingo," 635. Smith chaired the panel on Indian policy that reported to the Cabinet Council on Human Resources and sent it to President Reagan. Ibid.

28.	Ibid., 636–37.

29.	White House Press Release, "Statement by the President," Jan. 24, 1983, folder: Indians [2 of 5], file OA12749, box 3, Christina L. Bach Files, Reagan Library.

30. Although several White House aides proposed making the policy pronouncement a major event involving the president, Deaver called it "a candidate for worst schedule proposal of the week." Deaver and Baker thought Watt should meet with American Indian leaders and issue the announcement. Kotlowski, "From Backlash to Bingo," 639.

31. "Watt Sees Reservations As Failure of Socialism," *New York Times*, UPI, January 19, 1983. See, Andrei Znamenski, "Native American Reservations: 'Socialist Archipelago,'" *Mises Daily*, April 26, 2013, https://mises.org/daily/6416/Native-American-Reservations-Socialist-Archipelago.

32. Leilani Watt, *Caught in the Conflict: My Life With James Watt* (Harvest House, 1984), 149.

33. "Congress Criticizes Reagan's Proposed Cuts In Aid to Indian Tribes and Restores Funds," *Washington Post*, Aug. 19, 1983. Williams and Goldwater's remarks were acceptable, it would appear, because they came in support of their attack on President Reagan's budget. One journalist concluded that the Reagan administration budget cuts in Indian country, "replaced dollars with encouragement to Indians to nourish their entrepreneurial activities and to seek independence from the federal dole." Joseph G. Jorgensen, "Gaming and Recent American Indian Economic Development," *American Indian Culture and Research Journal* 22, vol. 3 (1998): 161.

34. Richard Reeves, *President Reagan: The Triumph of Imagination* (New York, 2005), 120. "U.S. Erred, 'Humored' Indians, Reagan Says; Tribes Outraged," *Arizona Republic* (Phoenix), June 1, 1988, A1.

35. A particularly poignant instance, that regarding venereal disease, and Secretary Watt's response to it, is provided by Leilani Watt. Watt, *Caught in the Conflict*, 153–55.

36. Ibid., 154.

37. Unfortunately, a press release issued by the program "Conservative Counterpoint" on which Watt appeared announced that he wanted to abolish reservations. Watt, *Caught in the Conflict*, 148.

38. In his final days in office, President Reagan sought to allay any concerns regarding his remarks in the Soviet Union when he personally "assured" American Indians leaders that "he shares their concerns about Indian programs." "There was a spirit of forgiveness by all of us," said Johnny Thompson, vice chairman of the Navajo Tribal Council...." Bill McAllister, "Reagan Holds Conciliatory Meeting With Select Group of Indians," *Washington Post*, December 13, 1988, A15. President Reagan wrote in his diary, "I met in Cabinet Room with 18 heads of Indian tribes. I think meeting went well. They want less bureaucratic control of tribes & more freedom. I'm for that." *The Reagan Diaries*, 678.

39. Kotlowski, "From Backlash to Bingo," 642–43. *Indian Self-Determination Amendments of 1987*, Public Law 100-472, *U.S. Statutes at Large*, 102 (1988), 3:2285–2299. The amendments required the Secretary of the Interior to begin a five-year Tribal Self-Governance Program.

40. The Indian Tribal Governmental Tax Status Act of 1982, (Title II of Pub. L. No. 97-473, 966 Stat. 2605, 2607-11, as amended by Pub. L. No. 98-21, 97 Stat. 65, 87 [1983-1 CB 510, 511, §1065 of the Tax Reform Act of 1984, 1984-3 [Vol. 1] Cumulative Bulletin 556, made permanent the rules treating Indian tribal governments, or subdivisions thereof, as states.

41. 25 U.S.C. §§ 2101-2108. One early beneficiary of the new law was the Crow Indian Tribe of Montana, which entered into an agreement with Shell Oil Company that brought the tribe $12 million in pre-production payments, plus annual royalties of $3 million. "Crow Tribe's Coal Mining Agreement with Shell Approved," Bureau of Indian Affairs press release, April 6, 1983. http://www.bia.gov/cs/groups/public/documents/text/idc-031939.pdf.

42. Kotlowski, "From Backlash to Bingo," 645. For other actions undertaken by Reagan's Interior Department, see *Interior Report 1983*, 31–33 and *Interior Report 1988*, 83–90.

43. For example, to address concerns regarding potential infiltration by organized crime, Assistant Secretary of the Interior for Indian Affairs Ross Swimmer, a Cherokee, issued guidelines in 1985. "Interior Issues Guidelines for Review of Tribal Bingo Management Contracts," U.S. Department of the Interior press release, April 14, 1986.

44. *California v. Cabazon Band of Mission Indians*, 480 U.S. 202, 218, 222 (1987).

45. Pub.L. 100-497, 25 U.S.C. § 2701 et seq.

46. David E. Wilkins, "Assessing the Presidents: Ronald Reagan," *Indian Country Today*, June 2, 2004, B2.

47. Kotlowski, "From Backlash to Bingo," 648.

48. "2011 Indian Gaming Revenues Increased 3%," National Indian Gaming Commission, Washington, D.C., July 17, 2012.

49. Adapted from Roderick Frazier Nash, *Wilderness and the American Mind* (Yale University Press, 2001), 161–81.

50. John Muir, *The Yosemite* (New York, 1912), 261–62. Muir believed he was preaching "the Tuolumne gospel" and that San Francisco was "the Prince of the powers of Darkness" and "Satan and Co." Nash, *Wilderness and the American Mind*, 167.

51. Representative Finly H. Gray of Indiana. *Congressional Record*, 63rd Cong., 1st Sess., 50 (August 30, 1913), 3991.

52. Elmo Richardson, "The Interior Secretary as Conservation Villain: The Notorious Case of Douglas 'Giveaway' McKay," *Pacific Historical Review* 41 (1972): 333–45.

53. Nash, *Wilderness and the American Mind*, 217.

54. Carl Pope, "Undamming Hetch Hetchy," *Sierra Magazine*, November/December 1987, 34–38.

55. *U.S. News & World Report*, August 31, 1987, 51.

56. Dan Morain and Paul Houston, "Hodel Would Tear Down Dam in Hetch Hetchy," *Los Angeles Times*, August 7, 1987. Hodel, labeling the response from Feinstein and others "astonishing" added, "I'm sorry that some people are so personally hostile to me that they are unable to look at the merits." Ibid.

57. Paul Nussbaum, "Atop Dam, Hodel Renews Hetch Hetchy Call," *Philadelphia Inquirer*, October 14, 1987.

58. Lee May and Dan Morain, "Water, Power Options Listed for Hodel's Hetch Hetchy Proposal," *Los Angeles Times*, November 11, 1987.

59. California Congressman Phil Burton, a Democrat from San Francisco, was an aggressive proponent of environmental set-asides across the country. In an infamous confrontation with Minnesota Congressman James Oberstar, a Democrat, Burton threatened to make all of Oberstar's vast congressional district "a National Park." Responded Oberstar, "I thought you already had." Arnold, *At the Eye of the Storm*, 182.

60. Morain and Houston, "Hodel Would Tear Down Dam in Hetch Hetchy," quoting Congressman Richard Lehman, a California Democrat.

61. Don Hodel, "Why we must restore Hetch Hetchy," *San Francisco Chronicle*, November 13, 2005.

62. Adapted from James H. Webb, Jr., *Micronesia and U.S. Pacific Strategy: A Blueprint for the 1980s* (Praeger Publishers, 1974), 78.

63. Ibid., 79, quoting Warren R. Austin, U.S. Representative to the Security Council, "Tens of thousands of American lives, vast expenditure and years of bitter fighting were needed to drive the Japanese aggressors from these islands...." *Digest of International Law*, I (Washington, D.C.: Government Printing Office, 1963), 771. See, for example, E. B. Sledge, *With the Old Breed at Peleliu and Okinawa* (Presidio Press, 1990). President Reagan's Bureau of Land Management Director Bob Burford, responded to comments that he was too conservative with, "I'm as liberal as a graduate of the Colorado School of Mines, a World War II Marine Corps veteran, and a lifelong rancher could be expected to be." Arnold, *At the Eye of the Storm*, 99. Several other Reagan appointees at the Department of the Interior were from the "greatest generation" and served in World War II and the Korean War: Assistant Secretaries Arnett (Captain, USMC, WWII & Korea) and Miller (U.S. Army Air Force, WWII); Solicitor Coldiron (Captain, U.S. Army, WWII) and Inspector General Mulberry (Major General, USMC Reserve, WWII, Korea, and Vietnam); and Directors Horton (U.S. Navy, WWII and Korea) and Dickenson (Captain, USMC, WWII).

64. Webb, *Micronesia and U.S. Pacific Strategy*, 79, citing Edward Friedman and Mark Selden, eds., *America's Asia: Dissenting Essays on Asia-American Relations* (New York, 1969), 155.

65. Webb, *Micronesia and U.S. Pacific Strategy*, 80. Webb reported that, of the eleven trust territories established by the U.N. at the end of WWII, only two remained; subsequently, "Papua New Guinea became self-governing in December 1973 and achieved independence on September 16, 1975."; http://www.state.gov/r/pa/ei/bgn/2797.htm#history.

66. Webb, *Micronesia and U.S. Pacific Strategy*, 81.

67. See, Arnold, *At the Eye of the Storm*, 234–36.

68. *Interior Report 1983*, 35.

69. Proclamation 5564, United States Relations with the Northern Mariana Island, Micronesia, and the Marshall Islands, November 3, 1986; *Interior Report 1988*, 77–78.

70. Reagan's Interior Department encouraged conservative initiatives such as portability of benefits and privatization of government entities such as the Ronald Reagan Marine Railway in American Samoa and utilities in Guam and the Commonwealth of the Northern Marianas. In addition, given the decrease in federal funds for capital projects, Reagan's Interior Department initiated industrial revenue bonds (IRB) to permit the governments to build projects without taxpayer funds. See generally *Interior Report 1988*, 78–82, and *Interior Report 1983*, 35–36.

71. *Interior Report 1988*, 78.
72. Ibid.
73. The Guam Organic Act of 1950, 48 U.S.C. § 1421 et seq., also made Guam residents citizens.
74. Webb, *Micronesia and U.S. Pacific Strategy*, 66.
75. Ibid., 68. "In addition to being the only piece of American soil directly affected by daily Vietnam commitments—[an almost continuous stream of aircraft takes off and lands]—Guam lost 73 citizens in Vietnam fighting [out of a native population of] about 65,000 people." Ibid., 68–69.
76. Robert F. Roberts, *Destiny's Landfall: A History of Guam* (University of Hawaii Press, 1995), 208–10.
77. In *Rice v. Cayetano*, 528 U.S. 495 (2000), the Supreme Court of the United States declared unconstitutional Hawaiian laws that limited participation in certain elections to native Hawaiians. Three members of the U.S. Civil Rights Commission, in their individual capacities, wrote President Obama to object. August 13, 2012 letter to President Barack Obama Re: Guam Political Status Plebiscite Voter Registration Requirements from Commissioners Peter Kirsanow, Gail Heriot, and Todd Gaziano.
78. The Reagan administration eschewed such overt racialism. The Native Hawaiians Study Commission, created by Congress on December 22, 1980 (Title III of Public Law 96-565) to "conduct a study of the culture, needs and concerns of the Native Hawaiians," published and released to the public a Draft Report of Findings on September 23, 1982. After a 120-day period of public comment, a final report was written and submitted on June 23, 1983 to the U.S. Senate Committee on Energy and Natural Resources and to the U.S. House of Representatives Committee on Interior and Insular Affairs. The report concluded that the United States does not owe an apology for actions that led to Hawaii becoming a U.S. territory and any special needs of Native Hawaiians should not be addressed on the basis of race. President Reagan appoints the Commission, September 11, 1981. http://www.presidency.ucsb.edu/ws/index.php?pid=44233.
79. *Davis v. Guam*, Civ. No. 11-00035, U.S. District Court, Territory of Guam. Colonel Davis is represented by J. Christian Adams, former Civil Rights Division attorney and author of *Injustice*: *Exposing the Racial Agenda of the Obama Justice Department* (Regnery, 2011).
80. James Webb, *Fields of Fire* (Naval Institute Press, 1978). "In my opinion, the finest of the Vietnam novels," Tom Wolfe.
81. James Webb, *Born Fighting: How the Scots-Irish Shaped America* (Broadway Books, 2004).
82. Webb's tale may be the worst of them all. See *Born Fighting*, "The Invisible People," 317–27. His Georgetown Law professor included in his final criminal law examination (100 percent of the grade) a hypothetical involving a Sergeant Jack Webb who stuffed jade in the wounds of his dead soldiers to smuggle it into the USA by escorting the remains home for the funerals. Question: "To what extent did the Fourth Amendment allow customs officials to search inside the holes of the dead bodies in order to find the jade?" Webb complained; the professor got tenure. Ibid., 320–21.
83. In April 1979, a group of Vietnam veterans established the Vietnam Veterans Memorial Fund, Inc., an IRC 501(c)(3) organization. Senator Charles McCurdy Mathias Jr., a Republican from Maryland, and Senator John W. Warner, a Republican from Virginia, cosponsored legislation that passed Congress and was signed into law on July 1, 1980, by President Carter (Public Law 96-297) authorizing a site for a Vietnam Veterans Memorial in Constitution Gardens, just northeast of the Lincoln Memorial.
84. "The wall is set into the earth so that as one walks along it, one gets the sensation of walking into a grave." Trust for the National Mall, Vietnam Veterans Memorial, http://www.nationalmall.org/sites-subpage-vietnam.php.
85. Digital.lib.lehigh.edu/trial/Vietnam/r3/may/, dated 7/7/1981.
86. Digital.lib.lehigh.edu/trial/Vietnam/r3/October/, dated 10/13/1981.
87. Ibid.
88. Days later Webb wrote, "At what point does a piece of architecture cease being a memorial to service and instead become a mockery of that service, a wailing wall for future anti-draft and anti-nuclear demonstrators?" James Webb, "Reassessing the Vietnam Veterans Memorial," *Wall Street Journal* (December 18, 1981), 22.
89. Meanwhile, Watt had heard from some Members of Congress who urged him to take action to ensure that the memorial will "honor those who served and died." Digital.lib.lehigh.edu/trial/Vietnam/r3/october, November 20, 1981. Later, Vietnam veteran Milton R. Copulos of The Heritage Foundation published a "Backgrounder," objecting to the design. Ibid., December 7, 1981. In

January 1982, Idaho Senator Steve Symms, a Republican, and three other Senators wrote to Watt objecting to the design; Digital.lib.lehigh.edu/trial/Vietnam/files/round3/october, January 18, 1982.

90.   Maya Lin "created the design for a class she was taking on funerary architecture." Maya Lin, "Systematic Landscapes," March 14-July 12, 2009, Corcoran Gallery of Art, unnumbered page 13, http://www.corcoran.org/sites/default/files/MayaLinTeachersPacket.pdf.

91.   Watt authorized work to progress on the Memorial; however, he instructed the National Park Service to erect an American Flag at the site. Official and unofficial ground breaking took place in March 1982.

92.   "Rick is, and I do not say this lightly, America's greatest sculptor," said Tom Wolfe. Tom Wolfe, "The Lives They Lived: Frederick Hart, b. 1943; The Artist the Art World Couldn't See," *New York Times Magazine*, January 2, 2000. Hart, a devout convert to Catholicism, had rare courage. When his deep bas reliefs and statuary of the Creation at the Washington Cathedral were stolen and blasphemed in the movie *The Devil's Advocate*, he sued Hollywood and won. Christopher Stern, "Settlement reached in 'Devil's Advocate' case: WB agrees to cut scenes from film in order to proceed with vid release," *Variety*, February 16, 1998.

93.   Rick Horowitz, "Maya Lin's Angry Objections," *Washington Post*, July 7, 1982, B1, B6. Phil McCombs, "Let Me Count the Ways," *Washington Post*, May 11, 1983, B7, in which Maya Lin continued to "rip" Frederick Hart's statue.

94.   "Over the past two months art mullahs of every description have begun a holy war against the addition of the statue." Tom Wolfe, "The Battle of the Vietnam Memorial: How the Mullahs of Modernism Caused a Stir," *Washington Post*, October 13, 1982, B1.

95.   Letter from Watt to J. Carter Brown, digital.lib.lehigh.edu/trial/Vietnam/r4/1982, November 24, 1982.

96.   In fact, Watt gave Reagan's Interior Department's approval to all three placement options; however, Watt stood by his earlier endorsement of the original agreement as to the location of the flag and the statue as one that "truly honors all those who served their Nation in the Vietnam War." He believed that the arts community would stand by the agreement it made with Hart and that the "good guys" had won. Letter from Secretary of the Interior James G. Watt to Mrs. Helen Scharf, Chairman, National Capitol Planning Commission, February 1, 1983. Arnold, *At the Eye of the Storm*, 239.

97.   President Reagan no doubt watched the battle by the arts community against the *Three Fighting Men* with a sense of déjà vu. In May 1978, he wrote of a similar battle between Dulles Airport and the Department of the Interior's Advisory Council on Historic Preservation and the Fine Arts Commission. *Reagan's Path to Victory*, 300–1.

98.   *The Reagan Diaries*, 277. President Reagan alone—Mrs. Reagan was in Phoenix—made his first unofficial visit to the Memorial on May 1, 1983 on his way back to the White House from church; he wrote in his diary: "On way home stopped by and put flowers at the Vietnam memorial. It's quite a place—a very impressive and moving experience." Ibid., 149. Despite incessant written and oral communications with White House staff by those who wanted to prevent Watt from representing the views of veterans who opposed the Wall, Watt was never contacted by "the White House." In fact, President Reagan did not officially visit the Memorial until the *Three Fighting Men* statue was in place.

99.   Tom Carhart, "The Memorial, the Mirror: A Reply," Letter to the Editor, *Washington Post*, November 12, 1984, A18: "[W]e have attained the addition of a powerful statue, an American Flag, and a fitting inscription to our memorial. Now it is a beautiful and complete memorial."

100.   The National Park Service refers to Hart's sculpture as "The Three Servicemen."; http://www.nps.gov/getaways/vive/. Others called it "The Three Soldiers."; http://en.wikipedia.org/wiki/The_Three_Soldiers.

CHAPTER TWELVE

1.   This is the title of Chapter 7 of Kengor's *God and Ronald Reagan: A Spiritual Life* (ReganBooks, 2004), 89–99. Kengor reveals that President Reagan traced the origin of the phrase, not just to John Winthrop's 1630 message from the deck of the *Arabella* off the Massachusetts coast, but also to Christ's Sermon on the Mount, specifically Matthew 5:14–16: "Ye are the light of the world. A city that is set on an hill cannot be hid. Neither do men light a candle, and put it under a bushel, but on a candlestick; and it giveth light unto all that are in the house. Let your light so shine before men, that they may see your good works, and glorify your Father which is in heaven." (AV). President Reagan stoutly defended his use of the "bully pulpit" of the presidency to defend the "Gospel of

Christ" when challenged by a Knight Ridder reporter in February 1984. Kengor, *God and Ronald Reagan*, 167.

2. President Ronald Reagan's Farewell Address to the Nation, Davis W. Houck and Amos Kiewe, eds., *Actor, Ideologue, Politician: The Public Speeches of Ronald Reagan* (Greenwood, 1993), 327. Nearly thirty-seven years earlier, in June 1952, Ronald Reagan declared, "I, in my own mind, have thought of America as a place in the divine scheme of things that was set aside as a promised land.... I believe that God in shedding his grace on this country has always in this divine scheme of things kept an eye on our land and guided it as a promised land for those people [who love freedom]." Ronald Reagan, "America the Beautiful," commencement address, William Woods College, June 1952, quoted in Kengor, *God and Ronald Reagan*, 95.

3. Bush added $4 trillion in 8 years, while Obama's contribution in just 4 years is nearly $6 trillion. Amy Payne, "Morning Bell," The Foundry, blog, The Heritage Foundation, September 5, 2012. Each taxpayer's portion of the debt is $111,414 and rising, and currently each child is born with a $50,000 share of the debt. Ibid.

4. "The actual liabilities of the federal government—including Social Security, Medicare, and federal employees' future retirement benefits—already exceed $86.8 trillion, or 550% of the GDP." Chris Cox and Bill Archer, "Why $16 Trillion Only Hints at the True U.S. Debt," *Wall Street Journal*, November 26, 2012. "It isn't what we don't know that gives us trouble; it's what we know that ain't so." Will Rogers.

5. "When you find yourself in a hole, stop digging." Will Rogers.

6. Harry Anderson et al., "The U.S. Economy in Crisis," *Newsweek*, January 19, 1981, 30–34.

7. In 2011, Steve Forbes concluded that the 1981 economy was worse than 2011. "Reagan came into the White House facing an economy as troubled as ours—one that had even higher unemployment, catastrophic interest rates (18% for mortgages) and a stock market that in real terms had fallen 60% from its mid-1960s levels." Steve Forbes, "Reagan's Legacy and the Current Malaise: Lower taxes and a strong dollar could spur growth once again." *Wall Street Journal*, March 22, 2011.

8. Phil Gramm, "Reagan and Obama: A Tale of Two Recoveries: How these two presidents responded to a deep recession reveals polar extremes in policy. And in results," *Wall Street Journal*, August 29, 2012. "Only twice since World War II has the U.S. unemployment rate reached 10%: It was 10.8% in 1982 and 10% in 2009." Fifty-five months after each recession started, Reagan "had created 7.8 million more jobs ... and real per capita gross domestic product [GDP] was up by $3,091" and for Obama "there were four million fewer Americans working ... and real per capita GDP was down $803."

9. "When he left office eight years later, the U.S. had become an economic miracle: 18 million new jobs had been created ... and the stock market was experiencing a bull run that, despite dramatic ups and downs, didn't end until the turn of the 21st century, after the Dow had expanded 15-fold. The expansion of the U.S. economy [through 2007] exceeded the entire size of West Germany's economy, then the world's third-largest," *Forbes*, "Reagan's Legacy and the Current Malaise."

10. For a single example, out of scores of potential regulatory horror stories, consider the cost of Obama's plans to impose redundant "fracturing regulations" on the most productive sector of the Nation's economy. The Western Energy Alliance estimates the cost of the new regulations at $1.6 billion a year according to John Dunham & Associates, an economics firm. "WEA questions cost of BLM's proposed fracking rule," *Oil and Gas Journal*, June 25, 2012. Taken as a whole, Obama's regulatory onslaught is devastating. Adam J. White, "Obama's Regulatory Rampage—Fasten your seatbelts, because the courts and Congress won't be able to slow it down much," *Weekly Standard*, January 28, 2013; Jeffrey H. Anderson, "The Cost of Obama's Regulatory Explosion—Nearly double the cost of the first three years of Bush and Clinton combined," *Weekly Standard*, January 30, 2013.

11. Jay W. Richards, *Money, Greed, and God: Why Capitalism is the Solution and Not the Problem*, (HarperOne, 2010), 202.

12. Vincent Carroll, "The anti-fracking goons in Boulder," *Denver Post*, December 7, 2012. Two female energy company employees had to call 911 and obtain a police escort to leave a Boulder hearing in safety after being attacked by anti-fracturing goons.

13. See Kengor, *God and Ronald Reagan*. "[Ronald Reagan's] political career expressed a historical and philosophical worldview that was Christian in a very traditional American sense." Hugh Heclo, "Ronald Reagan and the American Public Philosophy," in W. Elliot Brownlee and Hugh Davis Graham, eds., *The Reagan Presidency: Pragmatic Conservatism & Its Legacies* (University Press of Kansas, 2003), 20.

14. Charles W. Colson, Nancy Pearcey, and Harold Fickett, *How Now Shall We Live?* (Tyndale House, 1999).

15. Heclo, "Ronald Reagan and the American Public Philosophy," 25.

16. Throughout his life, Ronald Reagan believed God was in control. Kengor points out numerous instances. One stands out, his reaction to his survival of the attempt on his life. "Whatever happens now I owe my life to God and will try to serve him in every way I can." Ronald Reagan, *The Reagan Diaries* (Harper, 2007), 12.

17. Heclo, "Ronald Reagan and the American Public Philosophy," 21. "From Reagan's first to his last political utterances, God's unique relation to America was the central chord from which all else followed." Ibid., 20. This "theophanic view of the nation" had three major facets: [1] "God had chosen America as the agent of His special purposes in history." [2] "America undertook a mission charged with significance for all mankind." [3] "[America is to ensure] an end to the wreck of history and the beginning of a new time." Ibid., 21–22. As to Heclo's third point, Ronald Reagan makes clear, "America remains on a voyage of discovery, a land that has never become, but is always in the act of becoming." Speech to the Republican National Convention, August 17, 1992, Houck and Kiewe, *Actor, Ideologue, Politician*, 334.

18. Heclo, "Ronald Reagan and the American Public Philosophy," 29.

19. Houck and Kiewe, *Actor, Ideologue, Politician*, 5.

20. Heclo, "Ronald Reagan and the American Public Philosophy," 25.

21. Houck and Kiewe, *Actor, Ideologue, Politician*, 28.

22. Houck and Kiewe, *Actor, Ideologue, Politician*, 326; January 11, 1989, "Farewell Address to the Nation."

23. Houck and Kiewe, *Actor, Ideologue, Politician*, 152.

24. Ibid., 322–24.

25. "On my desk in the Oval Office, I have a little sign that says, 'There is no limit to what a man can do or where he can go if he doesn't mind who gets the credit.'" http://www.reaganfoundation.org/reagan-quotes.aspx. For Christmas 1982, President and Mrs. Reagan gave every cabinet secretary a gift of cut glass in a stand etched with those words so each one could have this "little sign" on the secretary's desk.

26. Madison declared, "If angels were to govern men, neither external nor internal controls on government would be necessary." *The Federalist Papers*, no. 51.

27. In a January 19, 1979, radio address entitled "Regulations," Governor Reagan spoke of Alexander Hamilton's warning of "laws so voluminous … , so incoherent … , [and subject to] such incessant changes that no man who knows what the law is today can guess what it will be tomorrow." Governor Reagan noted that Hamilton was writing of "laws written by our elected representatives. He had no way of foreseeing that multitudinous regulations having the power of law would be written by permanent employees of government who were not elected by us the people." Kiron K. Skinner, Annelise Anderson, and Martin Anderson, eds., *Reagan's Path to Victory, The Shaping of Ronald Reagan's Vision: Selected Writings* (The Free Press, 2004), 416, citing *Federalist Paper* no. 62.

28. Houck and Kiewe, *Actor, Ideologue, Politician*, 327.

BIBLIOGRAPHY

Books:

Adams, J. Christian. *Injustice*: *Exposing the Racial Agenda of the Obama Justice Department*. Washington, D.C.: Regnery, 2011.

Arnold, Ron. *At the Eye of the Storm*: *James Watt and the Environmentalists*. Chicago, IL: Regnery Gateway, 1982.

Arnold, Ron, and Alan Gottlieb. *Undue Influence*: *Wealthy Foundations, Grant Driven Environmental Groups, and Zealous Bureaucrats That Control Your Future*. Bellevue, WA: Merril Press, 1999.

———. *Trashing the Economy*: *How Runaway Environmentalism is Wrecking America*. Bellevue, WA: Merril Press, 1994.

Arrandale, Tom. *The Battle for Natural Resources*. Washington, D.C.: Congressional Quarterly, 1983.

Ashby, Eric. *Reconciling Man with the Environment*. Stanford, CA: Stanford University Press, 1972.

Aton, James M. *John Wesley Powell*: *His Life and Legacy*. Salt Lake City, UT: Bonneville Books, 2009.

Barker, Kenneth, ed. *The NIV (New International Version) Study Bible*. Grand Rapids, MI: Zondervan Publishing House, 1985.

Barrett, I. Laurence. *Gambling with History: Reagan in the White House*. Garden City, NY: Doubleday, 1983.

Bible, The Holy, (King James Version). New York: American Bible Society, 1980.

Bradlee, Ben. *A Good Life: Newspapering and Other Adventures*. New York: Simon & Schuster, 1995.

Brawarsky, Sandee, and D. Mark. *Two Jews, Three Opinions: A Collection of 20th Century American Jewish Quotations*. New York: Perigee Trade, 1998.

Brown, Keith, ed. *Encyclopedia of Language and Linguistics, Second Edition*. Oxford, UK: Elsevier Science Publishers, 2005.

Brownlee, W. Elliot, and Hugh Davis Graham, eds. *The Reagan Presidency: Pragmatic Conservatism & Its Legacies*. Lawrence, KS: University Press of Kansas, 2003.

Cannon, Lou. *Ronnie and Jesse: A Political Odyssey*. New York: Doubleday, 1969.

———. *Reagan*. New York: G. P. Putnam's Sons, 1982.

———. *Governor Reagan: His Rise to Power*. New York: Public Affairs, 2003.

Carr, Ethan. *Mission 66: Modernism and the National Park Dilemma*. Amherst, MA: University of Massachusetts Press, 2007.

Carson, Rachel. *Silent Spring*. New York: Houghton Mifflin, 1962.

Carter, Jimmy. *White House Diary*. New York: Farrar, Straus and Giroux, 2010.

Cawley, R. McGreggor. *Federal Land—Western Anger: The Sagebrush Rebellion & Environmental Politics*. Lawrence, KS: University Press of Kansas, 1993.

Clarke, Jeanne Nienaber, and Daniel C. McCool. *Staking Out the Terrain: Power Differentials Among Natural Resource Management Agencies*. Albany: Albany State University of New York Press, 1985.

Clause, George, and Karen Bolander. *Ecological Sanity*. New York: D. McKay, 1977.

Colson, Charles, Nancy Pearcey, and Harold Fickett. *How Now Shall We Live?* Wheaton, IL: Tyndale House Publishers, 1999.

Davis, Patti. *The Way I See It*: *An Autobiography*. New York: G. P. Putnam's Sons, 1992.

Drew, Elizabeth. *Portrait of an Election*: *The 1980 Presidential Campaign*. New York: Simon & Schuster, 1981.

D'Souza, Dinesh. *Ronald Reagan*: *How an Ordinary Man Became an Extraordinary Leader*. New York: The Free Press, 1997.

Durant, Robert F. *The Administrative Presidency Revisited*: *Public Lands, the BLM, and the Reagan Revolution*. Albany: State University of New York Press, 1992.

Easton, Robert Olney. *Black Tide*: *The Santa Barbara Oil Spill and Its Consequences*. New York: Delacorte Press, 1972.

Eckes, Alfred E. *The United States and The Global Struggle for Minerals*. Austin, TX: University of Texas Press, 1979.

Edwards, Lee. *Bringing Justice to the People*: *The Story of the Freedom-Based Public Interest Law Movement*. Washington, D.C.: Heritage Books, 2004.

Ehrlich, Paul R. *The Population Bomb*. New York: Ballantine Books, 1968.

Endangered Species Act, The (Stanford Environmental Law Society Handbook). Stanford: Stanford University Press, 2001.

Endicott, Eve, ed. *Land Conservation Through Public/Private Partnerships*. Washington, D.C.: Island Press, 1993.

Franklin, Benjamin, William Brownrigg, and James Farish. *On the Stilling of Waves by Means of Oil*. London: Royal Society of London, 1774.

Friedman, Edward, and Mark Selden, eds. *America's Asia*: *Dissenting Essays on Asian American Relations*. New York: Vintage Books, 1971.

Goldberg, Bernard. *Bias*: *A CBS Insider Exposes How the Media Distort the News*. Washington, D.C.: Regnery, 2001.

———. *A Slobbering Love Affair: The True (and Pathetic) Story of the Torrid Romance Between Barack Obama and the Mainstream Media.* Washington, D.C.: Regnery, 2009.

Golden, Marissa Martino. *What Motivates Bureaucrats? Politics and Administration During The Reagan Years.* New York: Columbia University Press, 2000.

Gore, Al. *Earth in the Balance: Ecology and the Human Spirit.* New York: Houghton Mifflin, 1992.

Gramling, Robert. *Oil on the Edge: Offshore Development, Conflict, Gridlock.* Albany: State University of New York Press, 1996.

Gulland, Daphne M., and David G. Hinds-Howell. *The Penguin Dictionary of English Idioms.* New York: Penguin Books, 1986.

Hayden, Richard Seth, Thierry W. Despont, Nadine M. Post, and Dan Cornish. *Restoring the Statue of Liberty: Sculpture, Structure, Symbol.* New York: McGraw-Hill, 1986.

Hayward, Steven F. *The Age of Reagan: The Conservative Counterrevolution 1980–1989.* New York: Crown Forum, 2009.

Heatherly, Charles L., ed. *Mandate for Leadership: Policy Management in a Conservative Administration.* Washington, D.C.: The Heritage Foundation, 1981.

Holland, F. Ross. *Idealists, Scoundrels, and the Lady: An Insider's View of the Statue of Liberty-Ellis Island Project.* Urbana, IL: University of Illinois Press, 1993.

Houck, Davis, and Amos Kiewe, eds. *Actor, Ideologue, Politician: The Public Speeches of Ronald Reagan.* Westport, CT: Greenwood Press, 1993.

Humes, James C. *The Wit & Wisdom of Ronald Reagan.* Washington, D.C.: Regnery, 2007.

Kengor, Paul, and Patricia Clark Doerner. *The Judge: William P. Clark, Ronald Reagan's Top Hand.* San Francisco: Ignatius, 2007.

Kengor, Paul. *God and Ronald Reagan: A Spiritual Life.* New York: HarperCollins, 2004.

Kinsley, Michael. *Curse of the Giant Muffins and Other Washington Maladies.* New York: Summit Books, 1987.

Kristol, Irving. *Two Cheers for Capitalism*. New York: Basic Books, 1978.

Kurtz, Stanley. *Radical-in-Chief: Barack Obama and the Untold Story of American Socialism*. New York: Threshold Editions, 2010.

Lamm, Richard D., and Michael McCarthy. *The Angry West: A Vulnerable Land and Its Future*. Boston: Houghton Mifflin, 1982.

Lash, Jonathan, Katherine Gillman, and David Sheridan. *A Season of Spoils: The Story of the Reagan Administration's Attack on the Environment*. New York: Pantheon Books, 1984.

Lazarus, Richard J., and Oliver A. Houck, eds. *Environmental Law Stories: An In-Depth Look at Ten Leading Environmental Law Cases*. New York: Foundation Press, 2005.

Maslow, A. H. *Motivation and Personality*. New York: Harper & Brothers, 1954.

McDonald, Stephen L. *The Leasing of Federal Lands for Fossil Fuels Production*. Washington, D.C.: RFF Press, 1979.

Meadows, Donella H. *The Limits to Growth: A Report for the Club of Rome's Project on the Predicament of Mankind*. New York: Signet, 1972.

Meese, Edwin, III. *With Reagan: The Inside Story*. Washington, D.C.: Regnery Gateway, 1992.

Miles, Austin. *Setting the Captives Free: Victims of the Church Tell Their Stories*. Buffalo: Prometheus Books, 1990.

Moreno, Barry. *The Statue of Liberty Encyclopedia*. New York: Simon & Schuster, 2000.

Muir, John. *The Yosemite*. New York: The Century Company, 1912.

Nash, Roderick Frazier. *Wilderness and the American Mind*. New Haven, CT: Yale University Press, 2001.

Nelson, Robert H. *The Making of Federal Coal Policy*. Durham, NC: Duke University Press, 1983.

Papritz, Carew, ed. *100 Watts: The James Watt Memorial Cartoon Collection*. Auburn, WA: Khyber Press, 1983.

Pendley, William Perry. *War on the West: Government Tyranny on America's Great Frontier*. Washington, D.C.: Regnery, 1995.

Pfiffner, James P. *The Strategic Presidency: Hitting the Ground Running* (*Second Edition, Revised*). Lawrence, KS: University Press of Kansas, 1996.

Pipes, Richard. *Vixi: Memoirs of a Non-Belonger*. New Haven, CT: Yale University Press, 2003.

Portney, Paul R., ed. *Natural Resources and the Environment: The Reagan Approach*. Washington, D.C.: Urban Institute Press, 1984.

Priest, Tyler. *The Offshore Imperative: Shell Oil's Search for Petroleum in Postwar America*. College Station, TX: Texas A&M University Press, 2007.

Reagan, Ronald. *Speaking My Mind* (*Selected Speeches*). New York: Simon & Schuster, 1989.

———. *The Reagan Diaries*. New York: HarperCollins, 2007.

———. *An American Life: The Autobiography*. New York: Simon & Schuster, 1990.

Reeves, Richard. *President Reagan: The Triumph of Imagination*. New York: Simon & Schuster, 2005.

Reynolds, Glenn H. *An Army of Davids: How Markets and Technology Empower Ordinary People to Beat Big Media, Big Government, and Other Goliaths*. Nashville, TN: Thomas Nelson, 2006.

Richards, Jay W. *Money, Greed, and God: Why Capitalism is the Solution and Not the Problem*. New York: HarperOne, 2009.

Roberts, Robert F. *Destiny's Landfall: A History of Guam*. Honolulu: University of Hawaii Press, 1995.

Rostvold, Dr. Gerhard N., and Thomas J. Dudley. *Report to Congress: New Perspectives on Grazing Fees and Public Land Management in the 1990's*. Malibu: Pepperdine University Press, 1992.

Safire, William, ed. *Lend Me Your Ears: Great Speeches in History*. New York: W. W. Norton, 1992.

Sayre, Nathan F. *Ranching, Endangered Species, and Urbanization in the Southwest: Species of Capital*. Tucson: University of Arizona Press, 2002

Schweizer, Peter. *Victory: The Reagan Administration's Secret Strategy That Hastened the Collapse of the Soviet Union*. New York: Atlantic Monthly Press, 1994.

Short, C. Brant. *Ronald Reagan and the Public Lands; America's Conservation Debate, 1979–1984*. College Station, TX: Texas A&M University Press, 1989.

Simon, Julian L. *The Ultimate Resource*. Princeton: Princeton University Press, 1981.

Skinner, Kiron K., Annelise Anderson, and Martin Anderson, eds. *Reagan, In His Own Hand: The Writings of Ronald Reagan That Reveal His Revolutionary Vision for America*. New York: The Free Press, 2001.

———. *Reagan: A Life in Letters*. New York: The Free Press, 2003.

———. *Reagan's Path to Victory: The Shaping of Ronald Reagan's Vision (Selected Writings)*. New York: The Free Press, 2004.

Slansky, Paul. *The Clothes Have No Emperor: A Chronicle of the American 80s*. New York: Fireside, 1989.

Sledge, E. B. *With the Old Breed at Peleliu and Okinawa*. Novato, CA: Presidio Press, 1981.

Smith, Phyllis, and William Hoy. *The Northern Pacific Railroad & Yellowstone National Park*. Germantown, MD: Keystone Press, 2009.

Stockman, David. *The Triumph of Politics: Why the Reagan Revolution Failed*. New York: Harper & Row, 1986.

Straughan, Dale. *Biological and Oceanographical Survey of the Santa Barbara Channel Oil Spill, 1969–1970*. Los Angeles: Allan Hancock Foundation/University of Southern California, 1971.

Trani, Eugene P. *The Secretaries of the Department of the Interior, 1849–1969*. Ann Arbor: University of Michigan Library, 1975.

Udall, Stewart L. *The Quiet Crisis*. New York: Henry Holt, 1963.

Vanderpoel, Sally. *Stan Hathaway: A Biography*. Huntley, WY: Wodehouse Enterprise, 2003.

Vietor, Richard. *Energy Policy in America Since 1945: A Study of Business-Government Relations*. New York: Cambridge University Press 1984.

Vig, Norman J., and Michael E. Kraft. *Environmental Policy in the 1980s: Reagan's New Agenda*. Washington, D.C.: Congressional Quarterly, 1984.

Viguerie, Richard. *America's Right Turn: How Conservatives Used New and Alternative Media to Take Over America*. Chicago: Bonus Books, 2004.

Watt, Leilani, with Al Janssen. *Caught in the Conflict: My Life with James Watt.* Eugene, OR: Harvest House Publishers, 1984.

Webb, James H., Jr. *Micronesia and U.S. Pacific Strategy: A Blueprint for the 1980s.* New York: Praeger Publishers, 1974.

Webb, James. *Born Fighting: How the Scots-Irish Shaped America.* New York: Broadway Books, 2004.

————. *Fields of Fire.* New York: Prentice-Hall, 1978.

Webster's Third New International Dictionary of the English Language Unabridged. Springfield, MA: G. & C. Merriam, 1969.

Wheeler, William Bruce, and Michael McDonald. *TVA and the Tellico Dam 1936–1979: A Bureaucratic Crisis in Post-Industrial America.* Knoxville: University of Tennessee Press, 1986.

Wyant, William K. *Westward in Eden: The Public Lands and the Conservation Movement.* Berkeley: University of California Press, 1982.

Government Documents:

Congressional Record

Energy Information Administration Reports

Federal Register

General Accounting Office Reports

Government Printing Office Publications

National Materials and Mineral Program Plan and Report to Congress

Office of Management and Budget Reports

Office of Technology Assessment Reports

Proclamation 5030 Exclusive Economic Zone of the United States of America 1983

State of Alaska Department of Natural Resources Division of Oil and Gas Report

United States Geological Survey–*National Water Summary*

United States Geological Survey Publications

United States Department of the Interior Reports, including:

- *1983—A Year Of Enrichment: Improving The Quality Of Life For All Americans* (Washington, D.C.: U.S. Government Printing Office, October 1983).
- *America: Our Treasure and Our Trust: The Legacy of President Ronald Reagan, 1981–1988* (Washington, D.C.: U.S. Government Printing Office, December 1988).

United States Office of Coal Mining Reclamation and Enforcement Reports

United States Senate Hearings and Reports

United States House of Representatives Hearings and Reports

Law Review Articles and Magazines:

American Behavioral Scientist

American Indian Culture and Research Journal

American Petroleum Institute Report

American Review of Public Administration

American Spectator

Annual Energy Review

Arizona Law Review

The Atlantic

Atlantic Monthly Press

Audubon

Boston College Environmental Affairs Law Review

Brigham Young University Public Law Review

Bureaucrat

Business Week

Congressional Research Service

Congressional Quarterly Weekly Reports

Digest of International Law

Energy Daily

Environmental Law Report

Environmental Law Review

Explorer

Federal Public Lands and Natural Resources Law

Forbes Land Use Planning Report

Forest Industries

Fortune

Harper's

Indian Country Today

inFocus Quarterly

International Affairs

Journal of Forest History

Journal of Mineral Law and Policy

Journal South African Inst. Mining & Metallurgy

Land and Water Law Review

Land Use Planning Report

Mountain Geologist

National Journal

National Magazine

Natural Resources and Environmental Policy

Natural Resources Lawyer

New Republic

Newsweek

New York Times Magazine

Offshore

Oil and Gas Journal

Pacific Historical Review

Public Land Law Review

Reason

Regulation

Rocky Mountain Magazine

Rocky Mountain Mineral Law Institute

Rolling Stone

Science

Sierra Magazine

Sports Illustrated

Time

New Yorker

U.S. News and World Report

Variety

Weekly Standard

Western New England Law Review

West Virginia State Journal

Wyoming Business Report

Yale Law Journal

COPYRIGHT ACKNOWLEDGMENTS

Areas Open for Energy Exploration under President Reagan's 1982 OCS Oil and Gas Leasing Program
- Institute for Energy Research, Washington, D.C.

Areas Closed to Energy Exploration under President Obama's 2012 OCS Oil and Gas Leasing Program
- Institute for Energy Research, Washington, D.C.

Clark Final Report to President Reagan
- William P. Clark, Paso Robles, California

Coal Produced from Federal Lands, FY1977–FY2012
- 1977–1984: U.S. Department of the Interior, Bureau of Land Management, "Public Land Statistics 1984" and prior issues;
- 1985–1993: U.S. Department of the Interior, Minerals Management Service, "Minerals Revenues 1993, Report on Receipts from Federal and Indian Leases" and prior issues; Energy Information Administration, Coal Production, DOE/EIA-0118, various issues; and Coal Industry Annual 1993, DOE/EIA-0584(93) (Washington, D.C., December 1994);

- 1994–2001: U.S. Department of the Interior, Minerals Management Service, "Minerals Revenues 1993, Report on Receipts from Federal and Indian Leases" and prior issues;
- 2003–2012: Office of Natural Resources Revenue, U.S. Department of the Interior, http://statistics.onrr.gov/Default.aspx.

Coal Production, FY1977–FY2012
- U.S. Energy Information Administration

Federal and Indian Lands Map
- Courtesy of National Atlas of the United States®

Federal Onshore Oil and Gas Leasing, FY1977–FY2012
- Oil and Gas Statistics, Bureau of Land Management, U.S. Department of the Interior; http://www.blm.gov/wo/st/en/prog/energy/oil_and_gas/statistics.html;
- 1985–1987: U.S. Department of the Interior, Bureau of Land Management, "Public Land Statistics 1987" and prior issues;
- "1983 – A Year Of Enrichment: Improving The Quality Of Life For All Americans," (U.S. Department of the Interior, October 1983), 16.

Herb Block political cartoon "Onward, Christian Soldier!"
- Reproduced by permission of The Herblock Foundation

Hodel Final Report to President Reagan
- Superintendent of Documents, U.S. Government Printing Office, Washington, D.C.

James G. Watt—photograph
- Fredde Lieberman

Jim Watt's Monday Morning Team
- William Perry Pendley, Washington, D.C., 1986

Land and Water Conservation Fund: Table and Graph
- Adapted from Carol Hardy Vincent, "Land and Water Conservation Fund: Overview, Funding History, and Issues," Congressional Research Service, August 13, 2010, 6–7. Source of data: DOI Budget Office; Land and Water Conservation Fund, MSExcel spreadsheet, on the Budget

Office's website at http://www.doi.gov/budget/budget_general/bgindex. html.

Mountain West States Onshore Oil and Gas Leasing, FY1988–FY2012
- Oil and Gas Statistics, Bureau of Land Management, U.S. Department of the Interior; http://www.blm.gov/wo/st/en/prog/energy/oil_and_gas/ statistics.html.

OCS Oil and Gas Leasing Acreage Offered for Leasing
- Bureau of Ocean Energy Management of the U.S. Department of the Interior, Washington, D.C.

Paul Conrad political cartoons:
"Mount Wattmore National Park"
"Batting for Watt and Playing Right Field.... "
"To Sec. Hodel, With Love"
"Watt Lives!"
- All reproduced by permission of The Huntington Library, San Marino, California, with thanks to Mrs. Kay Conrad for her generous permission.

President Reagan, joined by Secretary Hodel, Lou Gossett Jr., and Clint Eastwood, announces "Take Pride in America"—photograph
- Ronald Reagan Presidential Library and Museum

Proclamation 5030 (by Ronald Reagan)
- National Archives and Records Administration

Radio Address (by Ronald Reagan)
- Ronald Reagan Presidential Library and Museum

Ronald Reagan—Rancho del Cielo (Reagan ranch) cover photograph
- Newscom/Michael Evans

Ronald Reagan—official photograph
- Ronald Reagan Presidential Library and Museum

Three Soldiers, bronze statue © 1984 Frederick Hart and Vietnam Veterans Memorial Fund
- Frederick Hart Foundation and Vietnam Veterans Memorial Fund
- Photograph by Randy Santos/dcstockimages.com

Watt Final Report to President Reagan
  • Superintendent of Documents, U.S. Government Printing Office, Washington, D.C.

William P. Clark and Donald Paul Hodel—official photographs
  • National Park Service Historic Photograph Collection

Western Union Telegram
  • Dean A. Rhoads, Tuscarora, Nevada

INDEX